PRESIDENTIAL ECONOMICS

PRESIDENTIAL ECONOMICS

THE MAKING OF ECONOMIC POLICY FROM ROOSEVELT TO CLINTON

Third Revised Edition

Herbert Stein

American Enterprise Institute
for Public Policy Research
Washington, D.C.
1994

Library of Congress Cataloging-in-Publication Data

Stein, Herbert, 1916–
    Presidential economics : the making of economic policy from
    Roosevelt to Clinton / Herbert Stein. — 3rd rev. ed.
        p.   cm.
    Includes bibliographical references and index.
    ISBN 0-8447-3850-6
    ISBN 0-8447-3851-4 (pbk.)
    1. United States—Economic policy.   2. United States—Politics and
government—1933–1945.   3. United States—Politics and
government—1945–   4. Presidents—United States—History—20th
century.   I. Title.
HC106.S79   1994
338.973—dc20   93-40697
                                                                              CIP

The AEI PRESS
Publisher for the American Enterprise Institute
1150 Seventeenth St., N.W.
Washington, D.C. 20036

Printed in the United States of America

For my wife, Mildred

Contents

LIST OF FIGURES

PREFACE TO THE THIRD REVISED EDITION

Previous editions of *Presidential Economics* covered the period from the presidency of Herbert Hoover to that of Ronald Reagan. For the present edition, I have written a chapter on the economic policy of George Bush. I also include here two chapters that deal with the years 1990 to 1993: "This Peculiar Recovery" and "Another New Economics." The second of these originally appeared in slightly different form in the *Wall Street Journal*.

The tables and charts of economic statistics included in the previous editions have been brought up to date through 1992 on the basis of data available on July 1, 1993. Further information on the economic background of the period discussed in this book is provided in *An Illustrated Guide to the American Economy* (AEI Press, 1992) by Murray Foss and me. It is a useful complement to *Presidential Economics*.

I wish to thank Patricia McCloskey and Michael Krier for their assistance in preparing this revision.

ACKNOWLEDGMENTS

This book is largely the result of fifty years in Washington observing, commenting on, and for a time, participating in the making of national economic policy. Much of my debt is to the people who made this experience possible. First among these is President Richard M. Nixon, who gave me an opportunity as member and chairman of the President's Council of Economic Advisers to see policy making from the inside. By appointing me a member of his Economic Policy Advisory Board, President Ronald Reagan permitted some insights, if not so intimate, into his administration. For earlier periods I am indebted to the founders of the Committee for Economic Development—Paul Hoffman, Ralph Flanders, and others—who provided me a vantage point for twenty-two years of analysis of a wide variety of economic policy issues. In the past ten years I have benefited from the support of the American Enterprise Institute for Public Policy Research under four presidents, William Baroody, Sr., William Baroody, Jr., Paul W. McCracken, and Christopher DeMuth. Chapters 10 and 11 of the present volume consist of two essays first published in the *AEI Economist*.

I have received valuable secretarial and research assistance from Ilona Boina, Gretchen Chellson, Cathy Cromer, Glenn Follette, Richard Goldstone, Catherine Hill, Patricia Lewis, Marshall Tracht, Alan Viarda and Linda Wilson.

My son Benjamin has advised me about this book and about books in general. My daughter, Rachel Epstein, has been a steady source of good judgment. My deepest thanks go to my wife, Mildred, who read several drafts conscientiously, gave me wise counsel, and encouraged me to think it was worthwhile to add one more book to a world already full of books.

1

Introduction:
A Turn to the Right

THE ELECTION OF RONALD REAGAN in 1980 signified the end of an era in economic policy that had begun almost fifty years earlier. The old order, the Rooseveltian order, did not die in its prime. It had, in fact, been losing ground for almost fifteen years—almost from the moment of its greatest glory. But the coming of Ronald Reagan meant a decisive and total change—or so it seemed.

The new order which had been emerging and now leaped to the center of the stage was "conservative." We shall discuss later just what that means. Other terms were applied—"monetarist," "supply-side," "free market." But "conservative" is most usable just because it is least specific and therefore most easily includes the elements of thinking and policy which were coming to the fore.

The ideas that came together in conservative economics were negative. They were a call for less—less government spending, less taxation, less deficit, less monetary expansion, less government regulation.

Popular support for the conservative economic movement was

15

negative in its origins. It was a response to the observation that
things were not going well. People felt cheated by inflation. They
hadn't attained the living standards they thought their incomes
entitled them to, and they blamed the inflation for that. They
were worried about what inflation would do to them next. The
economy seemed always to be on the verge of recession, when it
wasn't in one. Even in good times unemployment was higher
than we were used to.

The most effective point candidate Reagan made about the
economy during the 1980 campaign was what he said to the
American people: "I think that when you make that decision
[about voting] it might be well if you ask yourself, are you better off today than you were four years ago?"[1] This was taken to
be a rhetorical question, to which the answer was obviously no—
although statistics would have made the answer arguable.[2] Also
this answer was assumed to have obvious policy and political
implications. It meant that the policy of the past four years—
and possibly the past forty years—had been mistaken if it had
led to these conditions. And it meant that the corrective change
called for was the change in the negative direction. This also was
arguable. Indeed, only a few years earlier, in 1974, 1975 and
1976, there had been interest in changes in the other direction—
toward more "planning." The inflation, recession and shortages
of those years were claimed by some to show the failures of the
free market system. But this was exclusively an "intellectual"
position, with little public support and attractive only to a few
politicians.

So dissatisfaction with the performance of the economy led to
a turn of economic policy in a conservative, negative direction.
At the same time dissatisfaction with other aspects of the American condition was rising, and this pointed to a conservative turn
in other, noneconomic, aspects of policy. There was dissatisfaction with what seemed to be America's weakness in the world,
signified by the growing military power of the Soviet Union, by
the futility of the American response to the invasion of Afghan-
istan, and most of all by the humiliation of the year-long holding
of American hostages in Iran. The resulting rise of nationalism,

support for a large military buildup and demand for a more
assertive posture in world affairs were the acceptance of a position that had, in the previous decade but not always, been a conservative position.

A third strand of conservatism which was raised to prominence, if not dominance, by the Reagan victory related to social
or private life in America. There had been rising dissatisfaction
with what were commonly regarded as liberal ways of living.
Many Americans were revolted by what seemed to be a wave of
sexual freedom, homosexuality, pornography, abortion, divorce,
drug use, indifference to religion and general slovenliness and
indolence. They wanted a restoration of conventional values and
sought leadership, including government leadership, to bring it
about.

To these three strands of conservatism—economic, national-
ist, social—must be added a fourth. This was a traditionalist
strand, mainly represented by a group of intellectual philoso-
phers, sociologists, historians—who had been writing conservative doctrine since the end of World War II and who had been
joined, or been taken over by, a more recent group who called
themselves neo-conservatives. Their ideas were elitist and traditionalist, importations from Europe to a country which had no
elites and little tradition. They tried to create an elite, from the
American entrepreneur, and to base themselves on the Judeo-
Christian tradition—a broad enough base for any purpose. They
were conservative in the sense that they resisted change, but they
did not like things as they were. This conservatism was less a
program than an attitude, but those who shared the attitude felt
they also had a victory in the victory of Ronald Reagan.

There were undoubtedly some people who thought themselves
to be conservative in all of these four senses. But in many respects conservative economics with which this book is concerned
was not comfortable in the company of these other conserva-
tisms. And conservative economics is itself a tent covering
diverse ideas. The conservatism of economists is basically derived from the British liberal tradition, and is basically still what
Europeans would call liberal. In fact, many of the economists

who are considered the apostles of conservative economics have been careful to disassociate themselves from the label "conservative." Friedrich Hayek, for example, wrote a famous essay entitled "Why I Am Not a Conservative."[3] Henry Simons worried about what to call himself, rejected the term "conservative" and settled, not entirely happily, for "libertarian."[4] The unifying theme was that society should be organized by free contract among consenting private individuals. The outlook which rejected tradition or authority in managing economic affairs did not readily accommodate them in managing social affairs. These economic conservatives, by and large, did not accept any elite, including the businessmen, and did not rely on their goodness or responsibility, but were suspicious of them. They did not, in principle, deny the responsibility of government for the national defense, but they accepted the implications of that as an unfortunate exception to their desire to minimize the role of government. At the extreme the Libertarian Party took a very narrow view of the role of government even in national security affairs.

But not all of the attitudes that are considered economic conservatism conform to these views of economists. There is the economic conservatism of the leaders of big business, which has been more tolerant of government intervention when that suited the perceived interest of business, which, of course, they identified with the national interest. At various times this conservatism has been, for example, protectionist, or supportive of government efforts to restrain wages. There is also a small-town, small-business, agrarian economic conservatism, which not only identifies its special interests with the general welfare but also retains respect for traditional symbols, like the balanced budget.[5]

Thus the term "conservative" has a variety of meanings in economics, and different meanings in economics than it has in other uses. Moreover, it is clear that a government which comes into office representing all of these versions of conservatism is going to be troubled by contradictions among them, as well as between any and all of them and the "real world."

All of that and many other problems were overlooked in the general joy which was felt, and not only by people who considered themselves conservatives, when Reagan was elected. The election of a new President is always an occasion for hope. It is like the first day of school when we have sharp pencils and new notebooks and teachers who do not yet know our deficiencies. Everything seems possible. This feeling of confidence is, of course, especially strong in the new President and his staff. They think that the world is different because they are in office and that problems that seemed difficult under the old regime will yield easily to their presence and their wisdom.

This new birth of confidence was especially great with the transition from Carter to Reagan because of the difference in personality between the two men. By 1980, Carter was exuding uncertainty, ineptitude and diffidence. We had come to think that Carter was the national problem, or at least that he was the bearer of our problems and would carry them off into the wilderness with him when he left. Reagan, on the other hand, represented clarity and self-confidence.

Alas, Ronald Reagan did not turn out to be our fairy godmother; the little package of conservative economic ideas with which he came into office did not solve our problems, as quickly became evident. That did not mean that the era of conservative economics ended a year or two after Reagan's election. It meant that the era had hardly begun. The package was only an approach, a point of view, and mainly, as already noted, a negative attitude to policies associated with earlier economic frustrations. The package was not a set of policies, programs and procedures for solving the nation's problems. The election of Reagan was not a mandate to put into effect a specific program. It was a mandate to develop a program, which would have certain general characteristics but whose chief characteristic would be to permit an affirmative answer to the question that had elected him—are you better off today than you were four years ago?

Reagan likes to compare himself to Franklin Roosevelt, and in some ways his position in 1980 was like that of FDR in 1932. Roosevelt was elected with one mandate—to get the country out of the depression. He was not elected because the country wanted him to pursue some particular program. His policy pronouncements during the campaign had been vague and contradictory. He came into office still in the early stages of developing a program. Much of what he did in the famous first hundred days, or in the first two years, was constructive and lasting, but much of it worsened the depression and some of it was declared unconstitutional. The test of the Roosevelt presidency was not the program of his 1932 campaign or the program of his first hundred days but his ability to develop and adapt actions to the existing and emerging conditions. Whether he should be given high marks on that score is still an open question.

Just so, the test of the Reagan presidency, which will also for some time be the test of conservative economics, will not be the validity of the program with which he came into office. One may take it as an axiom that the programs with which a President comes into office will be impractical, unrealistic and inadequate. The test for Reagan will be whether he succeeds in developing, within the framework of a general conservative philosophy, a program which makes significant progress against the nation's problems.

The economic package with which Ronald Reagan entered office was like the packages with which all Presidents enter office in one critical respect. That is, it promised benefits to everyone and costs to no one—or to almost no one. It would elevate growth, stability and freedom in the scale of national priorities—and demote government redistribution of income and government control over the allocation of output. But deemphasizing government's efforts to redistribute income would not injure the poor who were the presumed beneficiaries of those efforts. The stimulus to economic growth which would result from the economic package would help the poor, along with everyone else, and more than compensate them for the loss of government programs. In a phrase which the Reaganites loved to borrow from J. F. Kennedy, the rising tide would lift all the boats. Removing or relaxing government regulations ostensibly aimed at environmental purity and occupational safety would not make the air or water dirtier or the workplace more hazardous. These regulations were unnecessary anyway and only satisfied the ambitions of meddlesome bureaucrats.

The main engine of the Reagan economic program was to be a large cut of income tax rates. This would not, however, reduce the revenue or increase the budget deficit. Instead, the tax cut would stimulate the growth of output and productivity so much that the revenue would increase and the budget deficit would be eliminated. There was to be a large reduction of government nondefense expenditures, but no one was to suffer from that except the bureaucrats who administered the programs, because they were assumed to be the main beneficiaries.

The growth of the money supply was to be reduced and stabilized in order to restore reasonable price stability. But contrary to "Keynesian" notions, which were explicitly rejected, the transition to price stability would not entail a recession and increased unemployment; the Reagan program would so reduce costs and improve expectations as to make those pains unnecessary.

Of course, the world did not turn out to be so kind. The big tax cut was enacted, but it soon became obvious that it would greatly reduce, not increase, the revenues. The country was left facing enormous budget deficits which threatened the economic growth that was one of the program's main objectives. The inflation did come down, but not without the most serious recession since the 1930s. The amount by which government expenditures could be cut without pain to important elements of the American population—including essential parts of Mr. Reagan's constituency—was disappointingly small. The search for regulations that could be removed without controversy and cost turned out to be less successful than had been expected.

By 1983 the economy was recovering from the recession. Output was rising, unemployment was falling, and the inflation rate was low compared to the experience of previous years. There was a tendency to declare victory for the New Economics of Ronald Reagan. But we had been through such idyllic moments before. The American economy fluctuates, and in its cyclical movement it passes through a period, early in the recovery, when inflation is low and output is growing.[6] That does not mean that basic problems had been solved. What monetary policy would be most likely to keep the economy on a path of real growth without reviving inflation was highly uncertain. The consequences of the prospective deficits were commonly considered to be extremely serious, but no one expected them to be significantly reduced. The disagreement in the country about national priorities—about the division of the national output among defense, social programs, private consumption and investment—was sharper than ever before.

Despite the inadequacy of the ideas with which Mr. Reagan came into office—an inadequacy which was clear to many when he was elected and to many more within two years—they contained basic elements of validity. We did need to put more emphasis on economic growth and price stability. We did need to reduce those taxes that bore most heavily on growth and those expenditures and regulations that were least productive. The private economy needed more breathing room, and more assurance of stability in government policy.

These attitudes need to be converted into a program utilizing feasible and effective measures and balancing competing goals. That is an intellectually and politically difficult task. It is intellectually difficult because the experience of the past two years and of the past twenty years shows how little we know about what makes the economy tick. It is politically difficult because the program will involve sacrifice—for some people and perhaps temporarily for many people. This must be explained and people must be persuaded to accept such sacrifices in the interest of a larger and more lasting national objective. The future of conservative economics will depend on the ability of its champions to contribute to the performance of these tasks.

This book seeks to explain the current state of economic policy. The initial approach is historical. Today's direction of economics is a conservative response to a tendency of policy which began about fifty years ago. It is best understood if we first understand what that tendency was. Moreover, the political and intellectual requirements for a change of policy are clarified by an exposition of the processes by which the previous tendency developed.

This previous tendency, which we call liberalism, did not proceed at a constant rate from the inauguration of Franklin Roosevelt to the inauguration of Ronald Reagan. For our purposes, four periods need to be distinguished in those forty-eight years. There was a period of great activism in the Roosevelt years up to the beginning of World War II. After the war, in the administrations of Truman and, especially, Eisenhower, we went through a phase in which the experimental ideas of the Roosevelt period were moderated and accepted. Another period of activism came with the administrations of Kennedy and Johnson. This gave way to twelve years—the Nixon, Ford, Carter years—of conflict and ambiguity.

Having brought the story up to the election of Ronald Reagan, who promised a new and more radical brand of economic conservatism, eschewing such adjectives as "moderate" or "modernism," we describe the intellectual foundations of his policy and appraise its performance in operation in the first years of his presidency. The book will close with a discussion of the main economic issues now confronting the country and with suggestions for the direction that policy should take.

This book is a story of Presidents coping with economic problems. There is implicit in the book a certain view of the nature of the American economy, of what its main problems are and are not, and of what are the most constructive ways to deal with these problems. This view will probably be apparent to readers as they proceed through the book, but it may be helpful to summarize it here:

The great traumas of American economic history in the past half century or so have been associated with unemployment and inflation. They were the depression of the 1930s and lesser recessions, including the one through which we have been passing, and the inflation that began in the mid-1960s. These problems have been mainly caused by instability in the total demand for output or by excessive growth in the demand for output. Between 1929 and 1933, total demand, as measured by GNP in current dollars, fell by almost 50 percent. There would have been no Great Depression if that had not happened. Between the second quarter of 1981 and the fourth quarter of 1982, total demand rose at an annual rate of about 2.5 percent, after eight years in which it had averaged 10 percent annual increases. There would have been no serious recession if that slowdown had not occurred. Between 1965 and 1980, total demand rose at an annual rate of 9.3 percent. The consumer price index would not have risen by an annual rate of 6.6 percent during that period, soaring to 10.8 percent in 1977 to 1980, if the rise of demand had not been so great. In a nutshell, we get inflation because demand rises too fast and we get unemployment because it rises too unsteadily.

The magnitude of these excesses and fluctuations has been largely due to the behavior of the money supply. Between 1929 and 1933 the narrowly defined money supply fell by 26 percent. Between the end of 1980 and the middle of 1982 the money supply rose at an annual rate of 5.8 percent, compared to 7.5 percent in the previous four years. That decline contributed to the 1982 recession. Between 1965 and 1980 the money supply rose by 6.1 percent a year, compared to 3.1 percent in the previous six years. That rise was the main factor in the acceleration of the inflation.

Much of the history of presidential economics is the history of trying to cope with the unemployment and inflation problems without recognizing or being able to manage these relationships. This failure has led to many serious mistakes and aberrations of policy, from Roosevelt's NRA to Nixon's price and wage controls.

The strong performance of the American economy, despite serious deficiencies of government policy for managing aggregate demand, is evidence of the effectiveness of the underlying private economic system. Between 1929 and 1982, total output rose at an annual rate of 3 percent. The American standard of living increased dramatically. The proportion of the population in poverty fell to an extremely low level. One can expect that the private system will work even better if the government manages monetary policy better.

Nevertheless, there are other economic decisions to be made through government. In numerous ways the government affects the division of the national output among alternative uses—and should. It decides how much should be devoted to national defense, how much to providing assistance for the poor or other classes of the population and how much to take from various income classes in taxation. Through its decisions about the size of its budget surplus or deficit it affects how much of the national output will go into private investment.

These decisions constitute the budget problems. Essentially they are questions of what the national priorities are. Economists cannot tell the American people what their priorities should be, but economists should be able to advise about what the consequences of these decisions are, where these consequences are not obvious. These decisions have probably not given sufficient weight to long-run and indirect effects, and as a result there has probably been a tendency toward excessive budget deficits and excessively high marginal rates of taxation. There has, over the years, been much extreme and exaggerated talk about the evils of deficits and taxes, which now makes it difficult to get sensible consideration of the real consequences, but such consideration is necessary. This is a very rich country. It can afford to defend itself, to look after its poor and to meet other high-priority goals, even if the consequence is to slow down economic growth somewhat. The problem is to avoid impairing the growth of the economy for unworthy purposes.

Periodically through the period covered in this book there have been demands to impose upon the American economy a system of "planning," meaning comprehensive and detailed control or selective influence by government over investment, production, pricing, wage-setting and other decisions in the private economy. The current version of this demand is the call for "industrial policy." The American people have properly shown little interest in such proposals in peacetime, except for Roosevelt's NRA and Nixon's price controls. Planning has nothing to offer for the solution of America's real economic problems. It would interfere with the part of the economic system that works best—the private market—and divert attention from the need to improve what has not worked so well—government's conduct of its monetary and fiscal function.

I believe that the evidence confirms this view of the American economy and its problems, and that stated so broadly it would command a great deal of acceptance among economists. Some of the history told in this book supports this view, but I do not claim that this book demonstrates the validity of my viewpoint. I only aim to tell the story of Columbus' voyage to the Americas from the standpoint of one who believes that the earth is round; I do not aim to prove that the earth is round. I hope that readers will find my point of view congenial and persuasive. And I hope that others will in any case find my recounting of the history informative.

A portfolio of charts depicting key developments in the American economy from 1930 to 1980 is presented on pages 123 to 132. Statistical data for these same aspects of the American economy are in the appendix.

2

Hoover and Roosevelt: The Depression Origins of Liberal Economics

THE CONSERVATIVE ECONOMIC MOVEMENT of the 1980s is largely a reaction to the liberal movement which preceded it—to the excesses and failures of that movement and probably also to its successes and to boredom with it. The liberal movement in its turn was a reaction to the failures of a previous regime of policy which we can loosely call conservative, failures which became manifest in the depression of the 1930s. The liberal movement reached its finest hour—in terms of self-confidence and popular acceptance, as well as of achievement—in 1965. Thereafter, although it continued for many years to dominate policy, both its results and its intellectual foundations were increasingly questioned. Thinking and policy gradually edged away from it until by 1980 it was no longer dominant but clearly on the defensive.

To understand what the new conservative economics is, one must first understand what the liberal economics was. In fact, for some people the conclusive argument for the new conservative economics is that it is not the old liberal economics. That is not a good argument. There are many possible alternatives to liberal economics. Failure of the liberal economics does not point clearly to any particular substitute. Conservative economics is not the opposite of liberal economics, whatever being the opposite would mean. Conservative economics is a deviation from the preceding trend of policy, and although the general direction of the deviation is known, the specific forms and degrees of deviation are still the objects of search. Therefore we cannot describe conservative economics simply by describing liberal economics and imagining the opposite. But still it is essential to the understanding of the conservative movement to know what was the previous policy that is being modified or at least under newly critical scrutiny.

The beginning of the liberal wave in economic policy is usually placed at the inauguration of Franklin Roosevelt in 1933. That is, however, an oversimplification, just as it would be an oversimplification to date the conservative wave from the inauguration of Ronald Reagan—if, indeed, there is a conservative wave and not just a ripple. What came with Franklin Roosevelt was the acceleration of a trend that did not, however, begin on March 4, 1933.

When Ronald Reagan took office he hung the portrait of Calvin Coolidge in the Cabinet Room as a symbol of the restoration of conservative economics. But if we use as a test of conservatism the degree of government intervention in the economy, the Coolidge administration was not conservative compared to its predecessors. Coolidge presided over a New Era, and the era was new not only in the height of the stock market; it was also new in the economic role of government, and part of the confidence in the future of the American economy which was so strong in the Coolidge days was confidence in the cooperative policy of government. When Coolidge said that the business of America is business he did not mean that the business of government is to leave business alone. He meant that it is the business of government to help business. That was even more positively the idea of his activist Secretary of Commerce, Herbert Hoover. Coolidge did not undo the interventionist measures of the Theodore Roosevelt and Woodrow Wilson regimes. At the end of his term the federal budget was larger than in the time of, say,

William Howard Taft. He reduced income tax rates, but we still had an income tax, which we hadn't had fifteen years earlier. Perhaps most important, his term was a period of increasing acceptance of the responsibility of the Federal Reserve to help stabilize the economy.

Economic policy moved further in an interventionist direction during the unhappy presidency of Herbert Hoover. This was partly the reflection of the President himself. Hoover was a modern man, and the true-blue conservatives of the Republican Party had resisted his appointment to the Cabinet in 1921 on the grounds that he was too liberal. He was probably more up-to-date on the thinking of professional economists of his time than any other President of this century, and that thinking included a considerable role for the government to stabilize the economy by the management of its budget. The main force driving the government to take more responsibility for the performance of the economy was, of course, not the personality of Mr. Hoover but the fact of the depression which began early in his term.

It is impossible to overestimate the importance of the depression as an influence on thinking and policy in the United States over the whole half century from 1930 to 1980. A generation of politicians, economists and general citizens was obsessed by it. The recent change of economic policy away from the course on which we embarked fifty years ago is due in part to the fading of the memories of the depression and to the emergence into power of a new generation that has no memories of the depression. The ending of the obsession—the escape from the overhanging notion of depression as the normal or probable state of the economy—is a move toward realism. But to forget the depression, to think that it didn't happen and couldn't happen, would be a mistake. The ideas of the new conservative economics must be tested for their recognition of the fact that there was a depression and that policy must be prepared to prevent its recurrence.

Words and statistics cannot convey to people who did not live through it and do not remember it anything like an adequate picture of the depression. In fact, most of the statistics with which we now measure the performance of the economy did not exist in the 1930s, but everyone present could see without the statistics that the condition was tragic. We now know, which we didn't at the time, that in 1932 25 percent of the labor force was unemployed.[1] The highest unemployment rate for any year in the postwar period (up to the time of writing) was 9.7 percent in 1982. But the difference between the two conditions is not conveyed by the ratio of 25 to 9.7. When 25 percent of the labor force is unemployed, that will almost certainly include largely people who are heads of families. They will have been unemployed for a long time, and they will have lost confidence in their ability to find work soon. The difference between being one of 25 percent who are unemployed and one of 9.7 percent is the difference between tragedy and trouble. Moreover, when 25 percent are unemployed almost everyone is in or close to a family in which someone is unemployed. In the depression we all felt, or at least saw, the misery personally. We saw the unemployed, the breadlines, the foreclosed houses and the abandoned farms directly, and not through statistics or television film. When 25 percent were unemployed in 1932 there was no national unemployment compensation and few families with employed second workers.

This was a condition that demanded action by the federal government. One can imagine circumstances in which that would not have been the reaction—in which there was sufficient stoicism, or ignorance, or, some would say, wisdom so that the public would have accepted this condition without demanding federal action. But those were not the circumstances of the 1930s. The Republican administrations had enjoyed credit for the prosperity of the 1920s. They could not avoid responsibility for the troubles of the 1930s. That was unmistakable when the Democrats won control of the Congress in 1930.

Looking back from the 1980s one might ask why this demand for action by the federal government led to more positive measures—more intervention by the government in the management of the economy—rather than more negative measures—what we

later came to call getting government off our backs. That was
the remedy prescribed when we ran into economic difficulties in
the 1970s. And by the 1980s the view had developed, although
it was probably still a minority view, that even in the 1930s the
problem was too much government. There were some who
thought that the depression was due to too much effort of the
government to manage the money supply rather than follow
some neutral rule of constant monetary growth. There was also
a theory that the depression had been caused by an increase in
federal taxes, specifically by the Smoot-Hawley tariff, which had
been going through the Congress when the stock market crash
occurred in 1929.[2] Why didn't the demand for action by the
government take the form of a demand for the government to
stop manipulating the money supply and to stabilize its rate of
growth? Why didn't Andrew Mellon, the Secretary of the Treasury, whose earlier tax cuts were then and later credited with the
prosperity of the 1920s, propose more of the same medicine in
the 1930s?

While these are questions one might ask in the 1980s, they
were not realistic questions in the 1930s. For one thing, there
was not then in the country enough sophistication—or soph-
istry—to generate such questions. The money-supply or tax-cut
approaches to the problem of depression make sense only in the
context of a comprehensive economic system where action in one
corner can percolate throughout and have effects far from the
site of the original action. Even among economists, understanding of such a system was quite limited at the outset of the depression, although the country was to get some education on this
subject during the course of it. The prevailing attitude was that
if people are unemployed the remedy must be to give those people jobs, and if houses are being foreclosed the remedy must be
to stop those foreclosures. The indirect approach via aggregate
demand was not widely understood or appreciated.

This point may be made in a more general way. There was
not then (and may not be now) any general appreciation of the
way a free economy is supposed to operate, including the responsibilities, positive and negative, of the government in such a

system. What the public did understand was success. In the 1920s the policy of the government was understood to be a policy of very limited intervention in the economy, although, as I have said, the role of government was greater than before World War I. The doctrine preached by government was the doctrine of limited intervention. The people who were regarded as the nation's leading authorities on economic policy, heads of large corporations, preached the same doctrine. All of this was accepted as gospel while it succeeded, and while its preachers were seen to be succeeding. But then in the depression this policy failed. Many of its outstanding advocates failed quite literally— i.e., became personally bankrupt. There was not sufficient understanding of the system to lead people to ask what it was within the system that had failed or to seek solutions within the system.

The depression discredited the old policies and left the door open for new ones. Even if there had been no preference for governmentally managed solutions, a random selection among the available options would have turned policy in that direction. There wasn't much room for moving toward *less* government intervention, except in the very special sense that commitment to a monetary rule can be considered such a move, whereas there were large and varied possibilities for moving in the other direction.

There was no single ready-made alternative to take the place of the old one for managing the economy when the old one failed. Hoover, as I have said, did have modern notions of the proper role of government in dealing with a recession. That mainly called for increased government expenditures on public works and acceptance of a deficit. It also permitted him to reduce taxes at the onset of the recession despite the possible deficit. But when these measures failed to stem the decline of the economy, he was left with no theory of how to deal with a deeper and longer-lasting depression than the stabilization literature of that period contemplated. His position was not that he rejected possible options simply because they involved too much government action. He rejected options because he did not think they would work.

In the later days of his administration, Hoover took two main steps against the depression. He established a government corporation, the Reconstruction Finance Corporation, to make loans to state and local governments and to businesses that were in difficulty. That is an action so at odds with the cliché image of Hoover that most people forget it was Hoover who did it. In the late 1970s and early 1980s there were "liberals" who proposed the reestablishment of the RFC and they were embarrassed to be reminded that it was originally a Hoover creation.

The second major step he took remains in the history books, however, as a symbol of pure Hooverism—which is to say, traditionalism and know-nothingism. That was the proposal of a large tax increase in 1932. By the standards of latter-day Keynesianism, to raise tax rates at the depth of a depression was the height of folly. Even Reagan took this position during the recession in 1983. Of course, the people who had been saying that for a generation were similarly shocked by the proposal for a radical cut of tax rates in 1981 in the midst of a great inflation. But even the people who most enthusiastically supported the 1981 tax cuts thought that the 1932 tax increase had been a disaster. They were looking at the world through a different set of glasses than the Keynesians used, but they arrived at the same conclusion about the 1932 tax increase.[3]

In 1932, however, the decision to raise tax rates did not look like mere traditionalism or masochism. An argument could be made for it on sophisticated economic grounds, as necessary to get interest rates down, to inspire investor confidence, to induce the Federal Reserve to augment the money supply and to check the drain of gold out of the country. The decision was almost certainly a mistake, but it was the mistake of a President trying energetically to apply what was known of economics to the great problem of his time, not the mistake of a President engaging in an antediluvian reflex.[4]

Although beginnings of the movement to a more activist, interventionist economic policy can be seen in the Hoover administration, that movement became enormously more vigorous after the inauguration of Franklin Roosevelt. This shift of a trend of policy into higher gear when a new President takes office is a natural development, and occurred, for example, when Ronald Reagan succeeded Jimmy Carter. Policy was already turning under Carter, but the turn became much more radical with Reagan. This need not reflect any difference of ideology or personality between the old President and the new one. The new President is less inhibited by commitments to former policies and former officials, and he feels supported by a new mandate from the electorate.

Franklin Roosevelt surely came into office with a mandate to do something about the depression. But he did not have a mandate to do any particular thing. He received not a mandate to follow a particular policy but a free hand to do what he wanted. And he came into office without any clear idea of what he wanted. Some of his advisers had specific plans, but his different advisers had different plans. Some wanted to print money, some to set floors under prices, some to inaugurate big spending programs.

What survived in, say, 1946 as Rooseveltian, or New Deal, or liberal economic policy was not a blueprint that Roosevelt had in mind on inauguration day in 1933. What survived was the residue of a long list of varied measures and approaches that had been tried during the depression. The process cannot be called trial and error, for that would suggest that the test of survival had been success or failure, and that was surely not the exclusive determinant of survival. By 1946 there was little objective and convincing evidence of which among the New Deal measures had worked. Some had fallen by the way because they were unconstitutional, or politically unpopular, or out of step with the intellectual fashion. Some survived simply because they were there and there was no clear proof that they had failed.

I do not intend here to recount the history of economic experimentation during the New Deal.[5] It is worthwhile, however, to note some of the approaches that were discarded, or never followed up. They serve as a reminder of the tendency of governments to adopt, with much fanfare and great promises, policies having little rationale, and to abandon them when something else looks more attractive. They are part of the history that explains the great skepticism in the country about any of the new turns of economic policy which the government proclaims so frequently.

1. Roosevelt, like many other Presidents before and since, believed that the successful performance of the economy depended heavily on confidence and that he could inspire confidence by manipulation of words and symbols. That was presumably the basis of the most famous line in his first inaugural, "We have nothing to fear but fear itself." He said other things of similar intent later. The flags and parades that accompanied the National Recovery Program also had a mood-elevating purpose, and the President's own well-publicized "jauntiness" was probably calculated to serve the same end. All of this seems to have done something to make the country feel better, and that is not to be belittled. But it did not do much to bring about economic recovery. The confidence required for that was the confidence of investors and the business community. Roosevelt's symbolism could not obtain that, and he was unable, except in rare spasms, to do what was apparently necessary to gain their confidence.

2. During his 1932 campaign, Roosevelt attacked Hoover for failure to balance the budget and promised that he would do so. In the early days of his term he embarked upon a program of economy in government, but that was soon overwhelmed by the new spending programs he initiated. He continued to maintain his intention to balance the budget even while large deficits persisted. In 1937 when the partial recovery the economy had been enjoying gave way to a steep recession, Roosevelt flirted with the idea that this time he should really try to bring about revival by balancing the budget, and he sent his Secretary of the Treasury, Morgenthau, to reassure the business community on that point. But he quickly abandoned this idea when he got no favorable response. Thereafter deficits were accepted and rationalized by new economic theories. Until then, and possibly even later, Roosevelt believed that a balanced budget was a good thing, and he believed that the public thought so also, which was probably more important to him. His policy was somewhat influenced

by these notions, but they were not among the main determinants
of his policy.

(3) When Roosevelt came into office there was a considerable
body of opinion that the trouble with the American economy
was that it was "unplanned." There was no central authority to
see that the various branches of industry produced the right
amount of output and sold the output at the right prices, with
the result that production became unbalanced, gluts appeared,
and unemployment then developed. Some forms of this idea,
emphasizing the need for voluntary cooperation among the leaders of industry, and deriving in part from experience during
World War I, were, naturally, especially popular among leaders
of industry.

The most spectacular of Roosevelt's early approaches to the
depression, the National Recovery Act, was a reflection of this
idea of the need for planning. Industry committees would be set
up throughout the economy to assure that prices were set high
enough so that business could make a profit and would produce
and that workers would get wages high enough to buy the product. Throughout the past forty-five years economists have regarded this as a particularly foolish idea, because it did not deal
with the fundamental problem of a deficiency of demand, although the new supply-side economics may yet provide some
rationale for it. The program, although elaborately implemented,
showed no signs of bringing about a recovery. More important,
the Supreme Court declared it unconstitutional, saving Roosevelt the embarrassment of having to jettison it.

That particular form of planning did not reappear. The notion
of planning the American economy, but in a form more congenial to intellectuals than to businessmen, did, however, continue to fascinate some of the Roosevelt entourage. Between
1933 and 1939 Washington ran through a series of "planning"
agencies—the National Planning Board, the National Resources
Board, the National Resources Committee and the National Resources Planning Board. But these were essentially research organizations, without much influence on operations, and their
main effect was to provide a target for the conservatives who by

then were accusing Roosevelt of undermining the free, capitalist, system.

4. A strand of thinking in the Roosevelt circle that led to conclusions quite different from the planning strand was the emphasis on the need to promote competition. It was believed that the American economy suffered from a split between the competitive sectors and the monopolistic or oligopolistic sectors, with the uncompetitive sectors having priced themselves beyond the ability of the competitive sectors to buy their product, as a result of which there was excess capacity and unemployment in the uncompetitive sectors. The presumed remedy was to make the less competitive sectors more competitive, and the instrument for doing this was strict application of the antitrust laws. This turned out in practice, however, to be mainly talk, and the pro-competition movement became diverted into a movement to protect small business, which is quite a different thing.

Much hope was invested in these approaches to economic policy at various stages of the New Deal. But they all passed and left no lasting mark. The durable elements of the New Deal, which were the core of the liberal movement of the next generation, were the active use of fiscal policy to assure adequacy of total demand, the beginnings of a major effort to redistribute income toward the lower-income members of the population, and the increasing regulation of selected sectors of the economy.

Macroeconomics and Keynes

As I have noted, the idea that the way to deal with unemployment was to increase government spending, especially for public works, was well known and widely accepted when the depression struck. Hoover, for example, understood it. From the beginning of his administration, Roosevelt used this strategy, more vigorously than Hoover had done but not on what we would now regard as a massive scale. In his initial recourse to government spending as an antidepression tool, Roosevelt was neither encumbered nor assisted by any theories on the subject. That is, he did not worry about the possibility that government borrowing to pay for the increased expenditures would withdraw funds from the private sector and so depress private employment while public employment was being raised. Neither was he encouraged by the thought that if one person was put to work on the public payroll his expenditures would create demand which would put another person to work, and that his expenditures would employ another, and so on. Apparently these secondary effects did not occur to him. His approach was simpler. He saw that people were out of work and deprived of income and the most direct solution seemed to be to put them to work on the government payroll and pay them an income out of the Treasury. Calvin Coolidge had said that when people are out of work there is unemployment. Roosevelt's solution for unemployment was to put people to work. So he started the FERA, WPA, CCC and other employment-creating programs.

By 1936, Roosevelt had become aware of the positive secondary effects of government employment programs—that putting some people to work directly would put other people to work indirectly. During the 1936 campaign he explained this in the words of a then-popular song: "The music goes round and round and it comes out here."

Roosevelt's policy of increased government spending to reduce unemployment and get out of the depression has been called "Keynesian," in reference to the work of the famous British economist John Maynard Keynes and especially to *The General Theory of Employment, Interest and Money,*[6] published in January 1936. In fact, the term "Keynesian" has come to be used as an epithet by the conservatives of the 1980s (and earlier) to describe all the things they don't like about liberal economic policies. But Roosevelt did not have to learn about government spending from Keynes, and neither would Hoover have had to do so. Keynes provided a sophisticated rationale for what Roosevelt was doing anyway. He provided answers for questions that Roosevelt had never asked, although others had. How could so much unemployment persist for such a long time? Why did government spending work; why didn't it just crowd out private spending? Why wouldn't monetary expansion serve as well as government spending to raise the economy and reduce unemployment?

The answers that Keynes provided to these questions were not necessary for Roosevelt's efforts in the direction of expansionist fiscal policy. But as these answers came to dominate the thinking of economists, other intellectuals, and a new generation of politicians, they helped to make expansionist fiscal policy the major theme of liberal economic policy for about forty years after the publication of the *General Theory*. Without Keynes, and especially without the interpretation of Keynes by his followers, expansionist fiscal policy might have remained an occasional emergency measure and not become a way of life.

Keynes' explanation of the depression was simple, plausible and convincing. Demand was insufficient to buy the product that would be produced at full employment, or, put another way, people did not want to spend all of the income they would earn when there was full employment. The idea that unemployment and depression were due to a deficiency of demand was not invented by Keynes. It was one of the oldest and superficially most plausible of the explanations around. But sophisticated people had difficulties with that idea then, in the 1930s, and there are again, in the 1980s, sophisticated, or ultrasophisticated, people who have trouble with it. In fact, rejecting the demand-deficiency theory of unemployment was to become one of the tests of membership in a certain school of conservative economics in the 1980s.[7] So Keynes' explanation of the demand-deficiency theory was important in the 1930s and has become important again.

In 1935, when I was a graduate student, a distinguished economist, Harold G. Moulton, then president of the Brookings Institution, came to the University of Chicago to talk to us about the causes of the depression. He had a demand-deficiency theory. People were not spending all of their incomes and therefore the product could not be sold and people were unemployed. He could not, however, explain what happened to the income that people didn't spend, and so we regarded the explanation as unsatisfactory. But Keynes came along with an entirely satisfactory explanation of what happened to the income that wasn't spent. That income just never came into existence. The income earned in production would always be equal to the income that people spent to buy the production. If they didn't want to buy the production they wouldn't earn the income. Income and expenditure would always be equal at the level of expenditure. If when they had incomes of $1,000 billion people only wanted to spend $900 billion, then incomes couldn't be $1,000 billion but would be something less—enough less so that people would want to spend all of it. There wouldn't be anything left over—any unspent income.

Keynes also dealt with, or at least wrestled with, another aspect of the economics of his time that has been revived in the conservative economics of the 1980s. That was Say's Law, named for a French economist, Jean Baptiste Say, of the early nineteenth century.[8] Say was refuting the idea, already common in his time, that there could be a general "glut" of production, what we now call a deficiency of demand. He asserted that there could be no glut, no overproduction, because "supply creates its own demand." This is better understood as saying that supply *is* its own demand because the supply of something is an offer to provide it in exchange for something else and is therefore a demand for the something else. If workers offer to supply labor it is because they want to buy something with the wage. The supply of labor is a demand for the something they want to buy. Of course, this applied to goods in general. It did not mean that workers wanted to buy the particular goods they were producing, or that the demand for any particular good would be equal to its supply. There could be gluts of particular things. But they would not last for long. The price system would take care of that. If there was a glut of something its price would fall, less of it would be produced, and the labor engaged in producing it would shift to producing the things that workers did want when they offered their labor.

This did not necessarily mean that workers, or other earners of income, would want to spend all of their earnings on consumption. They would probably want to save some of it. But that caused no basic difficulty. Saving some of the income created a demand for capital goods, and for workers in the industries producing capital goods, just as spending some of the income on automobiles created a demand for automobiles and for workers in the automobile industry. The savers did not have to buy the capital goods directly. They could buy stocks or bonds, or put their money in banks or savings institutions which would lend it to the people who wanted to invest in factories or equipment or houses. Moreover, there couldn't be too much saving—at least not for long. The price system would take care of that. In this case the relevant price was the interest rate. If savers wanted to save more than investors wanted to invest at the existing interest rates, the interest rates would fall until all of the savings were invested.

There might seem to be a problem if workers and others who supplied productive resources didn't want to buy consumer goods or capital goods, even indirectly, but simply wanted to hold more money. Wouldn't this leave us with a supply of labor and capital for which there was no demand? Classical economists had an answer for that one too. First you might suppose that the system was using a commodity money, like gold. Then if people wanted to work for money, rather than for "ordinary" goods, wages would decline, because there wouldn't be enough work for them to do in ordinary production, but at lower wage rates it would be profitable to hire more of them in the production of gold. The supply of workers wanting to work for money would generate a demand for workers to produce gold. In the more usual case of a single country on the gold standard, an excess of supply of workers wanting to work for money would depress wages and prices in the country. That would stimulate exports, so that the excess of workers would be absorbed in production for export, which would bring a flow of gold into the country, and thus the workers would be employed in the production of money, which is what they wanted.

A problem arises when the money is managed by a government agency and there is no automatic mechanism by which an increased desire for money creates an increased supply of money.

In that case there might be unemployment, or a glut, if a certain amount of labor was offered not because workers wanted to buy goods and services but because they wanted to hold more money. But even for that case classical economists had an answer, or discovered an answer when the issue was raised in the 1930s. Again, if workers wanted to hoard their earnings in the form of money, rather than spending it for goods and services, prices and wages would fall. Although this would not increase the quantity of money it would increase its purchasing power—that is, it would increase the real value of the existing stock of money. Thus, the desire of workers and others to hold more money would be satisfied, but at a lower price level, and thereafter they could go on working for the purchase of goods and services.

Of course, economists before Keynes knew that the system did not always operate at full employment. The economy fluctuated, and from time to time there would be large unemployment. That was what the study of business cycles was all about, and the study of business cycles was a major part of economics. But this study concentrated on departures from full employment which were by their nature temporary, resulting from a delay of the economy in adjusting to some disturbance, such as a shift in the use of income from consumption to saving. The prevailing analysis left room for a permanent, or more or less permanent, condition of unemployment if wages did not adjust downward in the presence of unemployment and if the monetary system did not supply enough money. But it was thought extremely unlikely that wages would not adjust in time, even though they would not do so instantly. And if the unemployment resulted from the unwillingness of workers to accept wage reductions, should this really be called unemployment? In any case, an adequate monetary policy would be able to keep unemployment from persisting, even though it could not be so precise as to prevent short-run fluctuations.

In his *General Theory,* Keynes set out to explain why the mechanisms which his predecessors relied upon to prevent long-continued unemployment—declines of wage rates or increases of the money supply—would not work in some circumstances. In the first place, wages might not decline, despite unemployment, even in competitive labor markets without unions or government floors to wages. (Or they might not decline very rapidly. This ambiguity between what would never happen and what would happen only slowly has to be noted throughout the discussion of Keynes. He talked as if describing a condition that could go on indefinitely, and that was a large part of his claim to originality, whereas the argument is more plausible as an explanation for the slowness of adjustments.) Workers confronted with unemployment would not immediately accept lower wages. They would want to see how long the condition was going to last and what opportunities they might find by looking around. In a declining economy this process might never catch up enough to reverse the rise of unemployment.

A more critical point, however, had to do with money. Even if wages did fall, prices would presumably fall with them and the only effect would be to increase the real value of the money supply—that is, how much the existing quantity of money would buy. The key question, therefore, was whether an increase in the real value of the money supply, brought about by a decline of wages or by action of the monetary authority, would restore full employment. Keynes' answer was that in certain conditions it would not do so—or, at least, would do so only slowly. An increase of the money supply, in his view, would operate on the economy through its effect on interest rates. When people have more money, they use some of it to invest in assets that yield interest—like bonds—and that drives interest rates down. With interest rates lower, investment expenditure becomes more profitable, and increases, and that is the way the increase of the money supply increases total spending, and thus total production and thus total employment. But at some point, and in some conditions, Keynes argued, a further increase of the money supply would not depress interest rates further and so would have no effect in stimulating the economy. This would occur when interest rates had fallen far below what people thought they would be in the future and the risks of buying interest-yielding assets

were very great because of the possibility that a subsequent rise
of interest rates would depress their value.

Keynes provided an explanation for the persistence of a long
depression that did not tend to cure itself, or did so only with
intolerable slowness, and that could not be cured by monetary
expansion, or again only with intolerable slowness. The explanation rested on several assumptions, mainly about how people
responded to an increase in their holdings of money and about
how interest rates were determined. Whether the particular assumptions he made were true in the 1930s, or were ever likely
to be true, was not demonstrated then or since. This did not
diminish the appeal of the theory. Keynes had advanced a theory
which, if correct, would fill the logical holes in the most naive
view of what was causing the depression—namely that there was
too little demand—and the most naive view of what needed to
be done to correct that deficiency—namely for the government
to spend more money. It provided a rationalization for what the
government was doing and found easiest to do—namely to
spend more money. It had its attractions even for some conservatives, for reasons that I shall explain later.[9]

Looked at from the standpoint of the 1980s, a natural question
is why there was not more interest in a "monetarist," as distinct
from fiscalist, cure for the depression. In fact, the long list of
ideas that seemed eligible for consideration when Franklin Roosevelt came into office included unorthodox expansion of the
money supply. Congress enacted, early in 1933, legislation authorizing the President to issue unsecured currency—greenbacks
—up to the amount of $3 billion. This interest did not last long,
however. For one thing, a rapid expansion of the money supply
began without the need for any positive action to bring that
about. The increase in the price of gold, not initially conceived
as a way to increase the money supply, automatically increased
the reserves of the banking system. Thereafter a fairly steady
inflow of gold from abroad, partly due to political uncertainties
in Europe, generated a further large increase of bank reserves.
The increase in the reserves led to an increase in the money
stock. It also led to an increase in bank reserves in excess of the

legal requirements. Also, interest rates were low, relative to the rates experienced in the 1920s. In these circumstances it was natural to believe that efforts to accelerate the recovery by expanding the money supply would be futile. If more reserves were provided to the banking system, they would only increase the "excess," or if the banks did manage to find assets to buy, the public would only hold the additional money and would not spend or invest it. The low level of interest rates was taken to demonstrate that interest rates could not be pushed down further by monetary expansion and that, in any case, investment was not responsive to a decline of interest rates.

This belief in the ineffectiveness of monetary expansion to promote recovery was supported by Keynes' argument, but it had become commonplace before he published the *General Theory*. It was assumed to be a directly observable lesson of the experience of the first years of the depression. The view that monetary expansion would be futile—"pushing on a string"— was at least as dominant in the Federal Reserve as anywhere else. This conforms to a long self-protective tradition of the Federal Reserve, which never found itself responsible for the nation's economic troubles, whether depression in the 1930s or inflation in the 1970s.

Not only did the Federal Reserve not follow an actively expansionist policy during the New Deal, but its main worry most of the time was that the gold inflow was adding too much to the reserves of the banking system. A number of important steps were taken by the government, however, which paved the way for more positive management of the money supply, including inflationary policy in the postwar period. United States citizens were prohibited from holding gold, which insulated the monetary system against the possibility that U.S. citizens would limit money creation by asking for gold in exchange for paper money. The establishment of federal insurance of bank deposits greatly reduced the possibility that the course of the money supply would be disrupted by an effort of depositors to get out of bank deposits into currency. Reorganization of the Federal Reserve System increased the power of its board of governors in Washington in relation to the twelve regional banks and probably made the system more sensitive to political influences than it had previously been. It was these institutional changes, rather than any novelties of doctrine, that were the main legacies of the New Deal to future monetary policy.

Although Keynes was considered by the conservatives of the 1980s to be the leading spirit of the liberal economics they detested, in fact his position in the liberal-conservative spectrum is unclear. This is partly because the spectrum itself is unclear. I will take as the main dimension along which liberalism or conservatism is to be measured the degree and kind of government intervention in the economy that is contemplated. It is by that standard that the Keynesian doctrine is difficult to appraise.

Several views of Keynesianism may be distinguished:

1. Keynes was regarded by some as saying that the economic ills we were obviously suffering in the 1930s did not indicate a failure of the free market system. He did not propose any change in, or intervention in, the heart of that system, which is the market process for determining relative prices, outputs and incomes. He attributed our difficulties to the failure of government to discharge properly its essential function of managing monetary policy so as to assure an adequate and stable level of aggregate demand. His contribution, even then not novel but argued with new persuasiveness, was to say that in some circumstances this monetary policy could not be executed by conventional central banking measures. The government budget, its spending, taxing and borrowing, would have to be utilized. But this did not involve giving any additional powers to government. Only new rules for exercising the traditional and inescapable powers of government were required.

One must remember that in the 1930s the free market system was under intense attack. Radical alternatives to this system— communism and fascism—were being eyed with respect by some people. Even short of such extremes, there was widespread interest in structural "reform" of the system—involving planning, redistribution, regulation of prices and wages. In this environment,

Keynes looked to many like a defender of free markets. He said that structural reform was not needed to cure the major ills. All that was needed was to get the government's fiscal and monetary policies right. Radical reformers of the time scorned this aspect of Keynes. Many of my teachers at the University of Chicago who considered themselves conservatives in the old-fashioned, free market sense and did not accept his long-run theories agreed with him about the remedies for the depression. In fact, one of their main complaints was that he was getting a lot of credit for saying what they had been saying all along.

One can say, and it has been said, that Keynes and his philosophy gave free market capitalism a generation of unparalleled success, after a decade of failure which had threatened its survival.

2. Some conservatives even in the 1930s could not accept this bare-bones and sympathetic view of Keynes. This was true of many businessmen and some economists. The fact was that they were not satisfied with this purely macroeconomic or aggregative solution—the fiscal and monetary solution—to the economic problem. They *wanted* some "structural" reforms. They believed, for one thing, that unemployment was high because wage rates were too high. They had the support of classical economics in this belief. And they used this belief to support opposition to what they called Roosevelt's pro-labor policy, especially his promotion of labor organization through the National Labor Relations Act. Moreover, they relied heavily on the argument that government policy was anti-investment and as a consequence impeded recovery. They called for reforms that would reduce the taxation of corporations and a variety of business regulation.

Keynes was interpreted as saying that these anti-labor and pro-business reforms were unnecessary. His theory said that wage-rate reductions were not needed in order to restore full employment and might not even be helpful. Moreover, the stickiness of wages was not due to the power and greed of labor organizations but resulted from the natural response of workers in competitive markets. As far as investment was concerned, the government could supply that needed ingredient of total demand with its own expenditures. And if the government provided the necessary level of demand the private investment would be forthcoming anyway. So no special consideration of business was required.

It was not only the policy implications of Keynes' argument that businessmen resented. They also resented their removal from the central role in the performance of the economy. Of course, the depression itself had begun this process. The captains of industry had accepted credit for the New Era of the 1920s. They could not escape responsibility for the depression of the 1930s. In Keynes' system, businessmen were a passive element, sometimes erratic and unpredictable, but not responsible. They were like cows which might or might not give milk, and were valuable if they did, but they had no particular moral qualities. Responsibility and leadership went to the makers of government policy.

3. Although the Keynesian macroeconomic system, as it came to be expounded in textbooks, did not call for expansion of government functions beyond its traditional and inescapable ones with respect to money and the budget, it left room for such an expansion of the government role. That is, it tended to refute the argument that government intervention would impair business confidence or otherwise injure business investment and consequently prolong the depression. Keynesian argument said that the government not only didn't have to do what the businessmen and conservatives wanted the government to do but it could, if it wished, intervene in pursuit of all kinds of goals—such as income redistribution—without worrying about possible adverse consequences for employment. People who were unimpressed with the virtues of the free private economy were given assurance that any adverse consequences of government actions as far as employment was concerned could be offset by suitable fiscal policy—i.e., big enough deficits.

Keynes understood the power of the free enterprise system as an engine for economic—i.e., material—efficiency and growth. But he did not value that very highly. He imagined that in a foreseeable period—not over a hundred years—the economic problem would be solved, in the sense that everyone would have enough of the product of the economy for a good life, if the government played its part in managing the unemployment problem. He did not regard the unending expansion of material output as the way to a good life. Keynes' membership in the Bloomsbury set reflected an important part of his philosophy. This was a group mainly of writers and artists with whom Keynes was actively involved in the years before and after World War I. Its other famous names were Bertrand Russell, Virginia and Leonard Woolf, Lytton Strachey and Clive Bell. They were disciples of George Moore, a philosopher at Cambridge when Keynes was a student there, whose ideals for the good life were love and beauty. The members of the set felt able to cultivate these virtues without economic worries, since they all had upper-class incomes which they could take for granted.

This attitude to life led Keynes to a subordination of concern for, if not disdain for, the middle-class virtues that could be primarily valued for their contribution to economic growth—thrift and the work ethic—and to the policy reflections of those virtues—balanced budgets and care for the entrepreneur. Moreover, he did not assign high status to those who practiced these policies or preached these virtues—businessmen and conservative politicians. And this, of course, made the conservatives uneasy with him.

In the end, however, it was not Keynes himself or what he said that would be the great threat to the conservatives. It would be the ideas that his followers—the Keynesians as distinct from Keynes—extrapolated from his theories. Even more, it would be the consequences of these ideas when they came to permeate the political process. Some of the "Keynesian" ideas were already evident in the New Deal period, before World War II. The most important of these was to maintain that the conditions which Keynes considered to exist at the bottom of the depression were general and permanent conditions of "mature" economies like ours. Some of the political consequences of Keynesianism—especially inflation—were foreseen before the war, but not by many. In these earlier days few visualized in the 1930s what were to be the real consequences of Keynesianism as it came to be understood and practiced after the war. That was a Keynesianism simplified beyond the text of Keynes, generalized into a description of the natural state of the economy, rather than of an economy in an extraordinary depression, and applied to policy by economists who could only guess at the magnitudes which would have to be known for a precise prescription and by politicians who had their own fish to fry. Specifically, the simpleminded Keynesianism that a generation of economists learned in school and which became the creed of modern intellectuals assumed:

1. That the price level was constant, so that demand could be expanded without danger of inflation.

2. That the potential output of the economy, or the level of full employment, was given—that is, would not be affected by the government's policy to maintain full employment.

3. That we knew how much output was the potential output of the economy and how much unemployment was full employment.

4. That the economy had a tendency to operate with output below its potential and unemployment above its full employment level.

5. That output and employment could be brought up to their desirable levels by fiscal actions of government to expand demand—specifically by spending enough or by running large deficits.

6. That we knew how much spending or how big deficits would be enough to achieve the desired results.

7. That there was no other way to get to the desired levels of output and employment, the main implication of which was that monetary policy could not do it.

All of these assumptions were wrong. When used as bases for public policy they inevitably produced errors. But these errors would not be distributed at random. The political process would give a predictable bias to the results. Politicians naturally like to spend money, especially if they are not required to raise taxes to pay for it. The theory, as interpreted, told the politician that he could spend without taxing and in the process also do something else that he liked to do—that is, deliver full employment. Of course, the theory said that there were limits to how much taxing and spending he could do. But no one knew with confidence where these limits were. No one knew what was full employment or how much spending or deficit was needed to achieve it. Moreover, the consequences of exceeding the limit did not seem great, since the price level was considered to be "practically" fixed and the level of potential output was considered to be given by factors that would be uninfluenced by policy. So the politician was free to choose his fiscal policy within a wide range. That is, he could choose from among a wide range of estimates of the size of the spending or deficit the theory called for, and given the politician's natural biases he would choose the larger spending, the larger deficit and the more ambitious goal for the rate of unemployment. The result in the end would be a bigger government sector, slower economic growth and more inflation than would have been chosen if all the consequences of policy had been accurately foreseen.

As I have noted, few foresaw this danger at the outset. One who did was Jacob Viner, who said in his original review of Keynes that it would lead to a "race between the printing press and the business agents of the trade unions."[10] That is, Keynes' policy in practice would lead to an attempt to pump up demand to maintain full employment at whatever wage rates the unions insisted upon. This was not a necessary consequence of Keynes' theory, but it was a likely consequence of the way Keynes would be translated into policy. The likely political consequences of Keynes became clearer as Keynes' theory was increasingly translated into simpler and less qualified form and as rules for policy began to be derived from it. Keynes himself in the years just before his death in 1946 became concerned about the unintended lengths to which his theory was being carried in argument and in policy. By that time the risks had become much clearer in the United States, and I will return in the next chapter to the debates this generated.

To ask whether the later perversion of his theory, this extreme extension of it, was a necessary consequence of what he wrote, which he should have foreseen and for which he is to be blamed, may seem an academic exercise. But the question does have practical significance. Keynes' is not the only or last theory that may have unintended consequences. There is a lesson in the experience with Keynesianism for the process of public discussion of economic ideas, and of other ideas, in general. Keynes stated his theory, as he acknowledged, in an extreme and provocative way, in order to be sure of getting attention. His followers, exhilarated by being in at the beginning of a new movement, simplified it extremely to increase its accessibility to students, politicians and others. Economists in the government, eager for influence, exaggerated what they knew. Offered an attractive course of policy, politicians adopted it eagerly, without serious questioning. The lesson is that even good ideas can have bad consequences if irresponsibly exploited.

It would be wrong to ascribe the future course of government policy and its consequences, both helpful and harmful, entirely to Keynes and his theories or even to them and his disciples. The critical event was the depression, for which Keynes surely cannot be blamed. The depression, given the increasing democratization of politics and the expectations of prosperity that had been developed in the preceding generation, would have brought about a radical change of policy with or without Keynes. The country was not willing to endure disaster stoically. This could be seen in the landslide ouster of Hoover and in the uninhibited experimentation of the Roosevelt days. Even without Keynes the depression would have established the idea that the government had a responsibility to maintain full employment, which the private system could not be counted on to do by itself. The idea that a main instrument for doing that was the government budget would also have become accepted, partly as a result of the evident failure of other approaches and partly as a result of naive theorizing which existed independently of Keynes. The fact that willy-nilly we ran large budget deficits for ten years, before the war, and no disaster befell us, did much to relieve us of inhibitions about the need to balance the budget, even without the rationale that Keynes provided. The depression provoked Keynes' theory and provided a market for it. The fiscal policy extemporized during the depression served as an example for future generations. What was learned from the depression was not the only possible lesson. But if we look back to the 1930s, and to the discussion of that time, that was probably the most conservative of the available lessons. That is, it was the one that entailed the least departure from the prevailing economic structure.

Beginnings of the Tax-Transfer Explosion

The second strand of New Deal policy that was crucial for the future development of liberal economics was the early move toward a system of large transfers through the federal government, addressed mainly to low-income people, financed in part by higher taxes on upper-income individuals and on corporations. The biggest item on the transfer side was the social security system, initially providing benefits for retired persons and survivors and later to be expanded to cover disabled persons. The two other main transfer programs were unemployment insurance and federal support for welfare payments to poor aged and disabled persons and to families with dependent children.

The depression stimulated these moves in various ways. One of the common theories of the causes of the depression—a theory with a long history—was that the demand for output was too small to purchase the total output that would be produced at high employment because of the maldistribution of income. Too much of the income earned in production went to upper-income people who saved rather than to lower-income people who consumed. This was a favorite theory of socialists, who could use it to blame the depression on the capitalist way of distributing income. It also had a certain consistency with Keynesian theory. If the depression was caused by an excess of the saving that people would want to do under conditions of high employment over the investment they would want to do, one possible remedy would be to reduce saving by redistribution of income from savers to spenders. Keynes did not himself propose that solution. In his theory the problem could be solved simply by running a larger deficit. But "liberals" took pleasure in pointing out to conservatives that if they did not want deficits the problem of excessive saving could be solved by income redistribution.

This argument obviously supported a program of taxing the rich and giving to the poor. (Later research cast doubt on whether any significant reduction of saving could be achieved by this route, but at the time it seemed plausible.)[11] The social security system as originally planned was not good from this standpoint. The intent was to raise a reserve fund by payroll taxes, the income from which would be available to pay retirement benefits in the future when the people being covered by the system when it started would reach retirement age. The accumulation of this fund would be a big addition to national saving, and would compound the problem of excessive saving. There would have been an offset to that if the future beneficiaries of the system had reduced their private saving in view of their expectation that the social security system would look after them. But it was a basic premise of the program that people did not voluntarily save enough to provide for their old age, and it would have been inconsistent with that view to assume that the saving now being forced through the social security system would be offset by a reduction of private saving. In fact, as the social security system began to run a surplus in 1936 and 1937, concern was expressed that it was depressing the economy and contributing to the recession of 1937. Because of this, and also because of politicians' unwillingness to raise enough taxes to pay for future benefits, the system was changed in 1939. Only enough reserve would be accumulated to safeguard the program against brief contingencies, such as a recession when receipts might fall off. Future benefits, which would be much larger than present ones because a much larger number of people would have earned much larger benefits per retiree, would be paid for by higher taxes on future generations of workers.

This change in the system had important consequences. It created built-in pressure for increases of benefits. People already in retirement, or near retirement, had a strong interest in raising benefits, which they would not pay for, or pay for only to a small degree. Those who would pay, the future workers, were unaware of the burden being stored up for them, or at least were not sufficiently aware to be a great political force against the increase of benefits. Some who would pay were not yet born. Moreover, the change in the financing system tilted the scales of saving in the opposite direction from the original one. People were being promised benefits for their retirement, and their incentive to save for their retirement was being reduced. But the government was not doing any saving to compensate for the loss of private saving. Forty-five years later that would be put forth as a reason for the slowdown of economic growth in the United States.[12]

On the tax side of the tax-transfer system, the clearest expression of the anti-saving motivation was the undistributed profits tax of 1937. The theory was that taxing the undistributed profits of corporations at a higher rate than the distributed profits would force corporations to pay out more in dividends and so stimulate consumption rather than saving. The undistributed profits tax did not last for long, but the same reasoning was only a little less evident in the increase of the corporate profits tax in general and in the increase of the income tax in the upper brackets. These rates would be much further increased during the war and never returned to the New Deal levels. In fact, the Roosevelt tax acts of 1934 and 1936 did not raise upper-bracket income taxes as much as the 1932 act, during the Hoover administration. The Roosevelt tax increases were more resented, however, because they raised the upper-bracket rates while cutting those for middle-income taxpayers, unlike the 1932 act, which had raised rates across the board.

The antidepression argument for unemployment insurance was also clear. The payments to the unemployed would help to sustain the expenditures of those who had lost jobs and so would help to sustain economic activity. At the same time a payroll tax would be imposed on employers, and the level of that tax for each employer would depend on the amount of unemployment experienced by his workers. Thus there would be an incentive for employers to manage their affairs in a way that would reduce unemployment.

The economic arguments for expansion of the tax-transfer system were only part of the reason for it. The growing feeling about poverty and, what is not the same thing, inequality, was probably even more important. The poverty that came with the depression was especially moving to the national conscience and politically forceful for a number of reasons in addition to the fact that it was so widespread. There was the striking contrast with the prosperity of the 1920s. The poverty was not confined to rural and urban slums—out of sight of average citizens and the media. It was not confined to blacks or to recent immigrants, and could not be "blamed" on their special characteristics. It was not confined to people who could be called "shiftless." It had obviously far outstripped the ability of private charities or state and local governments to deal with it. Moreover, it could not be blamed on the inability of the American economy to produce enough to relieve the poverty. The situation at the time was commonly described as poverty in the midst of plenty, really meaning poverty in the midst of potential plenty. In the circumstances the remaining extremes of great wealth seemed more than ever intolerable. My professor Henry Simons, certainly no radical demagogue, found the inequality of income distribution "unlovely," not a fiery condemnation but one difficult to quarrel with.[13] Justification for extreme personal wealth as the engine of the general prosperity, which might have been accepted in the 1920s, was no longer acceptable when the engine had stalled. Many prominent captains of industry had lost their credibility as economic leaders by inanely optimistic statements or, worse, by criminal actions that brought them to prison. Populist, egalitarian movements were sweeping the country, with Huey Long, proclaiming "Every Man a King," as the most important leader.

The social security system, the program of federal grants to the states in support of welfare payments to the aged, the blind and dependent children, and the expansion of the progressive income tax were responses to economic, emotional and political conditions of the depression which lasted and grew during the postwar generation of prosperity. A related program of federal employment for people who could not find private jobs—the WPA and all its variants—faded away during the war and did not reappear until it came back in a much different form in the 1960s as part of the manpower programs initiated by the Kennedy administration. Of course, the welfare state which emerged in the United States in the 1930s had emerged in Europe much earlier. An important fact, usually considered a paradox but perhaps only natural, is that the beginning of social insurance goes back to Bismarck, the conservative Prussian Chancellor, in the 1890s. The emergence of the welfare state in the United States in the 1930s is probably easier to explain than its failure to emerge earlier.

Once the welfare state did come to America it grew rapidly. In 1929, total transfer payments by all governments—federal, state and local—except for benefits to veterans and pensions to government retirees amounted to about $250 million. (Those were days when we counted in millions.) Ten years later, without any intervening price inflation, they were a little over $1,750 million, or about seven times as much. As a fraction of GNP they had risen from .25 percent to about 2 percent. Most of the increase was in social security and unemployment compensation, which went from zero to 1.4 percent of GNP.

The development of the tax transfer system was hotly resisted by conservatives. The WPA became a national joke because of the commonly accepted picture that the work being done was useless and the workers indolent. Businessmen complained that the public employment and welfare programs kept wage rates up and so interfered with the revival of the private economy. (Labor unions criticized the low-paid government employment projects for driving down wages.) The social security system was attacked on grounds that would later seem bizarre. It was held that giving every covered worker a social security number would

introduce a police state, enabling the government to keep track
of, and ultimately control, the movements of every worker.
Workers were also warned that they were being required to pay,
through their social security "contributions," for promised pen-
sion benefits which they might never receive because Congress
could eliminate them by a stroke of the pen. (A realist might
have predicted, on the contrary, that the political process would
give them benefits they had never paid for.)

The most serious conservative complaint, however, was about
the tax side of the tax-transfer system. There was a little problem in this, because the conservatives were also opposed to the
budget deficits, and raising taxes seemed, to ordinary people, at
least, to be a way to reduce the deficit. Conservatives resolved
this difficulty then, as they had done earlier and would do over
and over again later, by claiming that the particular kinds of tax
increases proposed—mainly individual and corporate income
taxes and estate taxes—would depress the economy and so reduce rather than increase the revenue. Opposition was especially
strong to the undistributed profits tax. The business community
regarded that as an attack upon the growth of existing enterprises, and, indeed, one of the motives of its sponsors was to correct what they regarded as a bias in favor of existing enterprises
and against new ones. The undistributed profits tax was the only
New Deal enactment that conservatives succeeded in repealing.

Corporate profits tax liability rose from 13.7 percent of book
profits in 1929 to 20 percent in 1939. (As a percentage of "true"
profits—adjusted for under- or overstatement of the cost of re-
placing capital and inventories—the tax ratio rose from 15.1 percent to 27.0 percent.) The effects of the change in individual income taxation are less visible in the revenue figures. Individual
income tax as a percentage of personal income remained approximately stable at 1.4 percent in 1929 and 1.2 percent in
1939. Most personal income throughout this period was excluded from income taxation by high personal exemptions. The
income subject to taxes because it was above the exemption
levels was a smaller fraction of total personal income in 1939
than in 1929, and the average tax rate on that taxable income

was not only much higher than is suggested by the 1.6 percent and 1.4 percent figures but also had risen rather than declined.

The Spread of Economic Regulation

Although the American welfare state can be said to have its beginning during the New Deal, the history of federal economic regulation is much older.[14] The grandfather of it all, of course, was the protective tariff, which began with the new nation in 1789. In more familiar terms economic regulation can be dated from 1887, when we got the Interstate Commerce Commission to control the railroad industry, and 1890, when the Sherman Act to restrain monopolization was passed. There was another spurt of regulation during the administration of Woodrow Wilson, and some further steps even during the "conservative" Republican era following World War I.

Dissatisfaction with the performance of the economy in the 1930s naturally led to many proposals for increased government regulation. The National Recovery Act was the most comprehensive system of control attempted. That did not last very long, as already noted, and not only because it was declared unconstitutional. It was early seen to be an unworkable and unproductive system. Nevertheless, the New Deal did spawn a very significant extension of federal regulation of the economy.

What happened during the New Deal was not just more of the kind of regulation that had been going on since 1890. A new basis or justification for regulation was introduced on a major scale. Earlier regulation was designed either to preserve competition or to achieve the results of competition in circumstances where competition was considered not to be feasible, as in the case of railroads. There was some of this during the New Deal, with the establishment of the Civil Aeronautics Board and the Federal Power Commission. But the main new regulatory systems introduced by the New Deal had a different basis. They were intended to protect chosen sectors of the economy from competition.

The chosen sectors were labor, agriculture and small business. Presumably these sectors were disadvantaged in a competitive economy or, as was sometimes said, the competitiveness of these sectors put them at a disadvantage in an economy where other sectors were less competitive. There were several reasons for trying to do something about these "disadvantaged" sectors. One was the underconsumption argument, already mentioned. If a larger share of the national income could be directed to workers and farmers, a larger share of the national income would be consumed and the economy would operate at a higher level. Also, the disadvantaged were natural objects of sympathy, especially if their relatively low incomes were due to a defect in the economic system. Third, and certainly not least, workers, farmers and small businessmen made up a large proportion of the electorate and for that reason attracted the interest of politicians. (Small businessmen probably have a political influence that is more than proportionate to their numbers because they tend to be leading figures in almost every Congressional district.)

There were two main regulatory instruments for promoting the interests of workers. The National Labor Relations Act was intended to protect workers in the exercise of their right to organize in trade unions, and the Wages and Hours Act set for the first time a federal minimum wage. Farmers were the intended beneficiaries of a large body of legislation and regulation mainly working to raise farm prices by reducing farm output and by holding some of the output off the market. The Robinson-Patman Act was an effort to aid small businessmen by assuring that they could buy at prices not higher than those paid by larger firms.

Whether any of this ever worked as intended has always been subject to many questions. From the beginning, employers maintained that the Labor Relations Act was a limitation on the right of workers to abstain from unionization if they wished to do so and on the right of employers and employees jointly to agree on the best kind of relation between them. Economists have argued that the promotion of unionism has enabled a small elite fraction of the labor force to increase its incomes at the expense of other workers, and has increased rather than decreased the inequality in the distribution of income. The minimum wage can be looked at as a mechanism initially designed to prevent poor Southern workers from getting jobs at the expense of better-paid Northern workers, or as a device for keeping the Southern poor in their poverty. Later the minimum wage was to be extensively criticized for reducing the employment opportunities of disadvantaged youth, who were not sufficiently skilled to be employable at the minimum wage, and thereby preventing them from getting the work experience that would have made them employable at better jobs. The programs of agricultural regulation and price support were later seen to have mainly served the interests of the more prosperous farmers, and even more of landowners, at the expense of consumers and even of low-income farm workers who suffered from reduced demand for farm labor and did not share the gains in the value of the farmland.

Despite these serious questions about the consistency of their actual effects with the advertised intent, these regulations had great popular support. They persisted in the face of continuous conservative complaint and attack, although with some modifications in the postwar period.[15] The notion embodied in them, that the government had a responsibility to protect the incomes of selected groups of the population by regulation of prices or production, was extended to other sectors in the wave of regulation which came in the 1960s and 1970s.

The New Deal laid the basis for subsequent regulation of economic activity in another way that was probably even more important. The New Deal experience ended, apparently permanently, any constitutional restraint on the power of the federal government to regulate economic life. Before the New Deal the courts had limited the powers of the federal government in this field by a strict interpretation of the commerce clause and due process clause of the Constitution. On this basis the Supreme Court invalidated two of the key elements of the early New Deal, the NRA and the AAA. Roosevelt challenged the legitimacy of the court's action in striking down measures he considered necessary for the national welfare, and he proposed to get legislation which would permit him to appoint additional members to the

Supreme Court who would be more congenial. It never became necessary for him to push this proposal. The Court bowed to his popularity in the country and power in the Congress. Subsequent appointments to the Court, by Roosevelt and Truman, confirmed the fact that the power of the federal government to regulate economic activity would not be limited by any constitutional inhibitions.

The Legacy of the Depression, Roosevelt and Keynes

Whether the New Deal cured the depression is doubtful. The economy did recover after 1933, but slowly. In 1939, before the war began to dominate the economy, total output was still lower than it had been in 1929. The failure of the economy in a recovery to regain the level of output experienced ten years earlier had no parallel in our history. In the course of the recovery, and while it was still far from complete, we had a second recession, in 1937, one of the sharpest of our history. The New Deal did not yield a quicker or better recovery than we might have expected from the historical record. But we had had a deeper depression than the record would have led one to expect, and the relevance of the historical precedents is not certain.

One can reasonably argue, however, that once the pressure for contraction of the money supply had been relieved by the loosening of the tie to gold and the establishment of deposit insurance, and the gold inflow began to raise the money supply, a strong recovery was most probable. The increase of government expenditures may have tended to strengthen that course, but was probably not a dominant factor. On the other hand, many New Deal measures that tended to raise costs and prices—notably the labor and farm policies—tended to restrain the growth of real output while the tax and regulatory policies impeded the revival of private investment.

Only when combined with the theory of Keynes and the personality of Roosevelt does the New Deal look like a success and a lesson for the future. Keynes told us not to expect recovery as a natural development, because the system was capable of an extremely long depression, so that any recovery seemed a triumph of policy. He also told us that the essential policy for recovery was fiscal policy, and that other measures were of less importance, which also validated what the New Deal did.

But if the economic success of the New Deal was doubtful, its political success could not be questioned. No other President before or since has dominated the political scene as Roosevelt did. His personal triumph was more than a matter of votes. He made the nation feel better in miserable objective conditions, by the force of his own personality and behavior. What in others might have seemed vacillation and indecisiveness he made to seem bold experimentation. His defeats and failures were given the appearance of temporary setbacks at the hands of the enemies of the people against whom he would inevitably triumph.

The combination of the depression, Keynes and Roosevelt left us with many basic "lessons" which were to dominate policy for years to come:

1. The basic economic problem is unemployment—getting the economy to operate up to its potential.

2. That goal is to be achieved by assuring the adequacy of total spending—nominal demand—and that in turn is to be accomplished by management of the government budget.

3. If aggregate demand is managed properly, other aspects of economic policy—the tax-transfer system and regulation—can be used to redistribute income in favor of low-income groups or other "worthy" parts of the population—without concern for possible adverse effects on the total potential output of the economy.

4. There are no constitutional limits to the power of the federal government to regulate the economy.

5. An activist policy by the President—proposing strong and dramatic measures and maintaining constant communication with the public—will be appreciated by the public and will help to maintain the vigor of the economy.

3

Truman and Eisenhower: Postwar Consolidation

WHEN THE UNITED STATES ENTERED WORLD WAR II, President Roosevelt said that Dr. New Deal would be replaced by Dr. Win the War. This did not mean that domestic economic policy would be put in the deep freeze and reemerge unchanged when the war was over. The war years, when no immediate decisions about the "normal" peacetime operation of the economy had to be made, were a period of gestation for the ideas and controversies of the depression decade. Also, the economic experience of the war left behind changes of thinking and conditions which would not be entirely undone when the war ended.

The American economy performed brilliantly during the war. Total output rose by 77 percent from 1939 to 1944, or by about 12 percent a year. (This is according to present gross national product estimates, which cannot be taken literally for a period in which the composition of output changed as much as it did during the war, but the fact that output increased greatly cannot be questioned.) Unemployment fell to negligible levels. This experience tended to confirm the belief that there was nothing wrong with the economy that a sufficient expansion of demand brought about by government spending or government deficits could not correct. Everyone did not accept this conclusion. There was, after all, an unprecedented degree of government management of the economy during the war—with comprehensive price controls, rationing and materials allocations—and some drew from that the lesson that extensive economic planning was feasible and necessary. Others were concerned about the inflationary pressures which were associated with the demand expansion that had yielded the great increase of output and employment—pressures which had been only partially and temporarily restrained by price controls. But the prevailing lesson was that we could avoid a repetition of the depression by demand management without "structural" changes.

The war was a struggle of the free societies against totalitarianism. It was an occasion for remembering and reaffirming that freedom was the American way. This helped to restore acceptance of the idea that the way we organize the American economy is through the free enterprise system, after that idea had been called into question by the depression. The war tended to support the belief that we had to choose between free market systems and totalitarian systems, and this elicited and drew attention to a wave of powerful writing which warned of the direction in which the interventionist tendencies of the 1930s were taking us. The best-known example, whose title illustrates the thinking well, was Hayek's The Road to Serfdom.[1] This writing put the problem of the choice of economic systems in a more objective and historical context than had been done by the typical anti–New Deal pamphleteering of the National Association of Manufacturers during the 1930s. It was much more appealing to intellectuals and contributed to strengthening an intellectual free market or conservative movement, which had been weak during the depression (although Hayek, as already noted, did not accept the designation "conservative," preferring "liberal").

The war tended to moderate the negative and reactionary attitude which had characterized business leadership during the 1930s. Although some aspects of the wartime economic policy raised issues between business and the New Dealers who were still in the government, on the whole the war provided a breathing spell during which some of the earlier struggles could be forgotten. There was an atmosphere of national unity. Business had less to feel guilty about. And many businessmen came to work in the Washington war agencies and acquired a better understanding of the problems of government and of the people who ran it.

Keynesian economics was completing its domination of the economics profession. Keynesianism moved from a general theory to some abstract rules of policy—such as that government expenditures should be high enough to maintain high employment—to operational procedures for applying these rules in particular situations. One basic problem was to know how much to do in those particular situations. Keynes himself gave the lead in thinking about this problem in his pamphlet *How to Pay for the War,* which applied his reasoning to the British situation and data.[2] He estimated how much of the national output would be available for private consumption, in view of the demands of the war, how much income could be left to consumers so that they would not try to buy more than that amount, and what tax and savings programs were required to hold down disposable income and consumption to the permissible, noninflationary level.

The effort to quantify Keynesian policy was greatly promoted in the United States by availability of a new series of statistics on the gross national product (GNP), which began in 1941. For the first time we had a set of books on the American economy with income and expenditure sides that balanced. This permitted a comparison of the income that would be earned in production with the amount of output that would be available for private purchase. From this, on certain assumptions about how much of their income people would want to spend, it was possible to calculate a "gap"—the difference between desired expenditures and available output. On other assumptions one could then calculate what tax or other measures would be needed to close the gap. Moreover, it seemed only a matter of time before the accumulation of data would provide a solid empirical foundation under the assumptions needed for these calculations.

In World War II as in earlier wars the question arose of how to divide war finance between taxing and borrowing. In World War I, to say nothing of earlier days, there seemed to be no guidance for that question except such intuitive rules as fifty-fifty or political considerations of how much taxation the public would stand. In World War II the young Keynesian economists who were becoming important in the Treasury, Bureau of the Budget, Department of Commerce and Office of Price Administration tried to use their theory and new data to answer the question "scientifically." This did not mean, of course, that the President and the Congress would follow their prescription. Nor was there any demonstration that the prescription was correct. Nevertheless, there was growing confidence throughout the government that they knew how to do it, if given the chance.

In addition to these developments in the world of ideas the war brought two developments in the budget which would be influential for many years to come. The most important of these was that the nation acquired an enormously powerful new revenue-raising machine. For the first time we had a broad-based individual income tax, capable of nearly universal application. In 1939 a family of four with an income of $3,000 paid no income tax, with an income of $5,000 paid $48 and with an income of $10,000 paid $343. At the peak of wartime tax rates the $3,000 family was paying $275, the $5,000 family $755 and the $10,000 family $2,245. In 1939, federal personal income taxes were 1.2 percent of personal income. By 1945 the proportion had risen to 11.2 percent.[3] These rates would be reduced after the war, then raised again during the Korean War and subsequently reduced in a series of steps, mainly in 1954, 1964, 1970 and 1981. But they would never get anywhere near the low rates of 1939.

We could have what almost everyone regarded as a big tax cut after World War II and still be left with much more revenue, absolutely and relative to GNP, than the federal government ever had before. Also, with that tax system in place, even as reduced after the war, revenues would rise faster than GNP because of the interaction between the progressive tax system and economic growth, and that effect would be heightened by inflation. As a result, governments were in the position where they could continuously increase expenditures and cut tax rates from time to time without running deficits of a kind that they found unacceptable. This fact, plus the fact that so much of the revenue came in the form of weekly withholding rather than in annual declarations and payments, which made it all seem fairly painless, undoubtedly contributed to the growth of expenditures in the postwar period.

We ended the war with a federal budget much higher than it had been in 1939, not only absolutely but also relative to the GNP. But this increase was due entirely to purposes connected with the war and its aftermath. The defense establishment was much larger, and could be expected to remain so, now that we no longer rested behind the shield of the European Allies. We had large bills for veterans' benefits. Interest on the federal debt had been increased greatly by the wartime deficits. We had undertaken to make large expenditures in support of the reconstruction of Europe. Aside from these war-connected expenditures, federal outlays were a smaller fraction of the GNP than they had been in 1939—3.9 percent in 1946 compared to 7.3 percent in 1939.

There was a reasonable expectation that these war-connected expenditures would decline, if not absolutely at least as a fraction of the GNP. This did happen, although less than had been hoped when the war ended. This decline in the demands for war-connected expenditures was another factor, along with the natural growth of revenues from the existing tax system, that made it easy for nondefense expenditures to rise. Arithmetic suggested the possibility that total federal spending, as a fraction of GNP, would decline when the war-connected fraction declined. Politics suggested the unlikelihood of that picture. Especially when the revenue was rising strongly, the decline in the war-connected share left a vacuum into which nondefense spending rushed.

The higher level of taxes and expenditures left to us by the war had an important implication for "Keynesian" fiscal policy. In the 1930s that policy had essentially meant the government would decide from time to time what the level of government spending should be to maintain full employment. The budgetary situation after the war directed emphasis to taxation as an important variable, probably the most useful variable, for adjusting the budget to the needs of economic stabilization. Before the war the level of taxation was so low that there was little room for stimulating the economy by cutting taxes. After the war that was no longer the case. In fact, during the war the government began to withhold income taxes from wages at the time wages were paid. With that system larger flows of income could be manipulated in a short period on the revenue side of the budget than on the expenditure side. This had a substantial effect on the thinking of conservatives whose previous opposition to expansionist fiscal policy had been largely opposition to the increase of government spending it was assumed to imply.

A second consequence of the new budget situation was that large swings in the size of the deficit or surplus would occur automatically when the economy fluctuated. With large amounts of revenue coming from the income tax, and with Treasury collections being almost simultaneous with the earning of income, by virtue of withholding, there would be a large prompt increase or decrease of revenue when the economy rose or fell. On the other side of the budget, there would be a rise or fall of unemployment compensation payments as unemployment increased or decreased. Thus, there seemed to be an automatic stabilizing mechanism in the budget. This possibility had been observed earlier, but it became quantitatively important only when the level of taxation had increased and when pay-as-you-go income taxation brought fluctuations in tax payments much closer in time to the fluctuations in the economy. Such an automatic stabilization system was of great interest to conservatives who could buy the Keynesian theory but shied away from its implementation by politicians and bureaucrats, whom they mistrusted.

Postwar Schools of Economic Thought

In the days immediately after the war one could identify four main attitudes to the problems of economic policy.

1. Strict and exclusive Keynesians These were people, mainly economists, who believed that the only problem, or at least the main problem by far, was to maintain full employment. Moreover, they believed that the main, or sufficient, instrument for achieving that was the government budget. The devotion of fiscal policy to the maintenance of full employment was called "functional finance." Initially this had meant manipulation of the expenditure side of the budget, but there was no reason in principle for them to reject manipulation of the revenue side as well, and in a short time that became part of the accepted doctrine. They recognized that the implementation of a fiscal policy for full employment entailed certain difficulties of estimation and forecasting, but they didn't think those difficulties were serious.

In principle these early Keynesians recognized that expansionism could be overdone and cause inflation. But they were not greatly concerned about that either. They thought that inflation would be the result of an error—of generating more demand than was necessary for full employment. This could be avoided by good estimation of the amount of demand needed. They were not impressed with the possibility that if the level of demand was high enough to achieve full employment—which they assumed they knew how to measure—it might also be high enough to cause inflation. They thought that the inflation that might be caused by error could be reversed, and in any case they didn't think that on the scale that might be imagined in peacetime it would do any great harm.

They tended to regard monetary policy as ineffective, or at most only one-sidedly effective. That is, monetary restraint might serve to limit demand when it would otherwise be excessive, but it could not stimulate demand when it might be deficient.

I call these people exclusive Keynesians because their interest was almost entirely concentrated on the overall performance of the economy and on the overall behavior of aggregate demand. They were not much concerned with microeconomic matters, with the structure of the economy. They were not planners, in the sense of wanting to control production, investment, prices or wages in particular industries. They were not, however, strongly averse to price controls, either selectively or generally. They did not put great stock in the classical arguments for the price system, and if their demand-expansionist measures threatened to cause inflation they would be prepared to take direct steps to hold prices down. But they did not regard manipulation of prices as important to correct economic problems. They were not even much interested in selective regulation of this or that industry; although they felt no desire to reduce the regulation, regulation was not high on their agenda. Also, they tended to be income-equalizers, but they were not pushing that line of policy either. Given the structure of tax rates with which the country ended the war, there was not much point to discussing further increases of taxation of the wealthy. By and large, although these people tended to resist some of the claims made in the postwar years for reduction of income taxes on upper-bracket individuals and on corporations, they were not aggressively seeking to raise such taxes. Basically, they believed that the overwhelming problem was the execution of a fiscal policy for full employment, and they were not to be diverted from that by worrying about problems that might remain if such a policy was accomplished.

2. *Reformers and planners*   These were mainly leftover New Dealers who wanted to continue and expand the structural changes of the economy that they thought had been begun during the 1930s, for example, with the pro-labor and pro-farmer measures. They accepted the Keynesian prescriptions for macroeconomic policy, but did not think that was enough. They thought that more detailed government control, or influence, was needed to achieve "balance." By that they meant both balance between wages and prices, which would assure that the full-

employment product could be sold, and balance among industries, to avoid waste. They also supported major expansion of government transfer and subsidy programs, for housing and health, among other things.

3. Conservative macroeconomists This group of people has been called "commercial Keynesians," by critics who did not mean that as a term of approval. They agreed with the strict Keynesians that the maintenance of economic stability—of high employment without inflation—was the major problem. They also agreed that the stabilization of demand at an adequately growing rate was the way to solve that problem. They accepted the use of fiscal policy as an important instrument for the management of aggregate demand. But they differed from the conventional Keynesians in a number of respects. First, they thought that monetary policy was also important, being capable of both expanding and contracting demand. Therefore, they had more options for fiscal policy, because fiscal policy did not have to be exclusively dedicated to economic stabilization. Second, they were much concerned with inflation. This was partly because they thought that "full employment" might be inconsistent with price stability. They were worried by the experience of 1936–1937, when prices began to rise while the economy was still far short of full employment. Moreover, they mistrusted the political management of demand, thinking that it would have an inflationary bias even if that was not economically necessary. Third, they were skeptical of the claims of the Keynesians that they could reliably make the estimates and forecasts required for their fine-tuning management of the economy.

Like the Keynesians, they did not have microeconomic policy questions in the foreground of their concerns. But their basic leaning with respect to such questions was the opposite of the typical Keynesian. That is, they rejected ideas of government planning and intervention. But they did not have a long list of regulations they wanted to undo. Their concern in this field was mainly to prevent further intrusion by government.

4. Conventional conservatives These were the people, mainly leaders of business organizations and Republican politicians but also including some intellectuals, who were still fighting the battles of the New Deal. "Keynesian" was to them an obscenity. They waved the bloody red shirt of the totalitarian takeover. But behind or alongside the extreme rhetoric there were a few real things they wanted—especially lower taxes on corporations and upper incomes and some reduction of the powers given to labor unions under the Wagner Act.

Despite what seemed at the end of the war a wide range of opinion about national economic policy, a remarkable consensus was achieved in a few years. This was largely the result of an unusual process of discussion of economic policy that occurred near the end of the war and for about five years thereafter. The discussion was unusual in the degree to which it was realistic, operational, directed to national, long-run objectives and nonpartisan and nonideological. The process is important to recall, because progress today would be greatly assisted if we could have something like it again.

The basic condition was that the war had heightened the sense of common national destiny and purpose to a degree that is rare. At the same time, there was general acute concern about the possibility of falling back, after the war, into the depression from which only the war had extricated us. There was, therefore, a common willingness, and indeed eagerness, to think broadly about economic policy in the national interest, and to put aside partisan, special-interest or ritualistic arguments. The war had given us a feeling of competence to solve great problems, while the memory of the depression prevented us from complacency.

As the war drew to an end, postwar planning became the national occupation.[4] Among the proposals getting much attention were prescriptions from the National Planning Association, from Vice-President Henry Wallace, from the National Association of Manufacturers, and from a group of citizens in Minneapolis–St. Paul. Early in the postwar period the Twentieth Century Fund published a series of essays by well-known economists on maintaining postwar prosperity.[5] The American Economic Association, in an unusual step, established a committee to write a report setting forth the profession's views on economic stabilization. There were also many private, individual efforts, the most notable of which was Milton Friedman's "A Monetary and Fiscal Framework for Economic Stability."[6]

Special note must be made of the work of the Committee for Economic Development, because it epitomized both the spirit and the substance of the postwar consensus. The CED, established in 1942 with the blessing of the Department of Commerce, was a private organization of businessmen whose first concern was with the postwar transition. The leaders of this group considered themselves to be deeply devoted to the free society and the free economy and believed that the negative attitudes of business organizations in the 1930s had been unproductive from that standpoint. Those attitudes had not contributed to a solution of the economic problem, they had alienated business from the rest of society, and they had destroyed the influence of business even when it had something to say. Several of the business leaders of the CED had close connections with the University of Chicago. Of the founding members, one, the first chairman, Paul Hoffman, was a trustee of the university, one had been vice-president of the university, and one had been dean of the social sciences. The first three research directors, covering the period from 1942 to 1967, were Ph.D.s in economics from Chicago.[7] There was a strong influence of what I have called above conservative macroeconomics. That is, there was acceptance of government responsibility for stabilizing aggregate demand, with fiscal policy as an instrument for doing that but with monetary policy also important, but also with a need to constrain those policies to reduce errors and political bias in their management.

The Macroeconomic Consensus

Three developments were of major importance in arriving at the postwar consensus on macroeconomic policy.

1. The Employment Act of 1946   As the end of the war
came into sight, New Deal economists in the government and
their allies in the Congress initiated an effort to set postwar economic policy in a simple Keynesian mold. This was to be done
by the enactment of what was initially called the Full Employment Act. The act would declare the responsibility of the federal
government for maintaining full employment and establish a procedure and policy for discharging that responsibility. Essentially,
the Bureau of the Budget, where much of the thinking behind
the bill originated, would estimate the size of the government
deficit required to achieve full employment. (This deficit was
euphemistically called "investment.") The President would recommend this deficit to Congress, where it would be considered
by a joint committee to be newly created for this purpose. Once
this committee had decided on the proper size of the deficit, the
Congress was to be guided by that decision in acting on expenditures and taxes.[8]

This proposal stimulated a great debate. There were people
who rejected the whole idea, root and branch. But it was not
really practical in 1945 to deny the government's responsibility
for the level of employment. The real debate centered on more
operational issues.

—Did the notion of "full employment" imply a target so ambitious that it could be achieved only by harsh government controls or by inflation? There were arguments that a commitment
to full employment would require, or at least entitle, the government to force housewives out of the home into the factory. The
concern about inflation if the government tried to drive unemployment down to an extremely low level was more realistic.

—Did the formulation in the proposed legislation place too
much emphasis on manipulation of the budget, and especially of
the deficit, as a way of achieving full employment?

—Did the commitment to full employment authorize the government to direct or suppress the private economy?

—Did the proposal give too much power to the nest of Keynesian economists in the Budget Bureau who would presumably
make the estimates on which the whole operation was based?

On all of these issues compromises were reached in a conservative direction. The term "full employment" was removed from the bill and replaced by "maximum employment, production and purchasing power." While this might not in substance seem a great difference, in the context of the contemporary discussion it was understood as a move toward pragmatism and flexibility. References to the government deficit as the instrument of economic management were deleted. A sentence was inserted requiring that measures adopted under the act should be consistent with the free enterprise system. The Bureau of the Budget was removed from the implementation of the act. Instead a Council of Economic Advisers to the President, requiring confirmation by the Senate, was established. While many conservatives would have preferred an outside, nongovernmental council, the organization established at least held open the possibility of escaping the biases attributed to the Bureau of the Budget.

Given the experience of the 1930s, it was inconceivable that the government would fail to commit itself to maintaining high employment. That commitment was made in one way or another by governments all over the world. But the form that commitment took in the United States, as embodied in the Employment Act of 1946, could hardly have been more satisfactory to conservatives. That is, after a major national discussion the Congress rejected an overly ambitious, inflationary definition of the goal, rejected exclusive reliance on deficit financing as the means and reaffirmed its devotion to the free enterprise system.

Probably the most important lasting result of the act, which might not have occurred without it, was the establishment of the Council of Economic Advisers in the White House. The discussion at the time the act was passed did not imply that the members of this council would have to be economists. In fact, two of the three members of the first council, appointed by President Truman, were not professional economists. Starting with the three appointed by Eisenhower in 1953, however, all have been economists.

Whether the establishment of professional economists in a position so close to the President should be regarded as a plus or a minus from the standpoint of conservative economics is an open question. There are people who would unhesitatingly say that the answer is a minus, since they regard a majority of all economists and a still larger majority of the economists who take government positions as radicals of one degree or another. But a good case can be made for the opposite answer. On matters of government regulation and government expenditure the White House economists in all administrations have been a conservative force. On such matters the drive for expansion comes, within the government, from the spending departments and regulatory agencies, and anything that strengthens the President's hand is a force for restraint. On macroeconomic matters—particularly on inflation, deficits and controls—the history is more mixed. But it is probably true that on the whole the President's economists have been more cautious about these matters than the President—although undoubtedly not as cautious as they should have been.

2. The domestication of Keynesianism   The Employment Act of 1946 left open the question of the nature of federal fiscal policy and its relation to the maintenance of high employment. At the conventional academic level there was no question about this. Simple-minded Keynesian functional finance swept the colleges and universities. Generations of sophomores were being taught (fortunately, however, they soon forgot) that there was at any moment of time a size of government deficit, which the government knew and could achieve, which would yield full employment, and that the government should run a deficit of that size. Paul Samuelson's textbook *Economics: An Introductory Analysis,* which taught that lesson, dominated the field.[9] It had imitators but few dissenters.

At the level of policy, and at the more sophisticated level of economic thinking, things were not that simple. A critical element in the argument was, of course, the ability of the government to estimate reliably the size of the needed deficit. On this subject experience at the end of the war was enlightening—even shocking. The conventional forecast made by economists was that when the war ended and defense spending was cut back the United States would fall into a severe recession unless there was a big increase in nondefense expenditures of government. This didn't happen, and its failure to happen vividly illustrated three points:

1. The forecasting ability of economists was not adequate for the "functional finance" prescription.

2. The error in the postwar forecast resulted from a too exclusive Keynesian approach. The conventional forecasters ignored the effect on private demand of the big accumulation of money and other liquid assets that had occurred during the war. Economists who gave more weight to monetary factors did not make the same mistake. They believed that when wartime restrictions were removed, households and businesses would hurry to convert their liquid assets into real assets—which had been depleted during the war. That would create a demand for output and prevent a recession.

This experience tended to support the view that money mattered much more than was recognized in conventional Keynesian analysis. And that in turn had implications beyond the ability to forecast. It meant that there was no unique proper size of the deficit needed to achieve full employment. The proper size of the deficit for that purpose would depend on the monetary policy. There could be high employment with a deficit and tight money or with a surplus and easier money.

3. There was a suspicion that the error of the conventional forecasts was not simply a matter of chance or of mistaken analysis. These forecasts were made by people who wanted an increase of government nondefense expenditures and who were therefore biased toward making a forecast that would justify such an increase.

The implications of these points, and a proposal for dealing with them, were most clearly set forth by the Research and Policy Committee of the CED, notably in its 1947 statement "Taxes and the Budget: A Program for Stability in a Free Society."[10] The CED rejected the conventional functional finance prescription on the grounds that forecasting errors would make it destabilizing rather than stabilizing, and that political bias would lead toward inflation and increasing government expenditures. On the other hand, it rejected traditional budget balancing, which would require tax increases in recession and tax cuts in booms. That would probably be destabilizing, and, if not, certainly impractical and unnecessary.

The CED proposed as an alternative a policy of balancing the budget, or achieving a small surplus, at high employment. Departures of the economy from high employment would automatically yield deficits if the economy was below high employment, or a larger surplus than planned for high employment if the economy was in an exceptional boom. These automatic variations in the deficit or surplus would tend to stabilize the economy but they would not be subject to forecasting errors because they would be responses to *actual* variations of the economy, not to forecast ones. Also, the requirement that durable, noncyclical increases of expenditures be matched by increases of taxes would restrain the growth of expenditures, because the politicians' reluctance to raise taxes would affect their desire to raise expenditures. To the argument that a balanced budget might not on the average be consistent with high employment or that the automatic variations of the deficit or surplus might not sufficiently limit the fluctuations of the economy the CED replied that monetary policy would care for these deficiencies if they arose. (This implied that monetary policy would be not only powerful but also correct.)

Explicitly or implicity this became the standard approach to fiscal policy in the Truman and Eisenhower years and into the Kennedy years. Something like it was endorsed by the Douglas Subcommittee of the Joint Economic Committee in 1950[11] and by various officials or committees of the Eisenhower administration. Even without such endorsement it came to be commonly accepted that the normal practice would be to balance the budget in normal conditions, that the automatic variations of the deficit or surplus that came with variations of the economy would be accepted, but that except in extreme circumstances there would be no positive steps to change expenditures or tax rates to deal with actual or forecast recessions or booms. In a general way the actual fiscal policy of the years up to, say, 1965 can be described as conforming to these principles.

Despite broad acceptance, exception was taken to this standard doctrine from both sides. The Keynesian economists thought it was pretty good for a group of businessmen and a refreshing advance beyond traditional budget balancing. But they regarded the policy as still inadequate to the goal of full employment and an insufficient acceptance of modern economic analysis. The traditional conservatives, on the other hand, regarded the CED proposal as crypto-Keynesianism and a thinly disguised excuse for not balancing the budget. They carried on a campaign against the CED on these lines for many years.

Both objections were ironical. When the standard Keynesian economists came into office with President Kennedy they did not disdain to justify cutting taxes while there was a budget deficit by pointing to the fact that the budget would be in balance at full employment. That is, they were willing to make use of the vulgar prejudice in favor of a balanced budget, even if they did not share it.

The inconsistency in the traditional conservative position was more serious. Even though they held themselves out to be the champions of the balanced budget they never allowed that to stand in the way of their effort to get taxes—especially their own—reduced. Thus, there is the odd result that the traditional conservatives were all-out for tax reduction in 1947–1948 and 1953–1954, whereas the CED, constrained by its principle about a small surplus at high employment, was much more cautious about it. The conservatives in these cases rationalized their position by claiming that the tax reduction would increase the revenue—as they had done in the 1930s and would do again, notably in the 1980s. What stands out is that the balanced-budget argument, as commonly used, is an argument against government spending and for tax reduction, not against deficits that result from tax reduction.

3. The liberation of monetary policy The restrained view of the operation of fiscal policy was made more acceptable than it would otherwise have been by the belief that it would be supplemented by monetary policy. This idea required first of all overcoming the extreme interpretation of Keynes, that money didn't matter. As far as economic analysis was concerned, this occurred early in the postwar period. The evidence of the postwar forecasts has already been mentioned. But also, reflection indicated that the conditions specified by Keynes in which money would not matter were quite exceptional and did not exist in postwar America—if, indeed, they had ever existed. Wide differences remained in the economics profession about the size of the monetary influence. The great effort of Friedman and Schwartz to show that the monetary influence on total spending and on inflation was dominant and stable had not yet appeared.[12] Most textbooks, and most discussion by economists aimed at the public, still ran as if money didn't matter. But basically the profession accepted the idea that money did matter.

But to make monetary policy available as a supplement to fiscal policy required another step. During the war the Federal Reserve had accepted the responsibility of pegging the interest rates on government securities. That meant that the Federal Reserve would buy those securities whenever necessary to keep their prices from falling and their yields from rising. But when the Federal Reserve bought securities it increased the reserves of the banking system and so permitted an expansion of the money supply. As long as it remained committed to supporting the prices of government securities the Federal Reserve could not control the money supply in the interest of any other objective—such as to stabilize the price level.

When the war ended, a debate began over whether to continue this policy. There was nothing valid to say for it. But President Truman remembered that when he came home from World War I the Liberty bonds that he and other soldiers owned declined sharply in value. He didn't want that to happen again. Some banks that held large quantities of government securities were also opposed to letting them drop in value. Characteristically they identified this interest with the national interest. There was fear that if the bond price were not supported, interest rates would rise so high as to depress the economy.

Gradually the national discussion revealed the folly of this policy, especially when the Korean War revived the problem of inflation in an acute way. The Federal Reserve finally determined to end the bond support program. This led to a more open and explicit conflict between the President and the Federal Reserve than had ever occurred before or has occurred since. The upshot was an "accord" between the President and the Federal Reserve in which the Fed assumed some transitional obligations but basically achieved its freedom. This incident tended to establish the idea that the independence of the Federal Reserve is special—more sacred than the independence of other agencies. It did not advance any principle of how the Fed should use its independence. But it liberated monetary policy to act as part of a combined strategy for economic stability.

Thus, we achieved a national reconciliation on the issues that had arisen in the 1930s and that had divided and confused the country. The idea that the economy did not automatically stabilize itself and maintain a satisfactorily low level of unemployment was accepted, and so was the responsibility of government to contribute to stability and high employment. There was agreement that the basic requirement was stabilization of the growth of aggregate demand. The proposition that the government's budget was a useful instrument for doing this was accepted. But the idea that the budget was the exclusive instrument was rejected and a complementary role for monetary policy was accepted. Fears that a fiscal policy aimed at full employment might turn out to be destabilizing and inflationary and to yield excessive deficits and excessive government spending were recognized to have a real basis, and moderations of policy were accepted to avoid those dangers. There was also agreement that the stabilization of the economy did not require any radical change of its structure, or increase in the powers of government, but only more responsible use of the fiscal and monetary powers that government inevitably exercises.

Thus, we seemed to have reached a solution of the problem of the 1930s that was consistent with economic freedom, growth and price stability.

The Truce in the Microeconomic Struggle

As in the field of macroeconomics, many of the issues in other aspects of economic policy which had confused and divided the country simmered down in the 1950s. Conservatives continued to complain about government regulation and government spending, but with few exceptions these were abstract and ritual complaints. Business had learned to live with and accept most of the regulations it had strenuously opposed in the New Deal—the SEC, the minimum wage, the hours legislation, the FPC, CAB, FCC, etc. Still later, of course, this era when we had only the New Deal regulations would be looked back upon by business as the golden age of economic freedom. It is probably true that it is the newness and unfamiliarity of regulation that most disturbs the businessmen, and they regard the regulations they are used to as being freedom. But that says nothing at all about the real effects of the regulations on the economy as a whole and certainly does not mean that the regulations businessmen are used to and do not complain about are less harmful than the others.

On the other hand, there was little drive to push on with the movement toward regulation of business that had been begun during the New Deal. There was some flirtation with the revival of price controls, allocation of materials and selective credit controls, especially by the Democrats before the 1948 election, but it did not get far.

The one important exception to this general acceptance of the status quo with respect to regulation concerned the Wagner Act, designed to promote and protect collective bargaining. The Wagner Act seemed more menacing to businessmen and conservatives than the other regulations. The others imposed costs whose extent was known and which could be dealt with by lawyers, accountants and lobbyists. The Wagner Act exposed business and the business system to a dynamic, hostile and even violent force (as shown by the sit-ins of the 1930s) of potentially unlimited demands. Henry Simons, in one of his last articles, "Some Reflections on Syndicalism," pictured the free enterprise system as being devoured by labor unions.[13]

Conservatives launched a major effort to revise the Wagner Act when the war was over. The battle in Congress was furious. The upshot was the Taft-Hartley Act, which accomplished some but not all of the conservative objectives. It provided that in the event of a strike constituting a national emergency the President could seek an injunction prohibiting striking during an eighty-day "cooling-off" period, in which, presumably, reason would prevail. Limits were placed on picketing and boycotts. Probably the most controversial provision authorized states to pass legislation prohibiting employers from discriminating against workers for refusal to join a union.

The Taft-Hartley Act did not satisfy the conservatives and infuriated the unions. Each side continued for years to seek changes in it; these were never made to a significant degree. Whether the Taft-Hartley Act changed the course of unionism in the United States is uncertain. Its main importance for our story is that it is the only notable retreat from the regulatory legislation of the New Deal that occurred in the postwar period, and the only exception to the proposition that the period 1945–1960 was one in which the status quo was preserved in the field of economic regulation.

Conservatives continued to press for restraint or reduction of federal expenditures in the period under consideration here—from the end of World War II through 1960. On the other hand, proposals that would have increased expenditure substantially were constantly on the agenda—for federal aid to education, for housing and for health. But the conservatives were not advocating radical change in the New Deal program which had the greatest potential for raising outlays—namely, social security. That was accepted, in part because it was considered to be self-financing. And new expensive programs found inadequate support in Congress to get them adopted.

The result was approximate stabilization of federal expenditures relative to GNP. The level of this ratio was higher than it had been before the war, but this was entirely due to higher expenditures associated with national defense. The ratio of nondefense expenditures to GNP rose slowly, largely because of the increase in the number of people entitled to social security benefits and the increase in the average benefits to which their previous earnings entitled them. In 1960, federal nondefense expenditures were 9.6 percent of GNP compared to 8.4 percent in 1939, and social security expenditures were 3.4 percent of GNP compared to 0.9 percent in 1939. The approximate stability of the expenditure ratio did not satisfy the conservatives. They could and did argue that with private incomes growing strongly there was no need for as large nondefense expenditures as we had had at the end of the depression and that the ratio, if not the absolute level, should fall. The feeling about this was not intense, however. There had been two tax reductions—in 1948 and in 1954, from the World War II and Korean War levels—along lines congenial to business, and further tax reduction could be expected.

The performance of the economy in the first fifteen years of the postwar period was highly satisfactory by the standards of the prewar period. It also looks in most respects highly satisfactory from the perspective of the 1970s. The widely predicted sharp postwar recession had been avoided. The country had been through several recessions—in 1949, 1954, 1958 and 1960—but they were short and mild by comparison with the 1930s. Except in the first months of the Korean War there had been little inflation, at least by later standards. Total output in 1960 was 134 percent higher than in 1929—an average annual increase of 2.8 percent. Real disposable income per capita—income after tax and adjusted for inflation—was 44 percent higher than in 1929, an average annual increase of 1.2 percent. Differences of income among the regions of the country, and between the agricultural and nonagricultural economies, were declining. Although we didn't then have statistics on poverty, later estimates indicated that the proportion of the population in poverty was declining.[14]

This success is not to be attributed to the economic policy followed. It is mainly testimony to the vigor of the private economy. But at least one can say that the policy being followed was consistent with successful performance. The bundle of regulations and transfer programs left over from the New Deal, plus a fiscal-monetary policy aimed at economic stabilization but in a moderate way, did not seem to inhibit the effective working of the economic system. At the same time the performance of the economy did not seem to require a more active, ambitious, interventionist policy on the part of government. But, of course, we were about to turn in that direction.

4

Kennedy and Johnson: Activism Exhausted

IF THINGS WERE AS GOOD as I have just reported in the years up to 1960, why did the consensus break down and policy take off in a different direction? The answer has to be first in the realm of simple politics. John F. Kennedy wanted to be President. He could not become President by saying that things were great under Eisenhower. His opponent, Richard Nixon, had the best claim to the Eisenhower mantle, even though Ike gave it to him rather grudgingly. Kennedy had to identify unsatisfactory conditions in the Eisenhower years, which he could then promise to correct. Lyndon Johnson wanted to be a great President on his own, not living in the shadow of the popular young victim-hero to whom he was the accidental successor. He needed to find new conditions to correct, more ambitious goals and grander programs.

The Kennedy-Johnson situation was quite different from the one Franklin Roosevelt had faced. Roosevelt did not have to persuade the American people in 1932 that there was a massive economic problem. That was obvious. But Kennedy and Johnson did have to identify their problems and persuade the American people of the seriousness of the problems. That is not to say

89

that the conditions that they identified and offered themselves to correct were fabricated or unreal. The missile gap that Kennedy exploited in the 1960 campaign was unreal and may have been fabricated. The economic conditions to which he pointed as evidence of the need for a change did exist. The question about them was something else. We do not live in the garden of Eden. Even in the time of Dwight Eisenhower we did not live in the garden of Eden. There are always conditions that one could wish were different or better than they are. The relevant question is whether there is a cure for the condition which the candidate knows and can put into effect and which will not have consequences that are worse than the initial condition. This question Roosevelt did not have to answer in 1932. Kennedy and Johnson did not have to answer it in the early 1960s when they raised their problems to the top of the national agenda. The question would be answered only with the passage of time. The conservative economics movement of the late 1970s and early 1980s can be regarded as a response to the perceived failure of the liberals to solve the problems they identified. That is, it is a response to the belief that the policies initiated in the early 1960s to deal with the conditions that Kennedy and Johnson identified either did not cure the conditions or did so at costs that many people found unacceptable.

There were four main economic conditions which Kennedy and Johnson described as major national problems requiring active and aggressive federal policy, which they, of course, promised to provide.

1. Although, as has already been said, unemployment was much lower than it had been in the 1930s or than it would be again in the 1970s and early 1980s, there seemed to be a rising trend of unemployment. Unemployment had reached its highest postwar level in 1958—at 7.6 percent—and what was considered full employment had not been regained before unemployment began to rise again in 1960. The 1930s had left America acutely sensitive to the problem of unemployment, and the thought that unemployment was rising again, even though the numbers were

much lower then they had been in the depression, was alarming.

2. The long-term rate of economic growth, abstracting from cyclical fluctuations, had become, or been made into, a subject of national concern. Previously we had thought that our rate of secular growth, averaging about 3 percent a year, was one of the great marvels of the U.S. economy. Three percent a year is, after all, enough to double total output in twenty-five years. Moreover, at the end of the 1950s there was no reason to think that our growth rate was slowing down. Still, the growth rate became a national issue in the 1960s. There was nothing easier than to say that what had been 3 percent should be 4 percent or 5 percent. (There were even grown people who thought that an increase from 3 percent to 4 percent was a trifle—only 1 percent—whereas, of course, it is an increase of one-third.) The apparent reasonableness of such a goal was increased by comparison with the experience abroad. It was possible to show that several other countries were growing more rapidly than we. The most troubling comparison was with the Soviet Union, which had just given a demonstration of economic and technological proficiency by launching Sputnik. But there were also economic "miracles" in Japan, France, and Germany.[1]

3. Although the real per capita incomes of the American people were very high, by comparison with earlier periods or other countries, the charge was made that we were not using our incomes for the right things, and therefore were not getting the satisfaction out of them that we could get. The American way of life was said to be deficient, not worthy of us, in spite of our affluence. There were two lines to this complaint. The first was that the market system did not work satisfactorily to deliver the kinds of goods and services that the American people really wanted because the system did not adequately satisfy those wants that could only be satisfied collectively. The typical example was that of the American family driving in its 200-horsepower car to picnic next to a polluted river. The family would have preferred to spend a little less on the car and to spend something on cleaning up the river, but there was no way for a single family to make that choice. The benefit of its expenditures on cleaning up

the river would be largely reaped by other people and would be realized by the family to so small an extent that it was not worthwhile to make the expenditure. All who picnicked along the river would be better off if they each spent a little to clean it up, but there was no way for the private market system to yield that result. So we were said to be living in a condition of "private opulence and public squalor," in a vivid and influential phrase of J. K. Galbraith's.[2]

But the point was also made that if the system did respond to and satisfy the consumer's wants, those wants were not necessarily good wants. In fact, it was said, these wants could be, and to an unfortunate extent were, trivial, crass, selfish and otherwise unworthy. The standard example of the time was the automobile tail fin. So, the picture was drawn of an America that was rich in material terms but psychologically, aesthetically and spiritually impoverished. This line of thought was buttressed by Galbraith's argument that consumers' expenditures in the market did not reflect any original or autonomous desires of consumers but reflected wants created by producers, for their own benefit, through advertising. This argument tended to dethrone "consumers' sovereignty" and open the way for collective—i.e., government—action to determine the best uses of the national output.

4. The rise of average incomes per capita, the maintenance of fairly low unemployment, and the social security and welfare measures introduced during the Roosevelt era had combined to reduce poverty in the United States substantially by 1960.[3] Still, there were people in the United States who were poor. They were poor not only in the sense that they felt poor but also in the sense that many other people felt, or could be brought to feel, that the condition was a national concern about which something should be done. This feeling was probably heightened by a change in the distribution of poverty. Immediately after World War II, poverty seemed to be mainly a matter of the agricultural South, which meant first that most people rarely saw it and second that one could expect it to be cured either by agricultural policy or by migration from the farm. By 1960 much of the migration had occurred, and although that had reduced the depth

of the poverty it had also brought the poor into the cities, where the nonpoor were more conscious of them.

The Kennedy-Johnson liberal movement promised a leap forward on these four fronts—unemployment, growth, the "quality of life" and poverty. Now, there was nothing particularly new or "liberal" about the idea that these four areas were areas of legitimate collective and governmental concern. As pointed out in the preceding chapter, the idea that high employment was a proper objective of government policy was accepted after World War II even by those conservatives who had not previously accepted it. Economic growth was a particularly "conservative" objective. That is, when complaining about government policies they disliked—notably, high taxes—conservatives usually argued that those policies inhibited economic growth and therefore injured the whole population and not only the wealthy and the corporations, who might seem to be the only victims of those policies.

Conservative—that is to say, old-fashioned classical—economics had recognized for a long time the possibility that the private market might not adequately satisfy the wants of consumers because of the presence of what economists called "externalities." If the full benefit of a particular expenditure was not reaped by the consumer making the expenditure but was shared by others the individual consumer would not have an incentive to make expenditures in an amount whose benefits just equaled their cost. This was acknowledged to be an argument for government intervention of some kind. And, of course, there had been government intervention ever since the first regulations prohibiting throwing garbage into the street from second-story windows.

Moreover, the classical argument about the superiority of the free market system only maintained that such a system would satisfy the wants of the population efficiently, aside from the externalities just noted. It did not judge the merits of those wants, but took them as given. The free market argument did not exclude the legitimacy of a collective decision to affect the wants the economy served, either by education, regulation or government expenditure.

Finally, the classical conservative argument did not rule out government action to affect the distribution of income, presumably in an equalizing direction. The classical argument for free markets said that they would yield optimum results given the distribution of productive resources, which would determine the distribution of income. It did not maintain that the distribution of productive resources was itself optimal, and therefore did not maintain that the distribution of income was optimal. In general, classical economists had supported progressive income taxation as a means of reducing inequality and had supported measures to reduce poverty. By 1960, progressive income taxation on the one hand and income support measures for the poor on the other hand were accepted by all but the most unreconstructed conservatives.

Thus, what the Kennedy-Johnson liberalism brought was not the idea of a national concern with unemployment, growth, the quality of life or poverty. What it brought was the idea that the United States in the early 1960s was so backward in these respects that major changes of policy were required—meaning, of course, major changes in the occupancy of the White House—to "get America moving again." It created and exploited for its political advantage a much more ambitious set of goals for these four objectives than had existed earlier. The leaders of this movement in the early 1960s, Kennedy, Johnson and their political and intellectual associates, had no clear conception of the magnitude of the goals they were offering to achieve. They only promised "more." But they opened up a process in which the goals were likely to become more ambitious than was even vaguely visualized at the beginning, because of political competition. It was always possible to promise cleaner water and less poverty, and who could be against such goals? Moreover, the Kennedy-Johnson teams had no precise program for achieving the goals that they were raising to the top of the national agenda. They were, as they said, "pragmatic" about that, meaning that they had only slight reservations about using government spending, taxing and regulations for achieving their goals.

I describe this establishment of new goals as having mainly a political motivation of providing a platform on which the Democratic opposition could come into office. But it also had a considerable intellectual element. One should probably not say "but" in this connection, suggesting that the intellectual element is nonpolitical. It was partly political in the ordinary Democratic-Republican sense that it was concocted and promoted to serve a party purpose. But it was also political in the larger sense that it served the personal interests of its promoters in status, influence and ego satisfaction, and even in money. We had a standard Schumpeterian[4] case of the radicalization of the intellectuals who did not find themselves sufficiently appreciated by the society, even though the society was working well in other respects and even though they themselves enjoyed comfortable tenure in their universities or, in some cases, the luxury of Park Avenue apartments. In the more contemporary phrase of Tom Wolfe, we were experiencing the flowering of "radical chic" which had its milder origins in the admiration for Adlai Stevenson and became much riper in the Camelot of John F. Kennedy.

There were two elements in the intellectual underpinning of the new liberalism. One was basically Keynesian and reflected what by then was the mainstream of academic economics. By 1960 the young economists who had been hypnotized by Keynes when they were graduate students in the late 1930s were mature enough to be the advisers to Presidents and pundits to the nation. This included such people as Paul Samuelson, Walter Heller and James Tobin. They were primarily interested in the first two of the liberal goals—full employment and more rapid growth. They regarded the postwar consensus described in the previous chapter as progress but still far from the true gospel. They had much more ambitious goals for unemployment than the performance under the Eisenhower administration, they were much more confident of their ability to forecast and manage the economy, and they were ready and eager to put into practice the stereotype of Keynesian macroeconomic policy that was incorporated in the standard textbooks. Walter Heller later invented a name for that, "fine-tuning," which still later became a symbol of much that was thought to be wrong with the policy.

Contrary to what later became a common criticism of Keynesians, these people were not indifferent to the value of economic growth. They did not operate on the theory, which might have been reasonable during the depression, that the potential output of the economy was given, or at least of no concern, and that the only problem was to get the potential output actually used. They did, however, have their own view of how growth was to be promoted, which differed from the conventional businessman's view of that problem and from what later became the Reagan view. In the first place, they thought that maintaining a high level of demand and total output was absolutely essential, because businesses would invest in capital expansion only in that condition of the economy. Second, and again contrary to the cliché image of Keynesians, the preferred policy called for the government to run a budget surplus when the economy was at high employment. This surplus would add to the supply of savings available for private investment, keep interest rates down and stimulate growth by its favorable effect on investment. Third, the policy called for enlarged governmental investment in "human capital"—education, training and worker mobility. This might be called an anti-capitalist approach to economic growth. It would avoid having to pay high interest rates to capitalist savers, by providing for investment through the federal budget, both by running a surplus and by government investment expenditures. Moreover, it would add to the capital owned by the working class, in education that would increase their ability to produce and earn.

Again contrary to the common impression of them, the Keynesians of this period were not inflationists. Or, at least they did not think of themselves as inflationists. Their thinking had moved beyond the original and simple Keynesian model in which there would be no inflation while the economy was below full employment and nothing but inflation when the economy was above that level. They now thought of a continuous relation between unemployment and inflation, such that at lower levels of unemployment there would be a higher inflation rate and vice versa. (This relationship was called the Phillips curve, after the British economist A. W. Phillips, who had published a statistical demonstration of it.[5]) Thus, the government could choose among many combinations of unemployment and inflation. They could have, for example, 4 percent unemployment and 3 percent inflation, or 5 percent unemployment and 2 percent inflation, or 6 percent unemployment and 1 percent inflation, and so on. Basically, the Keynesian economists of this time thought that a fairly satisfactory choice was available. It would be possible to have something like 4 percent unemployment with, say, 3 percent inflation. Moreover, policy measures could improve this choice. Improving labor markets, by better training of workers for available jobs and assistance to worker mobility, would reduce the unemployment rate associated with a given inflation rate. "Incomes policy," the use of government "influence" to restrain wage and price increases, could reduce the inflation associated with any level of unemployment. The economists who came into office with Kennedy did not overlook the inflation problem. They only thought that they could manage it, like everything else.

The second strand in the 1960s liberalism, other than the updated and ambitious Keynesianism, was what might be called Galbraithianism. Whereas the Keynesian element was not radical in the sense that it did not require any serious departure from the free market system—whatever it might have led to in the end—the Galbraithian view was much more venturesome in this respect. It had little regard for "consumers' sovereignty"—a staple of free market economics—because it believed the consumer to be led around by the nose by the producer and advertiser. Therefore, those who held this view were quite prepared to alter the pattern of production that resulted from consumers' expenditures whenever they thought some better purpose would be served by government intervention. They scoffed at the idea that the American economy was governed by competition which yielded a high degree of efficiency and therefore had few qualms about extending government regulation. They did not accept the idea that the high rewards of capitalists and business executives were needed to induce saving, investment and business management on a satisfactory scale. So they were prepared for, and eager for, a large degree of government regulation of the economy and government redistribution of income. Unlike most of

the Keynesians they would not be satisfied with successful operation of the economy in the macro sense—with the maintenance
of full employment and rapid overall growth. They wanted that,
of course, but would have thought even such an economic performance to be deficient.

This kind of argument provided the motivation for, or at least
the justification for, the wave of regulatory and antipoverty programs of the 1960s. Although this involved a more far-reaching
departure from the free market system than was involved in the
Keynesian revolution, the case for it was put in a way that made
it peculiarly acceptable in America. There was no demand for a
new and different economic system. The ideological case for the
old system, the free market, capitalist system, was punctured by
the demonstration of exceptions to its general rules and claims,
and this opened the way for specific policy interventions and
measures of income redistribution without any visible limits.
This movement of the 1960s did not entail a turn to a "planned
economy." The American people were not asked whether they
wanted a radical change in their economic system. They were
only asked whether they wanted cleaner air and water, or whether
they wanted seventeen million Americans to go to bed every
night hungry. The answers to such questions seemed obvious—
but they were not the right questions. J. K. Galbraith was the
chief promoter of the intellectual attitude I am describing and
the chief example of the point I am making. He declared himself
a socialist, but did not fit the stereotype of a radical. He was a
member of the jet set, wintering in Gstaad and squiring Jacque-
line Kennedy around.

The interesting question about the idea that a sharp change of
policy was needed after the Eisenhower period is not why politicians like Kennedy espoused that idea. They clearly needed it as
a platform to run on. Neither is the question why a certain group
of intellectuals promoted it. They got the prospect of power and
vicarious glamour with the Kennedys, a chance to thumb their
noses at the anti-intellectualism of the Eisenhower regime, and
other psychological and material advantages. The interesting

question is why the public, which after all was well off under Eisenhower, bought the idea.

Part of the answer, of course, is that we don't yet know that they really did buy it in 1960. We still don't know whether Kennedy won the election in that year or was given it by Chicago's Mayor Daley, who was believed by many to have tampered with the election results in Illinois. In any event, the Kennedy victory was close, and could be explained by many things other than a general desire for a change of economic policy.

But still there seemed to be, in 1960, a certain readiness to accept a change of economics in a more activist direction, and there were several reasons for that. The possible changes of policy were not described specifically during the 1960 campaign, and there was no suggestion that anything radical was intended or that there was any threat to the system. Unlike the situation in the 1930s, nobody was talking about central planning or socialization of industries or any of the other big ideological concepts that Americans always distrusted. What seemed to be meant by getting America moving again was doing somewhat more, or doing more vigorously or more intelligently or more compassionately what we had been doing all along.

Moreover, as is always the case, the idea of change was put forward with no suggestion that there would be any cost. No one would have to give up anything. We were still operating with the idea that there was great unused potential output in the American economy. All that was necessary was to turn that potential into reality and we would be able to afford many new things without losing any old ones. We were getting used to the notion that was a little later to be called the "growth dividend," that the growth of the American economy automatically generated more national income and more government revenue each year, confronting us only with the problem of choosing how to use the additional national income and government revenue. There was, for example, no question that, barring war, the trend of tax rates was down. The only question was when the next step would come.

At the same time that the public accepted the idea that they had in the American economy a powerful instrument that could do a great deal costlessly, it was also coming to value less what the instrument was in fact accomplishing. We were then twenty years from the Great Depression. The facts of general prosperity with only occasional mild interruption by recessions, and continuing rises in the standard of living, were more ordinary and less impressive than they had been when memories of the depression were fresher. Popular willingness to believe that American economic policy needed alteration was fostered by the reports, whose significance was commonly exaggerated, of economic miracles being performed abroad. Although poverty was diminishing, poverty was becoming a more visible problem, as the location of poverty moved from Tobacco Road, where few people saw it except on stage or screen, to the ghettos of large Northern cities. And a new influence on popular thinking was beginning to make itself felt. That was television, with its persistent tendency to dramatize the negative, because it is more unusual in America, if for no other reason.

But looking back at 1960 one cannot miss the presence of another influence—boredom. There was a feeling that although life went on smoothly, or perhaps because it went on smoothly, something was missing. Nothing exciting or uplifting ever happened. One evidence of the searching for something more was the establishment by President Eisenhower of a Commission on National Goals.[6] This was intended to discover what the nation's goals should be. It reflected a feeling that the country should be after something but had no clear idea of what it should be after. There was much talk at the time about the lack of a "national purpose" and the need for one. It was partly to meet this need later that President Kennedy announced the goal of landing a man on the moon in the decade of the 1960s. In such a mood it was easy to accept the idea that something unspecified was missing in the performance of the economy and that new and interesting steps must be taken to fill the gap.

Once the new economic policies of the early 1960s were begun it was no surprise that they should gain in support during their early years. For most of the new initiatives the good parts came first and the bad parts, the costs, came only later. That, of course, is why these initiatives were politically so attractive. A drive to pump up the economy and reduce unemployment has its beneficial effects at first; if there are going to be adverse effects, like inflation, they will come later. Taxpayers will enjoy the pleasures of tax reductions before resulting deficits begin to trouble them. New spending programs promising attractive benefits can be launched and years may pass before the magnitude of the outlays to which the nation has committed itself becomes apparent. The public can savor the satisfaction of launching a war on poverty for years before the costs and casualties are recognized. This lag phenomenon helps to explain why, even though there was no great popular demand for a new economics in 1960, by 1964 it was held to be a great success and contributed to Lyndon Johnson's landslide. It also helps to explain, of course, why there was subsequent disappointment or revulsion, and support for a change of policy.

Kennedy Economic Policy

The new Kennedy team when it came into office approached economic policy in a conventional Keynesian way. Their main objectives were full employment and more rapid economic growth. They would achieve full employment by the expansion of demand. The achievement of full employment by the expansion of demand was also the main instrument for accelerating growth, on the ground that a full-employment economy was most likely to have a high rate of investment in productive capital, large private investment in training workers and flexible adaptation to more efficient methods of production. In addition, public expenditures for research, education, training and worker movement would contribute both to growth and to full employment.

Their preelection prescription for expanding demand by a combination of more rapid growth of the money supply with a surplus in the budget did not survive for long. The United States was running a large deficit in the balance of payments. Our payments to the rest of the world—for imports, investment abroad and foreign aid—were regularly exceeding our receipts. A traditional way to deal with this would have been to restrain demand at home, temporarily reducing the national income and ultimately reducing our price level, which would reduce our imports and stimulate our exports. That path was, of course, ruled out by the full-employment objective of the administration which was generally shared. The Kennedy administration's alternative was a different "mix" of fiscal and monetary policies, with tighter money and more expansive fiscal policy—i.e., no budget surplus—which was expected to yield the desired increase of demand with higher interest rates. The high interest rates would attract capital from abroad, or at least restrain our capital exports, and so relieve our balance of payments deficit. There was another reason, certainly simpler and probably more important in determining the policy. The budget-surplus-for-growth policy ran counter to the administration's promises and desires for increasing government expenditures, especially since a tax increase was, as almost always in peacetime, out of the question.

So the Kennedy administration became quickly committed to a policy of fiscal expansionism. But it did not move at once to the big tax cut that is still remembered as the great triumph of Kennedy economics. Although tax reduction was discussed by the Kennedy economists from the very beginning, over a year and a half passed before the President decided to make his move. There were several reasons for that. John F. Kennedy did not have firm views about fiscal policy, but such views as he had were conventional. A little persuasion would be required to get him to recommend a tax cut when the federal budget was already in deficit. Moreover, his administration had to consider that the Congress and the public might be even more conventional in this regard than the President, so that a move to increase what already seemed a worrisome deficit might be politically unwelcome. Also, the economy was apparently recovering from the recession of 1960. How far or fast the recovery might proceed without an additional boost from the government could not be

foreseen. Although getting back to full employment and staying
there was the first objective of the Kennedy economics team,
they were at the same time cautious about launching an initiative
that might overshoot the mark and lead to inflation. (Another
evidence of this caution, which we do not usually associate with
the Kennedy economists, is that they thought of full employment
as being 4 percent unemployment, whereas there were others in
the administration, especially in the Department of Labor, who
wanted to make 3 percent the goal. This disagreement was resolved by describing 4 percent unemployment as an "interim"
goal, with the implication that a more ambitious goal would be
pursued once the interim one had been achieved.) Finally, the
administration, or at least many members of it, preferred increasing expenditures to cutting taxes, because they were as interested in changing the allocation of the national income toward
a bigger share for government and for low-income people as in
getting the total income up to a higher level. This was more true
of the Galbraith wing of the team than of the more purely
Keynesian wing, which included Walter Heller, chairman of the
Council of Economic Advisers. Thus, there had to be an effort at
getting the expenditures up before a turn would be made to reducing the revenue. It should be emphasized that the Kennedy
administration was not strongly impressed with the case for tax
reduction as essential to provide incentives for work, saving and
investment. Although some deference was given to this argument, reducing taxes was regarded essentially as a way of putting money into the hands of people so that they would spend it,
and a rather inferior way compared with the beneficial expenditure programs that the administration could imagine.

　Thus, the big tax cut was, for the Kennedy administration, a
second best. By mid-1962 two things had become clear. The
idea that the economy might spontaneously rebound to what the
Kennedy people regarded as full employment had faded. Although there had been some recovery in the first months of the
administration the economy was flattening out in the summer of
1962 and there was fear that the country might be going into
another of the recesssions that occur before the previous boom

had fully matured, an occurrence that the Kennedy team had thought so typical of Eisenhower economics. Moreover, Congress was being extremely reluctant to go along with the new or increased expenditure programs the administration wanted. Something had been achieved in that direction, notably the beginning of new programs for manpower training and regional development, but on the whole the administration was unable to boost nondefense spending as it would have liked. This was not, as one might have thought, because Congress was averse to budget deficits or to an increase of government expenditures per se. Congress went along readily enough when the President asked for an increase of defense expenditures after the Soviets erected the Berlin Wall. The simple fact was that a large part of Congress did not like the particular things Kennedy wanted to spend money for.

The administration was coming face to face with the dreadful prospect that unless it changed course and got things moving along more speedily it might enter the 1964 election season with an economy in misery. This is a condition that frequently afflicts administrations in their second or third year and sets them to searching, open-mindedly or desperately, for new solutions. This happened to Nixon in 1971 and to Carter almost every six months after 1977.

The particular shape that the Kennedy administration's response to the worrisome economic situation took was greatly influenced by a number of developments during 1962. In its Economic Report at the beginning of the year, the Council of Economic Advisers had taken a new step to increase its room for expanding the economy without setting off inflation.[7] They described "guideposts" for price and wage behavior which they considered consistent with reasonable price stability and declared that businesses and labor had an obligation to abide by these guideposts. This was the farthest move yet made toward "incomes policy" or "voluntary price and wage controls" in the United States in peacetime, although there were precedents elsewhere, especially in Britain. This was not a particularly radical or liberal step, at least in its historical background. For many

years business leaders had been describing the irresponsible behavior of labor unions as the major cause of inflation, or inflationary danger, and pleading for leadership to restrain such
behavior. President Eisenhower had appealed for noninflationary
wage behavior by labor. Thus, traditional conservatives in business and politics were not in principle opposed to the idea of
some government intervention in the price and wage determination process, especially if that mainly meant the wage determination process, despite the horror of free market economists. But
both business and labor were dissatisfied with the specific guidelines announced in January 1962—neither side thinking them
fair, as usual. And the whole guideposts effort nearly exploded
when the steel industry raised its prices in April 1962 against
the wishes of the administration. The White House threatened
the companies involved in several ways, and the price increases
were rolled back after some tense days. The episode made the
business community furious with the administration. Combined
with a sharp drop in the stock market and the sluggishness of the
economy in the summer it convinced the administration of the
need to do something to mollify business if it was going to get a
durable recovery going.

The guideposts-steel controversy was a further reason for pursuing recovery by the "conservative" route of tax reduction
rather than by continued fighting for new spending programs.
In a sense there was implicitly the kind of "social contract" that
many had called for explicitly. The business community would
sit still for an incomes policy to restrain price increases if the
administration would give business what it wanted, which was
tax reduction. Moreover, the tax reduction would have to be of
a kind that the business community would like. In 1961 the
administration had proposed a package of tax changes designed
to increase business investment without reducing the revenue.
That would have provided a tax credit for investment in excess
of a corporation's depreciation allowances, combined with a
limit on the credit for foreign taxes and withholding of interest
and dividends. That did not satisfy business at all. They regarded
it as an attempt by the administration to drive business to invest

more without, on balance, giving business any tax relief. That proposal was rejected by Congress. In 1962, Congress enacted an investment tax credit in a form that was less objectionable to business but still not what they wanted. Business wanted more tax relief, and also wanted it as a recognition of business' just deserts, and not as an ingredient of a plan concocted by a group of liberal economists who might take the relief away if their econometric models changed.

As already noted, Kennedy was nervous about proposing a tax reduction while the budget was in deficit, partly because he had some vestigial qualms about deficits but more because he thought that others, "conservatives," worried about deficits. But as soon as he made the decision to go for the tax cut it became clear that the opposition on budget-balancing grounds would be small, and that there would be none from the business community. The business organizations and business leaders had been hesitant about getting out in front on this issue, and recommending a bigger deficit than the President did, although the CED made some steps in this direction before the President. But once the President proposed the tax cut, the business community was happy to go along. This was another confirmation of the principle that whatever businessmen's budget-balancing rhetoric may be, if given a choice between reducing their taxes and reducing the budget deficit business leaders will choose the reduction of their own taxes. In this they do not differ from others, except that most others do not talk so much about the evils of budget deficits.

The Kennedy economists at this juncture, when the large tax cut was being discussed, made much use of the concept of the "full-employment budget." That is, they emphasized that although the budget was actually in deficit it would be in surplus if the economy were operating at full employment, and would still be in surplus at full employment after the tax cut was made. The tax cut was defended as a way to balance the budget, on the ground that it would get the economy up to full employment, where the budget would actually be balanced. This use of the full-employment budget concept was new for the Kennedy economists. When the CED had first used the full-employment budget in this way the Keynesian economists had said that although there was analytical utility in measuring what the deficit or surplus would be at full employment there was no reason to say that the budget should be in balance or in surplus at full employment. Whether there should be a full-employment surplus, or a full-employment deficit, or how large they should be, would have to be determined from time to time in the light of economic conditions, with no presumption that balance was better than deficit. But now the Kennedy team recognized that there might be some people out there who cared about balancing the budget, and for them they offered the comfort that the budget would be balanced at full employment.

The Kennedy tax cut, which he proposed at the end of 1962 but which was not enacted until early 1964, after his death, was the largest tax cut in American history up to that time. It reduced individual income tax rates across the board, including a cut of the top marginal rate from 91 percent to 70 percent. It also reduced the rate of corporate profits taxation and liberalized provisions for the depreciation of capital. In total, estimates at the time were that the annual revenue loss from the tax cut when fully effective (it went into effect in two steps), on the assumption that it would not affect the national income, would be about $14 billion, or 2 percent of the GNP at the time.

In the 1960s the Kennedy-Johnson tax cut was regarded as the great achievement of the Keynesian New Economics and the demonstration of its validity. In *The Fiscal Revolution in America* I described the tax cut as "the act, which more than any other, came to symbolize the fiscal revolution."[8] I meant by that the revolution which was Keynesian in the sense that it relied upon the use of fiscal policy, by increasing government spending relative to revenues, to raise total spending in the economy and thereby to raise real output and employment. But the revolution was also tamed in a "conservative" direction by reliance upon tax reduction rather than expenditure increases, by considerable deference to the interests of corporations and wealthy individuals as taxpayers, and by some respect for a budget-balancing rule, however attenuated, in the form of the full-employment budget.

It is ironic that by the late 1970s the Kennedy-Johnson tax cut was appropriated as evidence and model for a group of economists and politicians, mainly Republicans, who considered themselves anti-Keynesians. In their language, which will be explained more later, they were supply-siders rather than demand-siders like the New Economists of the Kennedy days. They used the Kennedy-Johnson tax cut as evidence for their claim that a large reduction of income tax rates would not only increase the national income but also raise it enough so that the total revenue collected would increase rather than decrease. Moreover, this marvelous effect would be achieved by a distinctively supply-side process.

The New Economists of the Kennedy days had said that the tax cut would raise the national income, increase total output and reduce unemployment. That was what it was all about. They had mainly one particular view of how this would happen. Tax reduction would leave more after-tax income in the hands of taxpayers, individuals and businesses. Having more income available to spend, they would spend more for the purchase of goods and services, both consumers' goods and capital goods. This increase of spending would be, in the first instance, an increase in the dollar value of expenditure. But it would also be an increase of *real* expenditure, matched by an increase of real output and employment. This assumed that there were businesses willing to produce more, and workers willing to work more, at the existing real prices and wages, so that when spending in dollar terms increased, more output and labor would be forthcoming and the entire increase of spending would not be absorbed in an increase of prices and wages. That is what was meant by saying that the economy was operating below full employment or below potential.

The supply-side view of the way in which tax-rate reduction increases the real national income is different. It starts with the proposition that there are productive resources—labor and capital—not now being supplied and used because the after-tax return to working and saving is too small to make it worthwhile.

A reduction of tax rates will increase the after-tax return and increase the supply of labor and capital, which will increase total output. This is a rather modest proposition, although not entirely beyond question. It was not this modest proposition that made the supply-siders the *enfants terribles* of 1980 economics. It was the idea that the increase of total output would be large and prompt, large enough so that the tax cut would raise, not lower, the revenue. That had, of course, always been the argument of people who wanted their taxes cut but did not want to seem to be supporters of a deficit policy. The difference in the late 1970s and early 1980s was that the argument was used more flamboyantly by more important politicians and with more certification by professional economists.

The architects of the 1964 tax cut certainly claimed some supply-side benefit from the cut. It is almost always true that proponents of a policy claim all possible benefits from it. So they claimed that parts of the tax cut, specifically the cut in the top individual income tax rate from 91 percent to 70 percent and the reduction of taxes on corporations, would increase the incentives to private investment and cause a larger share of the national income to be invested. The higher rate of investment was expected, little by little, to raise America's capacity to produce, so that after some years total output would be larger. The cut of tax rates was also expected to increase incentives to work. But these effects were considered a minor and distant part of the total effect of the tax cut, which would mainly come from the additional expenditures of taxpayers who would have more money in their pockets.

In fact, total spending, total real output and total employment all rose after the tax cut and unemployment fell. The increases of output and employment and the decreases in unemployment were larger than in the years immediately preceding the tax cut. The crucial question is whether these developments were due to the tax cut and, to the extent that they were, how much of the effects was a demand-side effect and how much a supply-side effect? It is proper to start with saying that economists do not surely know the answer to this question. Many other things were going on besides the tax cut, and it is hard to disentangle the effects of the tax from the other effects. But still, the weight of the evidence is against the idea that the supply-side effects of the tax cut were dominant. There have been two periods of exceptionally rapid rise of production in the United States in the period after World War II. One was the period of the Korean War. The other was the period after the Kennedy-Johnson tax cut and running into the peak of the Vietnam War. The obvious conclusion is that the dominant factor in each case was the surge in total demand resulting from the way the wars were financed. All of the increase in the rate of growth of output after the 1964 tax cut went into effect resulted from the faster growth in the number of persons employed. Output per person employed actually grew more slowly after the tax cut than before, although one would have expected the reverse if the supply-side effects were dominant. That is, the supply-side effects should have increased capital per worker, research, innovation and all the things that speed up the rise of output per worker. But output per worker did not speed up.

The rise of the economy in the years after the tax cut is much more plausibly explained as a result of the growth of the demand side of the economy than as a result of the growth of the supply side. The dispute among economists at the time was about what had caused the acceleration of demand. Was it the tax cut or was it the stronger and steadier growth of the money supply which began in 1961? This question has never been resolved, and in the nature of the case it could not be resolved by looking at a single episode in which there was both a tax cut and monetary expansion. Economists have observed the behavior of aggregate demand, the money supply, fiscal policy and other variables over a long period. Some have concluded from that observation that the behavior of aggregate demand is closely determined by the behavior of the money supply. Those who have reached that conclusion naturally conclude that the expansion of the Kennedy-Johnson days was determined, or at least primarily determined, by the growth of the money supply. Those whose general theory and observation of history lead to a different conclusion, with fiscal influences playing a more important role and monetary influences unimportant or passive, naturally come to a different conclusion about the 1964 tax cut, being inclined to give it major credit for the economic expansion. One cannot tell from looking at the experience of the 1960s alone what caused the expansion. One needs a theory of what causes expansions in general.

Probably the general position of economists today would be that both expansion of the money supply and a large tax reduction contribute to expansion of total demand and, at least temporarily, to an increase of real output. The trend of thinking in the years since the 1964 tax cut has been to emphasize the monetary contribution, and particularly to emphasize that the effect of the tax cut is likely to be quite temporary, whereas an increase in the continuing rate of growth of the money supply can cause a permanent increase in the growth of demand. But in 1964 and 1965, after the tax cut went into effect, it was considered to be the main cause of the expansion. The good performance of the economy was considered to be the complete demonstration of the validity of the Keynesian theory. This was because the Keynesian theory was then the standard theory. It was the way in which almost everyone who thought about it looked at the world. The experience of the tax cut was not inconsistent with that theory, and therefore was thought to be confirmation of it. If the standard theory of the time had been that the behavior of the economy was determined by monetary policy, the experience of the early 1960s would have been seen to be not inconsistent with that and would have been taken as confirmation of it.

Tax revenues rose after the tax cut went into effect. This also has been frequently cited as evidence in support of the extreme supply-side theory that a general cut of tax rates will not only expand the economy, by increasing incentives to work, save and invest, but will expand it so much that the revenues rise even though tax rates fall. This, to repeat, is a proposition that "conservative" tax cutters regularly made long before the term "supply-side" was invented. But the rise of revenues after 1964 is not evidence for that proposition. In an economy like ours, the normal growth of the economy plus even the small amount of inflation we were experiencing before 1965 tended to raise the revenues year after year. There was nothing unusual about the fact that revenues rose after 1964. Even if the economy had continued to rise at only its normal rate, one would have expected the revenues to rise somewhat despite the tax cut. But in fact the economy and the revenues rose more than the normal expectation. This brings us back to the earlier question of the reasons for the strong growth of the economy, and the case for attributing that to the supply-side effects of the tax cut is weak.

Experience after the Kennedy-Johnson tax cut did much to make an extreme version of Keynesian economics standard doctrine for many years. What came to be believed was not only that fiscal policy could be used to moderate fluctuations of output and employment. The tax cut was thought also to demonstrate that continuous manipulation of tax rates could keep the economy at a quite ambitious level of full employment and could do that without inflation. The interpretation of the tax cut as an example of fine-tuning—the precise and flexible adaptation of fiscal policy to forecast economic conditions—is ironic. The decision to cut taxes was made in 1962 in response to the fear that the economy was going into recession. But by 1963 when the cut was being debated the economy was recovering. Indeed, there was some suggestion that the cut was no longer needed. When the cut went into effect, in stages in 1964 and 1965, the revival was already stronger. In fact, the whole period of the demonstrated "success" of the tax cut was short. By mid-1965 there were signs of incipient inflation, and by 1966 the economy was beginning to be dominated by the Vietnam War.

But the magic of the stabilizing tax cut remained. In 1965, President Johnson chose another dose, in the form of a small cut of excise taxes. When Vietnam War spending escalated, in 1966, the first response of the President's economic advisers was to propose a tax increase. Although the President rejected that, he did take some small and temporary revenue-raising steps later in the year. In each of the years through 1971 there were tax changes, up or down, permanent or temporary, proposed or enacted to stimulate or restrain the economy, and this was true in many of the subsequent years as well.

The high-water mark of the glorification of the New Economics was the December 31, 1965, issue of *Time*. The cover was a portrait of J. M. Keynes—the first time a person no longer living was so honored. The point of the article was that the New Economists had learned to apply Keynesian theory in a way that would maintain high employment and steady growth without inflation. *Time* quoted Milton Friedman, our leading non-Keynesian economist, as saying, "We are all Keynesians now." What Friedman had actually said was: "We are all Keynesians now and nobody is any longer a Keynesian," meaning that while everyone had absorbed some substantial part of what Keynes taught no one any longer believed it all. But the important fact was that Keynesian ideas had been incorporated into standard government policy to a much higher degree than ever before.

Johnson Economics

The big tax cut was finally enacted only after John F. Kennedy was assassinated and Lyndon B. Johnson became President. It remained, however, as a memorial to Kennedy which Johnson as loyal subordinate and accidental successor had helped in a minor way to complete. But Johnson wanted a monument of his own, and his monument in economics was to be the big growth of social expenditures. Or rather, that was to be one of his two monuments, the other being the inflation unleashed with the Vietnam War.

The most conspicuous, although not the most expensive, of the social expenditure programs of the Johnson administration were those measures that constituted the "War on Poverty." The idea of an intensified attack on poverty was active already in the Kennedy administration, reflecting some of the conditions and thinking noted earlier in this chapter. But the direct attack on poverty did not have a high priority then. The Kennedy administration's approach was largely the approach of economists, and macroeconomists at that. Their first goal was to get the economy moving again, reducing unemployment and curing poverty on the Kennedyesque principle that a rising tide lifts all the boats. Beyond that their aim was to increase education and training to lift the productivity of the disadvantaged, which they expected would also raise the national income and be costless for the rest of the population.

As the tax cut approached enactment, in the weeks before Kennedy's assassination, attention in the White House turned to what to do next, and a stronger attack on poverty was high on the list.[9] Public concern with poverty was rising—even though poverty was falling—and studies were revealing categories of poverty that would not be lifted by the general rising tide of the economy. There was also a feeling that the tax cut had been mainly beneficial to middle- and upper-income people and that it would be politically helpful for the administration to do something directly for the poor. However, John Kennedy never had the opportunity to test what he could do.

The attack on poverty meant more to Johnson than it had meant to Kennedy or probably would have meant to him if he had lived. Johnson had a great ambition to demonstrate his own leadership and have his own success. He could not stand living in the shadow of Kennedy. Moreover, leading the War on Poverty put him in the tradition of his mentor and hero, Franklin D. Roosevelt.

Johnson's proposals for increasing social expenditures had much more success in Congress than Kennedy's less expensive programs. Kennedy's assassination itself had much to do with this docility of Congress. It created an atmosphere in which resistance to programs associated with Kennedy, or to the Kennedy-like idea of positive, ambitious government, seemed disrepect for the fallen hero. Also, Johnson was a master in dealing with the Congress.

There was, however, more to the legislative success of Lyndon Johnson after the 1964 election. Johnson's landslide victory brought into office a large number of Democratic Senators and

Congressmen who owed their positions to Johnson's coattails. Although we had the first Southern President since the Civil War, we had the first Democratic majority in the Congress that was not dominated by traditional conservatives. The coalition of Republicans and conservative Democrats that had existed for almost thirty years broke down.

The War on Poverty programs initiated in the Johnson period would have a large effect on the federal budget and on the economy for years to come. But this continuing and growing impact was not mainly the result of a Johnson plan or intention. The program reflected a misconception of the long-run budget situation, if not a total neglect of the long run. The new spending measures were launched in an atmosphere still colored by the notion of the fiscal dividend. That is, policymakers were looking forward to the increasing flow of revenue that would result from the growth of the economy. That was considered more than an opportunity; it was a problem. The money, they thought, had to be returned to the private sector, in more spending or less taxes, or the economy would be depressed by deficiency of purchasing power. The Great Society programs were one way to solve that problem.

As it turned out, the economy did not grow as rapidly as had been expected, especially after 1973, when the increase of productivity slowed down. So the additional revenue counted on from that source was not forthcoming. The country did "afford" the new programs, and greatly expanded versions of social programs in general, but not in the way that had been foreseen. A major source of the money to pay for those programs came from inflation, which had not been predicted and which increased taxes by pushing people up into higher tax brackets. After 1973, part of the money to pay for the rising social programs came from the decline of defense spending relative to the GNP and relative to the revenues. That resulted, to some extent, from the antimilitary mood affecting the country after the Vietnam experience. And part of the money to pay for the social programs came from deficits and reflected increased tolerance of deficits.

So the country was able to pay for the social programs. But it was not able to pay in the way expected—out of growth and without higher tax burdens, without displacing defense and within the confines of a balanced budget.

Also, the social programs turned out to be much more expensive than visualized in the Johnson days. In 1965, the last year before the Vietnam War dominated federal finances, social programs cost $30 billion, 25 percent of the budget and 4.5 percent of the GNP. By 1980 these programs cost $280 billion, 48 percent of the budget and 11 percent of the GNP. In constant dollars the increase was 310 percent, more than five times as large as the percentage increase of real GNP. Of course, it was known by Johnson and his advisers that the social programs would grow, but they greatly underestimated the growth. There were several reasons for that. They did not foresee certain exogenous developments, mainly increased life spans which would greatly raise the cost of old-age insurance. They did not foresee the ways in which the availability of the programs increased the costs of the programs. The leading case was the health programs, Medicare and Medicaid. Ability to get medical care cheaply, or at no cost, increased the amount of medical care consumed more than had been expected. And the big increase in the demand for medical services, financed by programs in which the patient bore little of the expense, made the costs of medical care rise much faster than the general price level. The wider availability of more generous welfare payments also brought forth an unexpectedly large number of applicants. This was reinforced by deliberate efforts, sponsored by the government, to encourage applications.

Much of the big, unforeseen, increase in social expenditures after the Johnson administration was not automatic, except in the political sense. That is, the increase resulted from legislation that was enacted after Johnson was out of office but was stimulated by his example. He had shown how popular these spending measures were in the country and how feeble the political resistance was. They became an irresistible temptation for every officeholder and office seeker.

The fact is that a large part of the big increase in social expenditures that began in Johnson's term was not Johnson's but only Johnsonian. And although the Johnson War on Poverty was the kick-off for this development, the largest part of the increase in expenditures was not directed to "poverty" at all. Most of the money did not go to people who would have been poor without it—by the standard American definition of poor. Most of it went to middle-income people—primarily through old-age insurance and Medicare, but also through some smaller programs like educational assistance—and, of course, to the bureaucrats who administered it. Little of it went to rich people, but only because there are few rich people, not because rich people didn't get as much per capita as the average person.

Between 1965 and 1980, federal expenditures targeted on poor people and requiring a demonstration of need to qualify for benefits rose from 4 percent to 9 percent of the federal budget. In the same period, federal benefit payments not targeted on poor people and not involving a test of need rose from 24 percent to 40 percent of the budget. In 1980, only about 20 percent of federal benefit payments went to raise people who were otherwise below the poverty line toward or to it. The remaining approximately 80 percent went to people who even without it would have been above the poverty line.[10]

So Johnson's War on Poverty ended up as a gigantic program for transferring income to middle-income people—mainly old—from other middle-income people—mainly of working age. This should come as no surprise, considering the political power and increasing number of middle-income people who were at or approaching retirement age. These programs were always defended as being for the poor. That satisfied two needs at once for the politician and for the middle-class public—the need to feel compassionate and the need to minimize the cost of actually being so.

It is interesting to ask whether the big growth of social expenditures by the federal government was caused by the availability of a supply of revenue or whether the demand for these programs caused the revenue to be available. The answer is certainly some of both, although the proportions are uncertain. The revenue generated by inflation, by the willingness to cut the defense program, and by the tolerance of deficits would all have been there even if there had been no demand for social programs, and their presence encouraged the growth of the programs. On the other hand, if there had not been such a demand for social expenditures—partly initiated, as I have said, in ignorance of the future costs and revenues—there probably would have been more tax reduction, smaller deficits and, possibly, even a bigger defense program.

A more difficult question is whether the inflation that generated the revenues was itself the result of the increased social spending. The answer to that is probably negative. That is, the social expenditures could have been managed in ways that would not have been inflationary—with tax increases if one believes that deficits cause inflation or, in any case, by sufficient monetary restraint. But the connection might have been less direct. That is, the government may have followed inflationary policy as a way to generate tax revenues to finance the expenditures without having to make an open, and politically unpopular, decision to raise tax rates. There are people who believe that this happened. I do not find it plausible, not because it implies cynical behavior by politicians but because it implies more sophisticated behavior than is usual. The causes of the inflation lay elsewhere.

The Beginning of Inflation

In the years 1965 to 1968 a basic question about the New Economics of Kennedy-Johnson was to be tested. That economics called for vigorous, positive fiscal and monetary action to push the economy up to full employment whenever it tended to fall below the target. But the New Economics prescription had another half also. That was restrictive action when the economy rose into the inflationary zone. The first half of the prescription had been followed up until 1965. That was the easy part; that is, both the policy measure and the results were pleasant. The test would be whether the government would have the determination to follow this second half of the prescription when the time came for that.

In 1965 to 1968, the government failed that test. The test, it is true, came in exceptional circumstances because of the Vietnam War. But nevertheless the performance of the government raises serious doubts about whether the expansion of the economy would have been curbed before it turned into inflation, even if the policy situation had not been complicated by the war.

The basic fact was that the government was extremely sensitive to any sign of a slump that would raise unemployment, however slightly or temporarily, and would not persist in policy to restrain inflation when such a sign appeared. The administration was especially reluctant to adopt a restrictive policy in 1965–1968 because it feared that to do so would require giving up two efforts to which it was deeply committed. One was the Great Society program and the other was the Vietnam War. Each had strong opposition in the country. The logical step for the President when Vietnam War expenditures and budget deficits began to rise would have been to raise taxes. But the President was loath to take that step, and did not take it until 1968, because he did not want to confront a Congress that would prefer to cut either the Great Society programs or the war expenditures.

But too much weight should not be put on the war. Anti-inflation measures are always going to be unpopular in themselves—tightening money, raising interest rates, cutting expenditure programs or raising taxes. The test is of the willingness to take these unpopular measures. The Vietnam War versus Great Society, guns versus butter conflict was only the particular form the political difficulty took. It is doubtful that the President would have bitten the anti-inflationary bullet if the political difficulty had taken some other form, and that doubt is confirmed by the similar action of later Presidents in other circumstances.

The difference between the economics of the Vietnam War and the Korean War is instructive. In 1950, taxes were quickly raised, and after a little lag monetary policy was tightened. Price controls were imposed in 1951, but by that time the inflationary impact of the war had already been contained. The whole episode was dominated by the memory of the inflation of World War II and by the determination not to let anything like that recur. Vietnam War economics, on the other hand, was more influenced by the belief that unemployment was the great danger and natural tendency of the economy, to be resisted at all costs, whereas a serious inflation could hardly be visualized.

There were signs of inflation even before war expenditures began to rise visibly in the second half of 1965. At the end of the year, concerned about the strengthening boom, the Federal Reserve raised the discount rate. President Johnson did not, however, want his recovery snuffed out and invited William McChesney Martin, the chairman of the Fed, down to his ranch for a talk. As a result the discount rate increase was postponed.

Early in 1966 the picture of future increases of defense spending became clearer, although the full size of the probable increase was not revealed for many months. Suggestions that taxes should be raised became common, but the President resisted them. In discussions within the White House the President's economic advisers argued that he should raise taxes, but in public they supported his decision not to do so. The economic advisers supported the decision by pointing out that the full-employment budget was in balance, or nearly so. But by that time the balance was itself the result of the inflation that was raising the revenue. This was the first occasion on which it was demonstrated in practice that the full-employment budget can give a misleading picture of the impact of fiscal policy when inflation is going on. That is, a full-employment surplus, or even a rising full-employment surplus, may only indicate that policy is insufficiently restrictive to prevent an inflation that is generating additional revenues.

As the year 1966 proceeded, the inflation mounted. For the year as a whole the consumer price index rose by 3.4 percent— the biggest increase since 1951, the first full year of the Korean War. In response, the Fed did tighten money, raising a big hullabaloo about a credit crunch depressing housing. The President took some mild measures to raise the revenue, including a temporary suspension of the investment tax credit.

When the inflation rose during 1965 and 1966, President Johnson intensified efforts to restrain prices and wages directly, by incomes policy, to avoid the necessity for fiscal and monetary restraint. The use of sanctions against firms that violated the government's price guidelines became more overt. Violators were threatened with the loss of government contracts or with the sale of materials out of government stockpiles to depress prices. The prestige and influence of the White House were brought forcefully to bear in wage negotiations. But a moment arrived in 1966 when the International Association of Machinists found themselves in confrontation with the President, tested his power, and found that nothing happened to them if they defied his wishes. After that the incomes policy was entirely ineffective as far as wages were concerned. The administration maintained that it still had some influence over prices, but if so it was not visible to the naked eye.

By the beginning of 1967 the economy was in a slump. The slowdown of the economy was so mild that it never became officially designated a recession. For this year as a whole, the unemployment rate averaged 3.8 percent, the same as in 1966 and a little under the 4 percent that had been considered full employment for the preceding twenty years. But although the President recognized that the Vietnam War, if it continued, would require higher taxes, he considered that slump a reason to defer the imposition of the taxes. The full-employment budget went into a large deficit, about 2 percent of GNP. The Federal Reserve turned to a more expansive policy.

Consumer prices rose by 3 percent during 1967, the slump ended, and in 1968 the tax increase was finally proposed by the President. As he had feared, this precipitated a heated argument in Congress about his spending programs. In the end, after months of wrangling, Congress passed a tax increase to last until June 30, 1969, along with a ceiling on expenditures in the year that would end on that date. There were many holes in this ceiling, but the combination of the tax increase and the expenditure

ceiling frightened the administration with the possibility that restraint would be overdone. The common term for what was happening was "overkill." To avert the feared downturn of the
economy, at a time when the unemployment rate was below
4 percent and falling, the Federal Reserve renewed the monetary expansion it had interrupted earlier in the year. This was
seen to be a mistake before the year was out, and the Fed turned
to restraint again. The Johnson administration, with no more
elections to face, had no reason to object. They could now be
the champions of anti-inflation policy and promise, as they did
in their final economic report, that a little dose of restraint would
solve the problem.

But it was a late conversion. When Johnson left office the
inflation rate was about 5 percent, and no one could be sure
where it was going next.

Economic Indexes, 1929–1992

For data and sources, see appendix

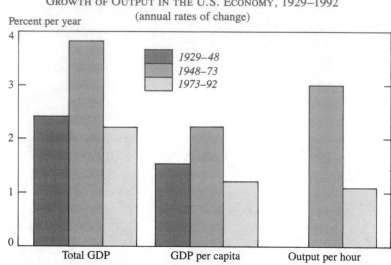

FIGURE 1
GROWTH OF OUTPUT IN THE U.S. ECONOMY, 1929–1992
(annual rates of change)

Percent per year

Legend:
- 1929–48
- 1948–73
- 1973–92

Categories: Total GDP, GDP per capita, Output per hour

SOURCE: Department of Commerce and Department of Labor.

FIGURE 2
TOTAL U.S. EMPLOYMENT, 1929–1992
(millions of persons)

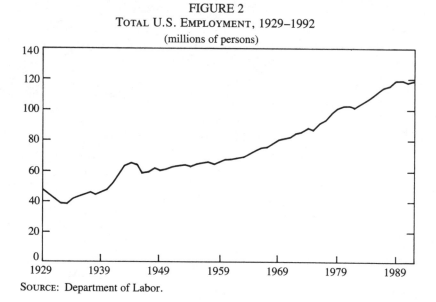

SOURCE: Department of Labor.

FIGURE 3
UNEMPLOYMENT AS A PERCENTAGE OF U.S. LABOR FORCE, 1929–1992

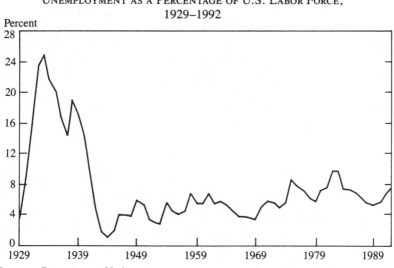

SOURCE: Department of Labor.

FIGURE 4
ANNUAL RATE OF INFLATION IN THE UNITED STATES, 1929–1992
(percentage increase of CPI)

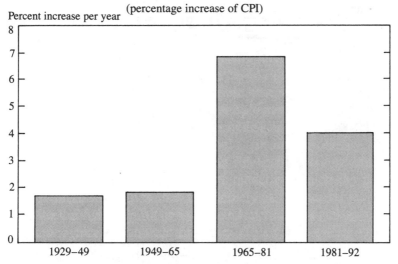

NOTE: CPI extrapolated back from 1959 to 1929 by use of CPI with 1967 = 0.
SOURCE: Department of Labor and author's calculations.

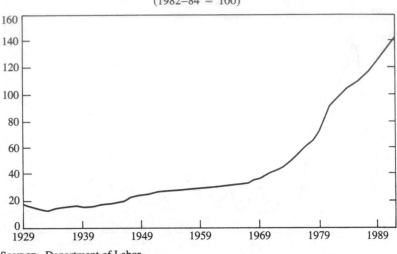

FIGURE 5
INDEX OF U.S. CONSUMER PRICES, 1929–1992
(1982–84 = 100)

SOURCE: Department of Labor.

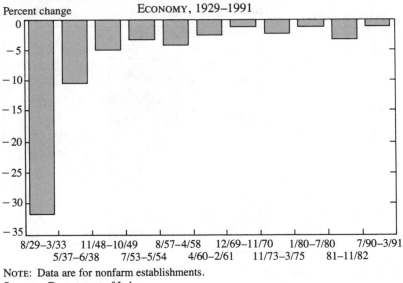

FIGURE 6
EMPLOYMENT DECLINES DURING CONTRACTIONS OF THE U.S.
ECONOMY, 1929–1991

NOTE: Data are for nonfarm establishments.
SOURCE: Department of Labor.

FIGURE 7

U.S. Government Expenditures as a Percentage of Gross Domestic Product, 1929–1992

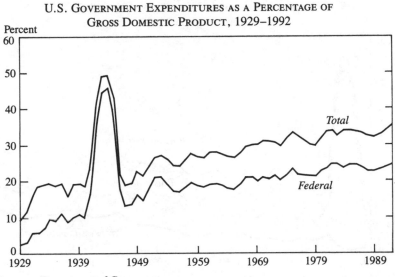

Percent

Total

Federal

SOURCE: Department of Commerce.

FIGURE 8

U.S. Government Receipts as a Percentage of Gross Domestic Product, 1929–1992

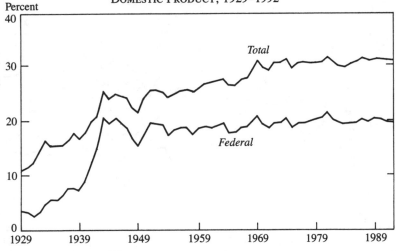

Percent

Total

Federal

SOURCE: Department of Commerce.

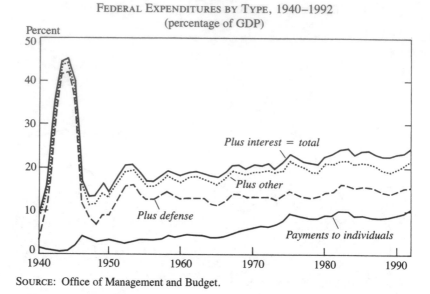

FIGURE 9
FEDERAL EXPENDITURES BY TYPE, 1940–1992
(percentage of GDP)

SOURCE: Office of Management and Budget.

FIGURE 10
FEDERAL RECEIPTS BY TYPE, 1940–1992
(percentage of GDP)

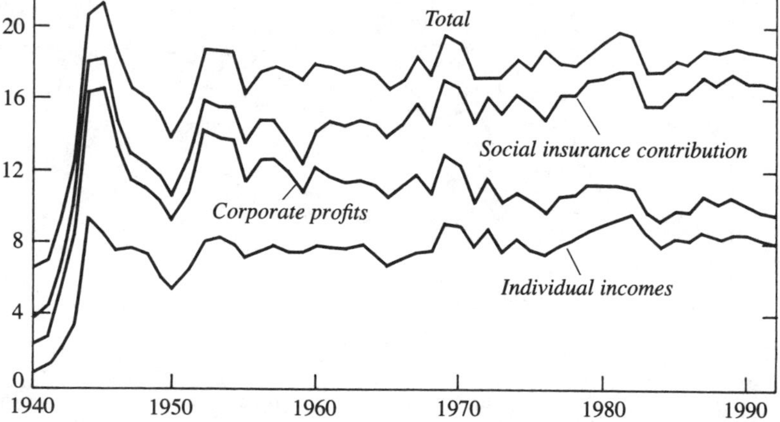

SOURCE: Office of Management and Budget.

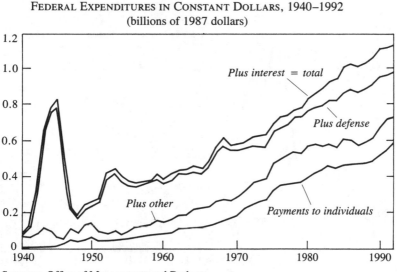

FIGURE 11
FEDERAL EXPENDITURES IN CONSTANT DOLLARS, 1940–1992
(billions of 1987 dollars)

SOURCE: Office of Management and Budget.

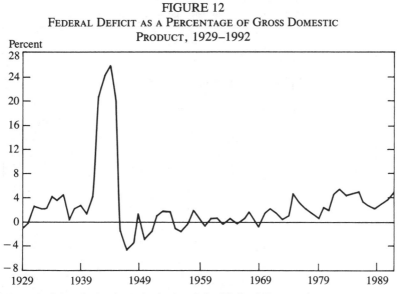

FIGURE 12
FEDERAL DEFICIT AS A PERCENTAGE OF GROSS DOMESTIC
PRODUCT, 1929–1992

NOTE: Deficit calculated on the basis of the National Income Accounts.
SOURCE: Department of Commerce.

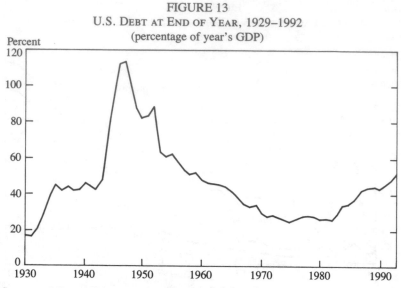

FIGURE 13
U.S. DEBT AT END OF YEAR, 1929–1992
(percentage of year's GDP)

SOURCE: Office of Management and Budget.

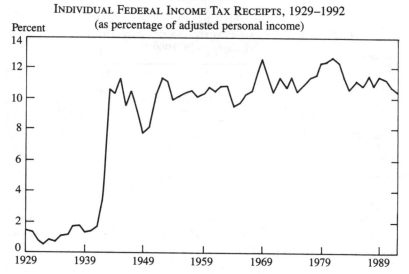

FIGURE 14
INDIVIDUAL FEDERAL INCOME TAX RECEIPTS, 1929–1992
(as percentage of adjusted personal income)

NOTE: "Adjusted personal income" equals personal income as defined in national income accounts less government transfer payments plus employees' contribution for social insurance.
SOURCE: Author's calculation from Department of Commerce data.

FIGURE 15
FEDERAL CORPORATE TAX ACCRUALS, 1929–1992
(percent of "real" profits)

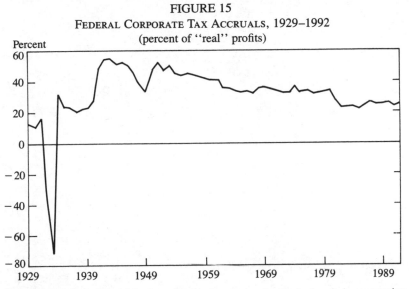

NOTE: "Real profits" equals back profits plus inventory valuation and capital consumption adjustment.

SOURCE: Author's calculation from Department of Commerce data.

5

Nixon: Conservative Men with Liberal Ideas

THE NIXON ADMINISTRATION WAS THE BEGINNING of a transition to more conservative economics. It was a stuttering and incomplete transition. By many measures the Nixon years were a period of retrogression from the conservative economic standpoint. The increase of government nondefense spending accelerated greatly. The federal deficit grew. Inflation increased. The extent of government regulation increased. The Nixon price and wage controls were an enormous peacetime intervention of the government in the American economy.

But despite this outcome—dreary from the conservative point of view—thinking and policy were changing in a conservative direction. In fact, the Nixon administration went through a considerable change during its not quite six years in office. Basically those were years of struggle between rising conservative ideas and the remaining Kennedy-Johnson ideas which, even though fading, were still dominant in the political process, or were thought to be. Indeed, the Nixon experience only served to demonstrate, not least of all to the Nixon team, how needed was a departure from Kennedy-Johnson liberalism.

133

Economic issues were not prominent in the 1968 campaign. The country had plenty of other worries—the Vietnam War, crime in the streets, busing, the new permissive morality. Moreover, the expenses of the war had for the time being put an end to the invention of new Great Society programs, so that kind of issue was quiet. The issue appeared in rarefied form as the question of the "Vietnam dividend." What would we do with all the money that would be available in the budget when the Vietnam War was over and military expenditures could be cut? This question divided the supporters of new social spending programs from the supporters of tax reduction. But this issue about the future did not excite the electorate in 1968.

Insofar as there was an economic issue it was inflation. By the time of the election the inflation rate (consumer price index) had risen to 5 percent. This was the highest rate since the beginning of the Korean War. But concern over it was not intense. The administration Democrats were still obsessed by the fear of unemployment, although the unemployment rate was only about 3.5 percent in the fall of 1968. As we have seen, when the anti-inflationary budget package was enacted in June 1968, the administration had become concerned about going so far in the restrictive direction as to raise unemployment. The administration and the Federal Reserve had then agreed on monetary expansion to offset the "deflationary" effects of the budget package.

On the Republican side, the inflation issue was a convenient platform for preaching the sermons Republicans always preached. That is, they blamed the inflation on Johnson's social spending and on Johnson's budget deficits.

Inflation was the key economic issue, but it was not an issue about which anyone felt deeply. The election was not a mandate to do anything specific about inflation, and not a mandate to do anything painful. Still, it was rising in the hierarchy of national problems, simply because there was more of it, and that would in time have serious policy implications.

Richard Nixon's own views when he came into office were fairly representative of the views in the country, partly because he was a close student of what the "country"—meaning the electorate—wanted. Probably the key words to describe these views are "mixed" and "ambivalent."

Nixon accepted the priority of the inflation problem, but he was allergic to unemployment. This became clear to me when I first met him in December 1968, on the day he announced my appointment as a member of the Council of Economic Advisers. He asked me what I thought would be our main economic problems, and I started, tritely, with inflation. He agreed but immediately warned me that we must not raise unemployment. I didn't at the time realize how deep this feeling was or how serious its implications would be. He attributed his defeat in the 1960 election largely to the recession of that year, and he attributed the recession, or at least its depth and duration, to economic officials, "financial types," who put curbing inflation ahead of curing unemployment. But in this attitude Nixon was not alone. He was certainly in tune with the conventional wisdom that the country valued continuous high employment above price stability.

This attitude, of recognizing the importance of price stability but at heart being committed to full employment, was part of a more general schizophrenia. Nixon felt that he ought to be for the traditional virtues. He regarded himself as the champion of the silent majority. But he wanted also to be a "modern" man and recognized as such by intellectuals and liberals. He was impatient with the dull, pedestrian and painful economics of conventional conservatism. He called that the economics of three yards in a cloud of dust, whereas he yearned for the long bomb.[1] In an early meeting in 1969 he said that we should have some "fine-tuning." He associated that term with sophistication and expertise, even though in the conventional conservative view he was praising the devil's prescription. A more public indication of his desires to be a modern man came in January 1971 when, on the occasion of submitting his budget, he proudly announced, "Now I am a Keynesian." This brought a flood of angry letters from conventional conservatives, to which I had to draft answers. The answer was that the President was recognizing that a recession would generate a budget deficit automatically and that it would be folly to try to prevent such a deficit by raising taxes in a recession. But he was not advocating an active policy to create deficits by raising government expenditures, and he was not ignoring the inflation problem.

Mr. Nixon "believed" in the free enterprise system. Or, more accurately, he was skeptical of and cynical about government interventions in the economy. He did not comprehend the economists' elaborate model by which free markets were shown to maximize efficiency. But he knew, or thought he did, how incompetent and venal government managers of the economy could be. This attitude seemed to go back to his early experiences as a low-level employee of the OPA during World War II.

This OPA experience was the source of one of Mr. Nixon's firmest opinions about economic policy. He did not like price and wage controls. J. K. Galbraith, who was deputy administrator of OPA, came away from that experience thinking it was a feasible and valuable program whereas Richard Nixon and I, who served at much lower levels, thought it was a great failure. This may reflect a natural tendency to think more of an enterprise in which one holds a high and responsible position.

In spite of being for free markets—some would say because of being for free markets—Nixon was no fan of big business. The big business establishment had never supported him, having consistently preferred Rockefeller or Scranton or Romney or almost anyone else for the Republican presidential nomination. He thought of them as hypocritical, wrapping themselves in the mantle of free markets and the national interest while being as eager as everyone else to use the powers of government for their own profit.

Partly because of this coolness toward big business, Nixon did not share the aversion to taxation which had obsessed the Republicans in the 80th and 83rd Congress and was to become a phobia in the Reagan administration. Of course, when he came into office, taxes relative to GNP were lower than they would be when Reagan came into office, if one excluded from the 1969 taxes the Vietnam surcharge that was generally expected to be temporary.[2] But there was more than that involved in explaining Nixon's rather indifferent attitude to the tax "burden." He did not accept the standard business argument about the way taxes were inhibiting investment and production because he didn't believe that a big business with a good lawyer would pay those taxes. Once in 1969 during a discussion of ways to close tax loopholes he said that whatever we did would not matter because sophisticated lawyers would find a way to beat the system. He attributed this wisdom to his recent experience practicing law in New York. He was willing to eliminate the investment tax credit, which the corporate establishment, having opposed it in 1962, had come to love by 1969. But he rejected the idea of limiting the deductibility of home mortgage interest. That would place a burden on suburban homeowners. They were "his" people, not only because they had voted for him but also because he sympathized with them.

Not being overwhelmed by the tax problem, Nixon was not overwhelmed by the spending problem either. He believed that much government spending was wasteful, his favorite example being the hordes of State Department cookie-pushers he had encountered at his stops at U.S. embassies around the world. But he did not have high hopes for cutting waste, believing that the bureaucracy would always defeat efforts to do that. He did not propose to spend much energy on this vain effort. Moreover, he didn't think it was terribly important to do so. He shared the common view that there would be a Vietnam dividend which, together with the revenues yielded by economic growth, would provide room for increases in nondefense expenditures as well as tax reduction. It was inconsistent with his image of himself as a conservative man with liberal policies for him to play the role of Scrooge on social expenditures. He was extremely critical of the Johnson War on Poverty programs, but not because they cost money. He thought that the particular programs adopted to carry on the war against poverty encouraged dependency, family breakup, idleness, hostility and the development of radical paragovernmental organizations. But he wanted to help the poor, and the not-quite-poor who were more likely to be his constituents, and was prepared to spend government money for that purpose.

Nixon understood that being a new conservative implied emphasis on monetary policy, as distinct from fiscal policy, as the lever which moved the economy. He was in touch with Milton Friedman, who was a strong supporter, and had been exposed to Friedman's line of thinking. He was, moreover, skeptical of the Federal Reserve, to which he attributed much of the blame for the 1960 recession and, in turn, for his defeat in the 1960 election. He always feared that the Federal Reserve was about to put the economy through the wringer, to the frustration of politicians in office, especially him. But he did not buy Friedman's simple and rigid rule for stable monetary growth.

One extremely important aspect of Mr. Nixon's initial attitude toward economic policy was that he did not want to have much to do with it. He had a remarkable capacity for retaining and using economic statistics and for grasping and synthesizing economic argument, but he did not consider economics as an area of his major competence, feeling much more able in dealing with foreign policy matters. He did not think it was a winning field for Republicans, because the traditional ideas to which Republicans were committed would never be popular. Moreover, it was not a field in which the public would be keenly interested—the subject being inherently dull and dismal—unless there was a great catastrophe.[3]

Thus, Richard Nixon, like the country, was not greatly absorbed with economic policy at the beginning of 1969. Inflation was a problem, but not a source of acute anxiety and not one to be dealt with by the sacrifice of other goals, especially high employment. Disillusionment with government "programs" was growing, but the remedy was reform, not radical surgery. Earlier enthusiasm about fine-tuning, Keynesian management of the economy, was fading, acceptance of the key role of money was rising, but the result was a call for more eclectic and less ambitious policy. Such a turn to conservatism as was occurring in public thinking, and as was represented in Richard Nixon, was a moderating trend, not reactionary or revolutionary.

The officials that President Nixon brought in with him fitted his attitudes well. His aim to be the conservative man with liberal policies was reflected in his two counselors—Arthur Burns and Daniel Moynihan. It was Moynihan who spelled out for Nixon the concept of the conservative man with liberal policies and introduced him to the classic models of that man—Lord Melbourne and Benjamin Disraeli. Moynihan's influence was to be seen mainly in Nixon's welfare and environment policies—efforts to use government power to serve two of the traditional purposes of the aristocratic conservative, assisting the poor and protecting the national heritage. Moynihan was Nixon's soaring kite reaching out for the liberal chic Eastern establishment, whose respect Nixon did not have but wanted. Burns was Nixon's anchor to conventional conservatism, which meant essentially to holding down government expenditures and trying to cultivate business confidence. He had particularly endeared himself to Nixon in 1960 by warning him that the Federal Reserve's tight monetary policy would worsen the recession and hurt his election chances.

Moynihan and Burns represented the liberal and conservative halves of Nixon, but the synthesis of the two was best represented by his Council of Economic Advisers and by his Secretary of Labor, George Shultz. The chairman of the Council of Economic Advisers was Paul McCracken, who had been a member of the council when Nixon was Vice-President. The other two members, Hendrik Houthakker and I, had never met the new President before the day he appointed us. We were all part of the small Republican branch of mainstream economics from which it was inevitable that Nixon would choose his advisers. McCracken used to say that we were the only three Republican economists that Nixon could find. That wasn't exactly true. But the number who would not be considered hopelessly antediluvian, or wildly eccentric and dogmatic, or rigidly committed to business interests, was not large.

McCracken and I, who would succeed him as chairman at the beginning of 1972, were of the generation who had been graduate students in 1936 when Keynes' *General Theory* was new, and who had been and remained greatly impressed by it. But we had been earlier than most of our contemporaries to develop an immunity to some of the more extreme manifestations of Keynesianism. We had both come to place much weight on monetary policy as the key to stabilizing the economy. But when a reporter asked him early in his term whether he was a Friedmanite, McCracken answered that he was not, but that he was "Friedmanesque." He thought that money mattered, but did not think that only money mattered. He saw and leaned toward Friedman's policy of a constant rate of growth of the money supply, but he could readily conceive of circumstances in which departure from the rule would be necessary.

Being Friedmanesque left room for believing that fiscal policy mattered for the stability of the economy as well as for other objectives. The distinguishing feature of Nixon's CEA in fiscal policy was its devotion to the idea of a rule for fiscal policy rather than the discretionary fine-tuning advocated by their predecessors. I had been the principal draftsman of the CED statements recommending and explaining the rule of balancing the budget at high employment, and McCracken had been an early supporter of that idea. But by 1969 we both recognized that the CED idea of 1947 was not entirely adequate. It was not sufficient in a world of inflation, because a budget that was balanced at high employment with a serious inflation going on, and balanced by the effect of the inflation itself, was not a satisfactory condition to aim at, especially if one started from a position where reducing a high inflation rate required going through a phase of lowered employment. So there was need for a better rule than the old CED rule, but this did not mean abandoning the idea of a rule.

Nixon's new Council of Economic Advisers was greatly concerned about inflation, and more ready than the President to recognize that reducing inflation would involve an increase of unemployment, at least temporarily, and more willing to accept that increase—if it was up to the council to accept it or not, which it wasn't. But it did not think the necessary rise of unemployment was very large or would have to last very long.

The CEA was influenced by Milton Friedman's theory of the natural rate of unemployment, which he had expounded in his presidential address to the American Economic Association in

December 1967. Friedman was answering the common notion that high inflation causes low unemployment and vice versa.[4] His basic point was that only an *unexpected* high inflation rate would make unemployment low, because an unexpected high inflation rate would yield prices that were high relative to wages, and that would hold unemployment down. But if the inflation rate remained high it would become expected, wages would adapt to it and unemployment would rise to its "natural" rate. The natural rate was the rate that would prevail when the actual inflation rate was equal to the expected rate.

The concept of the natural rate of unemployment, which would exist when the inflation rate was constant and fully anticipated, and the difficulty of estimating the natural rate were to be important for economic policy in the Nixon administration and continue to be important today. The concept meant that unemployment could not be durably reduced below its natural rate by inflationary policy. The inflation would become expected and would lose its effectiveness. How long it would take for the inflation to become expected was unknown, but there was reason to think that this period would shorten as people in the private sector became more sensitive to the inflationary consequences of expansionist policy. The concept did not imply that nothing could be done about the rate of unemployment. The natural rate would depend upon many factors, such as the suitability of workers for available jobs and the ability of workers to find and move to the available jobs. Thus, policies to train workers, to increase their mobility and to improve information about the labor market could reduce the natural rate of unemployment.

Even aside from policy measures intended to change it, the natural rate of unemployment would not be constant. It would change, for example, with changes in the composition of the labor force by age and sex. Young people and women tend to have higher unemployment rates than adult men. Therefore, even if the unemployment rates of young people, women and men are constant, the average unemployment rate will rise if the proportion of young people and women in the labor force is rising. Also, the natural rate of unemployment depends on the amount of time workers spend looking for the most suitable employment. Increases of unemployment compensation, and other improvements in workers' financial condition, would increase the ability of workers to spend time looking and so would raise the natural rate.

Since no one could be sure what the natural rate of unemployment was at any time, a policy of trying to achieve the natural rate by demand management policy was subject to error. If fiscal and monetary policy aimed at an unemployment rate that was below the natural rate, inflation would result, and if the policy persisted, the inflation would accelerate. On the other hand, if it aimed at too high an unemployment rate, the economy would be unnecessarily depressed. But the latter error was unlikely. All the political temptations would be in the direction of an overly ambitious unemployment goal and therefore in the direction of inflation.

The significance of the natural rate theory in 1969 was that reducing the existing inflation rate would entail a period in which unemployment would be above its natural rate. For example, if inflation had been running at 5 percent and that rate was expected to continue and was embodied in wage contracts, a reduction of the actual rate would mean for a while that inflation would be below its expected rate. During this period, unemployment would be above its natural rate. So the Nixon CEA accepted the proposition that its effort to reduce inflation would have the transitional effect of raising the unemployment rate. The problem was that no one knew what the natural rate of unemployment was in 1969 or how far or for how long the unemployment rate would have to stay above it to reduce inflation by any specified amount.

When Richard Nixon came into office the unemployment rate was 3.3 percent. With no hard evidence the CEA accepted the conventional wisdom of the time that the natural rate was 4 percent.[5] It believed that the inflation could be cured by a policy of demand restraint that would keep the unemployment rate only slightly above 4 percent, although possibly for a considerable period. It believed that this "gradualism," as McCracken called it, was not only feasible but also the policy with least economic damage and greatest political viability. The council was surprised and unhappy when the President, early in his term, sent a message to the AFL-CIO, via his Secretary of Labor, promising to control inflation without a rise of unemployment. But the council did not think the rise of unemployment would have to be large. As it turned out, this was a serious underestimation of the problem.

The CEA shared Nixon's deep aversion to price and wage controls. Indeed, the CEA was "purer" than Nixon in its aversion to "incomes policies"—efforts of government by persuasion or threat but without mandatory or comprehensive rules to restrain the wage- or price-raising decisions of companies and unions. The CEA regarded these measures as wicked in themselves and steps on the slippery slope whose logic led inevitably to controls. Nixon's attitude was more "pragmatic." As Vice-President he had negotiated some price restraint with the steel companies. He did not regard these companies as chips floating on a tide of market forces but thought they were powers to contend with. He did not like "incomes policies" and knew they did not fit with his basic ideological position, but he was prepared to think about the subject.

The CEA, from the beginning, considered incomes policies to be a critical issue for the Nixon administration. Even if our rather optimistic estimate proved correct there would be a rise of unemployment in the disinflationary process. As this appeared there would certainly be demands for incomes policies to ease the pain and hold unemployment down. This recourse to incomes policies had become part of the standard doctrine of liberal intellectuals during the Kennedy-Johnson years, despite the evidence of the apparent failure of such policies to prevent the inflation accompanying the Vietnam War. The Council of Economic Advisers of the Johnson administration had helped to assure that this would be a continuing issue by including in its final report, in January 1969, a statement on the need for incomes policy to reconcile high employment and price-level stability. Nixon's CEA therefore felt an obligation to keep the President informed of the various forms that incomes policy could take and of the arguments for and against them.

What some critics—such as J. K. Galbraith—called the CEA's "theological" aversion to price and wage controls was only the most obvious expression of its devotion to free market solutions. This was, it should be noted, more a desire for the government to perform its functions by market methods, or quasimarket means, than a desire to circumscribe the functions of government, although there was some of the latter in their position also. For example, the council believed that the government had a responsibility to try to prevent or correct poverty. It had no objection in principle to a War on Poverty. But, like Nixon, it was very dissatisfied with the Johnson way of conducting that war. It thought that the Johnson programs interfered too much with the lives of poor people. The programs gave poor people food stamps, housing subsidies, or medical care, whereas the CEA would have preferred to hand out money and leave the recipients free to spend it. Also it thought that the programs needlessly injected social workers into the lives of the poor.

Similarly, the CEA accepted the government's responsibility to clean up the environment, although it was concerned with the danger that this cleanup might be carried beyond the point where it was worth its cost. But the CEA's main interest was in utilizing pricing methods to reach the goals of environmental policy. Thus, it supported the use of effluent charges, which would impose a fee upon those who dumped pollutants into the water or air, rather than regulations which would limit pollution. Similarly, the council preferred a market solution—the volunteer army—to a draft as a way of providing military manpower, and another market solution—floating exchange rates—to capital or trade controls to bring international payments into balance.

The council shared the general view of the time that economic growth in the United States would continue at a high rate—4 percent per annum—for the next decade. It believed that public policy would have something to do with achieving this growth, but did not think that the public policy was critical. That is, it did not think that radical departures from existing policy were necessary to get that rate of growth. Believing this, of course, relieved the council of many problems. It could count on growth to raise the revenue sufficiently to avoid a fierce competition between claims for more government expenditure and for tax reduction. It was not necessary to cope with an insistent demand for reducing business taxes in order to stimulate economic growth. The council could and did also emphasize the need to do something for the very poor.

The most important people in Nixon economic policy, aside from the President himself, were not Burns or Moynihan or the members of the Council of Economic Advisers. They were George Shultz and John Connally. Connally was not on the scene at the beginning, and we will come to him later. Nixon had never met Shultz before the 1968 election. He had been recommended by Burns, on whose staff he had served when Burns was chairman of the Council of Economic Advisers. At the time he was appointed, he was dean of the Graduate School of Business of the University of Chicago. Few people, if any, appreciated the qualities Shultz had for high public office. These qualities developed greatly when he was in office and led Nixon to promote him from Secretary of Labor to director of the Office of Management and Budget to the combined position of Secretary of the Treasury and Special Assistant to the President for Economic Affairs. In this last position he was as much a czar over economic policy as anyone has ever been in this country.

Shultz was within himself the best representation of the range and ambivalence of Nixon's economic ideas. He was a close friend, admirer and disciple of Milton Friedman. His thinking was devotedly monetarist. He was also attached to the idea of balancing the budget at high employment. In both of these respects he was even "purer" than the Council of Economic Advisers, which was more impressed with qualifications to the basic rules. Shultz was also in principle a rigorous free marketeer and free trader.

At the same time his main field of specialization was labor

economics, he was on friendly terms with George Meany, the president of the AFL-CIO, and other labor leaders, and he was a former colleague and student of John Dunlop's and later brought Dunlop into the government. Dunlop's view of the economy was miles away from Friedman's. Friedman saw the economy as organized by exchange relations among individuals seeking to maximize a private goal—usually income. Dunlop saw the economy as organized by relations of power, status, rivalry and emulation. Shultz lived with both of these views, in different contexts and time periods.

There was a time when a free market economist of the University of Chicago would have had difficulty reconciling the existence of labor unions with his vision of a good economy. By the late 1960s that was no longer true. The free market economists had come to regard the power of government as the main, perhaps the only, obstacle to achievement of the competitive ideal. Large unions, like large corporations, were considered to cause only minor deviations from the optimum path of the economy. This view, of course, helped to reconcile the Friedman and Dunlop elements in the Shultz outlook.

Shultz's outstanding characteristic, however, which distinguished him from all the others I have named here, was his strong operational, managerial sense and skill. He knew that the object was to translate ideas into action. And he knew that this process would not be easy. If the conditions for doing it had been favorable it would probably have already been done. Therefore he was concerned with changing the conditions where he could, and where he could not, adapting the ideas so as to get as much as the unchangeable conditions would permit. This gave his action a malleability that his ideas might not have had.

Thus, both the Council of Economic Advisers and Secretary Shultz acknowledged some deviation from the straight and narrow path of academic conservative economics with its devotion to monetary and fiscal rules and competitive markets. But there were differences between them. The economists on the CEA were more impressed by the uncertainties of the strict conservative case; they accepted qualifications where they were not sure of the validity of the case in particular circumstances. Shultz was more impressed with the practical difficulty of carrying out the ideas in their pure form.

This was a team, from Nixon on down, that wanted to move economic policy in a conservative direction, but it was not a team that felt destined to make a conservative revolution. Nixon did want to leave his mark on history, but did not think that economics was the field in which he would make his mark. His economists, especially the CEA, considered themselves far apart from their liberal Democratic predecessors, but in fact they were only at the other edge of a rather narrow spectrum that was mainstream economics. Other advisers, Burns and Moynihan, had a little less eclectic view, but they were divided. Shultz had a fairly clear ideology, but he was continuously involved in adapting that ideology to the practicalities of life. At a critical point the team would be joined by a new, dominant player, John Connally, who wanted action to be decisive and dramatic but did not have firm convictions about the content of the action otherwise.

This mixed, ambivalent, eclectic character of the Nixon economic policy was much in harmony with the mood of the country in 1969. There were beginning to be complaints about the performance of the economy, but these were not very loud. The fact of inflation was beginning to seep into the popular consciousness, but not very deeply. Indeed, the Nixon CEA was troubled because the public generally was not sufficiently concerned about inflation. The Nixon administration was not in the position of having to meet a demand for solutions to widely felt problems. Instead it had to prescribe remedies, and painful ones at that, for a problem which the public—the patient—did not take seriously. That was not likely to encourage the doctor to prescribe radical therapy. Some questions were being raised about the validity of the pragmatic, fine-tuning, interventionist approach to economic policy. But this questioning was still confined to a wing of the economics profession. It had not reached other intellectuals or the media even to the extent that it would by the time of Reagan. Certainly it had not reached far into the political establishment.

Richard Nixon was the first President in the twentieth century to enter office without a majority of his own party in either house. And the Democrats in the Congress were no longer predominantly the Southern conservatives with whom Eisenhower had worked so congenially. Many of them were beneficiaries of the Goldwater debacle in 1964. Even though the intellectual basis of the Kennedy-Johnson economics was shaking, the conventional Democratic Senator or Congressman still regarded it as a great political and economic triumph. He was still moving in its direction—for more of everything: more ambitious goals for employment, more fine-tuning, and more government programs, such as comprehensive health insurance. The Republicans in the Congress were still shell-shocked by the Goldwater debacle and not eager to lead a conservative charge.

The timid movement of Nixonian conservative economics may have come into office at just the wrong time. If started in 1961, after Eisenhower's era of restraint had set the stage for an era of noninflationary expansion, a Nixon moderately conservative policy might have earned the credit for several good years—and deserved the credit at least as much as the Kennedy-Johnson policy that was actually followed. If started in 1981, after the failures of the old liberalism were clear, a moderately conservative Nixon policy might have had greater political acceptance and greater economic success than the Reagan policy did. But Nixon economics came into effect when the country was not yet prepared for the change of policy it required, and even the Nixon team was unprepared for the austerity that it would involve.

Tiptoeing Around the Inflation-Unemployment Dilemma

Throughout his term, President Nixon's economic policy was haunted by the inflation-unemployment problem. He had to struggle against inflation, and could not stand, or felt he could not stand, any significant increase of unemployment.

Everyone on the Nixon economic team was aware of this problem from the beginning, although, as I have noted, with somewhat different perceptions of its severity; no one thought that the problem could be escaped by settling for the inflation rate then prevailing. But no one thought that it would be impossible to manage. They believed that there was some combination of fiscal and monetary policies that would bring the inflation down with a rise of unemployment that would be moderate in size and direction. "Moderate" implied several things. It meant that few people would be seriously hurt. But it also meant that the transitional pain would be over before demand for incomes policy to cure the pain would become irresistible. And it meant most specifically that the pain would not be a critical factor in the 1972 election, or probably even in the 1970 election.

The Council of Economic Advisers believed that psychological preparation of the country would be helpful in getting through the transition to price stability. The American people needed education in the evils of inflation. Although they—or many of them—were being hurt, few of them appreciated that they were being hurt by inflation. The CEA initiated a study to pinpoint those groups of the population that were most injured, but the study was inconclusive. If anyone was being severely hurt, the available statistics were too crude to reveal it. The American people also needed, in the CEA's opinion, warning of the transitional costs of unemployment that would be involved in ending the inflation. The administration was not, however, inclined to make this warning very strongly, fearing the knee-jerk reaction that associated Republicans with unemployment.

The main requirement for a successful transition to price stability would be delicacy in the management of fiscal and monetary policy—meaning basically monetary policy. There had to be sufficient restraint of demand to get the inflation down but not so much as to push the economy into a serious recession. The numbers involved seemed to suggest that there would be some optimum path along which the inflation rate could be reduced without severe or prolonged unemployment. The inflation rate was about 5 percent at the beginning of 1969. It did not have to be reduced very far. Unemployment was only 3.3 percent. There seemed considerable room for an increase of unemployment without reaching a level that anyone could consider unusually high.

The administration had an ideal picture of the way in which the situation might develop. Unemployment would rise to a little over 4 percent, which was thought to be the rate of unemployment at which inflation would be stable. With a slight excess of unemployment above the 4 percent level the inflation would decline. This would occur gradually, but with increasing momentum as the expectation of a return to price stability gained force. When the inflation rate had declined sufficiently, and the expectation of price stability had become sufficiently strong, the economy would return to full employment (4 percent unemployment). But to accomplish all this required getting the monetary policy just right—tight enough to slow down the economy to just below 4 percent unemployment but not tighter.

(The CEA did not initially appreciate the importance of the rise of the natural rate of unemployment that was occurring as the proportion of young people and women in the labor force increased. Therefore we did not appreciate how far the unemployment rate would have to rise in order to end the inflation. In our January 1972 Economic Report we presented calculations showing that if the unemployment rate had remained constant at its 1956 level for each age-sex group of the population, the average unemployment rate would have risen from 4.1 percent in 1956 to 4.5 percent in 1971 because of the increase of women and young people in the labor force. The administration considered a public report to try to alter the conventional notion that "full employment" was 4 percent unemployment. The idea was discarded on the ground that it would be interpreted as an effort to conceal the true economic situation. Later administrations would be more free to alter the target, as 4 percent unemployment was left farther behind in history. By 1983 a common view among economists was that the natural rate of unemployment was between 6 and 7 percent.)

Monetary policy had turned in a restrictive direction before the Nixon administration came into office. As noted earlier, the Johnson administration's big move against inflation had been the temporary tax surcharge enacted in 1968. The Johnson Council of Economic Advisers, in its farewell report, predicted that the combination of tighter fiscal policy and tighter monetary policy would slow down the economy in the first half of 1969 enough to give a decisive check to inflation. Thereafter the economy could revive quickly to full employment without inflation. The new Nixon CEA regarded this as too optimistic, probably having been intended to paint the picture of an economy in which all steps had been taken by the Democrats for a painless transition to stability—thus leaving to the Republicans blame for all difficulties that might arise. In its first official statement the McCracken council said that fiscal and monetary restraint would have to be continued all year before the inflation could be licked and expansion renewed. This was thought by the council to be a realistic, even pessimistic statement.

Although the administration's public concern was with inflation, its continuing internal worry was that the Federal Reserve would be too tight for too long, causing a recession. This was the President's natural fear, left over from his 1960 experience. He was encouraged in this by Burns. (Burns would take over as chairman of the Federal Reserve when William McChesney Martin's term ran out in January 1970.) Shultz also expressed concern that the Fed had slipped into a depressive phase—following the argument of Milton Friedman, who believed that the Fed was always too tight when it wasn't too loose and saw in 1969 signs of excessive tightness. McCracken joined this position, warning the President that by the time it became obvious that policy had to turn in an expansionist direction it would be too late and that the turn had to be made earlier.

The administration went through 1969 in a state of increasing nervousness about monetary policy. The increase of the money supply had slowed down substantially, especially in the second

half of the year, and interest rates had leaped. Some of the pre-
liminary steps in the disinflationary process were occurring. The
rise of total spending (nominal GNP) was abating. The rise of
real output was also slowing down. Unemployment rose a little.
(In September the unemployment rate rose to 4 percent, leading
the CEA to think the necessary condition for lower inflation was
reached, but the rate then fell again to 3.4 percent by December.) The administration was unable, however, to find any convincing evidence that the inflation rate itself was diminishing.
This did not necessarily contradict the general strategy, in which
the decline of inflation only came at the end of the disinflationary
process. But the delay was worrisome. There was fear that the
Federal Reserve would keep tightening the monetary screw and
put the economy into a recession before the evidence of lower
inflation gave the signal to relax.

Throughout this period the question naturally and repeatedly
arose whether there was something less painful that could be
done to check the inflation. This was, of course, a question about
"incomes policy." The CEA prepared several reports on this subject for the Cabinet Committee on Economic Policy,[6] fulfilling
its duty to give the President all his options. The general tenor
of these reports, and the conclusion of these discussions, was that
incomes policies didn't work, that they were not consistent with
the general philosophy of the Nixon administration, and that an
attempt to use them by that administration would be particularly
incredible and ineffective.

And yet there remained in the administration a group of officials who were eager to do something less abstract and general
about inflation. Their attention focused on construction costs,
primarily on construction wage rates but also on lumber prices.
These costs were rising more rapidly than the general price level,
and there was fear that the rapid rise of construction costs would
spill over into the rest of the price level. These concerns were
most pronounced among some Cabinet members of the outer
circle—remote from the White House—such as the Secretaries
of Commerce, Transportation and HUD and the Postmaster
General. Two of these—Volpe and Blount—came from the con-

struction industry. The most significant member of the group, however, from the standpoint of later influence, was Arthur Burns, who was close to the White House.

The outcome of the concern with construction costs was probably harmless and ineffective. In September, a tripartite Construction Industry Collective Bargaining Commission was established as a forum for discussing labor problems in the industry. John Dunlop—the non-Friedman side of Shultz—was named its secretary. Steps were taken to increase the training of construction workers, to slow down federally financed construction work and to expand lumber output from federal lands. The main importance of this development was as a sign of the emergence within the administration of a group who wanted a "direct" attack on inflation.

By the beginning of 1970, the economy was clearly slowing down more than the administration had expected or desired— although the administration did not then acknowledge the existence of a recession. The administration view was that the slowdown would not necessarily be long or severe. It would probably continue moderately through the first half of the year. But if monetary policy would relax from the extreme tightness of 1969 the economy could begin expanding at midyear. Moreover, after the slowdown of the first half, output could expand and the inflation rate could decline simultaneously, because, although output would be rising, there would still be sufficient slack in the economy to keep inflation falling.

The CEA had essentially moved its earlier forecast forward by six months. The lull in the economy that had earlier been forecast to occur in the second half of 1969 and to set the stage for noninflationary expansion was now to occur in the first half of 1970. During 1970 and the first half of 1971 the CEA went through a series of recalculations of the disinflationary path. The CEA would estimate a level of output below which the inflation rate could be expected to subside. Actual output would then fall below that level without any significant decline of the inflation rate. Another econometric calculation would then be made, taking account of this new information. From this the CEA would draw another picture of the necessary disinflationary path, in which output would have to fall a little further in order to begin reduction of the inflation rate. The successive estimates never gave sufficient weight to the effect of the continuing inflation in hardening inflationary expectations and so making it more difficult to get inflation down. Thus, the CEA saw the inflation as getting more and more stubborn, but never quite as stubborn as it would turn out to be.

Each time the administration looked at the problem its strategy called for a gradual expansion of demand at a pace that would raise output but not interfere with the reduction of inflation. This management of demand was to be primarily the responsibility of monetary policy. (The role of fiscal policy in this period will be discussed subsequently, but it may be pointed out here that this "fine-tuning" management of demand was not mainly to be carried out by fiscal policy.) By February 1970 the control of monetary policy was in the hands of Arthur Burns, President Nixon's friend and appointee. Burns, however, turned out to be no less independent than his predecessor—in fact, if anything he was more independent. He did not share the "Friedmanesque" ways of looking at monetary policy espoused by the CEA and Shultz. That is, he did not believe that it was desirable to fix the path for the rate of change of the money supply for a considerable period of time—either in obedience to a long-term rule or in conformity to a medium-term objective such as reducing the inflation rate. Instead he believed in continuously looking at all the evidence and continuously adjusting the instruments of monetary policy in the light of all the evidence.

In any case, Burns did not accept for monetary policy the primary responsibility for bringing about a noninflationary expansion. He thought that the role of monetary policy would be facilitating only—permitting an expansion when other conditions were ripe to bring it about but not actively generating a recovery. Like all his predecessors as chairman of the Federal Reserve he placed great weight on fiscal policy and was a tireless advocate of holding down government spending as a way to inspire business confidence and, therefore, recovery.

During 1970 and 1971 the Federal Reserve did in fact provide an increase in the money supply which would have been sufficient for the recovery the administration desired, if the average relation between money and economic activity had prevailed. But this average relation is subject to a good deal of variability, and in this period the growth of the money supply did not yield as much expansion as might have been expected.

The critical role of Arthur Burns in this period, 1970–1971, was the encouragement and legitimacy he gave to the push for "some kind of incomes policy." Burns had been opposed to the Kennedy-Johnson guidepost policy for holding down price and wage increases. But shortly after he became Fed chairman he revealed in a speech that he had come to the conclusion that the economy was no longer operating as it used to.[7] Restraint of demand would not suffice to slow down increases in wages and prices, which were being driven up by powerful unions and corporations. Something more than fiscal-monetary policy would be required to curb inflation. In a number of speeches Burns indicated what that would be. He suggested the establishment of a wage-price review board of distinguished citizens who would give their judgment on the appropriateness of major wage and price decisions. These judgments would have no legal force but presumably they would exert moral suasion on businesses and unions and gradually establish standards to which others would conform.

Burns was not the only advocate of ideas like these. The circumstances made the idea of incomes policy naturally attractive. The Nixon administration's promises that the slowdown of the economy would soon bring a reduction of the inflation rate were being disappointed month after month. The President's critics, who were numerous, for reasons not connected with the economy as well as because of his economic policy, were claiming that the country was suffering "the worst of both worlds"—high unemployment and high inflation. (The unemployment rate in mid-1970 was 5 percent and the inflation rate was also around 5 percent.) The political opposition had a great interest in pointing out that there was another, less painful, route to price stability, which Mr. Nixon was too ideological to follow. Incomes policy filled this bill very well. It was identified with the Kennedy-Johnson economics. Moreover, it appealed to the naive idea that the simple and direct way to deal with inflation is to ask or tell businesses and unions not to raise prices and wages so much.

The idea of incomes policy was particularly appealing at this time to many business leaders. They were under pressure from their labor unions for large wage increases, following the pattern of increases begun with the inflation in 1966. But with the economy in recession their ability to pass the wage increases on in higher prices had diminished. So the business leaders wanted the government to help them withstand the demands of their unions, which they did not think they could do by themselves.

Thus, there would have been a clamor for incomes policy even if Burns had never said anything. But his position was important. He was well known as a "conservative." He was obviously well-informed. And he was a friend of Nixon's. Every editorial writer who wanted to recommend some kind of incomes policy could say that "even" Arthur Burns was in favor of it. Incomes policy could not be dismissed as the idea of liberals or ignoramuses. Moreover, Burns' position encouraged some people within the administration who also leaned toward an incomes policy. These people included some economists in the Treasury and the Budget Bureau, who wanted to distinguish themselves from the "purist" ideology of the CEA. The whole situation was awkward for the White House.

From this point on, from the spring of 1970 until August 1971, the administration and the economy were engaged in a race. The question was whether the administration's disinflation program would be *seen* to be succeeding before disappointment with its failure made the demand for incomes policy irresistible. A generally recognized deadline hung over this race. The administration could not enter the active period of the 1972 election with an economic policy that was not working and that did not utilize all measures that might make it work. In the spring of 1970 this did not seem a very rigorous deadline. But still it would not be desirable to go through the next two years continuously in the position of resisting ameliorative measures for which there was a great popular demand.

This raised a difficult strategic question. On the one hand it might be desirable to make some concessions to the calls for direct measures, to blunt the charges of obstinacy. On the other hand there was danger that concessions would only be taken as admission that the basic demand-management policy was inadequate and so serve to intensify the clamor for more direct measures. The policy adopted—as it played out—was to make a series of concessions at intervals. As I described it at the time, the administration was like a Russian family fleeing over the snow in a horse-drawn troika pursued by wolves. Every once in a while they threw a baby out to slow down the wolves, hoping thereby to gain enough time for most of the family to reach safety. Every once in a while the administration would make another step in the direction of incomes policies, hoping to appease the critics while the demand-management policy would work. In the end, of course, the strategy failed, and the administration made the final concession on August 15, 1971, when price and wage controls were adopted.

To say that the demand-management policy did not work and that the general strategy failed is, of course, to say something about what the standards for success were. In fact, appraisals of the success of the policy were mixed at the time and remained mixed subsequently. The recession in 1970 was not very deep— in fact, it was the most shallow of the postwar period. There were already signs of recovery by the end of the year before the economy was knocked down again by a long strike at the General Motors Corporation. The ending of the strike was accompanied by a sharp spurt of output in the first quarter of 1971, but that spurt contained temporary elements and the rate of increase of real output subsided again. Although the unemployment rate fell during the post-strike months it then rose and was flat during the spring and summer at around 6 percent. Meanwhile, the inflation rate had fallen and then risen again, but even after the rise, inflation was below its earlier levels.[8] The fluctua-

tions in the inflation rate also had transitory elements, like variations in food prices connected with the weather, so that it was
difficult to be sure of the trend.

Probably a reasonable judgment of this policy—which can
never be firm because the policy was not carried through to a
final test—was that it was working in the sense that it was getting the inflation down at the price of a recession which, at least
by later standards, seems moderate. The course of the economy,
however, was so irregular that it was impossible to project any
trends and thus to establish any confidence that the policy
was working. Moreover, performance was measured against a
set of expectations which, in retrospect, seem unrealistic. These
expectations were in part the residue of the extraordinary performance of the economy in the Kennedy and early Johnson
days. That experience had left the impression that the combination of low unemployment and low inflation through which
we passed briefly in the transition from Eisenhower's restraint
to Johnson's expansionism was par for the course—not only
in the long run but also in the transition in the other direction.
The Nixon administration reinforced these expectations by
promising a speedy return to full employment—still meaning
about 4 percent unemployment—and price stability. Moreover,
as time passed and the 1972 elections drew closer, the administration's goals and forecasts became more demanding. The
administration felt obliged to describe a path of the economy
which would deliver fairly high employment and low inflation
by the summer of 1972. Although a case could be made for
the feasibility of such a path there was always a considerable
risk of falling behind this optimum path. This happened repeatedly. And when it did it provided ammunition for those who
mistrusted the whole strategy and wanted something more—
namely, incomes policies.

Although Nixon, and the CEA and Shultz, never had any
confidence in incomes policies, the President felt the need to appease the demand for such measures from time to time—to
throw a baby to the pursuing wolves, in the simile cited above.

The first of these steps was taken in the President's speech of June 17, 1970.[9] Much hope was invested in this speech. An earlier speech on the Vietnam War was regarded by the White House as highly successful in turning around public attitudes on the war. There was hope that a speech could also turn around public attitudes on the economy. The drafting of the speech—by William Safire—became a major arena for struggle on incomes policy within the administration. The outcome was superficially impressive, ambiguous and in the end ineffective. Aside from the restatement of the basic demand-management policy there were three concessions to the incomes policy position.

First, the President established a National Commission on Productivity, with members from government, labor, management and the general public (code term for professors). This was a Shultz idea. It had the advantage of meeting the need for some kind of labor-management forum but for using it on a subject to which labor could not object, productivity. There were people who hoped that when the representatives of the four parties sat down around the table they would begin to talk about wages and prices and gradually evolve into a wage-price review board to execute a voluntary incomes policy. At the first meeting, however, George Meany, president of the AFL-CIO, made clear that this was not to be. From that time the National Commission on Productivity and its successor bodies, which survived for many years, settled into irrelevance.

Second, the Council of Economic Advisers would issue periodic "Inflation Alerts," calling attention to economic developments that were causing inflation. Again there were people who regarded this as the entry into a more ambitious incomes policy. They thought that the CEA might be drawn into commenting on the appropriateness of pending major wage and price increases and that these comments might in time reveal a common set of standards or guidelines. The Council of Economic Advisers had no intention of establishing a system of guidelines, however. The reports the council issued were general, statistical and analytical and contained no recommendations about specific wage and price decisions. This disappointed the proponents of incomes policy but still served for some months to give the impression of action.

Third, the President established a Government Procurement and Regulations Review Board to try to correct government actions—like import controls—that tended to raise costs and prices. This was one of a long series of such committees that would be set up. They dealt with a real but not large problem. They were not very effective, because the price-raising measures they tried to correct had much political support. That was why they existed. Economists called such measures "sacred cows"—suggesting how much resistance there was to exterminating them.

The actions announced in the June 17 speech blunted the attack on the administration's economic policy for a while, but by fall the President felt the need for another move. The rise of gasoline and heating-oil prices was getting much attention. So the President made a speech in which he announced steps to increase importation of oil from Canada and to relax limits on the production of oil on federal offshore lands.[10]

In January 1971 the administration went through what had become a ritual process with the steel industry. Some of the major steel companies announced a big price increase. The administration denounced this action and said that it would initiate studies of what was wrong with the industry. The companies then cut the size of the price increase in half. There was suspicion that the initial price increase had been set in the expectation that the government would complain and there would have to be a rollback.

From January to March 1971 the administration launched its most serious venture in incomes policy before it went all the way to controls in August. Wages in the construction industry were a subject of great concern. Some local unions were getting wage increases that were far above the national pattern. That was beginning to worry the national leadership, partly because they feared the rising popularity of the local union heads who were getting the big increases. The President temporarily suspended the Davis-Bacon Act, which required the government to pay prescribed wages (usually union wages) on government construction contracts. A month later, the national leadership of the construction industry agreed to participate in a Construction Industry Stabilization Committee which would pass on wage increases in the industry. It would also do something, never clearly spelled out, about the fees charged by construction contractors. This operation was only getting under way when it was folded into the comprehensive price and wage control system in August.

These steps did not visibly affect the course of the inflation and were not expected by the White House to do so. They were intended to divert and defer the popular pressure for stronger measures of incomes policy while the demand-management strategy was working. If evidence of the success of the demand-management strategy had been forthcoming in time this might have been an effective approach. But evidence of the decline of inflation remained at best ambiguous through the summer of 1971. It is therefore uncertain whether the steps the administration took strengthened the administration's hand or weakened it. The steps taken were an admission that there was something in the argument for a direct attack on inflation, but the steps did not satisfy the critics for long. There were always more possible steps to take, like a wage-price review board, which the President had not taken but which, it could be claimed, would solve the inflation problem painlessly.

In August 1970 the Congress (which was, of course, Democratic) made certain that the President could not escape the sole responsibility for failing to stop the inflation by direct means and so avoiding unemployment. Legislation was enacted which gave the President discretionary authority to impose comprehensive wage and price controls. From that moment the decision not to impose controls was the President's alone; he could not claim lack of authority.

Congress was not at that time recommending that controls be imposed. A motion in the House of Representatives to impose controls received only eleven affirmative votes. In fact, among "responsible" people there was a considerable reluctance to recommend mandatory controls, especially comprehensive and durable ones. Sophisticated people were supposed to know that durable comprehensive mandatory controls were beyond the pale in a society like ours. So their call was for something more voluntary and selective. As I said at the time, the call was for a nonfattening hot fudge sundae—a policy that would have all the good effects of controls but none of their disadvantages.

A new and critically important character entered the story in December 1970 when the President appointed John Connally Secretary of the Treasury. This appointment signaled the desire of the President to change the image of his economic policy. He was tired of being on the defensive all the time, of the "three-yards-in-a-cloud-of-dust" strategy. He wanted a more aggressive, dramatic and leading role. But he didn't think he could produce that himself, and he didn't find that he got much help in that direction from his scholarly and low-keyed team of economic advisers and officials.

Connally, whom Nixon met for the first time in April 1969 as a member of a commission on executive organization, filled Nixon's bill perfectly. He was tall, handsome, forceful, colorful, charming, an excellent speaker in small and large groups and political to his eyeballs. The facts that he was a Democrat, had been Secretary of the Navy under Kennedy and had been wounded when Kennedy was assassinated were to his advantage, further signs of breaking out of the gray, Republican rut.

The appointment of Connally did not imply a decision by Nixon to work his way to controls. He wanted to change the image of his economic policy but not necessarily to change the policy itself. Connally did not take office with any preconception in favor of controls. In fact, he did not seem to have any preconception in favor of any particular policy. One of his favorite expressions was: "I can play it round or I can play it flat, just tell me how to play it."

Nevertheless, the arrival of Connally contributed greatly to the probability that the Nixon administration would end with controls. For the first time there was an important member of Nixon's economic circle—indeed, the most important member—who had no strong philosophical aversion to controls. Moreover, with the coming of Connally the most critical issues of economic policy were no longer decided by a process of discussion in which a number of people participated. This kind of committee process tended to caution, compromise and gradualism. But for a time the decision-making process moved inside, into a one-on-one relation between Connally and Nixon. In this atmosphere Nixon's ideological aversion to controls could be more easily overcome by his desire for the big political gesture, a desire in which Connally would fortify him.

Connally found himself the head of a Treasury that already included a number of officials who had a leaning toward "incomes policies" and who were in conflict with the purists—the CEA and Shultz—on that subject. He was determined to assert the primacy of the Treasury in economic matters, and this naturally made him the champion of a more active direct approach to inflation.

Whether Nixon would ever have moved to mandatory, comprehensive controls without Connally is doubtful. The President was not disposed to take big unconventional actions without strong support from inside his own team. The imposition of controls is sometimes compared to the opening of relations with China or detente with the Soviet Union as a step that would not be expected from a Republican but that only a Republican could take. But Nixon felt more confident of his own judgments in foreign policy than in economics. His turns toward the USSR and China were not so strange for him; he had floated such ideas before he became President. He had Kissinger to tell him they were the things to do. But the turn to controls was alien to him, not only on general principles but also personally because of the way he had interpreted his wartime experience with the OPA. He probably could not have brought himself to so radical a step if his only inside advice had come from the likes of Shultz and Mc-Cracken. But he probably would not have brought Connally into the Cabinet if he had not wanted to liberate himself from such advice.

Connally was the link between Nixon and controls in another respect—in addition to personal style and politics. As Secretary of the Treasury he was primarily responsible for the international financial position of the United States. That position had been deteriorating for over ten years. That is, the United States had been running deficits in its balance of payments. We were spending more dollars abroad, for imports, for military operations, and so on, than we were earning abroad by our exports and the income on our foreign investments. As a result, foreign treasuries and central banks were accumulating large quantities of dollars, and, under the system then in force, the United States had an obligation to convert those dollars into gold on demand at a price of one ounce of gold for $35. But the amount of foreign-held dollars outstanding had become far larger than the value of the U.S. gold stock at that price. Everyone knew that if the foreign holders presented their dollars for conversion there wouldn't be enough gold to go around. So there was a tacit understanding among foreign treasuries and central banks not to ask for gold lest doing so precipitate a run. But the situation was unstable. Every country had to be concerned that some other one would get to the gold window first and draw out the gold while it lasted—or while the United States remained willing to keep the window open.

The obvious remedy for this situation was for the United States to declare that it would no longer pay out gold, or no longer pay it out at the price of $35 an ounce. If that was done the value of the dollar would decline and might float freely—being determined by supply and demand in the market. Foreign governments could not be expected to continue to hold dollars and to buy them from their citizens at a fixed price if the United States rejected any obligations to convert them into anything.

On this subject there had been a significant development in "conservative" thinking. For a long time the standard doctrine of free market economists, led by Friedman, had favored floating, or free, exchange rates. They regarded the exchange rate—the price of pounds or marks or yen in dollars—as a price like others to be determined in the market. They also observed that the effort of governments to maintain a fixed exchange rate for their currencies often took the form of interferences with trade and capital movements. Thus, a free exchange rate seemed to be a necessary condition for freedom in other international economic transactions. On the other hand, as recently as 1960, conventional conservative thinking on these matters, the thinking of the Wall Street banking community, was all for fixed exchange rates. This was partly because the bankers thought that they would have great difficulty doing business with variable rates. But they also believed that the obligation to maintain fixed exchange rates served as a discipline on governments, keeping them from inflationary policy in general and from big expenditures in particular.

By 1970 and 1971 the attitude of the banking community had changed considerably and had become much more receptive to variable rates. This was in part a concession to the intellectual argument. But it was also a reflection of experience with what the government actually did in an effort to defend the exchange rate. Specifically, the government was limiting the outflow of capital by a tax on interest earned abroad and by ceilings on foreign lending by banks. In other words, the Wall Street financial community was bearing part of the burden of maintaining fixed exchange rates. This did much to convince the conventional conservatives of the virtue of free exchange rates.

By 1971 there was an immediate application of the principle that free exchange rates were the necessary condition for freedom in other aspects of the international economy. The government was becoming greatly exercised over the "Japan" problem. The United States was running a deficit in its balance of trade with Japan, and, more significant politically, a number of industries were complaining about Japanese competition. Ideas of quotas or other restraints on Japanese imports were being seriously considered. To the free market people in the government, closing the gold window and allowing the dollar to decline in value relative to the yen was a much better solution.

There were, however, difficulties with ending gold convertibility and allowing the dollar to depreciate. The decline in the value of the dollar would itself be inflationary in the United States, because it would raise the dollar price of imports. Also, there was a danger that people at home and abroad would regard the ending of gold convertibility as a sign that the United States had given up on the fight against inflation and was cutting the last link to price stability. Finally, to abandon the gold standard would look like a confession of failure, of inability to meet our commitments, and the failure would be mainly a failure of the U.S. Treasury—which meant of John Connally.

Ending gold convertibility would go down better if it was packaged as part of an independent, positive American economic policy, especially one that looked strongly anti-inflationary. In a word, ending gold convertibility was a natural partner of a move to mandatory price and wage controls. In the spring, Nixon and Connally agreed that if a foreign demand for gold should force them to close the gold window they would at the same time impose price and wage controls. There was still a good deal of discussion in the government, as in the country, of an intermediate step, such as a wage-price review board. But Nixon knew that if he took any intermediate step he would almost immediately be criticized for not having done more. Therefore he decided that if he moved he would, as he said, "leapfrog them all." He would move so far that no one could complain that he hadn't gone farther. That meant the mandatory, comprehensive freeze.

The Nixon-Connally decision was in turn communicated to Shultz and McCracken but not to others. Of course, the decision was still contingent on international financial developments. It was imperative that the program not be known before it went into effect. Otherwise all the gold would have gone out before the window was closed and prices and wages would have been raised before the freeze was imposed.

(The secret was well kept. In July the *Washington Post* ran an article by J. K. Galbraith recommending the imposition of controls and then asked Shultz to write a reply. Shultz demurred and suggested that I do it. But the *Post* had just published an article by me and did not want another one so soon. So it was arranged that the reply would be by McCracken but that I would draft it since McCracken was too busy. Before we sent in the article, McCracken and I discussed the possibility that Nixon would decide to impose controls, which would leave us like outsiders—the worst fate for a White House employee. We concluded that as long as the President was publicly committed not to impose controls our obligation was to make the best possible explanation of that position. If he decided to change his mind he could easily disown his advisers who had been out of step.)

As June and July passed, conditions combined to push the administration into activating its contingent decision. The economy was not getting worse. The unemployment rate was stable, and it was not clear whether the inflation rate was going up or down. But the economy was clearly not on the track of rapid improvement that the administration had promised. Republicans in Congress, becoming worried about running in 1972 with the economic issue against them, petitioned the President for action. Business leaders asked for help in resisting union demands. The national media kept up a drumfire of complaint about the President's stubborn ideology. (The White House, constantly immersed in *Time, Newsweek,* CBS, the *New York Times* and the *Washington Post,* could not help thinking the media represented a popular demand for direct action, but in fact that was probably an exaggeration of the public attitude. Polls almost always show that the public is "for" price and wage controls, just as they always show that the public is "for" balancing the budget and cutting government expenditures. But the public apparently does not care very much in any of these cases.)

Finally, in the week of August 9, the British representative came to the Treasury and asked for $3 billion of gold. On Friday, August 13, the central economic officials of the administration helicoptered to Camp David, and returned on Sunday, bringing a New Economic Policy, which included a mandatory comprehensive freeze on prices and wages.

Clearly, to explain how this "conservative" administration— the administration of Nixon, Shultz, McCracken and Stein—got to such a radical departure from conservative, free market philosophy involves a combination of factors. It must be recognized that the number of people who had any strong aversion to "some kind of incomes policy" was small. The President had very few allies in a strong policy of resistance. Even conventional conservatives, including business leaders, were for something in that direction. Most of them would have denied that they were for mandatory controls. But their failure to defend the free market approach helped to undermine the President's position and to leave him exposed to continuous demands for more action. Possibly the President's step-by-step concessions to these demands only weakened his position and encouraged demands for more. This pressure on him would, of course, not have been great if the demand-management policy had seemed to be successful. But on this point the administration contributed to its own frustration. By its optimistic predictions for the simultaneous reduction of inflation and unemployment the administration helped to create expectations that it could not meet. The condition of the economy was not so bad as to explain, let alone justify, such drastic action except by contrast with unrealistic expectations which the administration itself fostered. Some responsibility must be assigned to Nixon's personality. He had a great longing for the dramatic gesture, for which he found a perfect supporter in John Connally. He also tended to worry exceedingly about his reelection prospects and so to feel impelled to extreme measures to assure his reelection. Finally, as we shall see, no one involved in the decision to impose controls foresaw how long they would last or how rigorous they would be.

We shall come next to the experience with the controls. But before turning to that we must report the evolution of fiscal policy, which also moved a long way, although less dramatically, from the traditional conservative position.

Richard Nixon had run for President on the standard Republican position that Lyndon Johnson's deficits had been a primary cause of inflation and that balancing the budget should be a major object of policy. Mr. Nixon did not, however, have a strong feeling about this, and neither did his economists. Being "Friedmanesque," his economists put much more weight on the money supply as cause of the inflation. They did not, however, feel sufficiently confident of this position to go against the combination of conventional wisdoms—both Republican and Keynesian. The Nixon team encountered a test on this matter even before it took office. Lyndon Johnson was preparing his final budget message, and the question was whether he would recommend extension of the Vietnam War tax surcharge, due to expire on June 30, 1969. He was reluctant to do this if Nixon would immediately repudiate the idea, leaving him solely responsible for this unpopular suggestion. The issue was brought to Nixon's newly chosen economic officials, who were not yet installed. There was some inclination among them to say that the temporary tax surcharge was irrelevant to the inflation problem and there was no reason to continue it. But in the end the decision was not to take so unorthodox a position, which would have been hard to explain either to those Republicans who believed in balancing the budget for its own sake or to all those people who had been taught by the new Keynesian economists that tax increases were anti-inflationary. At that point, in January, all that Mr. Nixon had to say was that he would consider continuing the surcharge in the light of the budget as it looked in the spring.

The issue became more acute in the spring, when the decision was Nixon's to make. Efforts to cut expenditures had not turned up much. If the budget was to be balanced in fiscal 1970 the surcharge would have to be continued. Moreover, there was still no sign of the inflation abating. Again, the President's economic advisers recommended continuing the surcharge, out of deference to the possibility that their confidence in the power of monetary policy might be mistaken.

The Nixon CEA did not share the traditional conservative devotion to budget balancing as a moral principle—a devotion which in any case was more honored in rhetoric than in action. Neither did it share the confidence of its Kennedy-Johnson predecessors in fine-tuning the budget to stabilize the economy. It did, however, want a rule of fiscal policy and saw an important place for balancing the budget in such a rule. At an earlier stage it had supported the CED rule that the budget should be set to balance or yield a moderate surplus at high employment, a rule that I had helped to formulate and explain. The CEA saw in this several advantages. When the economy was operating at its desirable level the government would not be absorbing private savings to finance a deficit but would be augmenting private savings with a surplus, which would be good for private investment and economic growth. Expenditure decisions would be disciplined by the requirement to provide revenues equal to expenditures. And insofar as there was any stabilizing effect in variations in the size of the deficit or surplus this effect would be automatically obtained to a considerable degree by the natural response of the deficit or surplus to the level of employment and economic activity, without the government's being required to take deliberate actions.

In the early months of the administration this line of thinking was not critical. There was high employment and inflation. All lines of thinking—traditional, Keynesian or high-employment balance—pointed to the desirability of balancing the budget or coming as close to that as the situation would allow.

By 1970, however, with the economy falling into recession and the budget deficit climbing, the rationale for fiscal policy did become critical. The high-employment balance rule would permit, and even welcome, a deficit up to a certain size. But the CEA was grappling with problems in that rule which had become more and more apparent with the Vietnam War inflation. This experience had demonstrated that with the economy at high employment, inflation would generate more and more revenue. If the policy was to keep the budget in balance inflation would permit an increase of expenditures without an increase of taxes— undermining the disciplinary effect of the budget-balancing rule. Also there was no stabilizing effect against the inflation because the rule did not require a surplus under inflationary conditions unless unemployment was below the target rate, then considered to be 4 percent. The whole system was asymmetrical. It permitted deficits when the economy was below full employment but did not require surpluses when the economy was in an inflationary state.

Pursuing this question led the CEA to a more sophisticated

view of the underlying rationale of the high-employment balance rule. The basic principle was that the budget should be in balance when the economy was in its desirable and achievable condition—when it was on what the CEA called the optimum feasible path, or OFP. It would be the goal of monetary policy to keep the economy on the OFP, and while that goal would not be constantly achieved, the OFP would be the most probable path of the economy, because monetary policy would be seeking to achieve it. Consequently, if the budget was set to yield a surplus when the economy was on the OFP the most probable result over a period of time would be a surplus, satisfying the interest in promoting private investment. Fluctuations of the economy around the OFP—fluctuations both in the price level and in output—would generate variation of the deficit or surplus that would tend to restrain the fluctuations of the economy. As contrasted with the high-employment balance rule, the OFP balance rule was also stabilizing against inflation. That is, additional revenue generated by inflation was not to be spent but was to be added to the surplus. This had the further advantage that inflation would not permit the government to raise expenditures without having to raise tax rates.

The OFP would not always be at high employment. Specifically, in the conditions of 1970 the OFP would run through a period in which unemployment would be high, because that was temporarily necessary to get the inflation down. The earlier CED formulations had not visualized the possibility that in some circumstances "high employment" might not be the optimum condition of the economy. As the Council visualized the OFP in 1970 there would be a period in which the unemployment rate was rising, say to 5 percent, after which it would decline to reach 4 percent in 1972. During this time the inflation rate would decline to, say, 2 percent, also by 1972. After that the unemployment rate would be stable at 4 percent, output would grow at its normal rate, thought to be 4 percent a year, and inflation would be stable at a low rate.

This scenario made the achievement of budget balance on the optimum feasible path in 1970 and 1971 more difficult than achievement of budget balance at high employment in those years, because the OFP involved a higher level of unemployment and less inflation. Higher taxes or lower expenditures would have been required to balance the budget on the OFP.

But, the council's notion of the optimum feasible path was too complicated to explain to other members of the administration, including the President. And even if they had accepted it they would have been unable to explain it to the public. Moreover, as these ideas were developing in the council, time for decision was growing short. With the recession deepening, the actual and prospective deficits were increasing. To try to eliminate these deficits by raising taxes or cutting expenditures made sense to hardly anyone and was probably not feasible.

Some explanation of this situation was necessary that was not a surrender to the fine-tuning, no-holds-barred expansionist policies of the Democrats and which retained some link to traditional Republican budget balancing. To meet this need, Shultz, who had become director of the Office of Management and Budget on July 2, 1970, persuaded Nixon to adopt the high-employment balance standard. The idea that the budget should be balanced at high employment had, of course, considerable currency before Nixon adopted it. As we have pointed out, officials of the Eisenhower, Kennedy and Johnson administrations had used it as an explanation or rationalization of their budget policies. But still the idea had remained somewhat exotic, part of the language economists and other experts spoke to each other. Before the budget that Nixon submitted in January 1971 no budget document had ever contained estimates of the high-employment budget, although annual reports of the CEA had contained such estimates since 1962. No President before Nixon had endorsed the high-employment budget standard as conspicuously and as definitely as he did.[11]

The President's State of the Union Message in 1971 listed a noninflationary recovery as one of the President's main goals and the full-employment budget as the major instrument for achieving it. The message said:

"To achieve this, I will submit an expansionary budget this

year—one that will help stimulate the economy and thereby open up new job opportunities for millions of Americans.

"It will be a full employment budget, a budget designed to be in balance if the economy were operating at its peak potential. By spending as if we were *at* full employment, we will help to *bring about* full employment."[12]

The President probably, and his speechwriters certainly, tended to exaggerate the effect of balancing the budget at high employment. They seemed to regard it as a "self-fulfilling prophecy," with the idea that acting "as if" we were at full employment would bring us to full employment. This was claiming too much. But still the President's pride in what he had done was legitimate. He had adopted a policy which was both innovative and conservative—conservative in that it incorporated a rule which set a limit to fine-tuning and expansionism.

It was in the euphoria of this announcement that the President said, in an interview with Howard K. Smith after the message was delivered, "Now I am a Keynesian," as I have already noted.[13]

In general, Nixon's espousal of the idea that the full-employment budget should be kept in balance received little praise. That the liberals would scoff at it was natural enough. They regarded it as a limit on the increase of spending or reduction of taxes to pump the economy out of the recession, and they were not prepared to accept any limit. That the traditional conservatives—the leaders of the business and financial community—should reject it was a little more surprising. They did not recognize or accept it as a restraint on more expansionist policy—on even bigger deficits—that prevailing ideology and politics would have delivered. And they ridiculed the idea of balancing the budget with phantom revenue—the revenue that would have been collected under conditions that didn't exist. (That was, of course, a caricature of the idea. There was no claim that the budget would be balanced. Deficits of a certain size were recognized as acceptable when the economy was below full employment. The function of the full-employment balance rule was to tell how big an actual deficit was acceptable—namely, as big an actual deficit as would result if the expenditures did not exceed the revenues that would be yielded at full employment. A main point of the whole exercise was not to pretend that the budget was balanced but to keep deficits from exceeding this size.)

Ten years earlier the notion of balancing the budget at full employment had been a major item in a conservative-liberal consensus. By 1971 it was acceptable to hardly anyone. What had happened in the interval? In the 1950s, full-employment balance had widespread acceptance as second-best. The liberals and thoroughgoing Keynesians regarded it as the best they could get out of an old-fashioned conservative establishment. The conservatives, or some of them, regarded it as an acceptable limit on what they saw as a strong intellectual and political tendency to endless deficits and limitless expenditures. The CED had not seen the policy in this light. It did not like to call it a compromise. It preferred the term "synthesis," believing that the policy retained the best elements of functional finance and budget balancing and was the first-best, not the second-best. But others were for the time willing to accept the full-employment balance rule as the best they could do, while their hearts were elsewhere.

By 1971 no one was willing to settle for second-best. The thoroughgoing Keynesians had their appetites whetted by the apparent success of their policies in the Kennedy-Johnson days and saw no reason any longer to make concessions. The conservatives, on the other hand, felt that the Kennedy-Johnson people had used the full-employment balance idea as an entering wedge for a more activist fiscal policy, and didn't like to have their man, Nixon, endorsing it. There was probably another factor at work as well. By 1971 there was a new generation of business leaders who had not been so much affected by the depression and had less firsthand experience with the unrealism of the conventional budget-balancing doctrine.

In any case, the failure of Nixon's venture into "modern" fiscal policy—the rule of balancing the budget at high employment— to win any support in the country greatly diminished its force within the administration. From the President's standpoint, the high-employment balance rule was a limitation upon his own freedom of action that he accepted in an effort to reestablish some discipline and responsibility in fiscal policy. It was a rule that in 1971 was keeping him from raising expenditures or cutting taxes and possibly speeding up the economic recovery. If he was to get no credit for this self-restraint, and especially if the self-proclaimed custodians of fiscal responsibility dismissed his proposal, there was little incentive for him to be bound by it. The full-employment budget remained something for the Nixon economists to look at, and it might be used as window dressing when convenient. But it would not be a governing standard of budget policy.

By August 13, 1971, when the Nixon economic team went up to Camp David, there had been radical and surprising changes from the conceptions of economic policy with which they had entered office. The role of "conservatives" in bringing about these changes is interesting evidence of the diversity of attitudes which is covered by the term "conservative."

The administration was about to impose mandatory, comprehensive price and wage controls. From the standpoint of the free market conservatives, a group consisting mainly of economists, nothing could have been more distasteful. But more conventional conservatives, including many business leaders, participated in the demand for direct action which led to the controls.

The administration was about to cut the last link of the dollar to gold. This was a move that free market economists had wanted for a long time. It was a move that the business and financial community had only recently come to accept.

The standard Republican conservative notion of balancing the budget as the rule of fiscal policy had not survived the recession of 1970 any better than it had survived other recessions of the previous forty years. The conservative economists had hoped that some more realistic version of the balanced-budget rule, like balancing the budget at high employment, could be established. Nixon had tried this. But the idea had not caught on, partly because of the coolness of the business and financial community. So the government was left without any guiding principles of fiscal policy.

Although the administration placed great weight on monetary

policy as an instrument of economic stabilization, the management of that instrument was in the hand of a friend and a conservative who did not share the administration's views of the way that instrument should be used. This forced the administration into more reliance on the manipulation of fiscal policy than it would have preferred.

The Price Control Interlude

The meeting at Camp David on the weekend of August 13–15, 1971, was one of the most exciting and dramatic events in the history of economic policy. That was not only because the participants knew they were making extremely big and startling decisions. It was also because of the atmosphere in which the decisions were to be made. The group in attendance was small— sixteen people—and they had the feeling that being there was a sign of their importance. They were on a mountaintop—even though it was not a very high mountain. The Camp David establishment was arranged to give the participants the sense of their unique value. Although the physical structure and furnishings were not luxurious but simple, every provision was made for the wishes of the participants—any choice of food and drink, tennis, swimming, skeet shooting, bicycle riding, horseback riding and so on. Moreover, the Navy personnel in attendance were unfailingly helpful and courteous, treating everyone as if he were a full admiral.

Most of this was part of the "usual" Camp David atmosphere. Probably the distinctive thing about the August 13–15 weekend was the secrecy. The group was totally cut off from communication, in or out, with the world below, in recognition of the damage that could result from any leaks of the deliberations.

The whole atmosphere, and particularly the isolation from the outside, served to separate the group from the realities of economic and political life. They acquired the attitudes of a group of scriptwriters preparing a TV special to be broadcast on Sunday evening. The announcement—the performance—was everything. It had to be as dramatic and smooth as possible, with no loose ends trailing. But it was not regarded as a step in a continuing process of government. After the special, regular programming would be resumed.

(The analogy of the TV scriptwriting conference was made especially pertinent by the attention that some of the participants—notably Nixon and Haldeman—gave to the mechanics of the TV speech that the President would make announcing the program. The President was at first reluctant to make his speech on Sunday evening because he did not want to irritate a large part of the public by preempting *Bonanza,* which was then one of the most popular programs. He was, however, persuaded that the announcement had to be made before the markets opened on Monday morning.)

This suspension of realism enabled the participants to overlook a number of questions that would have been considered at length if the decision had been made in a less exotic environment. It was agreed that there would be a freeze of up to ninety days on prices and wages. The OMB and the CEA had done a small amount of thinking, on a contingent basis, about the operation of such a system—staffing, regulations, enforcement and so on. But this revealed only a small fraction of the problems that would be encountered. More important, there was little consideration of what would happen after the freeze, which obviously could not last for long. There was a general assumption that after the period of the freeze the system could be greatly relaxed, turning into some variant of a voluntary wage-price review board limited to a few large corporations and unions. What would happen during the ninety-day freeze to make that possible at the end of it, when it was not possible at the beginning, was not thought through very rigorously. Insofar as there was any underlying theory it was that the inflation was persisting stubbornly because of the inflationary expectations which had developed during the previous six years. A period of price stability would dispel these expectations and allow the economy to proceed at high employment without inflation. But even if the theory was correct no one knew how long the price stability would have to last in order to dispel the inflationary expectations. And the result was especially uncertain if the period of price stability was brought about by a process—direct controls—that did not change the underlying conditions and that would surely be temporary. The imposition of the freeze was a jump off the diving board without any clear idea of what lay below.

There was also agreement at Camp David that the United States would close the gold window—that is, that we would no longer be committed to converting dollars into gold, even for foreign treasuries and central banks. But there was no agreement on what was going to happen next. There were two possibilities. One was that the exchange value of the dollar would decline and be fixed at a new level, which we would try to maintain. If this was the course the question of the desirable new level of the dollar had to be faced. The other possibility would be that the dollar would float, with the exchange rate determined in the market. Little consideration was given at Camp David to the alternatives.

Finally, there was agreement at Camp David on a fiscal policy intended to stimulate the economy. The policy was dressed up to consist of equal expenditure reductions and tax reductions, so that it did not seem to increase the deficit. There was a reasonable expectation that the actual tax reductions would exceed the amount proposed by the President—the natural tendency of the Congress being to cut taxes more than the President proposed. Also, the nature of the expenditure cuts and tax cuts was such that the stimulative effect of the tax cuts might be expected to exceed the restraining effect of the expenditure cuts.

But there was no careful calculation of the desirable amount of fiscal stimulus. One of the arguments the Nixon economists had regularly made against controls was that they seduced governments into excessively expansionary fiscal and monetary policies which overran the controls and caused new inflation. Now that they were about to impose controls they thought they had room for more stimulus. In fact, the CEA had wanted more stimulus even without the controls. But nothing was done to establish guidelines that would keep our government from falling into the same expansionist error which had helped to undermine previous controls systems.

And although the future course of monetary policy would have a major effect on the success of the New Economic Policy, monetary policy was one subject not considered at Camp David. The New Economic Policy would temporarily suppress inflationary forces by price and wage controls and would remove one conventional limitation on inflation, gold convertibility. Whether the result would in the end be more inflation would depend on monetary policy more than on anything else. But no attention was paid to this critical monetary component of the policy.

Despite these deficiencies in the preparation for the future they were opening up, the participants at Camp David accomplished a great deal in forty-eight hours and returned to Washington on the afternoon of August 15 in a state of exhilaration. This was true even for those participants—probably a majority of those present—who did not like the controls. As my son said to me after the program was announced, "Ideologically you should fall on your sword but existentially it's great." Something of the high spirits with which the participants came down from Camp David was reflected in the mock "Fact Sheet" that I wrote to accompany the President's August 15 speech.

"Fact Sheet"

On the 15th day of the 8th month the president came down from the mountain and spoke to the people on all networks, saying:

I bring you a Comprehensive Eight-point Program, as follows:

First, thou shall raise no price, neither any wage, rent, interest, fee or dividend.

Second, thou shall pay out no gold, neither metallic nor paper.

Third, thou shall drive no Japanese car, wear no Italian shoe, nor drink any French wine, neither red nor white.

Fourth, thou shall pay to whosoever buys any equipment ten percent of the value thereof in the first year, but only five percent thereafter.

Fifth, thou shall share no revenue and assist no family, not yet.

Sixth, whosoever buyeth an American automobile, thou shall honor him, and charge him no tax.

Seventh, thou shall enjoy in 1972 what the Democrats promised thee for 1973.

Eighth, thou shall appoint a Council of Elders to consider what to do for an encore.

(The eight commandments referred to the price-wage freeze, the closing of the gold window, a surcharge on imports, an investment tax credit, deferral of certain proposed expenditure increases, elimination of the excise tax on automobiles, and a new Cabinet Committee, the Cost of Living Council, to manage the program.)

The country apparently shared the excitement and instant satisfaction with the new program. The imposition of the controls was the most popular move in economic policy that anyone could remember. The President had been concerned that the closing of the gold window might be interpreted as a confession of national bankruptcy. But he had presented the move as an attack by the United States on international speculators, and the public cheered him on. The daily quotations on the dollar were closely watched, and declines of the dollar were regarded as signs of success. The Dow-Jones Average rose 32.9 points on Monday after the President's announcement—the biggest one-day increase up to that point. Most important, the man and woman in the street felt great satisfaction and relief. They believed that at last the government was entering the market on their side—to defend them against landlords, grocers and other scoundrels. Only a few economists—and those mainly from the University of Chicago—objected.

This reaction is important to the history of economic policy in America. It shows how shallow was the general support in principle for the basic characteristics of a free market economy. This situation did not change, moreover, during the nearly three years when the controls were in effect. Complaints would multiply, of course, but these were almost all complaints from particular interests—particular industries and unions—about the way in which they were treated. There would be some public indignation about what seemed one or another especially shocking consequence of the controls, like the drowning of little chicks when ceilings were placed on chicken prices. And in the end there was disillusionment about the controls, because prices were rising rapidly, but there was no clear public impression of whether that was an inherent defect of controls, or was due to the particular attitude of the Nixon administration, or was due to the accidents of the Soviet crop failure and OPEC aggressiveness. Enthusiasm for controls had vanished but there was still no strong opposition to controls in principle.

The popular enthusiasm for the controls in August 1971 had a major effect on the administration's planning for the period that would follow the ninety-day freeze. (That period immediately became known as Phase II, and in the materials prepared for public distribution at the end of the ninety days it was so described. The President decided, however, that the public would not understand the word "phase," so all the documents were rewritten, using "Stage II" or various circumlocutions. The press and the public nonetheless continued to say "Phase II," and the government soon returned to that designation also.) When the team returned from Camp David, I volunteered to work on the transition out of the freeze. My main interest was in getting out of the controls promptly and in orderly way, and I believed that my experience, especially with World War II and Korean decontrol, qualified me. I was made chairman of a little task force to analyze and prepare options for Phase II to be considered by the Cost of Living Council—the Cabinet committee set up to run the controls—and then by the President. The Phase II task force began with a range of options from total decontrol, through various kinds of voluntary incomes policy, to continued mandatory controls with relaxed standards and limited coverage to continuation of the freeze. But it became clear at once that the public atmosphere would not tolerate either immediate decontrol or a severely limited and voluntary system. The public shock of being so suddenly returned to the tender mercies of the market after the comfort of the freeze would have been too great.

Only two general alternative standards could be seriously considered by the Cost of Living Council. One was to stay close to the freeze for a longer period. The other was to allow wage increases of a moderate amount—which turned out to be up to 5.5 percent—with the expectation that productivity growth would keep the rise of unit labor costs and of prices to something less than that—specifically, 2 to 3 percent. Even the more relaxed system would require a compliance staff of three thousand people, regular reporting by hundreds of thousands of firms, and elaborate Washington organization to pass on exceptions and appeals and penalties lurking in the background.

The President chose the more relaxed system. It was the one that had at least a chance of inducing the labor unions to cooperate for a while, and it was also a step into getting out of the controls entirely. But even the more relaxed system was an embarrassment to President Nixon that he felt the need to explain, at least to the free market ideologues of his team. He would explain that much as he disliked imposing the controls, if he didn't do it the Democrats would win the presidency and they would impose permanent controls. Or, as he said to Shultz and me when he approved the Phase II plan, it was fortunate that the controls were imposed by people who didn't really believe in them because they would strangle the controls in their cradle if they threatened to live too long.

But it was not going to be easy to get rid of the controls, even though the administration was determined to work its way out of them. The administration's theory, in 1971 and 1972, was that the inflation was being propelled by expectations and by long-term wage contracts rather than by any current pressure of demand. That is, the inflation was not proceeding at an equilibrium rate but was a lagged response to earlier demand conditions. The controls would hold the actual inflation down until these lagging factors were outgrown, after which the controls could be removed and the inflation would remain at its low equilibrium rate. But the story did not work out like that. If the expectation of inflation was a major factor in the inflation, the expectation was not corrected by the controls, which seemed only to generate the expectation that prices would rise sharply when the controls ended. And if the inflation was not an equilibrium condition in 1971—that is, if it was not required by an excess of demand then—it became an equilibrium condition in the latter part of 1972 and 1973. Thus, instead of entering a situation in which the controls would be redundant and could be phased out, leaving the inflation floating freely at a low level, the ceilings became more and more the effective limits, holding prices below their equilibrium levels, and the probability of a big price explosion when controls were removed became greater and greater.

There were three reasons for the rise of the equilibrium inflation rate—i.e., the rate that would have prevailed without the controls. The first and most important was the revival of demand, partly brought about by fiscal and monetary policy and partly spontaneous. Of course, some revival of demand was part of the exercise; that was what would raise employment while inflation stayed low. But it was also part of the exercise that the revival of demand should be restrained. The Nixon team prided themselves on being alert to the error which other governments had fallen into and assured themselves and others that the controls would not seduce them into excessive expansionism.

But they did fall into the trap. During the freeze and up to the end of 1971, unemployment remained at 6 percent while inflation was negligible. The administration became uneasy about the failure of unemployment to fall and believed that there was much room for increasing demand without reviving inflation, especially since the controls had, as the administration thought, favorably affected inflationary expectations. The President, on the advice of his economists, decided that government expenditures should be rapidly increased during the first half of calendar 1972—the last half of fiscal 1972—after which they would be restrained. The deficit for fiscal 1972 was going to be large anyway, and there would be no complaints about making it larger, as long as the budget for next year, fiscal 1973, would be in balance, at least on a high-employment basis. This was an old FDR trick, to combine expansionism with the appearance of fiscal prudence by making this year's deficit so large that future deficits would look moderate by contrast.

President Nixon explained this policy with amusement to the Cabinet at a meeting early in January 1972. He told the Cabinet members that whereas he had regularly in the past urged them to be economical in their expenditures he was now urging them to get out and spend. He recognized that this instruction would seem strange to them, as it did to him, but he passed on the assurance of his economists that it was the right thing to do. As it turned out, most of the Cabinet members were no better at spending money than at saving it and only the Defense Department managed to carry out the President's expansionist policy for the first half of 1972.

At the same time, at the beginning of 1972, the Federal Reserve began to increase the rate of growth of the money supply, which had been quite low in the second half of 1971. Its reasoning was like that of the administration. Unemployment was high and steady, inflation was low, there was room for expansion. The Fed was encouraged in this move by the administration.

For a time everything worked beautifully. In the early part of 1972, real output rose strongly, unemployment began to fall, and inflation remained low. This pattern of rising output and low inflation is not unusual in the early days of a recovery when unemployment is still high and productivity is rising. But the combination was extraordinarily favorable, perhaps because of the controls.

The economic expansion would, however, be quite strong. This was partly because the money supply continued to grow rapidly through the middle of 1973 and partly because the rest of the world was entering a boom at the same time. And as happened again and again during the Nixon administration—and subsequently—the government continued at least until the end of 1972 to think that there was so much slack in the economy that demand could increase a great deal before inflationary conditions would be encountered. This mistake was shared by many others. In fact, during 1972 the standard criticism of the government's fiscal-monetary policies was that they were too restrictive too early.[14] And at the beginning of 1973 the common view of business economists was that there was much excess capacity in the basic industries. By the middle of 1973 at the latest, and possibly earlier, the United States was in the grip of a classical demand-pull inflation against which the controls were powerless.

Two other more special factors tended to raise the rate of inflation, both operating from the supply side. One was crop failures, notably in the Soviet Union, which raised world food prices sharply. The other was the rise of world petroleum prices, which began slowly early in 1973 but escalated steeply after the Arab oil embargo was instituted in the fall of that year. The controls could not keep the prices of food and oil from rising without causing severe shortages. And once food and petroleum prices were rising, other prices and wage rates could not be kept from rising without causing shortages and strikes. If demand had been rigorously controlled by tight fiscal and monetary policy, the rises of food and petroleum prices might have been absorbed by an offsetting decline of other prices, but demand was not rigorously controlled. Moreover, such a process would have required forcing other prices down below the levels authorized by the control system.

Although the administration's early hope was that the ending of controls would be accompanied by the stabilization of inflation at a low level, its determination to phase out the controls was not dependent on the realization of that hope. Even when the hope was seen to be vain the administration proceeded with the decontrol process. It had no stomach for a continuing effort to hold the rate of inflation below its equilibrium level.

There is no need to trace the process of decontrol through its succession of steps and phases leading up to the final abolition of the system in April 1974. It is sufficient to say that almost every step of decontrol until mid-1973 was widely criticized as being premature and as reflecting the ideological obsessions of President Nixon and his free market economists. There were, of course, always people who wanted some specific decontrol on relaxation. Landlords wanted rents decontrolled, unions wanted the 5.5 percent guidelines for wages raised, businesses wanted bigger profit margins. But hardly any interest was expressed outside the administration in gradually getting rid of the system until the second freeze in 1973 demonstrated the futility of the whole effort.

The second freeze was an exception to the continuous push for decontrol. In the spring of 1973, with food prices rising rapidly, the President, under mounting personal attack in connection with Watergate, began to long for the euphoric days when he had imposed the first freeze. I warned him, citing Heraclitus, that you can't step in the same river twice. Nixon replied that you could, if it was frozen. He tried for months to get his economic advisers to recommend the reinstitution of the freeze but did not succeed. Finally, in June, he decided to do it anyway. The effort this time was a total disaster. There were all the visible symptoms of a price control system gone wild. Cattle were being withheld from market, chickens were being drowned, and the foodstore shelves were being emptied. The freeze was then lifted in steps, beginning within a little more than a month after it had been imposed. From then on, everyone knew that the system could not last much longer. The controls ended on April 30, 1974, when authority for them expired, and the President did not ask for their renewal.

There was another exception, not so big but more lasting and probably more important in the end, to the continuous process of decontrol. That was the treatment of oil prices, which I discuss below (pp. 190–193).

Whether the controls reduced the inflation, if one considers the whole period of their life plus, say, six months thereafter, no one will ever know. From the middle of 1971 to the end of 1974 the general price level rose by an average annual rate of 6.6 percent, much more than in the years before the controls were imposed. But we don't know what would have happened without the controls. The answer depends primarily on what fiscal and monetary policy would have been like if there had been no controls. One possibility is that in the absence of the controls, fiscal and monetary policy would have been more restrictive because the inflation would have been more obvious and direct means to deal with it not available. This is the standard answer and probably the correct one. But it is not the only possibility. Perhaps if the administration had not achieved its popular, though temporary, triumph with the imposition of the controls in 1971 it would have felt the need for even more expansionist policies before the 1972 election, and that might have been even more inflationary than our actual experience. There was also a more admirable alternative, which would have been to recognize and accept the necessary pain of the transition to price stability and stick with tight fiscal and monetary policy until the transition was over. But then one would have to ask, as Nixon would surely have asked, whether McGovern would have been elected and how inflationary that would have been.

Still, to say one doesn't know whether the controls succeeded in their primary mission of restraining inflation is a considerable indictment, in view of the national travail, the administrative costs, public and private, the interference with investment in basic industries and economic distortions they caused. No one objected to the end of the controls. But the experience did not leave the country with a strong commitment to the free market, monetarist way of restraining inflation. The attraction of the direct approach remained. Comprehensive mandatory controls were discredited, at least for the time, although some people believed that they would have worked if they had been administered by officials who "believed" in them more than the Nixon team did. But the idea that "some kind" of controls, but usually not called controls, had a major contribution to make remained a part of standard liberal, intellectual doctrine and, according to polls, remained acceptable to a majority of the public.

The Old-Time Religion

When the President launched his big push to increase expenditures in the first half of calendar 1972, he announced that in the next fiscal year he would return to balancing the budget at high employment. The administration, especially the economists, wanted to get to the discipline of some budgetary rule. Moreover, they were anticipating the arrival of the day when policy would have to turn in a more restrictive direction if it was to become possible to get out from under the controls without an inflationary explosion.

The case for a turn to more restrictive fiscal policy became stronger as 1972 proceeded. The economy was rising sharply, and although there was a general belief that considerable room existed before inflationary pressures would be encountered, planning for a fiscal year that would end on June 30, 1973, had to take account of that. There was, moreover, a political argument as well. The good behavior of the economy took the President off the defensive on the political issue. And since he had an opponent who was engaged in irritating the American people on all traditional values, it was convenient for Nixon to emphasize his own devotion to the traditional values, including fiscal prudence and balancing the budget.

The President's drive for fiscal restraint was obstructed for a while by the political ambitions of Wilbur Mills. The Congressman visualized himself as a possible presidential candidate. As chairman of the Ways and Means Committee the best thing he could do to further his ambition was to sponsor and push through a big increase in social security benefits. This he did, tying it to an extension of the federal debt limit which the President could not veto even if political considerations in an election year would have permitted him to do so.[15] Mills did not, of course, get the nomination but he did defer the reduction of the deficit.

But still by calendar year 1973 the budget deficit had been substantially reduced. The President had proposed an expenditure ceiling of $246 billion for fiscal 1973, and despite overruns in some categories the total actually came in at $246 billion.

The best picture of the tightening of fiscal policy in these years is probably given by the movement of the high-employment deficit—that is, the changes of the deficit which were not due to the fluctuations of the unemployment rate. On this basis the deficit went from 1 percent of GNP in calendar 1972 to 0.7 percent in calendar 1973 to zero in calendar 1974. Much of this move was due to the inflation. That is, the inflation was raising the revenue, but expenditures were not raised to match and there was a shift from deficit to budget balance.

Monetary policy did not turn to restraint until about the middle of 1973. This delay was not unusual. The common experience has been that as the economy expands, interest rates tend to rise, and the Federal Reserve tries to moderate this rise by increasing the supply of money, until inflation has gathered momentum, at which time—sometimes too late—the Fed shifts to restraint. In 1972 the turn to monetary restraint may have been impeded by a repeated Congressional threat to impose ceilings on interest rates.

But in any case by mid-1973 the government—the administration and the Federal Reserve—was in the third stage of its five-year struggle with the inflation-unemployment problem. The first, which lasted until August 1971, was an attempt to find the narrow path of fiscal and monetary policy which would reduce the inflation rate gradually, permanently and substantially while unemployment rose only slightly and briefly. The second, which lasted from August 1971 until the second freeze broke down in July 1973, was an attempt to make the earlier policy succeed by supplementing it with initially strong and gradually relaxing controls intended to overcome the inflationary expectations and contracts that had defeated the first approach. The third reflected a recognition that the controls were not going to serve that purpose and that there was not going to be any painless way out of the inflation. Demand would have to be restrained by fiscal and monetary policy and the resulting unemployment and other pain would have to be accepted until the inflation was substantially eliminated.

This was not a masochistic policy. The pain was not desired for its own sake. And efforts could be made to cushion the pain. But the emphasis had shifted to a much more determined approach to the fight against inflation and a much greater willingness to recognize and accept the costs. This was the lesson that all in the government, from the President down, had drawn from their previous efforts, whether delicate or strenuous. It was this lesson that I called the old-time religion. The President and his advisers lived by this rather stoically through the remainder of his shortened term.

Nixon on Regulation

Richard Nixon regarded himself as an opponent of government regulation of the economy. His economic advisers and most of his economic officials were even more strongly of that view. The outcome was disappointing. Probably more new regulation was imposed on the economy during the Nixon administration than in any other presidency since the New Deal, even if one excludes the temporary Nixon foray into price and wage controls. But the administration did succeed in removing some regulations and in furthering a process that would lead to more deregulation later.

There were two main areas in which the Nixon administration extended federal regulation: energy and the bundle of matters that economists call "externalities," including the environment, occupational health and safety, and consumer product safety.

The energy regulations had at their core control of the price of most domestically produced oil. They were a textbook example of the regulatory system which develops, almost inevitably, in an effort to compensate for the distortion and irrationalities that result from price control. By 1973, under the control system, there were two prices of oil (later there were many more); there was a controlled price on some of the domestic supply and a free market price for the imported oil and the rest of the domestic oil. The free market price was variable but always higher than the controlled price. Within any market, however, gasoline at the pumps had to sell at the same price, regardless of the source of the oil, and that was true of all other sales of petroleum products to the final purchaser. But different refiners had access to controlled and free market oil in different proportions, and therefore at widely different costs. So a complicated system was required to equalize the costs of different refiners. Moreover, the situation obviously required conservation of energy, but the price controls frustrated what could have been the most effective force for conservation—a high price. Therefore the need was felt for direct regulatory measures to effect conservation, such as gas mileage requirements for automobiles, various tax incentives and innumerable appeals for voluntary cooperation. Also the price mechanism for assuring efficient allocation of oil products among different distributors and different regions did not work, so a direct bureaucratic allocation system was imposed. This worked poorly, and as a result from time to time Americans in various parts of the country found themselves lined up for hours at their gas stations seeking a few gallons of the precious fluid.

Thus, we had managed to produce a shortage of energy in the richest country in the world. We had made "energy" one of the great national problems—at a level with national security and inflation. President Carter would later say that the effort to deal with the energy problem was the "moral equivalent of war." An immense Rube Goldberg structure of controls was erected simply to deal with the problems created by unwillingness to let the prices of oil rise to a free market level, and the structure was dismantled only when Ronald Reagan freed oil prices.

This system was the most obvious and irksome legacy of the Nixon price-wage controls. The whole thing began innocently enough, or naively enough, in 1973, when world oil prices began to rise significantly above the domestic price control level. We could not control the import price—at least not without giving up the imports. And it seemed obviously irrational to refuse to give domestic suppliers the price we were willing to pay Arabs, Venezuelans and other foreigners. The "energy experts" of the Cost of Living Council devised the two-price system. The idea was not to raise the price for "old" oil, which came from existing wells, on the theory that such oil would be supplied anyway and did not require any price increase to attract it. The price of "new" oil would be allowed to rise freely, so that production of it would not be limited by the price ceiling. In fact, the price of "new" oil would rise to the import price level. The authors of this plan were not in fact energy "experts." Within a few months, when the Arabs imposed the oil embargo, we all became energy experts. As I said in a speech at that time, an energy expert was a person who knew that Abu Dhabi was a place and Qaddafi was a person. They had the energy desk at the Cost of Living Council only at a time when that did not require any special knowledge. Also they were not economists, and were disdainful of the *a priori* reasoning of economists which warned against the plan. No one involved foresaw the full consequences of the policy. No one foresaw how big the difference between the controlled price and the free market price would be. And no one foresaw how long the energy controls would last—well beyond the duration of the other price controls.

There was a moment, in December 1973, when there seemed to be a real possibility of getting out from under the energy controls. The Arab oil embargo and the rise in the world oil price had underlined how counterproductive the oil price control was. By keeping a ceiling on the price of domestic oil and by selling petroleum products in the United States at a price which averaged the controlled domestic price and the free import price, we were encouraging oil imports, increasing our dependence and making it easier for OPEC to charge us a high price.

In the near-hysteria that accompanied the oil embargo and the OPEC price increase the President had established a Federal Energy Office and given it authority to control oil prices, an authority that, by subsequent legislation, would not expire on April 30, 1974, as the general price control authority would. This transfer of authority from the Cost of Living Council to the Federal Energy Office was to take place in December at a moment when the Council of Economic Advisers and many economists in the Treasury were urging decontrol of oil prices or, if that was not possible, an increase in the ceiling big enough to make the control nugatory.

Secretary of the Treasury Shultz called a meeting in his office on December 18 to discuss this issue. The director of the Cost of Living Council, John Dunlop, the head of the Energy Office, William Simon, and I were present. There was general recognition of the case for a large increase in the ceiling prices. But the group present could not agree on taking the step. The difficulty was partly economic—unwillingness to heighten, even temporarily, the rising tide of inflation. But the main problem was probably political—fear of being accused of sacrificing homeowners and commuters for the profit of the oil companies.

Being unable to reach agreement, Shultz adjourned the meeting and took the issue up to Nixon that evening. The President approved a small increase in the ceiling, from $4.25 a barrel to $5.25 a barrel. As Shultz explained it to me the next morning, the President was also afraid of the Congressional reaction, especially since Congressmen opposing the price increase would have been able to quote Nixon's own Cost of Living Council on their side. What the President thought would be the real effect of Congressional anger was unclear. His relations with Congress were already about as bad as they could be. Perhaps Congress would have passed legislation establishing a ceiling of $4.25 or even less. That would have been an unusual step, since Congress is commonly reluctant to enact such specific numbers into law. But even if that had happened it might have been a worthwhile education.

In saying that the oil price controls, and the myriad of auxiliary regulations put into place to support them during the years 1973–1981, were a legacy of the Nixon general wage and price controls I am suggesting that there would not have been oil price controls if the general system had not been in effect at the time of the 1973 oil shock. That is not certain, of course. Other industrial countries did not impose price controls at that time, but they did not have significant domestic oil production whose price they could control. We might have imposed price controls anyway in 1973, but the fact that we had the law, the machinery and a staff quite prepared to manage oil price controls made the controls inevitable and, as we have seen, their termination difficult. The energy regulation experience is an example of the unforeseen consequences that can result from changes in the ideological, political and bureaucratic atmosphere produced by general price controls.

Unlike the general price controls or the oil price controls, the

environmental regulations imposed by the Nixon administration
had a traditional and legitimate role in conservative, free market
economics. Regulations against dumping garbage in the streets
of English cities went back several hundred years. The argument
that some government intervention was appropriate when the
costs of private decisions were not borne by the private decision-
maker, as when the steel mill emits pollutants into the air, was
standard classical doctrine. A similar although less clear case
could be made for interventions to protect worker and consumer
safety on the ground that workers and consumers could not efficiently obtain the information needed to protect themselves.

So in establishing and developing the Environmental Protection Agency, the Occupational Safety and Health Administration, and the Consumer Product Safety Commission, President
Nixon was not only playing his part as a modern man, following
up the movement that had started in the Kennedy administration. He was also being consistent with free market ideology.
The problem, however, was how far the policy should be pushed
and by what means it should be implemented. The "externality"
argument does not say that no pollution should be emitted from
the stacks of steel mills. Beyond some point the cost of reducing
the pollution is more than the benefit of doing that. And there
are generally several different ways of achieving any desired
degree of environmental purification. Policy should seek to get it
done in the most economical way. There is a considerable body
of economic analysis to support the view that the most efficient
way to reduce pollution is by charging the polluters a fee per
unit of pollutant, which would bring home to them the cost of
pollution and induce them to seek the most economical way of
reducing pollution.

The Nixon administration tried to establish limits to the requirements for environmental purification that would conform to
the balancing of costs and benefits, and to use regulatory instruments that provided an incentive for efficiency. But its efforts
foundered on a tide of Congressional demagoguery and sentimentality plus bureaucratic zeal. The Council of Economic Ad-

visers argued that making the nation's streams 99 percent pure, rather than 98 percent pure, would have a cost far exceeding its benefits, but Congress was unmoved. The argument that standards for permissible pollution might be different for Idaho than for New York was considered an insult to Idaho, and suggestions for emission fees were regarded as the sale of licenses to infect babies with deadly diseases. The juggernaut of environmental regulation proved not to be controllable by the Nixon administration.

On the other hand, significant steps toward deregulation were taken in several areas.

The free market economists of the Nixon administration, and the President himself, regarded the draft for military service in peacetime as an intolerable infringement of personal liberty and an extremely unfair tax. One of the President's early acts was to establish a commission to study the matter. In April 1970, on the recommendation of the commission, he sent a message to Congress proposing an end to the draft, and it did end on June 30, 1973.

In August 1971 the administration stopped the presumed convertibility of the dollar to gold and allowed the exchange value of the dollar to fall. In March 1973 it moved to a "floating" exchange rate, under which the value of the dollar was determined by market forces. Thus it deregulated this key price in the economic system, which had long been a goal of many economists. This move made others possible. When the Nixon administration came into office the export of capital was under control as a means of supporting the dollar. These controls were gradually relaxed and then ended when the dollar was devalued. Also it is clear that if the gold window had not been closed there would have been restrictive measures against imports, especially from Japan, because of national anxiety about our adverse trade balance. Undoubtedly other restrictions on trade and capital movements would have been imposed if the effort to sustain the exchange rate of the dollar had continued.

During 1972 and 1973 all controls limiting the production of food crops were removed. These controls had been in force for almost all of the preceding forty years. Their elimination was made politically possible by exceptionally high world food prices, resulting from poor crops around the world. And their elimination was made economically necessary by the administration's price-wage control program, since the rise of food prices threatened to undermine the effort to restrain wages.

In 1973 the administration proposed legislation authorizing renewed negotiations for reduction of tariffs and other barriers to international trade. The act, which was passed in 1974, did broaden the range of circumstances in which U.S. producers might obtain protection against imports, and these provisions of the act were later used in a restrictive way. But on the whole the negotiations permitted under the act, the Tokyo Round, led to trade liberalization.

Early in his administration the President set up an interagency task force—of which I was chairman—to study the federal regulation of interest rates paid by banks, savings and loan associations, and other financial institutions. As might have been expected, the task force recommended that these regulations should be ended. As might also have been expected, the Treasury recommended that steps to end the controls be taken slowly. More time and argument would be needed to persuade or wear down or bypass the lobbies of the financial institutions, especially the savings and loan associations, which could be expected to object. So, in the classic government style, a commission was set up to study the matter. Then there were hearings and more discussion. The process dragged on for years. Finally, by 1983, almost complete decontrol was achieved, and the efforts made in the Nixon administration had been a step to accomplishing that.

Much work was done in the Nixon administration, as, indeed, in the Johnson administration, looking to deregulation of air, truck and rail transportation. Studies were conducted, legislation was drafted, and hearings were held. This work came to fruition only later, mainly in the Carter administration, but the earlier efforts were useful in the end.

Spending and Taxing

As I have said earlier, Richard Nixon did not come into office with great zeal to reduce either the expenditure or the revenue side of the budget. He did not think that the country was suffering from excesses on either side. He was, however, confronted with a number of specific problems on both sides of the budget.

He expected to get rid of the temporary tax surcharge that had been enacted in 1968 to help finance the Vietnam War. Thus, he expected to run the government with a somewhat smaller tax system than the one in place when he entered office. The decline of Vietnam War expenditures was counted on to make that possible.

The Johnson administration also left Mr. Nixon a ticking time bomb in the form of a demand for "tax reform," meaning measures to assure that rich people paid more taxes. In testimony three days before Lyndon Johnson left office his Secretary of the Treasury, Joseph Barr, presented evidence showing that twenty-one people with incomes of $1 million or more and 155 with incomes above $200,000 paid no federal income taxes in the previous year. This fact caused a sensation in the country, and it became the battle cry of the Congressional Democrats who thought that Richard Nixon could be skewered as resisting tax reform that would hit the rich people who were presumed to be his friends. The Nixon administration would have to deal with that for political reasons, if for no other.

Mr. Nixon also inherited a number of programs with strong built-in tendencies for expenditure increases—even without any further legislation. The leading case was social security, where the aging of the population and the increase in their earnings records were continuously raising outlays for benefits. Medicare outlays would also rise rapidly as the existence of the program attracted more and more claims and also raised medical costs. Also there seemed to have been a breakthrough in public attitudes toward government benefit programs, nourished by Johnson's War on Poverty, which led potential beneficiaries increasingly to seek every dollar they might claim, and that was ballooning the costs of the programs. But even beyond the cost increases built into the programs themselves, the Johnson programs had demonstrated their political effectiveness and strengthened the tendency of ambitious politicians to exploit the popularity of bigger and bigger benefit programs.

When Richard Nixon came into office there was national anticipation of the Vietnam dividend, which would permit large expenditure increases or tax reductions once the war expenditures ended. During his first month in office the President set up a Committee of the Domestic Policy Council to examine the Vietnam dividend. I was chairman, and there were members from the Treasury, the Bureau of the Budget and other agencies. We discovered that the cupboard was bare, or, rather, that the funds that would be made available by the ending of the war expenditures would be fully absorbed by the built-in increases in the costs of programs already on the books. We reported this in a meeting with the President in San Clemente in August 1969, after which Patrick Moynihan, director of the Domestic Policy Council, told the press: "The Vietnam dividend is as evanescent as the clouds over San Clemente."

So even if the President had no strong desire to cut government expenditures, he had a major problem in trying to limit their increase and keep them within the bounds of the available revenue. This was made especially difficult because he did have some definite desires about the composition of the budget, desires that were not shared with many in Congress and elsewhere. Therefore he found himself bargaining to get what he wanted in the budget, and often what he had to pay was acceptance of expenditure increases that he would have preferred not to make.

A major plank in a "modern" Republican platform when Mr. Nixon came into office was revenue sharing. The basic rationale for this in Republican thinking was that the efficiency of the federal government as a revenue collector should be used to supplement the resources of the states and localities but that the federal government should not intrude in state and local decisions as it did under several hundred specific grant-in-aid programs. Revenue sharing was intended as a substitute for part of the existing grant programs, to increase the freedom and responsibility of the lower levels of government without depriving them of funds. But the existing "categorical" programs all had their supporters in the Congress and in the country. Moreover, it was impossible to devise a way to substitute revenue sharing for categorical grants that would not reduce the payments to some local governments, unless the total expenditure was increased. So general revenue sharing turned out to be largely an addition to the budget. Similarly, the President's objective in reform of the welfare system was to make it more objective in giving support to poor people on the basis of their poverty, with less intrusion by social workers into their lives and less discouragement of work effort and family solidarity. The intention was to hold down total outlays as much as possible and to redirect the existing funds. But this turned out to be politically impossible, because every beneficiary and every unit of government had to be "held harmless." That is, nobody could lose. In that case redirection could occur only with an increase of total expenditures.

The disagreement between the President and the Congress on the division of the budget between defense and nondefense purposes was another force tending to propel the total budget upward. The President was constantly trying to get bigger defense appropriations than the Congress was willing to provide and trying to resist nondefense appropriations that the Congress wanted. The net result was a compromise in which the President accepted more nondefense spending than he wanted and the Congress accepted more defense spending than it wanted and total spending was larger than either wanted. Each party was willing to subordinate its preference about the total size of the budget to its preference for particular expenditures.

From time to time in an effort to hold down nondefense spending, the President "impounded" funds—that is, declined to spend amounts that Congress had appropriated. President Lyndon Johnson had done that frequently, and the practice had a still longer history. It had always raised complaints, from Congress and from program beneficiaries. The complaints were especially loud against President Nixon's impoundments, partly because they were larger than the earlier ones and partly because in the second term he seemed vulnerable. In fact, the impoundments were cited as an example of Nixon's grasping for power that was covered by the term "Watergate." Many suits were brought against the President to require him to spend the money that had been appropriated.[16]

The impoundment issue would not be settled by the courts, but would be settled by legislation. The basic fact was that Congressional procedures did not provide any way for making and carrying out a decision about the total amounts of expenditure and revenue. Separate decisions were made in a large number of appropriation and revenue bills without assurance that they added up to totals on each side of the budget that anyone preferred. The President, therefore, was the only person who could impose an explicitly chosen limit on total expenditures, and to do that he had to be able to refuse to spend some of the Congressional appropriations. If he was to be denied that power a Congressional procedure to limit the totals would be needed. Recognition of this dilemma led to the Congressional Budget and Impoundment Control Act of 1974. This limited the President's authority to withhold expenditures except in conformity to procedures that required Congressional approval. It also established new Congressional procedures and institutions intended to enable Congress to make decisions about the totals in the budget and force the specific decisions about appropriations and taxation to conform to those totals.

Mr. Nixon's initial consideration of taxation concentrated on the question of the extension of the Vietnam surcharge, which was due to expire in 1969. He decided within a few months that he would have to ask for the extension, since there was no immediate way to cut military spending and efforts to cut nondefense expenditures had yielded slight results. Beyond that the administration only planned some steps to respond to the furor that had been raised by the revelation that a few people with high incomes had been paying no income tax. These necessary steps were not expected to have any important budgetary or economic impact. Shortly after the Nixon administration took office I called the Assistant Secretary of the Treasury who handled tax matters and told him that the Council of Economic Advisers would like to participate in discussions of tax policy. He assured me that the Treasury was only contemplating some technical corrections and that he would let us know if any economic questions arose. (Many months passed before the Treasury recognized that economic questions were involved.) When the discovery was made that there would be no Vietnam dividend, a new element came into the tax picture. It would be necessary to protect the revenues. There would be no room for tax reduction after the temporary surcharge expired.

These three elements—extension of the surcharge, tax reform and preservation of the future revenue—were entangled in a struggle between the administration and the Congress that went on all year. Although the tax surcharge was President Johnson's idea, and he had recommended its extension, the Democrats in Congress wanted a price from Richard Nixon if they were to agree to its extension. The Treasury's Congressional liaisons informed Nixon that he would gain one hundred votes in the House in favor of extension if he would agree to ending the tax credit for business investment. This was also ironic, since the tax credit was a John F. Kennedy initiative that had at first been opposed by business leaders. By 1969, however, the Democrats were taking an anti-corporation, anti-wealthy line in opposition to a Republican President who they thought was on the other side.

As Paul McCracken was out of Washington when the issue arose, I wrote the memo for the President on the economics of the investment credit. I argued that the credit should be eliminated, mainly on the grounds that the stimulation of business investment was then less important than obtaining more revenue to provide assistance to the poor and to states and localities and to reduce the budget deficit, which we considered an impediment to housing finance. The President complimented me on the memo, perhaps because he found it refreshing to get such an argument from a Republican economist and perhaps because it rationalized what he wanted to do anyway—make a deal with Congress in which the surcharge would be extended in exchange for repeal of the investment tax credit. The President's message supporting the repeal made the priorities arguments that had been in my memo.

Congress was not satisfied with repeal of the investment credit as the price for extension of the surcharge. The President had proposed a minimum income tax designed to make sure that very wealthy persons did not entirely escape federal income tax. Congress wanted to go much further than he in raising taxes on investment income. The President had also proposed a low-income allowance that would have relieved from federal income tax persons whose income was below the poverty line. Congress wanted to give more relief than that to low- and middle-income people, including an increase in the personal exemption to be phased in over a three-year period. The President's tax proposal would have raised the revenue in the long run, because of the elimination of the investment credit. The Congressional revisions converted the package into one that would reduce the annual revenue substantially by the time all the scheduled exemption increases were phased in.

The administration and the Congress struggled over the shape and size of the tax package during the last months of 1969. The President tried to get the future revenue loss reduced while also relieving investors and businesses of some of the additional tax burdens involved in the Congressional program. To some extent he succeeded in this. But still the tax bill that Congress passed and sent to him in December was unsatisfactory in both respects. From his standpoint it reduced future revenues too much by cuts in the income tax on low-income and middle-income individuals and raised burdens too much where they would hurt saving and investment. On the other hand, the bill did extend the tax surcharge, at a reduced rate, into 1970 and so eased the immediate deficit problem. The President had to choose between signing the bill, which would obtain the revenue he wanted for 1970, and vetoing the bill, which would avoid the revenue loss in the future.

After much discussion in which his advisers were divided, he signed the bill, with a message indicating his reluctance to do so.

The irony is that after all the dispute with the Congress and the agonizing debates within the administration, the President changed his mind in less than two years. When the President decided—at Camp David in August 1971—to adopt a new economic policy, part of that policy would be to cut taxes in order to stimulate employment. The President then recommended that the investment tax credit, which he had helped to repeal in 1969, should be restored. He also proposed that part of the rise of individual income tax exemptions scheduled to take effect on January 1, 1973, should be advanced to take effect on January 1, 1972. Thus he now welcomed the main revenue-reducing measure at which he had balked in 1969 and undid his main revenue-raising measure of that time.

The course of taxation during the Nixon administration was influenced less by the President's struggles with Congress in 1969 and his abrupt turnaround in 1971 than by two developments that passed almost unnoticed. One was the effect of the inflation on the tax burden. The other was the gradual rise in social security taxes that was quietly accepted by everyone as the counterpart of the rising benefits.

Although there were substantial increases of personal income tax exemptions and allowances, the ratio of personal taxes to personal income rose from 10.8 percent in 1967 to 11.8 percent in 1974, as the inflation raised taxpayers into higher brackets.[17] This entailed a considerable shift of the income tax burden, as the exemption increases mainly relieved low-income persons whereas the inflation mainly increased the burden on middle- and upper-income people—except for the very-highest-income people. At the same time, changes in the tax law were reducing the tax burden on the book profits of corporations, but the inflation was substantially reducing real profits relative to book profits, so that the burden on real profits increased a great deal. Total profits taxes relative to GNP fell substantially, because real profits fell substantially relative to GNP. Social security taxes rose over

35 percent relative to GNP, as a result of increases in rates and coverage.

In sum, if we compare 1974 with 1967—to take the year before the imposition of the Vietnam tax surcharge—federal receipts rose from 18.8 percent of GNP to 20.1 percent. But federal receipts other than social security contributions fell from 14.2 percent of GNP to 13.8 percent. This small decline resulted from two conflicting tendencies. On the one hand, changes in the law tended to reduce both individual and corporate burdens, and the decline of corporate profits relative to GNP was also holding down receipts. On the other hand, the inflation was raising the revenue, relative to GNP, by pushing individual income taxes into higher brackets and by artificially raising the corporate tax base.

Most of the increase of the revenues, relative to GNP, between 1967 and 1974, went into reducing the deficit, and little of it was used to finance an increase in the expenditure/GNP ratio. While revenues as a percent of GNP rose by 1.3 percent the deficit fell by 0.9 percent, from 1.7 to 0.8 percent of GNP. (This is even clearer on a high employment basis, if we factor out the effects of the 1974 recession. The receipts that would have been collected at high employment rose by 1.4 percent of GNP as the high-employment deficit fell from 1.9 percent of GNP to zero. High-employment expenditures fell relative to GNP.[18]) Behind this stability of the ratio of expenditures to GNP there was a marked shift in the composition of the budget. Total expenditures rose only from 20.5 percent of GNP to 20.9 percent, but defense expenditures dropped from 9.0 percent to 5.4 percent and non-defense expenditures rose from 11.5 percent to 15.5 percent. Most of the increases of nondefense expenditures were in social insurance programs, for retirement, disability, medical care and unemployment, which rose from 4.1 to 6.3 percent.

Superficially the budget seemed to be reaching a stable and satisfactory situation during the Nixon administration. Expenditure growth was slow and revenues were rising rapidly enough, despite some tax decreases, to cover the expenditure increases and approximately eliminate the budget deficit. But, of course, the development had major unsustainable, even explosive, elements. The growth of total expenditures was held down only because defense expenditures were declining, not only relative to GNP but also absolutely when adjusted for inflation. That could not continue. When defense expenditures stopped declining, and especially if a time came when the need for more defense was accepted, the total budget would rise dangerously unless the trend of nondefense expenditures changed radically. At the same time, the rise of revenues could not be projected into the future. That rise depended on the inflation, which could not continue. And even if the inflation did continue, the taxpayers could not be counted on to sit still for the surreptitious increase in their tax burdens that the inflation was yielding.

So there was a looming conflict among the prospective expenditure commitments and needs, the apparent unwillingness of the country to tax itself explicitly, and conventional notions of the requirement to balance the budget. The administration had a foretaste of this conflict when its earliest budget projections showed that there would be no Vietnam dividend. That had accounted for Mr. Nixon's effort to defend the revenue in 1969. But that attitude toward the budget was submerged in the attempt to deal with the economics of the 1970–1971 recession and the politics of the 1972 election. In 1973 and 1974 the administration, in what I have called its old-time religion phase, returned to active concern about the budget situation, now focused on the expenditure side. Great anxiety was building up about commitments to future transfer payments. But the administration was unable to attack the problem effectively. It was bargaining, as I have already noted, for higher defense appropriations from Congress. The President's influence was not great. And the situation did not yet seem critical to many people, perhaps because the deficits were not large. So the problem remained when the Nixon administration left in 1974, and remains —and is more obvious—ten years later.

Summing Up

Mr. Nixon did not come into office to make a conservative revolution in economic policy. He had certain conventional leanings in that direction but did not feel strongly about it and it was not his main interest. Moreover, the economic situation in 1969 did not call for a revolution—only for moderate reforms and cautions.

Mr. Nixon's economists regarded themselves as conservatives and were very conscious of differences between themselves and their predecessors—the Hellers, Ackleys and Okuns of the Kennedy-Johnson regime. But in fact, the differences between them were not great.

So there was no reason to expect a conservative revolution from the Nixon team. But still the actual developments were surprisingly different from what might have been expected. One might have expected:

1. More emphasis on inflation and some success in getting the inflation down.

2. More emphasis on monetary policy, and particularly on stable growth of the money supply.

3. Reliance on a stable rule of fiscal policy.

4. Moderate reduction of government regulations, or at least slowing down their proliferation.

These things did not happen. There are several reasons why they did not. Probably the most important is that everything turned out to be more difficult than it seemed in advance. That was notably true of the effort to check inflation. No one knew how much the anti-inflation fight would cost. When they got some inkling of the cost, they—the President and his advisers—were unwilling to pay it and also thought the public was unwilling to pay it. So they all went chasing off after panaceas.

The idea of a "Friedmanesque" policy of stable monetary growth ran into a number of difficulties. The policy may be the most appropriate one for keeping an economy stable when it is in a position where it should be kept stable. But the problem of 1969 was not to stabilize the economy; it was to reduce the on-going inflation. That called for a reduction in the rate of monetary growth, but the "stable money" rule provided no guidance about the speed with which monetary growth should be decelerated. Moreover, the Federal Reserve did not share the "stable money" view of monetary policy and was not inclined to follow such a policy, even if its quantitative meaning had been clear. Finally, even if the ideal monetary policy had been known and followed, it would not have guaranteed a painless transition from inflation and subsequent return to high employment. The prolonged, even though not very deep, recession encountered in 1970, and the eagerness to regain high employment diverted the Friedmanesque economists in the administration from the intentions with which they had entered office.

Inability to achieve the desired results from monetary policy tended to push the administration in the direction of attempts to manipulate fiscal policy as an instrument of economic stabilization. There were two other reasons for frustration of the hopes to establish a "modern" rule of fiscal policy. Such rules have the merit, if they are good ones, that they yield better results on the average over long periods than *ad hoc* fine-tuning, but Presidents do not live or get reelected on the average over long periods and they cannot resist the attempt to beat the averages in their particular short run. Also, the traditional conservatives from the financial and business world who might have been expected to support a disciplinary rule of policy spurned the administration's proposal.

Finally, the great paradox of the Nixon administration, and by its own standard the great sin, was the price and wage controls. The reasons for falling into this were numerous and have been recited earlier in this chapter. But the critical failure was the failure to recognize that all things conspired to drive the country into controls. A positive and active program would have been needed to resist. The tide was not running toward freedom, but the administration did not foresee or imagine what would happen and did not build dikes against the tide.

6

Ford and Carter: The Uncertain Transition

THE YEARS 1974–1980, the Ford and Carter years, were a time of turmoil, anxiety and dissatisfaction in the economy. The dominant, continuing factor was the inflation. In 1974 the inflation rate zoomed to the highest level seen in the United States since 1919 at the end of World War I. This spike in the inflation rate was heightened by the big increase in the OPEC oil price, by the end of price and wage controls and by bad crops depressing the world food supply. After 1974 the inflation rate subsided, but it began to rise in 1977 and reached another peak in 1980, again heightened by the oil price increase. Despite the occasional abatement of the inflation rate, the concern about inflation never subsided but the fear of inflation as a threat to the stability of every household became stronger and stronger.

In the midst of this inflation the country suffered the worst recession of the postwar period up to that time. In May 1975 the unemployment rate rose to 9.2 percent—two percentage points higher than the previous postwar high.

During this period also the American people encountered the first real shortages they had ever met in peacetime. At various

209

times during these six years they lined up for gasoline and were reminded of what a totally disorganized economy could be like.

And as the years passed it became clear that productivity was rising at an exceptionally slow rate compared to our previous experience. This threatened the increase of living standards to which Americans had become accustomed.

As is usually the case, these problems dominated perceptions of the economy and thinking about economic policy, even though in some respects the economy was performing well. There was a large rise of employment, as the number of young people reaching working age increased rapidly and more and more women entered the labor force. Because of this rise of employment, total output increased at about its usual rate despite the slow growth of output per worker. These two developments, the rapid increase of employment and the slow rise of productivity, were connected. The increase of employment meant that a larger fraction of the work force was inexperienced and relatively unproductive. Also, the increase of employment held down capital per worker. With an increasing fraction of the population employed, output and income per capita increased about as rapidly as ever.

Still, the inflation, the recession, the slowdown of productivity growth and the actual and potential energy shortage were real problems with which public policy was expected to cope. By and large the government's effort to cope during this period, 1974 to 1980, relapsed into the form of conventional, *ad hoc,* pragmatic fine-tuning. And it was dissatisfaction with the results of such a strategy that led to a movement in a more conservative direction even before Reagan—that is, in the last years of Carter.

As we have pointed out, by the beginning of 1974 the Nixon team itself was disillusioned with its effort to achieve noninflationary high employment by a combination of fiscal-monetary variable expansionism with price and wage controls. Their alternative—perhaps their atonement—was the "old-time religion." They would stick by fiscal and monetary restraint to control inflation, would not be diverted by recession and unemployment and not be seduced by the idea of direct controls over inflation. The main ingredient in this prescription was holding down government expenditures. What it meant for budget policy—for the size of the deficit or surplus—was less clear. In early 1974, in discussion of the fiscal 1975 budget among the Nixon officials, there was general agreement that the policy should be to balance the budget for that year. That would, presumably, give the country a "signal" of the seriousness of the intent to mend the old ways and stop the inflation. It was pointed out that they could not really promise to balance the budget in fiscal year 1975. If there was a severe recession there would be a deficit, and no one would want to take the steps needed to prevent that. All that the administration could say was that it would balance the budget at high employment, or some such condition. But the new enthusiasts for the old-time religion regarded that as equivocation and rejected it. Secretary of the Treasury Simon said that their policy should be "Balance the Budget, Period!" meaning balance the budget no matter what. Of course, they could not and did not do that, but the expression indicated the prevailing sentiment.

The old-time religion also implied something about monetary policy—something like firmness and stability. There was, however, no articulation of what that meant operationally.

The Nixon team had the opportunity to show their devotion to the old-time religion as the economy went into decline at the end of 1973. This decline was mostly, if not entirely, caused by the oil embargo and price increase. There immediately arose a demand for fiscal and monetary stimulus to keep the economy rising. The administration resisted these demands, except for minor steps to encourage home building. The President said there would be no recession, although the Council of Economic Advisers was more cautious, and I said, "We're going to have the littlest boom you ever saw."

The Nixon economists maintained that what was going on was not a conventional recession because it did not originate on the demand side of the economy. Output was falling, they said, because the oil shortage was limiting the ability of many enterprises to produce. Critics of this analysis claimed that the high oil price, causing a big increase in the payments of Americans to foreigners, was cutting the demand of Americans for American products. But the Nixon economists were unmoved by this. The argument was not really about this analysis. The basic point was the determination of the administration to turn over a new leaf and stay on a steady, disinflationary course—whatever the passing statistics might show. This attitude was apparent in Richard Nixon's last public speech before his resignation. Although not pure—Presidents' speeches always have something for everybody—the speech emphasized the intent to stick to a steady long-run policy.

In fact, the government's policy during the remainder of 1974 was quite restrictive, probably more restrictive than what the government might have chosen if it had known precisely what was happening. The budget moved into surplus as the sharp rise of prices and incomes raised revenues unexpectedly. The inflation reduced the real value of the money supply. We were getting the built-in anti-inflation reaction of fiscal and monetary policy to a degree not expected. Moreover, the available statistics did not reveal how large was the buildup of inventories during the early part of 1974 and therefore how great was the possibility of a severe recession.

Whether the Nixon team's turn to austerity would have survived in the face of the recession that was to develop was, of course, not tested. On the afternoon of the day he was sworn in, August 9, 1974, the new President, Gerald Ford, met with his economic officials to review the situation. William Simon was Secretary of the Treasury, but he was not the Special Assistant to the President for Economic Affairs, as Shultz had been; that position was held by Kenneth Rush. I was present, but my departure had been announced, and my replacement, Alan Greenspan, was also present. The budget director, Roy Ash, and Arthur Burns were also at the meeting. Although the discussion at the meeting was quite diffuse, the memoranda that the participants were asked to submit afterward showed a clear consensus. Unemployment would rise, but only to about 6 percent within a year. No strong action was recommended; there were some suggestions for improving unemployment compensation. No one foresaw that the unemployment rate would hit 9 percent in nine months.

With that view of the economic prospect it was perfectly natural that the administration should continue its focus on inflation. In September the White House launched the Inflation Summit—a series of conferences at which economists, bankers, businessmen, labor leaders and others met, at first separately and then, through representatives, in joint sessions, to talk about the ways to fight inflation. The conferences were fully covered by the media, which explains in part why they consisted mainly of declarations of long-standing positions with little attempt at a meeting of minds. Probably the only memorable utterance in many days of talk was that of George Shultz, attending as a private citizen, who said that the whole range of economic forecasts could be covered by a hat. It was not only the government economists who did not foresee the depth of the recession that was coming.

In October, with the unemployment rate rising, the President went up to Congress and submitted his full-scale economic program.[1] It presumably reflected the findings of the Inflation Summit Conferences, but in fact was standard fare—what a group of government economists, politicians and public relations experts would have produced without any Summit. The program was "balanced." It emphasized the fight against inflation but showed concern for the rising unemployment by proposing extended unemployment compensation and moderate jobs programs, assistance for the housing industry and a tax stimulus for business investment. The employment aids were to take effect when and if the unemployment rate reached 6 percent—as it did in the month when the President was speaking, but that was not yet known. There was, on the other hand, a plea for expenditure restraint by Congress and a recommendation for a tax increase to pay for the costs of the antirecession measures. There was also what later would be called a supply-side element in the program—measures to increase food production, conserve energy and stimulate domestic production of it, promote competition and get rid of excess government regulation.

But one part of the program was unusual, or at least given unusual prominence. That was a call for voluntary cooperation by all Americans to fight inflation by saving, working, conserving energy and sharing with the less fortunate. This effort was to be symbolized by a button, saying WIN, for Whip Inflation Now, that the people were invited to wear. The button immediately became an object of ridicule and a symbol of vacuity in economic policy.

In retrospect, the policy of 1974, aside from the WIN button, seems to have been consistent with the strategy of a stoical acceptance of the transitional costs of getting the inflation down from the 12 to 14 percent rate it reached that year. The puzzling question about the policy is how much of it was accidental—a result of failure to appreciate either the severity of the coming recession or the stringency of the fiscal and monetary position. Would the policy that did finally contribute to driving the inflation rate down substantially have been continued through 1974 if the government had known what the result would be in unemployment? No one can answer that, but the administration's language did not indicate that degree of determination.

By the end of 1974 the steepness of the decline was evident, and some positive response was required from the government. The response was an extreme example of fine-tuning. There would be a temporary tax cut, designed to give the economy a shot in the arm in the second quarter of 1975 but not to continue long enough to imperil a subsequent move to a balanced budget. There would be a rapid increase in the growth of the money supply for several months, after which money growth would subside again. This response may be looked upon as a departure from the old-time religion of stable, nonexpansionist policy. But in the light of the severity of the recession the surprise is that the response was so mild. Liberal economists loudly called for more expansionist policy. But these calls did not generate much action, even from a Democratic, activist Congress. The big news of 1975 was that the country reached 9 percent unemployment with much less complaint, much less excitement in the streets or in the Congress, much less pressure for expansionist measures, than would have been predicted a year or two earlier. At least for the time being the extreme inflationary experience of 1974 had made the government and the public cautious about expansionist policy and content with the prospect of a more stable price level.

The severe restraint of 1974, however accidental, and the limited stimulus of 1975 may be counted a success. At least the inflation came down substantially, recovery began and the recovery did not, at least during 1975 and 1976, revive the inflation. The increase in the consumer price index over the previous year fell from 11 percent in 1974 to 9.1 percent in 1975 and 5.8 percent in 1976. The decline of inflation was to some degree a transitory fall from a transitory peak that had resulted from special oil and food price situations and the end of price controls. The slowdown of wage increases, which would have been required for a permanent decline of inflation to a low level, was small, but there was some.

The country enjoyed, in 1976, the best of conditions, as is usually the case in the early stages of a recovery. Inflation stays low while output rises and unemployment falls. The key question is how long that combination can be maintained. That in turn depends on whether a demand-management policy can be maintained that does not push the economy up too fast and too far. We do not know whether a Ford administration, if kept in office after 1976, would have persisted in such a course of moderation. But we do know that the basis for the persistence of such a course had not been laid. There was no agreement in the country on rules of policy that would keep the government on such a course and little understanding of the need for such rules. Although the public in its first recoil from double-digit inflation would tolerate a policy of caution in pumping the economy up again, that patience might not persist as the memory of the inflation peak faded. The Ford administration might have followed a noninflationary policy. It made little effort to fix upon the national mind any general principles of policy that would prevent the return of inflation. Its own actions, however successful in 1975 and 1976, could be interpreted as an unusually skillful or lucky exercise in adaptation to changing forecasts and developments rather than as the carrying out of any objective and predictable rules. Certainly the Federal Reserve denied the utility of such rules. With such a philosophy, the success of the policy would depend on the good luck or wisdom of the policymakers who happened to be in office.

After 1976—that is, after the Carter administration came into office—either the luck or the wisdom departed. The policy of forecasting the course of the economy and adapting actions to the forecast did not work so well as the economy approached the zone where expansion could be inflationary and as policy fell into the hands of people with overly ambitious goals.

The Carter team did have such goals. They had come to repeat the Kennedy achievement of "getting the economy moving again." They would do this by fiscal and monetary expansionism, cutting taxes and speeding up the growth of money to reduce interest rates. When expansionism began to threaten the revival of inflation they would invoke incomes policy to hold prices and wages down.

There was, however, a crucial difference between the situation Kennedy had faced and the situation Carter faced. Upon arrival in the White House, Kennedy had behind him a period of reasonable price stability that President Eisenhower and Federal Reserve Chairman Martin had achieved. Carter had behind him ten years of Johnson-Nixon inflation. Kennedy could exploit the expectation of price stability, which allowed him to get a great deal of output increase and only a little bit of price increase by raising demand. Carter had no such margin. The expectation of inflation had remained despite the brief Ford interlude. This expectation would be turned into critical price and wage increases very quickly by a policy of expanding demand. That is, Carter would get much more inflation and much less output per dollar of demand increase than Kennedy got. Moreover, after ten years of price and wage controls in various forms, all more or less ineffective, the Carter incomes policy would be a paper tiger.

In January 1977 when Jimmy Carter took office, the unemployment rate was 7.4 percent. The new team regarded that as much too high and believed that as long as unemployment was in that neighborhood there was no danger of reviving inflation. The Ford Council of Economic Advisers, in their final economic report that month, had wrestled with the problem of defining "full employment." They estimated that if 4 percent had been full employment in the 1950s the change in the age-sex composition of the labor force would have raised the full employment rate to 4.9 percent by 1977. They pointed to other factors that might have raised the rate to 5.5 percent, and that even that rate was highly uncertain. In general, the tendency of the analysis was to avoid commitment to any number as a target of policy. The Ford CEA did not, however, positively reject the policy of directing fiscal and monetary policy at achieving a full-employment target. That policy had been responsible for much of the inflation of the previous decade as the government had aimed at an excessively ambitious employment target. But to reject the employment goal clearly would have seemed excessively hard-hearted, even though aiming at "full employment" had not durably yielded the desired result.

The Carter administration made the unemployment target a centerpiece of its policy. That is, they acted as if called upon to get to this arbitrarily defined full employment in two or three years. They "accepted" 4.9 percent as the full-employment goal, attributing it to the Ford Council of Economic Advisers and without recognition of the numerous qualifications the Ford council had placed around that number. True, that was a politically difficult time for trying to educate the American public about the pitfalls of full-employment targeting. Mr. Carter had run for election on the promise to lift the economy out of the Ford doldrums. He could hardly be less ambitious than Ford. Also, in these years—1976 to 1978—a conspicuous piece of legislation, the Humphrey-Hawkins Bill, was moving through Congress. That would have required the government to attain all manner of good things, no matter how unattainable or inconsistent with each other. One of the good things to be attained was 4 percent unemployment. Every informed person knew that the whole idea—including the 4 percent unemployment—was nonsense and that the bill could be stomached only on the assumption, which proved to be correct, that it would be forgotten as soon as enacted. But no political person, certainly not one dependent on the traditional Democratic constituency, found the courage to say so. Although the Carter administration tried to moderate the bill in the end, it also had to act as if the 4 percent goal was in some long-run sense reasonable.

The Carter administration not only participated in but also took the lead in creating an atmosphere in which rapid movement toward a low level of unemployment was the overriding test of the success of national economic policy. The predictable results followed.

The administration began 1977 with a major fiscal program for stimulating the economy, relying heavily on a temporary tax cut. The one-shot tax cut was rejected, but most of the other parts of the program survived. There was a considerable increase in the budget deficit in the second half of 1977, especially significant because it occurred in the face of a rising economy. Thereafter deficits subsided for a time, mainly because the rising tide of inflation was generating revenue faster than the government was spending it. Deficits rose again in late 1979 and early 1980 as expenditures surged.

But the stronger force at work was the growth of the money supply. The growth of the money supply (M_1) was greater in the three years 1977, 1978 and 1979 than in any other three-year period of the postwar era. The administration was known to be urging the Fed to greater expansion. In February 1978, Arthur Burns was replaced by Carter's own man, G. William Miller, as chairman of the Fed. The performance of the Fed was not, however, chiefly a reflection of the personalities involved. It was a response to a prevailing attitude in the country about the goals of economic policy.

The rapid increase in the money supply in these years 1977–1979 was associated with, and probably caused, an extremely rapid increase in total spending—nominal GNP—in the same three years. And this big increase in demand mainly accounted for the return of inflation to double-digit figures by 1979.

Leading up to the 1980 Campaign

By 1979 the time had clearly come for a turn in economic policy. This was partly because of two objective conditions. The inflation had accelerated again, reaching 13.3 percent from December 1978 to December 1979, as measured by the consumer price index. And the slowdown in the growth of output per worker, on which the improvement of living standards ultimately depends, had persisted for six years. From 1947 to 1973 the average annual rise of output per worker hour had been 3.0 percent; from 1973 to 1979 it was 0.8 percent. One could no longer think that the slowdown might be a statistical aberration or an entirely cyclical fluctuation.

The objective conditions by themselves do not explain the intensity of the feeling that policy had to change, or the direction in which changes were thought to be needed. Perception of the harm done by inflation bears no close relation to the harm that is objectively done, although it is hard to tell whether the perceived harm is greater or less than the actual harm. Probably the answer is that the perception exaggerates the harm currently being done and underestimates the dangers being built up for the future. People measure the injury they suffer from inflation by the rise in the prices they have to pay. They overlook the fact that most of the prices they pay are received as income by Americans, including themselves. On the average and in the short run, incomes do keep up with prices. There is some redistribution as a result of inflation—some people gain and some people lose. But clichés about who the gainers and losers are do not have much foundation. A recent study has concluded that the main losers are upper-income people, whose assets decline most in real value during inflation.[2] One redistribution to which much attention has been paid is the transfer of income from taxpayers to the government as a result of the progressive income tax schedule, which in a time of inflation raises revenue automatically more than in proportion to the amount of inflation. In the end this is, of course, not a net reduction in the incomes of private individuals, since the revenue the government gets is paid out again in government expenditures.

Nevertheless, the fact is that most people feel that they are hurt by inflation. They are disappointed and offended because although they are receiving larger incomes, in dollars, than they used to receive they are not nearly as rich as they think they should be with such large dollar incomes. Moreover, they are frightened by the inflation. Even if they realize that they are keeping up with the inflation they have little confidence that they will keep up in the future. These disappointments and anxieties are real—and politically important—even if the objective facts are misunderstood.

On the other hand, inflation has long-run effects which are not well understood. Probably most important, a high rate of inflation is bound to be an uncertain rate of inflation, and that uncertainty depresses long-run investment and retards the growth of productivity. Moreover, if a high rate of inflation is tolerated it will probably escalate, but the escalation will not be allowed to go on forever, and its ending will almost certainly involve a recession with increased unemployment.

Despite the inflation, and despite the slowdown in productivity growth, real per capita income after tax, probably the best simple measure of economic welfare, increased between 1976 and 1980. Indeed, it increased just about as much in that period as in the preceding four years. Still, public opinion polls supported common observation of great dissatisfaction with the state of the economy. When Ronald Reagan, campaigning for the presidency in 1980, asked the American people to ask themselves whether they were better off than they had been four years earlier, he could count on a negative answer, despite the economic statistics. Candidates in 1980 promising a change in the economic policy could take that dissatisfaction for granted; they did not, like Kennedy twenty years earlier, have to create the problem they would promise to solve.

The objective circumstances did not dictate that the policy change would be in a conservative direction. There were explanations of the economic difficulties that, if correct, would have called for solutions requiring more government controls of the economy. The inflation was blamed on high oil prices, high prices for medical care and high food prices. And the prescription offered was more control of oil prices and medical costs and specific measures to stabilize food prices. The slowdown of productivity growth could be blamed on the lack of government leadership in economic affairs—by contrast with Japan, for example. There were some who regarded the Nixon, Ford and Carter administrations as representatives of conservative and monetarist policies and who held those policies responsible for the state of the economy.

But such attitudes were not credible in 1979 and 1980. There had been a flurry of interest in economic planning, meaning much more systematic and detailed government control, in 1975 when the combination of a severe recession, the oil embargo and recent extreme inflation led some people to believe that the failure of the free economy had been finally demonstrated. This turned out to be a brief fad, however. As usual, the American people were not interested in grand plans to change the system.

By 1979 the case for going in the other direction seemed obvious. We were at the end of two decades in which government spending, government taxes, government deficits, government regulation and government expansion of the money supply had all increased rapidly. And at the end of those two decades the inflation rate was high, real economic growth was slow and our "normal" unemployment rate—the rate we experienced in good times—was higher than ever. Nothing was more natural than the conclusion that the problems were caused by all these government increases and would be cured by reversing, or at least stopping, them.

This attitude was reinforced by a common grievance about taxes. The inflation had boosted many taxpayers into brackets that they had thought were reserved for the rich—i.e., for other people. They didn't like it. They were not comforted to know that the government had "offset" this bracket creep by cutting some taxes or by paying out money to some people.[3] The tax cuts were mainly for the poor, and the spending increases they thought of as being mainly for the very poor. And while they sympathized with the "deserving poor" they felt that much of their money was going to support indolence and family breakup.

The shift to traditional, conservative attitudes in economic policy was part of a more general shift of attitudes. By 1979 the "liberalism" of the 1960s and 1970s had become associated with immorality and indifference to America's interests in the world. The rejection of liberal economics was reinforced by a widespread desire to come home in other aspects of life.

This popular attitude toward the economic policies of the 1960s and 1970s was, to some extent, accompanied by a shift in the mainstream of thinking among economists. The basic change was in the new emphasis on the long run. Keynes had belittled attention to the long run, saying that in the long run we are all dead. But by 1979, forty-three years after the publication of Keynes' *General Theory,* we woke up to discover that we were living in the long run and were suffering for our failure to look after it.

The earlier emphasis on the short run had two main implications. It focused attention on the problem of getting the actual level of output up to the level that we were capable of producing. In the short run what could be gained by closing the gap between actual and potential production was much larger than what could be gained by raising the rate of growth of potential. But even what seems a relatively small change in the rate of growth of potential output per year makes a big difference in the level of output after many years.

In addition the short-run view encouraged concentration on the possibilities of raising the level of output, relative to potential, by demand expansion, even though that might be inflationary. Such a policy would not work in the long run. It worked by surprise—by the actual inflation rate exceeding what people had expected, which made employers willing to hire more workers. But people could not be surprised indefinitely; they would catch on and then the inflation would lose its power to lower unemployment.

Economists had known for a long time that the prescriptions

they were offering were good for the short run only. At least they had known it in the back of their minds. It would be wrong to say that the New Economists had ignored longer-term considerations. But still they gave advice mainly on the basis that the long run was a succession of short runs.

The second half of the 1970s showed the fallacy of this outlook. Even though a short-run connection between inflation and unemployment could still be seen, the dominant fact was that *both* inflation and unemployment were trending up. We did not have less unemployment with more inflation, except for brief periods. Moreover, the marked slowdown in the growth of productivity made clear that the long-run strong upward trend of potential output could not be taken for granted. It would have to be nourished. The experience of those years did more than mountains of journal papers to restore economists to concern with the long run.

Rediscovery of the long run contributed to many changes of thinking about economic policy. It strengthened the tendency already under way to regard control of the money supply as the essential means of controlling inflation. Although the connection between the money supply and inflation had been generally recognized by economists (restoring the pre-depression doctrine), that connection was also recognized to be rather loose in the short run. If the rate of growth of the money supply increased from 5 percent to 10 percent between one year and the next, one couldn't be sure that the inflation rate would rise by 5 percent between the two years, or even that it would rise at all. And if there was a tendency to more inflation it could be offset by fiscal measures, such as a cut of government expenditures. But if the increase in the rate of monetary growth were to last for, say, a decade, there was little doubt of a significant inflationary effect which could hardly be prevented by fiscal action. So as our experience forced us to look at inflation continuing and accelerating over a long period, monetary policy moved to the center of the stage.

At the same time, concern with long-run growth changed ideas about budget policy. One way in which the budget could contribute to increasing long-run growth was to run a budget surplus which would provide funds that could be invested by private business. This meant that we would have to give up, or at least deemphasize, reliance on variations of the budget surplus or deficit to stabilize the economy. Instead of being complementary or alternative ways of achieving the same objective, fiscal and monetary policy would have more distinct functions. Monetary policy would be addressed to achieving a reasonably stable price level, and fiscal policy would be addressed to assisting a more rapid growth of real output in the long run.

Moreover, attitudes toward taxes and expenditures had to be changed. As long as economic growth at a rate around 3 percent per annum was taken for granted, conservative arguments that high tax rates on income earners and large benefit payments to nonearners interfered with economic efficiency and growth could be disregarded as fanciful ideology. But once a significant continuing slowdown in economic growth became evident, this argument had to be taken more seriously.

Two other developments in economics—other than the rediscovery of the long run—had a major influence on policy thinking. One was the increased attention to the role of economic expectations. In fact, notions about expectations, under the more common term of "confidence," had played a part in discussion of economics for a long time. When Herbert Hoover was faced with the depression, one of the concerns was with the reestablishment of "confidence," meaning the expectation that conditions would improve. The implication of this seemed to be that policies should be followed which the business and financial community would find congenial, even though the policies would be counterproductive aside from those attitudes. Keynes' argument in the *General Theory* relied heavily on the influence of expectations. But the argument about confidence remained the property of traditional conservatives and was one of their main responses to liberal proposals. Mainstream economists after Keynes used a more mechanical line of reasoning in which what people thought was a reaction to what happened in the economy and not to their impression of government policies.

Interest in expectations revived after Friedman's presidential address in 1967, which has already been discussed. His main point was that unemployment tended to be low when inflation was high because high inflation tended to be a condition in which the actual inflation rate was high relative to the expected rate. What made the unemployment low was not the absolute rate of inflation but the excess of the actual over the expected rate of inflation. That was why inflation would not permanently keep unemployment low. Expectations would catch up to the actual inflation rate.

Friedman was describing a world in which the expected rate of inflation depended on experience with the actual rate of inflation. If people have experienced 10 percent inflation for some time they will continue to expect it. That could make reducing the inflation rate difficult. If, after some years of 10 percent inflation, the government tries to reduce the rate, the private sector will continue to expect 10 percent. Workers will demand wage increases to match and businesses will try to get price increases to match. The process of disinflation will entail loss of output and higher unemployment until a lower inflation rate comes to be expected. Neither Friedman nor anyone else knew how long that would take.

The assumption that expectations of inflation depended entirely on the inflation experienced in the past was soon recognized to be too limiting. One might realistically think that people would take account also of the government's intentions and policies, as they interpreted the probable effect of the intentions and policies. Thus, if a government disinflation effort was believed to be an interlude to be followed by another surge of inflation, expectations of inflation would remain high even if the actual inflation rate should subside for a while. On the other hand, if the policy was credible, expectations would adapt more quickly and the disinflationary process would be less painful. This made commitment, steadiness, perceived durability, clear and enforceable rules—all the things that might contribute to the desired change of expectation—very important.

Finally, developments in the methodology of economics helped to create skepticism about many of the government programs that had been adopted in the 1960s and 1970s. There was a great wave of measurement and estimation by economists, who had some new data plus more sophisticated theories and techniques to work with. Much of this measurement and estimation was applied to the costs and benefits of government programs—both expenditure programs and regulatory programs. The result was to cast grave doubt on the worth of many of these programs— whether their benefits justified their costs. In principle, these studies did not have to come out that way. They could have showed that all the programs were worthwhile and that there was, in fact, a long list of additional programs whose benefits would exceed their costs. The fact that the studies did not come out that way revealed a bias in the government's decision-making process. The benefit expected from programs tended to be direct and obvious, especially to the beneficiaries. The costs of any particular program were likely to be more diffused and were exposed only by analysis. Moreover, we had been through a period of sentimentality about many problems, of extraordinary confidence in the ability of government to do things, and of admiration for activism as a sign of leadership on the part of government. Therefore, the wave of cost-benefit analysis, coming at this particular time, revealed a great deal of unjustified spending and regulation. This same kind of analysis at a different point in history might have produced a different result.

How Sharp a Turn?

By 1979, as the country wound up for a presidential election, the stage was set for a change in economic policy, and the direction of the change was clear. There would be a shift of national priorities—toward greater price stability, faster growth and greater freedom for individuals in the use of their own money and management of their own affairs, and away from higher employment, the redistribution of income and the promotion of particular industries and uses of the national income as the primary objectives. This shift of priorities called for:

1. Slower, more stable and more predictable monetary growth.
2. Reduction of federal deficits.
3. Slowing down the growth of federal spending.
4. Reducing some federal tax rates, especially those bearing heavily on investment and savings.
5. Reducing the burden of federal regulation.

This agenda would have been accepted by all the leading candidates for the presidency in 1980—from Senator Kennedy to Governor Reagan. Nevertheless the agenda raised two serious problems. One related to the side effects of the process of disinflation.

In the standard view, reducing the inflation rate by slowing down the growth of the money supply would involve a transitional period in which unemployment would rise. No one knew how long this period might be or how high unemployment would go. This obviously was a serious problem for the country, to which politicians were naturally sensitive. It had become essential for politicians to say that they would not use unemployment to cure inflation—a formulation which left little room for accepting unemployment as an unfortunate but inevitable by-product of curing inflation.

There were a number of possible ways to deal with this difficulty, or at least to seem to deal with it. One was incomes policy. This notion, that businesses and workers could be induced to slow down price and wage increases without being forced to do so by the restraint of demand, and therefore without an increase of unemployment, had been around in America for over twenty years and had been tried on several occasions. At an earlier stage, such a policy was thought by some to eliminate the need for monetary and fiscal measures to restrain demand. By 1979 that would not be said anymore. The need for demand restraint was recognized. But the incomes policy was expected to avoid the

need for an increase of unemployment while demand was restrained, by bringing down the rate of price and wage increases
quickly.

At the other extreme was a policy called by some "cold tur-
key" or "sudden death." Growth of the money supply would be
cut drastically, to get the inflation rate down at once, or almost
at once, to zero. This might be such a shock as to put an end
immediately to inflationary expectations and to force prompt re-
negotiation of all contracts to bring them into line with the new
reality. This idea had more popularity in academic circles than
in political ones.

The other options required some combination of gradualism
and commitment in reducing the growth of the money supply
and restraining demand. The point of the gradualism was to try
to keep the pace of the demand restraint close to the pace of the
inflation slowdown, in order to minimize unemployment. The
point of the commitment—a firm and credible evidence of the
government's intent—was to bring about a prompt change of inflationary expectations, to facilitate the disinflation. The problem was that the gradualism and the commitment did not go well
together. The more the government emphasized that its policy
would be applied gradually, over a long period and with opportunities to modulate its pace if unemployment rose, the less
credible the strategy was. And the more the government lashed
itself to the mast and insisted on sticking to a preannounced path
of disinflation, the greater was the danger of being unable to
back off if the policy led to unemployment.

The second problem was how to achieve simultaneously the
various new goals for the budget. Reducing deficits and, if possible, balancing the budget were important for promoting economic growth by keeping the government from absorbing a large
share of private saving to finance the deficit. To some extent—
and there was disagreement about the extent—reducing deficits
would contribute to curbing inflation. At the same time, promotion of growth required cuts of some tax rates. Cutting tax rates
would reduce the revenues, or this was the conventional thinking, although a few people were beginning to deny it. This left

the need to reconcile eliminating the budget deficits with reducing the revenues. The obvious answer to this was to cut expenditures or substantially reduce their rate of growth. As is well known, however, this is much easier to talk about in general than to do in particular. The difficulty was compounded by the need, generally recognized, to raise defense spending, not only absolutely but also relative to the GNP.

All candidates for the presidency had to decide what to say about these two problems—the disinflation-unemployment connection and the fact that budgets have to add up, so that expenditures minus revenues equals the deficit. But one candidate had to do more than decide what to say about these problems. He had to decide what to do about them. That, of course, was Jimmy Carter, the President of the United States. Since he was the President, and was doing things, all the other candidates had to react to his policies.

Carter did not decide by himself what to do about these problems. He had a number of associates. The most important of these was Paul Volcker, the chairman of the Federal Reserve Board. One should not get the picture of Volcker and Carter sitting down together to devise the new economic policy. Volcker was the independent head of an independent agency, with important although limited functions. He had to take account of Carter's policy and Carter had to take account of his.

The Carter-Volcker policy of 1979–1980 was an attempt to feel a way through the difficulties of the transition to a less inflationary world by extremely cautious, tentative and reversible steps—which were nevertheless steps in the indicated direction. The first move was Volcker's. On October 6, 1979, he announced, on behalf of the Federal Reserve, a change of procedures, in which more attention would be paid to controlling bank reserves and less to controlling interest rates. That did not necessarily signify any change of objectives. But in the circumstances there seemed little doubt that the move reflected a sterner determination to check the inflation. The money supply had been rising rapidly—beyond the Fed's targets—and the inflation rate was accelerating. The foreign exchange value of the dollar had fallen to a low level. Foreign central bankers had been emphasizing to Volcker the need to check our inflation. Volcker returned from Europe to Washington and almost immediately announced the new policy, which was generally interpreted as a significant shift in an anti-inflationary direction.

The Carter administration announced its support for the Federal Reserve's new policy. In his January 1980 Economic Report the President emphasized his conviction that inflation was the number-one economic problem and proposed a four-part program for attacking that problem:

1. Fiscal and monetary restraint, including support for an anti-inflationary monetary policy and reducing the budget deficit. Real federal government expenditure, which had risen at a rate of 3.6 percent per annum from 1974 to 1979, would rise by 2.8 percent per annum from 1979 to 1983. The annual rate of increase of nondefense spending would be cut in half—from 4.9 percent to 2.5 percent. The budget deficit, estimated at $40 billion in the ongoing fiscal year, would be reduced to $16 billion in the next year and converted to a $5 billion surplus in the year after. Achieving that would require that tax reduction be forgone.

2. An incomes policy to achieve voluntary cooperation of business and labor in holding down price and wage increases.

3. Increase of productivity.

4. Insulation of the economy against external shocks, such as those which from time to time had raised oil and food prices.

This had the look of an orderly and comprehensive program. It made a decision about what the top priority was—inflation—and seemed willing to sacrifice at least one popular bit of candy—tax reduction—in order to curb inflation. But a little reflection and a little experience revealed that the program was mainly a facade. The 1980 incomes policy was only the last gasp of an approach that Carter had been trying without visible result for several years. Improving productivity and insulating the economy against "shocks," one a good idea and the other one not so good, were not going to contribute significantly to checking inflation for years to come.

The hard core of the program was this fiscal and monetary restraint. But the fiscal part was itself mushy and unconvincing. The movement toward a balanced budget depended on a number of unrealistic or unacceptable assumptions. Real output was projected to grow at a high rate and inflation to continue at a rate which itself implied that the disinflation effort would be only minimally successful. By pushing people into higher tax brackets the inflation would raise the ratio of taxes to GNP by 1982 to the highest figure since World War II. The allowance for increasing the national defense expenditures was small. The estimates were highly suspect at many other points.

The publication of the budget in January 1980 was immediately followed by cries of "Foul" from the financial community and by sharp declines of bond prices. The fall in bond prices was widely attributed to the shock of investors at discovering that the budget was not coming into balance. Carter's budget did not inspire confidence as a pillar of an anti-inflation program. The President revised the budget in March to meet some of the criticisms, but that was taken to indicate lack of steadfastness.

The monetary restraint was the real element in the program. But in 1980 one could not be sure how real it was. The Federal Reserve made no long-term commitments about the money supply or about the price level. The administration had announced its support for the new monetary policy in October 1979, but the historical record made such support seem unreliable. The new policy called for concentrating attention on the supply of bank reserves, rather than on the level of interest rates. But when interest rates rose, after the budget came out in January, the Federal Reserve, at the initiative of the administration, imposed credit controls. This threw a monkey wrench into the machinery and made it impossible to interpret the course of monetary policy for the remainder of the year.

Thus, Carter by 1979–1980 had assumed the look of a conservative in economics. He had elevated inflation to the top of his list of economic problems. He had endorsed a new anti-inflationary monetary policy, proposed a slowdown of government expenditures and laid out a path to a balanced budget. For the sake of fiscal responsibility he was resisting the politically popular move of tax reduction. But the policy was not acceptable or credible, especially to people who considered themselves conservatives.

One possible alternative to Carterism, in 1979–1980, was "Thatcherism." Mrs. Thatcher had become Prime Minister of Great Britain in May 1979 on a platform which had as its distinctive characteristic the willingness to tell the public that a policy to correct the ailments of the economy would be painful for a considerable period before its benefits appeared.[4] There were people here who thought this was the truth and who were encouraged by Mrs. Thatcher's election to think that telling the truth would be politically tolerable and possibly even attractive in the United States. Moreover, this appeared a peculiarly "conservative" outlook. The liberal policies of the preceding two decades had gone to excess by failure to recognize limits to the potentialities of even as strong and flexible an economy as ours, and by unwillingness to accept the short-term pains required for long-term health. A conservative program should try to avoid and if possible correct these errors. Two touchstones of conservative economics are the Long Run and No Free Lunch. Both might lead to the conclusion that redirecting economic policy would not be painless but would be worthwhile.

In the circumstances of 1979–1980, Thatcherism in the United States could have taken the form of a position like this:

"Inflation is the primary problem, and progress against other problems will have to be deferred where there is a conflict. To get the inflation rate down significantly, the rate of growth of the money supply will have to be slowed down. In the process of reducing the inflation rate, unemployment will rise for a while, and no one can say how far or for how long. The rise of unemployment will be smaller and shorter if the government's commitment to reducing the inflation is clear and firm, and it will be our intention to stick by this commitment and by the monetary policy required to implement it. This time we will not turn to pump the economy up again at the first sign of trouble.

"The budget deficit will be gradually reduced and eliminated over the course of the next five years or so as the disinflation proceeds. This program is important for two reasons. First, although there is disagreement about whether deficits cause inflation, confidence in the anti-inflation effort will surely be strengthened if there is a credible plan for eliminating the deficit. Second, eliminating the budget deficit will assist in promoting economic growth by making more funds available to finance private investment.

"In order to reduce the budget deficit while making necessary increases in defense expenditures, two things will be required. First, tax reductions will have to be deferred except in a few cases where taxation bears most heavily on private investment. Second, there will have to be cuts of some expenditures that affect mainly middle-income Americans, such as social security. Aside from defense, that is where most of the money is and most of the increase of spending in the past two decades.

"This program involves a period of pain for many people. There will be unemployment, business losses and sacrifice of some expected benefits from government programs. But that is the price we must pay to correct past excesses and put the country on the path to stability and prosperity from which all will benefit. We will try to protect disadvantaged people from severe injury, but we cannot promise a painless transition."

No politician, no candidate, adopted this position. Some, notably George Bush, made a certain bow to it, emphasizing that there is "no quick fix" and reserving their promises for the long run. Bush publicly accepted the possibility that ending the inflation would involve a transitional period of higher unemployment. Although he could not entirely disassociate himself from the yearning for tax reduction, he was cautious about its proper amount. But on the whole, practical, political conservatives in 1979–1980 rejected Thatcherism. Instead they chose the economics of joy. Ronald Reagan, although not the originator of that attitude, became its chief spokesman and came into the presidency with it, if not necessarily because of it.

7

The Reagan Campaign:
The Economics of Joy

THREE OF THE MAIN ELEMENTS in the new conservative approach to economic policy, by 1979–1980, were to get the inflation down by restraining monetary growth, to balance the budget and to reduce government expenditures or at least retard their growth. Each of these elements in the approach ran into a serious problem:

1. Reducing inflation, by restraining monetary growth or by any other feasible means, would raise unemployment for some period.
2. Balancing the budget would require forgoing or deferring tax reduction, given any realistic estimate of expenditure limitation.
3. Reducing the growth of total government expenditures, given the need to increase defense spending, would require cutting into benefits that many Americans, including middle-income Americans, enjoyed.

There were three ways of dealing with these three difficulties:

235

1. *Carterism*—pursuing each element in the approach so tentatively and flexibly that no harm would be done to anyone, but no significant good either.

2. *Thatcherism*—recognizing the costs of the objectives being pursued and being willing to pay them.

3. *Reaganism*—denying that the objectives being pursued had any costs.

Reaganism was the rejection of traditional Republican policies of "austerity"—sometimes called castor-oil economics or deep-root-canal economics. But it was more than that. It was an assertion that these policies could be rejected without also rejecting many conservative objectives or totems. This rejection rested upon three propositions:

1. There is no necessary connection between inflation and unemployment, even in the short run, and inflation can be reduced without a transitional period of increased unemployment.

2. Reduction of tax rates will not prevent balancing the budget but will actually contribute to balance, because reducing tax rates will raise the national income enough to increase revenues.

3. Government expenditures can be reduced significantly without injuring anyone except government bureaucrats, because the budget is full of waste, fraud and counterproductive programs.

The political utility of these ideas is obvious and was becoming increasingly obvious to the Republican Party as the 1970s went on. Goldwater had campaigned on the economics of austerity, or at least was so perceived. Although he emphasized the glory of liberty and economic growth in the long run, what stood out in his rhetoric was antipathy to Santa Claus and the free lunch. He was overwhelmingly defeated in 1964. After a narrow victory over a war-torn Democratic Party in 1968, Nixon returned in 1972 with a most un-Republican policy of price-wage controls and fiscal expansionism and won by a landslide. Ford tried to return to the old-time religion in economics and lost in 1976 to an unknown from Georgia who talked Kennedy-Johnson economics.

Supply-Side Economics and Politics

The transition from the old-time religion to the economics of joy came first in Congress and in the Republican National Committee, spurred and supported by certain movements in the intellectual community. The feeling was developing, in Republican circles and in some of its intellectual auxiliaries, that with their economics of austerity conservative Republicans could never come to power except in a crisis. Once in power, devotion to their traditional values, even though meritorious in the long run, gave them a Scrooge-like appearance which assured that their tenure would be brief.

A group of Republicans in the Congress were determined to break out of this pattern. The instrument of their escape would be tax reduction. Jimmy Carter was hemmed in by the inflation and by standard Keynesian notions of how to deal with it, and by the deficit and conventional notions of how to deal with that. He could not be the champion of tax reduction, however popular or, in some theories, economically useful. The Republicans would pick up the tax reduction ball and run with it.

This was nothing new for the Congressional Republicans. They had controlled the Congress twice in the previous fifty years. On the first of these occasions, 1947–1948, they had pushed through a major tax cut against the opposition of President Truman. On the second occasion, 1953–1954, they had pushed through a major tax cut despite the reluctance of President Eisenhower.

These earlier Republican tax cuts did not, however, provide comforting precedents for the Congressional Republicans in 1977 and 1978. The economic and budgetary conditions were quite different. On both of the earlier occasions the economy was in, or thought to be entering, a recession and the Republicans used, rather coyly, Keynesian arguments about curing recession by tax reduction. Moreover, in the 1947–1948 period the budget was coming into balance—some people even worried about too large a surplus—and in the 1953–1954 period the deficits were small and one could think they were disappearing. In 1978, inflation was the main problem, not recession, and in any event use of tax cuts to prevent recession was unfashionable, especially among Republicans. The deficit was large and there was great skepticism about forecasts that it would decline. The idea of a fiscal dividend produced by the inexorable growth of the American economy had become a wry joke.

There was another reason for not relying on the precedent of the 80th and 83rd Congresses. Truman had campaigned against the 80th Congress in part on the ground that it had enacted a "rich man's tax bill," and the Republicans lost control of the Congress. The Democrats had campaigned against the 83rd Congress on the ground that it had enacted a "trickle-down" tax bill—one from which the people at large would get indirect, doubtful and trivial benefits as a consequence of big benefits given to the rich. The Republicans then lost control of the Congress and had not regained it twenty-four years later. The Republican losses in elections were surely not entirely due to their success in cutting taxes. But cutting taxes, at least cutting them in the Republican way, did not look like a prescription for winning.

So the Republicans during the Carter administration needed a tax cut that would be popular and not easily attacked as a giveaway for the rich. That meant that their typical ideas, then being promoted by a number of Republicans including Congressman Jack Kemp, would not suffice. That is, it would not do to have a tax bill which mainly reduced taxation of investment income, however strong the case might be that such tax relief would be most beneficial for the economy. It had to be a tax bill that would give direct, immediate visible benefits to a large proportion of the electorate and that would have a chance to be defended as fair.

This requirement seemed to be met by an equal percentage cut in all income tax rates, the cut being large enough to be appreciated even by people in the lower rate brackets. The program hit upon was a cut of 10 percent a year for three years. That would, for example, cut the top 70 percent rate to 50 percent and the bottom 14 percent rate to 10 percent. One could still argue, as some would later argue, that this tax cut was unfair, because the tax cuts for the rich were not only absolutely larger than those for the poor but also larger relative to their incomes. Indeed, there were people who paid no tax and would have to be satisfied with the benefits that would trickle down. But a great many people would get enough relief to recognize and appreciate it.

This, however, created a serious problem. If the tax relief was going to be large enough to be appreciated by all or almost all income taxpayers, it would *seem* to cause a large reduction in the federal revenue. But there was already a large federal deficit. The feeling that this was a bad thing was evident in the movement for a constitutional amendment requiring a balanced budget, which was sweeping through the states. A large number of Republican Congressmen and Senators had endorsed the amendment. Aside from that, inflation was recognized to be the number-one national problem, and many people, including many conservatives, attributed the inflation to the budget deficits.

A tax cut that would greatly increase the deficit was not acceptable to the Republicans or salable to the country. It was at this point that "supply-side economics" came to the rescue. According to supply-side economics, a large across-the-board equal cut of income tax rates would not reduce but would raise the revenues and so would not increase the deficit but would reduce it. This wonderful consequence would be produced by a large increase in the taxable income base—large enough so that the revenue would be larger even though the tax rates were lower. The large increase in the taxable income base would come about mainly because of a large increase in the total national output and income, resulting in turn from an increase in the quantity of labor and capital supplied when tax rates were reduced and the after-tax return for working and saving was increased. This was not the only source of the additional tax base. Some income would come out of shelters or out of the underground economy. But mainly there would be more supply of output and more income.

This idea was just what the "conservative" Republican tax cutters needed. This was not quite a case of necessity being the mother of invention. The idea in its late-1970s form had been invented a few years before the Congressional Republicans had the need for it, and if it met anyone's need it was not theirs but more likely the need of the economists who invented it. But the idea was quickly bought by politicans because they needed it. The idea was not foreign to conservatives, who had always argued that the particular tax cuts they most wanted would raise the revenue. But this new argument applied to cuts across the board. Moreover, whereas the earlier trickle-down theories had been scorned by intellectuals, the present idea was supported and promoted by certified intellectuals who were most eager and articulate in explaining it. This was important protection against the argument that the idea was only a rich man's toy. The idea had the further merit that, unlike the tax-cutting theories of the Kennedy-Johnson days, it did not rely on an increase of demand that would result from leaving more income in the hands of taxpayers. In 1978 that would have been considered inflationary. Instead, the new idea relied upon an increase in the supply of labor and capital called forth by lower tax rates. That could not be made to look inflationary. On the contrary, one could claim that it was anti-inflationary. For good measure, the whole idea could be described as an escape from Keynesianism, which by this time had become a term of disrepute.

The only trouble with the idea was that it was almost certainly not true. But that would not be generally recognized for some time.

The term "supply-side economics" has been attached to a spectrum of ideas—some of them old, conventional and probably true. Among these are that the capacity of the economy to produce is very important, the most important determinant of living standards and a basic subject of economic study. More-

over, the capacity of the economy to produce is not given forever by nature but depends to some extent on public policy, and
is a legitimate object of public policy. Also the "supply-side"
proposition that the level and character of taxes affect capacity
to produce is certainly valid, as is the implication that these effects should be considered in deciding tax policy. The idea that
a cut in the tax rate on the production, sale or importation of a
certain commodity will increase the amount produced, sold or
imported is as old as economics. Almost as old is the idea that
the increase in production, sale or importation can in some cases
be so large that the total revenue from the tax will rise, even
though the tax rate is reduced.[1]

The advocates of the supply-side theory could legitimately
claim that in the period beginning with the depression and with
inspiration from Keynes, economics had concentrated too exclusively on the demand side of the economic equation. That emphasis needed to be corrected, and the supply-siders were contributing to the correction. Most specifically, economics needed
to get away from the practice of looking at fiscal policy as
mainly an instrument for manipulating aggregate demand. When
I coined the term "supply-side" in April 1976 in a paper delivered to a meeting of economists I was classifying economists
in their attitudes toward fiscal policy.[2] I called one group "supply-side fiscalists" on the ground that they concentrated on the
effects of taxes, expenditures and deficits on the total supply of
output. Although I was later said to have used the term "deri-
sively" that was not the fact. I recognized that as a legitimate
way to look at fiscal policy. By itself, of course, it says nothing
about what the size or even the direction of the effects of fiscal
changes on supply would be.

To slide from these conventional or neutral propositions to the
specific supply-side idea that a general cut of income tax rates
from the rates prevailing in the United States would increase the
revenue was easy. It was, however, also misleading. The supply-
side thesis of the 1970s depended upon specific quantitative relations. These could not be demonstrated by any *a priori* principles or homely analogies. What was missing was any reason to
believe that these specific quantitative relations between the size

of the tax rate cut and the change in the tax base held in the United States in the 1970s and 1980s.

The critical point may be illustrated by a few cases. Take the case of a person whose whole income is from personal services, who earns, before tax, for convenience of calculation, $100 an hour and who has considerable flexibility in determining his hours of work. He might be a psychiatrist. Let us suppose that he works thirty hours a week, forty weeks a year, and thus has gross income of $120,000 a year. His personal exemptions and deductions amount to $20,000, leaving him a taxable income of $100,000. At 1980 tax rates he would have paid about $40,000 in federal income tax. He would have been in a 50 percent marginal tax bracket, since the law set a ceiling of 50 percent on the tax rate for personal income. That is, for every additional hour he worked he would have received $100 of which he would owe the Internal Revenue Service $50.

Now suppose all tax rates are cut 30 percent. Then if he continues to work the same number of hours and earn the same income before tax, his tax will decline by $12,000 and his after-tax income will rise from $80,000 to $92,000. His after-tax income per additional hour of work will rise from $50 to $65— or 30 percent.

The question is how he will react. He may decide that since his total after-tax income has increased he will work a little less. He can live better than he did before and still work a little less. On the other hand, since he retains more after-tax income for an additional hour of work he may decide that it is worthwhile to work more. The supply-side argument implies that he will work more, although that is not the obvious answer. But it is not sufficient that he should work more. If the tax cut is not to reduce the total revenue he must work 343 more hours per year. He must increase his hours of work 28.6 percent in response to a 30 percent increase in his after-tax return per hour of work. (In fact, the tax program later enacted did not decrease the marginal rate for most people in the 50 percent bracket, like our sample psychiatrist, because it did not lower the 50 percent ceiling on the tax on personal income. The psychiatrist would have had a reduction of $6,000 in total tax but no reduction in the tax on another dollar of earnings and no incentive to work more or earn more.)

We may now consider the case of a taxpayer with about an average income. He earns $13 an hour, works 1,920 hours a year and makes about $25,000 a year before taxes. After exemptions and deductions he has $20,000 of taxable income. At 1980 tax rates he paid $3,225 of taxes and was in a 24 percent tax bracket. That is, out of the $13 he would make on an additional hour of work he would pay $3.12 in taxes and keep $9.88 for himself.

If all tax rates are cut 30 percent and he continues to work 1,920 hours a year his tax will decline by $967 and his marginal tax rate will fall from 24 percent to 16.8 percent. Thus, after-tax income for an additional hour of work will rise from $9.88 to $10.82—or about 9.5 percent. As in the psychiatrist's case he may either work less because he has more income or work more because he keeps more of his pay for an hour's work. If he is going to work more so that his total tax payment doesn't decline he has to work 381 more hours a year. That is, with a 9.5 percent increase in after-tax income for an hour of work he must increase the number of hours he works per year by about 20 percent. (All of these calculations start with the progressive rate schedule of 1980.)

These examples illustrate the basic point about the supply-side doctrine. Its validity is not a matter of conservative or liberal philosophy. It is not even a matter of the idea that if you tax something more you get less of it although that isn't necessarily true. The point is that the validity of the doctrine depends on certain quantities, not on general philosophies or directions. In the psychiatrist's case it depended on the percentage increase in work being 95 percent as high as the percent increase in after-tax pay. In the case of the middle-income taxpayer it depended on the percentage increase in work being more than twice as high as the percentage increase in after-tax pay.

Neither economists nor anyone else knew or yet knows with

confidence what these ratios are. It is very difficult to make the kind of experiment that would be needed to find out. But there have been a number of efforts to estimate such ratios, by methods that are necessarily crude. The results have varied, but none has come close to suggesting that an across-the-board reduction in the income tax rate on labor income would raise the amount of labor enough to prevent the revenue from declining.[3]

The same conclusion holds for the effects of the reduction of the tax rate on income from capital. Economists have always been uncertain about whether an increase in the after-tax return on capital would increase or decrease the amount of saving. Much saving is done by people who are providing for a specific future objective, like their retirement or the education of their children. An increase in the after-tax return would reduce the amount of saving required to provide for the objective and could reduce the amount of saving done. On the other hand, the increase in the after-tax return would raise the benefit from saving and might increase the total amount of saving done. Attempts by economists to estimate the effect of a cut in tax rates on saving were inconclusive, even as to the direction of the effect. And those estimates that produced the largest positive effects—the biggest increase of saving in relation to the size of the tax cuts—did not suggest an effect large enough to yield an increase in the revenue until tens of years had passed.[4]

A large tax cut might nevertheless be defended if it increased the national income by increasing work and saving even if it increased the deficit. But the Republicans did not want to be the advocates of larger deficits. Moreover, if the tax cut increased the deficit one could not be sure that the tax cut would increase the national income at all. The deficit would have a negative effect on the national income. Some part of the savings that would have been available for private investment, which would have contributed to the growth of the national income, would be absorbed in financing the government deficit. There would be a favorable effect on the national income only if the positive effect from the increase of work and saving was large enough to offset the negative effect of absorbing more saving in financing the budget deficit. This was a less demanding test than that the tax cut should increase the revenue.

Some economists who gave great weight to the positive sup-ply-side effects of tax cuts, and considered themselves supply-siders, nevertheless did not expect those effects to be large enough to keep the revenue from falling and the deficit from rising. They argued, however, that the tax cuts would raise savings by enough to finance the deficit, thus avoiding the crowding out of private investment. This was, for example, the position of Norman Ture, who later became Under Secretary of the Treasury in the Reagan administration. While it was more plausible than the all-out sup-ply-side position, there was no empirical evidence for this posi-tion either.

On some occasions supply-siders described their position as if the factor that delivered the increase of the national income were not a tax cut but an expenditure cut. The argument ran like this: The national income is produced by private individuals and busi-nesses. Their incentive to produce it is the part of the national income they receive. This cannot exceed the national income but it can fall short of the total national income by the amount the government uses in ways that do not provide an incentive to pro-duce—for example, in giving income assistance to nonworkers. The government use of the national income—the government's expenditure—is, in the supply-siders' language, a "wedge" be-tween what the private sector produces and what the private sec-tor gets. The bigger the wedge, the less incentive to produce and the less production.[5]

The wedge argument led directly back to the old-time religion of cutting government expenditures. But that was not the kind of argument the Republicans were looking for. They needed to show that there could be a big tax cut *without* a big expenditure cut and without an increase in the deficit. The basic supply-side proposition provided them with a way to show that.

The early history of the idea need not concern us much. In its present incarnation it was developed by Arthur Laffer, an economist at the University of Southern California, with some inspiration from Robert Mundell, an economist at Columbia University. Laffer explained it to Jude Wanniski, an editorial writer for the *Wall Street Journal*, who became its enthusiastic proponent. He sold it to the editors of the *Wall Street Journal*, who made it the constant theme of their editorials. Wanniski also wrote a long tract explaining and supporting the idea, *The Way the World Works*.[6] Wanniski, supported by Irving Kristol, a New York intellectual and leading neo-conservative, brought the idea to the attention of Jack Kemp, Congressman from Buffalo.

Once the idea entered the Republican Congressional bloodstream it spread rapidly. Kemp and Senator William Roth of Delaware incorporated the idea in a bill which called for across-the-board 10 percent cuts of individual income tax rates each year for three years. In September 1977 the Republican National Committee endorsed the bill, and in the summer of 1978 the committee decided to make it the highlight of the Congressional campaign. Teams of supporters would fly around the country to promote it and the Republican candidates.

The great convenience of the supply-side arguments for Republican politics has already been explained. Still, the question remains why the idea was so quickly and widely adopted if its validity is as improbable as has been suggested here.

Part of the answer is that the idea is extremely plausible. Arguments can be made for it that are correct and almost, but not quite, relevant. The leading example is the Laffer Curve, devised by Professor Laffer to show that a reduction of tax rates could increase the revenue. Laffer started with the proposition that a tax rate of zero would yield no revenue and that a tax rate of 100 percent would yield no revenue. But there are tax rates between zero and 100 percent that do raise revenue. Therefore, reducing the rate below 100 percent must increase the revenue, but reducing the rate beyond some point, toward zero, must reduce the revenue.

Laffer illustrated this proposition with a curve showing the relation between the tax rate and the revenue which looked like this:

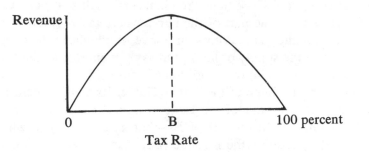

This was intended to show that in the range of tax rates between B and 100, the revenue would be higher the lower the tax rate. There were some minor problems with the general idea. It was not true of all kinds of taxes that they would yield no revenue at a tax rate of 100 percent. A tax of 100 percent on the price of cigarettes would yield revenue. Presumably the curve applies only to income tax rates (or to taxes where the base includes the tax). Also, we do not have one income tax rate in the United States. There is a schedule of rates, ranging in the late 1970s from zero to 70 percent. What rate is supposed to go into the Laffer Curve is unclear.

Nevertheless the Laffer Curve does illustrate a relevant question. But it does not answer the question. The question is whether the existing tax rate lies above B or below B. If above B, reducing tax rates increases the revenue; if below B, it reduces the revenue. To answer the question the shape of the Laffer Curve must be known. The conventional picture in which the curve is symmetrical and reaches its high point at 50 percent has only an aesthetic justification. The curve might look like this:

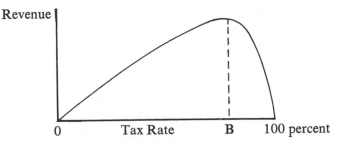

If the curve looks like that, the chance is small that our existing tax rates lie in the part of the curve where tax rate reduction raises the revenue. The discussion above of whether rate reduction increases the supply of labor and savings enough to raise the revenue is not a denial of the existence of a Laffer Curve. It is a discussion of the shape of the Laffer Curve. Its usual conclusion has been that the shape of the Laffer Curve is such that our existing tax rates lie to the left of B—that is, in the range where rate reduction reduces the revenue. But many observers jumped from the fact that tax reduction *can* increase the revenue to the conclusion that tax reduction from where we are *will* increase the revenue.

Another plausible but not relevant argument relied on experience of certain limited areas. For example, it was said that Puerto Rico reduced tax rates on business and so stimulated the Puerto Rican economy that total Puerto Rican revenue increased. But this only demonstrates that if a certain limited area reduces its tax rates relative to its neighbors it can attract enough capital and business from its neighbors to raise its revenues. It is not evidence that the United States can do the same thing.

A similar plausible but inconclusive argument relates to experience with particular taxes. It may be that reduction of the capital gains tax will for a period at least increase the revenue. People who were holding stocks, for example, until they could be passed on tax-free in their estates would take the opportunity afforded by a cut in capital gains tax rates to make some transfers, which would increase the volume of transactions and raise the revenue. But this kind of tax cut, affecting the timing of transactions, is different from a cut which depends for its effects on changing basic work and savings practices permanently.

These plausible arguments made acceptance of the idea, so convenient in every way, easy for people who were not used to economic reasoning. There was another consideration which led to acceptance of the idea. Although the odds on the idea being valid were low, they were not zero, since the quantitative relations were not known for certain. There was a chance that an across-the-board tax rate cut might increase the revenue. Betting on this chance was a gamble—what Senator Baker later was to call "a riverboat gamble." But in the conditions of the years before 1980 the proponents of the idea risked little on the gamble. The Republicans did not control either the White House or the Congress. There was no possibility that the Democratic Congress or President Carter would allow the Kemp-Roth Bill to become law. At least for the next few years the proposal would not have to demonstrate its economic validity. It served, without risk to the Republicans, as a way to force the Democrats to take the position of refusing to give the taxpayer the relief he wanted.

There was also little risk, and much possibility of gain, for the few economists and other intellectuals who originated or endorsed the idea and gave the politicians the scholarly seal of approval. Mainstream economists or other academics would scoff at them, but would be unable to "prove" to the lay world that they were wrong. They would be understood by the public to be the leaders of one of those many schools of economics or social science that were always fighting with each other, that all had an equal chance to be right and that one could choose among as one's taste, politics or pocketbook dictated. Important politicians would appreciate them, as would big taxpayers. They would be in demand as consultants and lecturers. And if the supply-side idea should explode or wither away, they would remain celebrities and prophets—a status never achievable by living within the framework of the standard textbook.

By 1977, supply-side economics had become Congressional Republican doctrine. It had its political captain, Jack Kemp; its economic guru, Arthur Laffer; its editorial voice, the *Wall Street Journal;* and its chief intellectual, Irving Kristol. It still did not have Ronald Reagan. Before we come to the connection between supply-side economics and Reagan we should look at the other two distinctive economic ideas that were to go into the Reagan 1980 program.

The Inflation-Unemployment Trade-off

The prospect that anti-inflationary policy would increase unemployment had consistently prevented the government from taking an effective stand against inflation during the 1960s and 1970s. By the late 1970s no one any longer believed, as many economists had believed twenty years earlier, that there was a *permanent* trade-off between inflation and unemployment. That is, it was no longer thought that the country could choose to have a low rate of unemployment forever by accepting or creating a high rate of inflation. Unemployment would be low when inflation was high only as long as the high rate of inflation was unexpected. But that would not go on forever. Moreover, we had before our eyes the sight of higher inflation rates than we had experienced for a long time and also the highest unemployment rates since the depression. This seemed to confirm the view that in the longer run inflation did not make unemployment low.

But it was the standard opinion of economists that the transition from a high inflation rate to a low one would involve a period in which the unemployment rates were high. And while it was true that in 1978 both the inflation rate and the unemployment rate were higher than in, say, 1973 or 1968 it was also true that between 1960 and 1978 the unemployment rate had risen in every year when the inflation rate had fallen with only two exceptions, 1972 and 1976. One of these exceptions was a year of price and wage controls.

Politicians needed a formula which would allow them to promise a cure for inflation without a transitional period of high unemployment. President Carter's formula was "incomes policy," but that was, of course, unacceptable to the Republicans—as well as being ineffective. Here again, as in the convenient assertion that cutting taxes would increase the revenue, economics provided a useful, or at least a plausible, answer. Indeed, it provided four different answers, all serving the same purpose.

1. Some answers simply ignored the short-run experience. They looked at the long-run connection of high inflation rates and high unemployment rates—for example, both being higher in the 1970s than in the 1950s—and concluded that this was a causal relation, which applied in the short run as well as in the long run, and in the disinflationary direction as well as in the inflationary ones. Therefore they were prepared to assert that unemployment would fall, not rise, as inflation came down.

2. There was a theory, expressed, for example, by the Joint Economic Committee of the Congress, that supply-side economics held the key to painless reduction of inflation.[7] The argument started with the proposition that inflation was caused by an excess of the demand for output over the supply. This led to the assertion that the conventional method of fighting inflation, which had for one consequence a reduction of output, could not cure inflation. On the other hand, tax rate reduction, which would stimulate the supply side of the equation, would reduce the excess of demand over supply and so check the inflation. Moreover, supply-side measures would increase productivity—output per hour of work—which would slow down the rise of labor costs and therefore of the price level.

This line of argument was quantitatively unrealistic. With the demand for output rising by 12 percent a year, productivity rising by 2 percent and total output by 3 percent, there was no way of getting results on the supply side that would make a significant dent on the inflation rate.

3. Some supply-siders denied the notion, conventional by then in mainstream economics, that a high level of unemployment was due to the expectation of a rate of inflation which was high relative to the actual rate. On this theory, the expectation of high inflation made workers demand wages too high for employers to pay, and that caused unemployment. Therefore, when the actual inflation was forced down by demand restraint, unemployment would rise until expected inflation fell as much as the actual inflation, which would take some time.

Extreme supply-siders rejected this explanation. They held

that people were unemployed because high tax rates made it unprofitable for them to work, or because high welfare benefits made it profitable for them not to work. Reduction of tax rates and of welfare benefits would cause unemployment to go down, whatever was happening to inflation. This argument, however, mixed up the long-run effects of changing tax rates and benefits, which might be favorable, with the effects of disinflation, which would dominate in the short run.

4. As already noted, the prevailing explanation for the temporary rise of unemployment during a disinflationary process was that wage increases would continue to be high because of previous experience of high inflation. If wage increases slowed down step by step with inflation there would be no rise of unemployment. But it was unrealistic to assume that workers and employers based their expectations solely on past experience with inflation. They would also be influenced by what they perceived to be the firmness of the government's intention to stop inflation and the probable effectiveness of its policies. If people in the private sector believed that the government would really stop the inflation the expectations acquired during the previous inflationary period would disappear. Inflation could then be reduced with little or no increase of unemployment.

This line of thinking led to a great deal of interest in ways by which a government could generate credibility. But few economists believed that after fifteen years in which promises of government had been repeatedly broken a new government could immediately establish complete credibility for a promise to end inflation. The difficulty of establishing credibility was compounded by the general realization that the reason for past failure to stick to anti-inflationary policy was government fear of unemployment. There was a Catch-22 situation in that the only way the government could achieve credibility and thus be able to reduce inflation without causing more unemployment was to make quite clear that it would not be diverted from the disinflationary path by an increase of unemployment if that occurred.

None of these arguments created a convincing case for the

possibility of reducing the inflation rate substantially without a transitional increase of unemployment. But taken all together they provided a plausible if superficial case. Again, as in the extreme supply-side theory, one couldn't be 100 percent sure that the case was invalid. And this slight probability was enough for politicians to buy and sell it.

The No-Fault Expenditure Cuts

For many of the supply-siders there was no need for the Republicans to recommend a substantial cut of federal expenditures. Congressman Kemp, for example, warned the Republicans against trying to repeal the New Deal and the welfare state. It was precisely to avoid the image of the party of castor oil that they had embraced supply-sidism.

But on the whole, the Republicans could not abandon the expenditure-cutting posture, even though they believed that tax-rate reduction would raise the revenue. In one respect, cutting expenditures would be an extension of the supply-side principle. Giving benefits to people who didn't work was a kind of tax on working. Cutting the benefit would not only reduce expenditures; it would also raise the national income as a consequence of the former beneficiaries' going to work, and that would raise the government revenue.

There were other reasons for the Republicans to cling to their expenditure-cutting stance. Even if they accepted the supply-side effects on the revenue side, some had their fingers crossed and liked the idea of expenditure-cutting as insurance against the possibility that the revenue increases might not emerge. Some didn't like particular expenditures, quite aside from the budgetary consequences. And there was a desire not to shock the traditional Republicans by omitting the usual call for cutting expenditures.

The Republicans needed to be able to recommend large expenditure cuts without leaving themselves open, any more than necessary, to the complaint that as usual they were enemies of the people. This was an especially dangerous charge because by 1978, 60 percent of the budget, excluding defense and interest, was going to social security and Medicare, whose beneficiaries no one wanted to offend. There was no elaborate theoretical construct for getting the Republicans out of this dilemma, as there was for the tax cut–budget deficit conflict or disinflation-unemployment conflict. Instead reliance was placed on the proposition that the budget was filled with waste and extravagance, from which large amounts could be cut without loss to anyone.

If the concept of "extravagance" was broadly interpreted, a good deal of it was being revealed by analysis of programs in the budget. This analysis often concluded that particular expenditure programs did not, in the long run, yield benefits that were worth their costs. Programs aimed at poverty, including training and welfare programs, seemed especially vulnerable to such evaluations. This was not, of course, the same thing as saying that these programs were not worthwhile to their beneficiaries, and even less as saying that their beneficiaries did not think them worthwhile or would not feel aggrieved by their elimination.

Nevertheless, for the time being, and while the Republicans did not have the responsibility for preparing a budget or specifying where cuts were to be made, the argument that large savings would be obtained by eliminating waste and extravagance was sufficient.

Reagan Comes to the Economics of Joy

In 1982 and 1983 some of his supporters—from the radical right and extreme supply-side edges of the spectrum—became alarmed at what they considered moderating or softening influences on President Reagan. "Let Reagan be Reagan!" became their battle cry. But Ronald Reagan had not always been "Reagan." And even after he became "Reagan" the meaning of that was not constant or clear.

Until the late 1940s or early 1950s—that is, until he was

about forty years old—Ronald Reagan was a conventional New Deal, FDR liberal, although at the end of this period becoming more and more distressed by the Communist influence on Hollywood "liberalism." He voted for Harry Truman in 1948 and Helen Gahagan Douglas in 1950. His conversion to conservatism became clearest after he went to work as spokesman for the General Electric Company in 1954. In its economic aspects the brand of conservatism he embraced was about what has been called here the "old-time religion." It has also been called, by people who consider themselves true Reaganauts, "deep-root-canal economics." This promised a great future for America, but only if we went through a purge of all our easy and soft policies first. Its distinguishing credo was "No Free Lunch."

The political leader of this school of conservatives was Barry Goldwater. During most of his political life Reagan was a Goldwater Republican, as distinguished from a Nixon Republican or a Rockefeller Republican. A speech he made for Goldwater during the 1964 campaign brought him his first national political attention. On the subject of great interest for Reagan's economic policy, Goldwater had made his position clear in 1960:

"While there is something to be said for the proposition that spending will never be reduced so long as there is money in the federal treasury, I believe that as a practical matter spending cuts must come before tax cuts. If we reduce taxes before firm, principled decisions are made about expenditures, we will court deficit spending and the inflationary effects that invariably follow."[8]

When Reagan made his own first big drive for the presidency, before the 1976 election, he was clearly still in the "austerity" school. He made one speech proposing that federal expenditures should be cut $90 billion a year, as the precondition for a tax cut. There was no suggestion that the tax cut could raise the revenues. In another speech he raised the idea of making social security voluntary. Both of these speeches, especially the one about the $90 billion expenditure cut, were used by his opposition within the party as evidence that Reagan was another Goldwater, who would have no chance to win if nominated. These em-

barrassing statements, probably contributed to Reagan's failure
to win the nomination.

Even after his frustration in 1976, Reagan's natural responses
tended to the austerity philosophy. He told friends that the nation faced a big "belly ache" of unemployment and recession as
punishment for its inflationary binges. Still in 1978 he was saying, "Frankly, I'm afraid this country is going to have to suffer
two, three years of hard times to pay for the binge we've been on."

But by 1978 Reagan was beginning to move from the austerity position. As noted above, the Republican National Committee had already moved in that direction, motivated partly by
political considerations and partly by conviction. The RNC at
that time, since the Democrats were in the White House, was
mainly the Congressional wing of the party. And that wing of
the party was used to advocating tax cuts first, no matter what.
It had done that in 1947–1948 and in 1953–1954. The presidential wing of the party had been more cautious. Both Eisenhower and Nixon, as Presidents, had felt obliged to resist Congressional pressure for tax reduction.

In 1978 Reagan was the first of the prominent candidates for
the Republican nomination to endorse the Kemp-Roth tax cut
bill. Although the economics of joy was clearly to be the Republican position in the two years before the 1980 election,
Regan was the major candidate who took that position earliest
and most vigorously. He was led in that direction by his political
managers, notably John Sears. His managers saw the proposal of
the big tax cut and the optimistic promises of the results that
would follow from it as ways to appeal to the ordinary voter.
They also saw this position as permitting Reagan to neutralize
the appeal of Jack Kemp who was attracting attention from the
right wing of the Republican Party by his dynamic campaign for
supply-side economics. It might even be possible to add Kemp
to the Reagan team.

The political attractiveness of the economics of joy must have
been just as obvious to the other candidates as it was to the
Reagan camp. There were several reasons why the position may
have been more congenial to Reagan than to the others—Bush,

Baker, Anderson and Connally. Reagan needed this position more than the others, because he had greater need to separate himself from the Scrooge-like, and disastrous, image of Barry Goldwater. Also, unlike the others he had no experience in the federal government. He was less inhibited by what might be called either the realism or the defeatism that comes with Washington experience. Moreover, he had a strongly optimistic temperament and tended to believe that things would work out despite the obstacles that lesser people might foresee. He also believed that presidential optimism was good for the country.[9]

To say that Ronald Reagan's conversion began for political reasons is not to deny that the conversion was genuine. As far as anyone can see, it was genuine. Politicians generally believe what they say. One of the main ways by which politicians learn what they think is through listening to what they say. In any case, the question of "sincerity" is of little importance. What a candidate says during the campaign has effect if he is elected, whether he meant it or not, because what he says creates expectations and commitments.

The real question about Ronald Reagan's conversion is what he meant by it. The answer to that would influence his policy when he became President. Clearly, he now gave much more weight to tax reduction than he formerly did, no longer making it a tail to follow expenditure reduction. But he was not a consistent Kemp follower—a thoroughgoing believer in the proposition that cutting taxes would raise the revenue. He was off and on in his devotion to this idea during the campaign.

During the middle months of 1979, Reagan drew close to Kemp and the supply-siders. Martin Anderson, who had been Reagan's economic adviser for many years, was cool to these ideas. At the height of Reagan's flirtation with Kempism, Anderson left the campaign. But when Reagan made his formal announcement of his candidacy, on November 13, 1979, caution had set in again and the speech was not strong on supply-side arguments.

After the surprising loss to Bush in the Iowa caucus of January 1980, the team turned again to the supply side as a way to revitalize Reagan's drive. The candidate made a number of television spots emphasizing the value of cutting taxes and calling attention to the fact that revenues rose after the Kennedy tax cut. But on the day in February when Reagan won the New Hampshire primary he dismissed Sears as his campaign manager. Thereafter the extreme supply-side influence faded.[10]

When the Illinois primary of March 18 confirmed that Ronald Reagan would be the Republican candidate, the nature of the economic discussion changed. The heightened possibility that he would become President focused closer attention on what he had to say about economics. He could no longer address himself entirely to the priorities and prejudices of Republicans. Moreover, he had to show responsibility in dealing with economic issues and ability to obtain and use respected expert judgment, especially since he had no experience of his own in national economic affairs and some of his economic ideas had been criticized as wild by other Republicans.

Mr. Reagan then gathered around him a group of economic advisers including George Shultz, Milton Friedman, Arthur Burns, Alan Greenspan, Charls Walker, Walter Wriston, Paul McCracken, Arthur Laffer and Jack Kemp. Only the last two were thoroughgoing supply-siders. Several had publicly dissociated themselves from the idea that an across-the-board tax cut would increase the revenue. Many had at one time or another expressed reservations about the Kemp-Roth tax bill, some wanting to spread it out over a longer period, others preferring a more investment-oriented tax cut, and some approving the bill only as part of a package which would include a commitment to expenditure reduction. But by this time the Kemp-Roth tax bill was not negotiable as far as the candidate and many of his closest aides were concerned. The bill was, in fact, incorporated in the Republican platform.

As the campaign progressed, more and more doubts were expressed about the realism of Reagan's promise to cut taxes sharply, increase defense expenditures substantially and balance the budget within a few years while cutting only "waste and extravagance" from the expenditure side of the budget. There was need for a set of numbers that would show the feasibility of this combination. That created a certain difficulty, because most of the economists then around Reagan were reluctant to put into the picture a big increase of revenue from the tax cut. When Reagan assembled a group of advisers on September 3 to work on his major economic speech, there were no supply-siders present. Alan Greenspan, one of the advisers most involved in the campaign numbers exercise, had publicly estimated that only about 20 percent of the gross revenue loss from a tax cut would be recouped through additional revenue yielded by the resulting expansion of the economy. That is, if taxes were cut by $100 billion there would be a net revenue loss of $80 billion. He could not suddenly discover that there would be no revenue loss.

This difficulty was overcome for the purpose of the September 9 speech by starting with a set of economic forecasts that had been used by the Senate Finance Committee in August. On the basis of these forecasts the committee had estimated the revenue of the existing tax system and the outlays of the existing expenditure programs. This showed that the budget would come into balance in fiscal year 1982 and reach a surplus of $182 billion in fiscal year 1985. Thus the Reagan estimators started with a good deal of money available for tax reduction. To this they added unspecified reductions of spending rising from 2 percent of expenditures projected for 1981 to 7 percent of expenditures projected for 1985. They also added an amount of revenue due to the additional growth to be caused by the Reagan tax cuts, which would rise to about 20 percent of the tax cut. When this had been done there was room for making the promised tax cut, balancing the budget in 1983 and achieving a surplus of almost $100 billion in 1985, out of which, presumably, defense expenditures could be increased.

There was one major flaw in this picture. The economic assumptions used, borrowed from the Senate Finance Committee, implied 8.7 percent per year annual inflation from 1980 to 1985. This was inconsistent with the Reagan promises for conquering inflation, but it was a major source of revenue. Basically, their forecasts abstained from the supply-siders' unrealistic estimates of the revenue-raising effects of a tax cut and relied instead on the revenue-raising effects of an all-too-realistic, but undesired, inflation. The argument was as unrealistic as the supply-side argument, but it was unrealistic in a more conventional way.

These numbers did, however, serve to subdue the criticism that the Reagan program was arithmetically impossible. It was shown to be arithmetically possible, even though under higher inflationary conditions. President Carter campaigned hard against what he called the Reagan-Kemp-Roth tax proposal. He repeated the charges Harry Truman had made against the Republican tax cut of 1948. He said it was a rich man's tax bill, which would give much more to the upper-income people than to the middle-income people. But by 1980 the middle-income people were so eager for what they would get themselves that they were not offended by what the rich would get. Carter said that the tax cut would be inflationary, but he may not have been accepted as an authority on that subject. He did not attack Reagan-Kemp as bad arithmetic and bad economics. Perhaps he knew that no one cared.

The big tax cut was the distinctive feature of "Reaganism" in the field of economics. But the meaning of that was unclear. There were several ways by which one could reach the position that there should be a tax cut. One was the extreme supply-side route. Another was extreme Keynesian—relying on the tax cut to raise the *demand* for output and so raise the national income enough to raise the revenue. A third was the belief that cutting the revenue would automatically force an equal reduction of expenditures. A fourth was that a President like Reagan would be able to get the expenditures down. A fifth was that budget deficits were of secondary significance. A sixth was that the critical thing was to get elected and that worry about the budget arithmetic could come later.

Every one of these ideas was probably represented in the team around Reagan during the 1980 campaign. Probably most if not all of them were in the mind of Reagan himself. Only later, when he faced the budget arithmetic, would he and the country discover what he "really" meant and which ideas were compelling to him. And if he decided at various points to support tax increases, as he did in 1982 and 1983, no one could be sure that he was not the real Reagan.

A similarly wide, if less varied, range of interpretation can also be given to other elements of Reagan campaign economics. He was for cutting or restraining expenditures, balancing the budget, reducing inflation, sound monetary policy, deregulation and economic growth. In these respects he was for a difference of leaning or priorities from his predecessors. But whatever may have been true of any one of his various advisers, he did not have a precise, comprehensive, internally consistent, durable model of the economy and of economic policy in his mind.

What was true of Reagan has been true of Presidents generally. They are not programmed by any economist's model, and it would be unjustifiably conceited for an economist to consider that a fault. My favorite example of a President's attitude comes from Franklin D. Roosevelt. In his 1933 inaugural address he promised an "adequate and sound currency." At a press conference later he was asked what that meant. He replied: "I am not going to write a book on it." Presidents don't write books, at least while in office. After they leave office they write books, looking back and discovering what they meant all along.

The Turning Point

By 1980 the country was ready for a more radical turn of economic policy to the right than had been seen since 1896—possibly ever. There was a greater feeling than at any time in forty years that prevailing policy had failed—and that was conventional liberal policy. And the country elected a President who was deeply devoted to such a radical turn. He was no "modern" Republican or "moderate" conservative—terms which in his world had come to mean liberal in disguise.

The general meaning of the turn was clear. There was to be more growth and more price stability, achieved by more monetary restraint, lower taxes, lower spending, lower deficits and less regulation. That was clear to all, and Ronald Reagan stood for it more clearly than anyone else in public life.

But there were problems, too. Anti-inflationary monetary policy raised the probability of increased unemployment for a time. Cutting tax rates raised the probability of larger deficits. Cutting expenditures would deprive some people of benefits they valued.

More generally, the turn to the right did not mean that we had discovered a new way to have more of everything at once. The turn was mainly a change of priorities. It meant that we had raised some things—growth and price stability—in our scale of priorities. That meant that we had demoted some other things. It implied willingness to give up some things to get more of what we now valued more.

The campaign had not prepared either the public or the candidate for that. They would face that challenge after November 1980. They would have to deal with these difficulties, finding ways to minimize the sacrifices as far as they could not be avoided. How well they did that would do much to determine how durable the turning to the right would be.

8

The Reagan Presidency: Encounter with Reality

ALL NEWLY ELECTED ADMINISTRATIONS come into office full of confidence, especially when they bring a change of party. People do not become President unless they have a great deal of confidence in their ability or their star. In the course of a campaign they have convinced the public of their superior competence, compared to their rivals, and this process has strengthened their own conviction on the point. Once in office the President and his aides are impressed by their power and the resources at their command and the blank page they see laid out before them.

This feeling of confidence and mission was probably greater in the Reagan administration than in many others. They had a longer historical vision of themselves than many. They came to correct the errors not only of the past administration but of the past fifty years. In the field of economics their program was articulated with unusual clarity (although the rationale was less clear), and embracing the program had been a loyalty test for membership on the economics team. Some members of the team had a strong personal identification with this program, so that its success, or at least its coming into being, was indistinguishable from their success.

The new team set about to implement its program with vigor. Like many earlier administrations, all sharing in the mystique of Roosevelt's Hundred Days, they wanted to hit the ground running. They wanted to announce their program in specific detail quickly and immediately initiate its enactment and implementation. The reason for this was partly political and partly economic. Mr. Reagan would have a "honeymoon" at the beginning of his term. The chance of getting what he wanted through Congress would be greater then than later, especially since he did not control the House of Representatives. On the economic side, they were impressed with the need to take steps at the outset which would change expectations sharply. They thought they saw the economic situation deteriorating fast. As David Stockman, the new director of OMB, had put it in a memorandum that was given to Mr. Reagan shortly after the election, the country was facing an "economic Dunkirk." The main signs of the approaching catastrophe were the rising estimates of the budget deficit, the soaring interest rates and a renewed acceleration of inflation.[1] The new administration could not do anything immediately. They did not have at hand any counterpart of Roosevelt's emergency actions of closing the banks and suspending gold convertibility. In fact, their whole philosophy was against "emergency" action. They had come to reverse a trend of fifty years, not to manage a momentary crisis. Their watchword was long-run consistency of policy, not short-run maneuverability. But they hoped by a prompt, clear and credible statement of their long-run policy, and demonstration of sufficient political strength to enact the policy, to change expectations from the outset. They would show the financial community that they would get the deficit down and get inflation down, and while these results would be for the future the anticipation of them would reduce interest rates at once. Also, by showing the workers and employers that they would get inflation down they would lead them to settle for lower wage increases, which would in turn help to get the inflation down.

The campaign had made clear what the basic elements of the program would be:

1. A big tax cut—10 percent reduction in the individual income tax each year for three years, plus significant reduction of the taxes on income from business investment.

2. A large reduction of planned nondefense expenditures.

3. Slower and steadier monetary growth, to help get the inflation down.

4. Substantial reduction of government regulation.

And not included in the customary listing of the four pillars of Reagan economics, but essential parts or constraints of the program:

5. A large increase of defense expenditures.

6. Bringing the federal budget into balance in a period of a few years.

The elements of the program were considered to be tightly related to each other. The administration emphasized that it was not possible to pick one part of the menu without the others. The mechanism by which the parts of the program were tied together was not fully articulated by the administration, but its logic was approximately as follows:

Slowing down the rate of growth of money would slow down the rate of increase of total spending, nominal GNP, which was the necessary condition for reducing the inflation. To slow down spending and reduce inflation without increasing unemployment—indeed, while significantly reducing unemployment—two things would be needed. There would have to be a marked abatement of inflationary expectations and there would have to be a substantial acceleration of productivity, in order to curb the rise of unit labor costs. The correction of inflationary expectations would come about as a result of the announcement of the administration's commitment to monetary restraint and to budget balancing. Productivity growth would be speeded up by the incentive effects of the tax rate cuts and by the reduction and elimination of government deficits, which would leave more of the nation's savings to support private, productivity-raising investment. The stimulus to productivity and production resulting primarily from the tax rate cuts would increase the national income, and that would offset a large fraction if not all or more than all of the revenue loss that the tax cuts would cause. This offset, plus the reduction of nondefense expenditures, would permit the budget to be balanced despite the big increase of defense expenditures.

Thus, the parts of the program were tied together not only in the sense that all the parts had to be put into place but also in the sense that they all had to work. The announcement of the program had to have the desired effect on expectations. Otherwise, the monetary restraint would cause an economic contraction, which would, among other things, keep the budget from coming into balance, and that would impair the growth of production and productivity, further affecting the revenue and the deficit and so on in a general unraveling. Similarly the tax rate cuts had to have the promised effects on the supply of output on the desired scale and time schedule. If they didn't, the budget would not come into balance, investment would be held back, productivity growth would be sluggish, the monetary restraint would cause unemployment and the whole scenario would unravel from a different direction.

The edifice was delicately balanced on a set of simultaneous policy actions and a set of equations describing the effects of the policy actions on the economy. A failure at any point could cause collapse at others. But this would not necessarily be fatal from the standpoint of all supporters of the program. There were some who regarded disinflation as the primary objective. They believed that monetary restraint would deliver that. If complementary policies were adopted and worked well the disinflation would be less painful than otherwise; but painful or not the disinflation would be achieved. There were others who believed that getting the real or supply side of the economy moving again was the primary objective. They believed that reducing tax rates would accomplish that, even if the disinflation program did not work and even if the budget was not brought into balance.

These views were represented in the administration. But the administration was not in a mood to compromise, or set priori-

ties, among its objectives and promises. It promised the whole
package—painless disinflation, revived economic growth, balanced budgets and greatly strengthened defense. The question
whether this could all be done at once had been the skeptical
question of 1980, to which the Reagan team had confidently
answered "Yes." In 1981 they intended to show that it could all
be done.

The Reagan Budgets

The problem of showing that it was all simultaneously possible
was encountered in earnest in the drafting of the budget that
President Reagan would submit in February 1981. This problem
was now much more difficult than it had seemed when the Reagan campaign produced a set of numbers in September 1980
which added up to a balanced budget. There were several reasons for that. The budget deficit from which the new program
had to start had grown. In September the Reagan team had estimated that existing taxes and expenditure programs would yield
a deficit of $23 billion in fiscal 1981 and a surplus of $2 billion
in fiscal 1982. By the time President Carter submitted his
budget in January 1981 these figures had changed to a deficit
of $55 billion in fiscal 1981 and a deficit of $28 billion in fiscal
1982. This was almost entirely due to the increase in estimated
expenditures under the existing programs.

Moreover, the new administration's estimates of the required
defense expenditures were higher than had been included in the
1980 calculations. And now the administration could no longer
say, as it had in 1980, that it would cut expenditures by per-
centages rising from at least 2 percent in fiscal 1981 to at least
7 percent in fiscal 1985 and aim to do much more than that. It
was time to say where the cuts would be made. The new director
of the Office of Management and Budget tackled that problem
with great vigor, but he was unable in the time available to
identify the amount of cuts that had been promised during the
campaign. And only a small fraction of the cuts he did identify

could be strictly described as eliminating "waste and extravagance." Careful study of the budget revealed that large cuts were
impossible without sacrifice by other people in addition to bureaucrats.

Finally, the new administration, now having the resources and
responsibility of the government, could no longer rely on (or
hide behind) an economic forecast made by the Senate Finance
Committee as had been done in the September 1980 speech on
economic policy. It had to produce its own forecast. And it
could not produce a forecast which envisaged an average of 8.7
percent inflation for five years; at least, it couldn't do that without undercutting its own claims about curing the inflation.

So, the administration faced the problem of squaring the
budget circle. It accomplished this, or so it seemed, by four steps.

1. The date for balancing the budget was deferred from fiscal
1983 to fiscal 1984.

2. A new element—an asterisk—was introduced into the
budget, standing for expenditure cuts which would be proposed
later but were not yet specified.

3. The date for starting the three 10 percent cuts of individual
income tax rates was postponed from January 1, 1981, to July
1, 1981.

4. A strong growth of real output, averaging 3.8 percent per
annum from 1980 to 1985, was forecast.[2]

The last two of these decisions were hotly debated within the
administration. Some thought that clinging to the January 1
starting date, which had been promised in the campaign, would
show firmness of purpose and would help to bring about the
radical change of expectations that was desired. It would show
that a new era had come and the time of muddling through was
over. On the other hand, others thought that deferring the tax
cut until July, or until October, the beginning of the fiscal year,
would show a proper and encouraging concern for keeping deficits down. They maintained that the delay would not signifi-

cantly postpone the economic effects of the tax cut, which depended more on the anticipation of future tax relief than on today's tax relief.

The effective date of the tax cut was one of the main items on the agenda of the President's Economic Policy Advisory Board, a group of supportive economic experts, at its first meeting in February 1981. The issue was discussed mainly in terms of its effects on expectations and psychology in the financial markets, and through that on interest rates. One respected, hardheaded observer of the financial markets was certain that an effective date of January 1 would inspire the markets. Another equally respected and hardheaded member said just the opposite and urged delay until October 1. The fact was that no one had evidence for his opinion, except introspection. The discussion was a forecast of what were to be two key elements in all considerations of Reagan economics—loyalty to an assumed pure Reagan doctrine and speculation about what the financial markets would think.

The decision was mainly procedural. There was no way to get the tax cut through the Congress before midyear and no advantage to making the tax cut retroactive by six months. In the end the legislative process delayed the effective date until October 1.

The argument over the economic forecasts underlying the budget involved three points of view. Some thought that the tax rate cut would unleash a spurt of productivity that would permit an extraordinarily high rate of real growth for five years. Some thought that during a period in which monetary growth was restrained in order to get inflation down the growth of real output could not exceed the normal rate but would most likely be short of it. And others thought that the main objective was to devise a plausible forecast of the economy that would yield a plausible forecast of a balanced budget by 1984. This was the argument that prevailed. The forecast that emerged was an effort to combine the highest amount of inflation that would still look like the route to price stability and the highest amount of real output that could possibly be associated with the approach to price stability. The result strained credulity. It showed from the beginning a willingness to take great risks with balancing the budget in order to push the tax cut and the increase of defense spending.

When the administration's economic program and budget were published in January and February it was mainly the proposed expenditure cuts that were the news. The tax proposals had been well known in advance. And even though the Reagan team had promised big expenditure cuts, there had been much skepticism among people who were used to the ways of Washington. The size of the cuts now specified was surprising, even though it did not come up to the amounts projected during the campaign. There was, moreover, admiration for the quality of the work done in getting the proposal for cutting the budget together in a short time, admiration even from people who were not sympathetic to the cuts.

There was, however, much skepticism about the program, and the rationale given for it, from economists.[3] There were four main points to this criticism:

1. The forecast of rapidly rising nominal GNP for the next four years was inconsistent with the administration's own principle that the growth of the money supply should gradually subside over the same period in order to get the inflation down.

2. Even if the Federal Reserve would provide enough monetary expansion to make nominal GNP rise at the rate projected in the budget, that would be undesirable and would not actually yield the results the budget forecast, because there would be more inflation and less real growth.

3. The tax rate cuts would not yield the gains in productivity and output that the administration's scenario required.

4. The expenditure program still relied on large cuts not yet specified—the asterisk. Presumably the cuts which remained to be made were the more difficult ones, and they would probably have to be achieved after the Reagan honeymoon was over. Thus, the target cuts were by no means assured.

The net of all this was that the conservative budget problem had not been solved. The conservative position was to yearn for a balanced budget, partly because that was the traditional conservative symbol of fiscal prudence but also because it was thought to contribute to growth and price stability—also conservative values. A way had not been found to make the big tax cut and the defense increase plausibly consistent with balancing the budget. The administration was not prepared to make an explicit choice among its inconsistent objectives. But a choice was implicit anyway. The administration would not give up anything in order to balance the budget, except for a small delay in starting the tax cut. Its main recourse for keeping alive the prospect that the budget was on its way to balance was an unrealistic economic projection.

These complaints about the Reagan program were mainly confined to economists. The business and financial community, popularly considered to be great worriers about the budget, suppressed its anxiety on this occasion—being so eager to have their taxes cut. When the tax bill was passed, in August, that was celebrated as a great victory for the President. Yet there was never any doubt that a tax bill very much like the President's would pass. It is, after all, one of the hoary axioms of political life that a Congressman should and will vote for every tax cut. When the tax cut provides some relief for all taxpayers, and when it is certified as essential by the most conservative President in fifty years, its adoption is assured. The Democrats made halfhearted efforts to give the tax bill some characteristics of their own, but insofar as these characteristics would have limited the size of the tax cut they were destined to failure. In the discussion of the tax cut leading up to its passage it was almost as if there was a conspiracy on all sides not to look at the reality of the budget deficit. The administration was scheduled to issue a midyear review of the budget on July 15, and that would ordinarily have been the occasion for revising the economic forecast and showing what the effects were on the budget. By that time it was already clear to the administration economists that the budget forecasts used earlier in the year were too optimistic. The administration decided, however, not to revise the forecasts, because that would have shown the deficit for the next year to be larger than previously estimated and they did not want to throw that fact into the tax deliberations then nearing conclusion.

The bill that was passed cut taxes by about as much as the President had proposed. This should not have been a surprise. There is usually little Congressional motivation to cut taxes less than a President says is prudent. What was unusual was the nature of the changes the Congress made. Ordinarily Congress tilts a presidential tax bill to give a little more to the low-income taxpayers, among whom are so many voters. In 1981, Congress took the step of immediately reducing the highest tax rate, 70 percent, to 50 percent. The administration favored that move but had considered it politically unwise to propose. Congress also added a number of provisions beneficial to middle-class savers.

The character of the changes made in the tax bill reflected the alteration of the conventional political wisdom that had occurred by 1981. So did the fact that the large expenditure cut proposed by the administration was mostly approved by the Congress. The administration had been wise in concentrating cuts in areas which did not impinge seriously on the great bulk of active, middle-class voters. Its initial proposals barely touched social security and Medicare, for example, but took relatively large amounts out of employment and training programs and out of food stamps. Moreover, OMB director Stockman was wise to use the Congressional procedure in a way which forced Congress to act on the whole package of expenditure cuts at once, rather than item by item. This focused attention on the package as an instrument for doing something good about the national economy rather than as a series of separate extractions from one after another beneficiary of government programs.

So the President's budget package was adopted. The 1981 tax legislation would reduce receipts by over $100 billion, or 4 percent of GNP, in fiscal year 1985. The President celebrated the budget as a great triumph.[4] And up to a point it was. Three main items of the conservative agenda had been achieved in less

than seven months—a big tax cut, a big increase in defense
appropriations and an encouraging cut in nondefense spending.
But one haunting, traditionally conservative question remained.
Where was the money going to come from?

Shortly after the President signed the tax-cut bill this question
surfaced with a vengeance. It was as if once the bill had been
safely signed people were free to recognize how big the future
deficits were likely to be. And the consequences of that were not
waiting until the deficits appeared but seemed to be felt immediately. The stock market fell 11 percent between mid-August and
mid-September. Long-term interest rates rose substantially. This
distressing behavior of the financial markets, so different from
the results the new policy was supposed to yield, was believed to
be connected with anxiety over the budget prospect. Moreover,
there were already signs that the economy was slowing down.
The index of industrial production fell every month after July.
Unemployment rose in every month after July. There was concern that the fall of the stock and bond markets portended a
frustration of the administration's forecasts that after a brief
period in which the economy would be "soggy" (the term of the
chairman of the Council of Economic Advisers) the economy
would take off on a strong expansion. Moreover, the prospect of
continuing large deficits was embarrassing to the administration.
It was the first generally recognized sign of internal inconsistency
of the Reagan economic plan. The first serious loss of confidence
of the enthusiasts inside the administration was connected with
this and was finally revealed in interviews with David Stockman
published in the December *Atlantic,* which created a public
sensation.

This situation presented the President with three options.
First, he could deny that any basic change was required. The
immediate deficit problem could be blamed on failure of Congress to enact all of his expenditure cuts and to a temporary lag
of the economy, leaving the longer-run prospect unchanged. He
could use this diagnosis to prescribe small changes in the budget.
Second, he could propose a radical change in the budget, including cancellation of some of the tax cut that had just been

enacted. Third, he could substantially defer or abandon achievement of the balanced budget, saying it was not worth the sacrifice of other parts of his program that would have been required to achieve it.

The President chose the first of these options. On September 24, 1981, he proposed small tax increases, euphemistically called "revenue enhancements," to the general amusement. He also proposed small expenditure cuts. None of this happened, and if it had happened it would not have changed the basic situation.

By December the problem had become more acute. Economic conditions had deteriorated. Unemployment in the fourth quarter was 8.3 percent, compared to the 7.7 percent the Reagan administration had forecast in February. And word was leaking out of the administration that the deficits for the next few years would run around $100 billion a year. This was shocking news at a time when real interest rates were still very high and considered to be a major impediment to economic recovery.

The administration seemed unable to make up its mind about how to respond to this fact. At a public discussion of the $100 billion deficits, a member of the Council of Economic Advisers, William Niskanen, offered a number of reasons for not being worried about the deficits.[5] Doubt was expressed about whether deficits caused inflation or high interest rates or would crowd out domestic private investment. This appearance of insouciance caused consternation, especially among Republicans, and the administration hurried to say that it really did care about deficits. These same reasons for not being worried appeared in the council's Annual Economic Report when that was published in February 1982. But after these reasons were cited the report concluded that deficits were bad after all.

The administration wrestled with the problem of reducing the prospective deficits, in preparation for the February 1982 budget message. The President limited this wrestling match within a small ring by ruling out of bounds any cuts of the defense budget and social security and any retreat from the tax reductions that had been enacted in 1981. The argument narrowed down to tax increases that did not undo the 1981 cut—specifically, increases of excise taxes. On the one hand there were people who thought that some tax increase was a necessary part of a bargain with Congress that would also include expenditure reductions, and that such a bargain was essential to restore "confidence" to financial markets and permit the economy to recover. On the other hand there were people who thought that any tax increase would be a betrayal of Reagan principles and there were other people who just didn't like to pay taxes.

As usual, the decision was some of each. The budget contained a little tax increase, a little more expenditure cutting, some overestimate of revenues and underestimate of expenditures and an economic forecast which stretched the bounds of plausibility. All of this reduced the deficits to $98.6 billion in 1982, $91.5 billion in 1983, $82.9 billion in 1984, and $71.9 billion in 1985. This succession of deficits was explained as resulting from the administration's success in getting inflation down, the Carter administration's failure to prevent the recession, and the reluctance of Congress. But in any case the administration claimed credit for getting the deficits on a downward path.

Coming from the administration which a year earlier had said that it would balance the budget in 1984, this would have been staggering enough if anyone had believed it. But in fact hardly anyone did believe it. The estimates were too improbable and the recommendations too unlikely to be adopted.

There began a period of negotiation, name-calling and struggle between the President and the Congress, the House and the Senate, the Republicans and the Democrats, the old-time-religionists and the Kemp-follower conservatives. The object of all this activity was first to avoid responsibility for the deficits and second to reduce the deficits insofar as possible without sacrificing anything of value. By the middle of 1983 the administration's own estimates of the deficits for each of the fiscal years 1983, 1984, and 1985 were twice as high as it had estimated at the beginning of 1982—even on the assumption that all its recommendations were followed.

By the beginning of 1983 the administration was clearly

changing its fiscal course, and there is no need to trace its budget struggles in more detail. But it is necessary to evaluate the experience of the first two years. The budget program of the administration clearly had, by that time, four "accomplishments" to its credit. It had significantly reduced tax rates below where they would have been otherwise, it had lowered the trend of nondefense expenditures, it had moved budget deficits to a new, higher level, absolutely and relative to GNP, and it had left the country without any principles of fiscal policy. Each of these developments requires evaluation.

The main question about the big tax cuts is whether they worked, or what light experience during the early part of the Reagan administration throws on the likelihood of their working. The answer is that little if anything has been learned about that.

The common assertion that "supply-side economics failed" is not supported by the facts, if the assertion applies to any proposition which had a reasonable chance of working. The tax rate cuts and changes should not have been expected to produce a prompt increase in the national income of such size as to increase the revenue, and of course they did not. They should not have been expected to produce a prompt increase of productivity so large as to alter the trend of unit labor costs markedly and so permit a decline of the inflation rate without more unemployment, and they did not.

A more reasonable expectation was that they would gradually and significantly raise the rate of growth of productivity and output, and that would recoup a substantial part of the revenue that would otherwise have been lost.

In the latter part of 1982 a rise in productivity was apparent and in the first half of 1983 a general increase in output began. However, this did not seem to be much more than cyclical behavior. There was no sign that any distinctively supply-side result attributable to the tax cut was being obtained. But the evidence was not conclusive for several reasons:

1. In 1982 federal individual income tax in relation to personal income was higher than in any year of the 1970s and was

only slightly lower than in 1980. A large part of the individual income tax rate cut had been offset by the effects of continuing inflation in pushing taxpayers into higher brackets. In addition, there was an increase of social security taxes. The most that should have been expected was avoiding the further decline of output and productivity that would have resulted if tax rates had not been cut. Taxpayers with income from labor services high enough to keep them in the 50 percent maximum tax rate bracket did not have any cut in their marginal tax rate. All that should have been expected to operate in a positive way was the part of the tax program that provided incentives for business investment and for some forms of personal saving.

2. By the end of 1982 only half of the income tax rate cuts had taken effect. Some supply-siders claimed that the prospect of further cuts to come had a negative effect on economic activity by inducing businesses and workers to postpone income-generating activity until the rates came down. Even if this was dismissed as insignificant and farfetched, one would expect adjustment of work and savings patterns to take time.

3. The tax cuts came into effect during a major recession which swamped the supply-side effects of the tax cut, especially with respect to incentives to invest.

4. The tax cuts came into effect alongside very large budget deficits that raised interest rates and offset the effects of tax incentives on private investment. Of course, the tax cuts also contributed to the deficits.

Thus the experience of 1981–1983 did not disprove moderate supply-side contentions. It was still possible that in the long run, in a period of prosperity, and if accompanied by sufficient expenditure reductions the tax rate cuts would make a significant contribution to the national income and offset a significant part of the revenue loss that would otherwise result from the rate cut. The experience of 1981–1983 threw no light on that, one way or the other. Some supply-siders grasped at small increases in the personal saving rate as evidence that the tax cuts were working, but these increases were too small and short-lived to demon-

strate anything. In fact, the more economic analysis was, be-
latedly, devoted to the supply-side claims, the weaker the case
for them looked. The original Treasury team, devoted to the
supply-side view of taxes and now possessing the data resources
of that department, failed to deliver any empirical evidence in
support of the idea that the output response to tax cuts would
be prompt and large. That contributed to dwindling faith in the
earlier supply-side claims for the benefits of cutting taxes. By
mid-1982 the most conspicuous supply-siders had left the government.

Belief in the supply-side benefits of tax reduction remained
part of the administration's language. But it played less and less
a part in its calculations and decisions. Estimates of future levels
of output did not count on any departures from past trends as a
result of the tax rate cuts. When large deficits loomed in 1982,
no one proposed tax cuts as a way to raise the revenue and reduce the deficits. In fact, the President supported a large tax increase in mid-1982. At the end of the year he also proposed an
increase in the gasoline tax, and early in 1983 he was pleased
with a bipartisan social security program that included substantial tax increases and accelerations of tax increases already scheduled. His January 1983 budget also contained a proposal for
large tax increases to apply to the years 1986–1988 if certain
conditions were met.

Despite these "lapses" the President retained a general posture
of opposition to tax increases. The argument, however, was no
longer that tax increases reduce the revenue and that tax reductions increase the revenue. To some extent the new Reagan argument was old-fashioned Keynesianism—that raising taxes in a
recession would reduce private purchasing power and prevent recovery. But the basic argument was that keeping revenues low
would force a reduction of expenditures, which was the true objective. Fear of the actual or prospective deficits would induce
the government to cut expenditures. To some extent this may
have worked in 1981, although the President and the Congress
were then operating under the assumption that the budget was
going to come into balance in 1984 and into surplus thereafter,

and so the deficit picture did not look terrifying. By 1982 the deficit picture did look terrifying, and undoubtedly did exert pressure, first on the President and then on the Congress, to cut expenditures. It also exerted pressure on the President and the Congress to raise taxes. Indeed, in 1982, increasing taxes seemed to be the way to get expenditures down. The Congressmen who were most defensive of the expenditure programs were unwilling to cut them unless the sacrifice was shared by taxpayers through a tax increase. They were not so worried about deficits that they were willing to make a unilateral sacrifice to reduce them.

The Reagan administration's "preemptive strike" of getting a big tax cut first and then negotiating about the budget almost certainly contributed to a reduction of nondefense expenditures. The reduction was not as large as the tax cut, however, and certainly not as large as the tax cut plus the defense spending increase. That is, the deficit increased. That is not necessarily a fatal flaw in the policy. Possibly the deficits exerted a restraint on expenditures and thus on the increase in the deficit. But that is not the only possibility. The prospect of deficits operates to hold spending down only if decision-makers fear deficits. But that fear seems to relate only to deficits of a size that is not yet customary. In January 1982, deficits of $100 billion were shocking, but $60 billion would not have been. By mid-1982, deficits of $150 billion were shocking, but deficits of $100 billion were regarded as a triumph of fiscal prudence. By 1983, a deficit of $200 billion was accepted as equivalent to zero—par for the course. Large deficits may temporarily restrain expenditures but more durably breed tolerance of large deficits, and in the end tolerance of more expenditures.

The result of the Reagan policy of tax cuts was first that during some period expenditures would be lower than they would otherwise be and deficits higher. The longer-run outcome was uncertain. How the interim consequences should be appraised depends on what evaluation is assigned to the reduced expenditures and to the enlarged deficits. There are people who consider any reduction of expenditure a gain, without regard to the size of deficit that forced it. But that is a view not shared even by all "conservatives."

Estimating how much President Reagan had cut the nondefense budget by the middle of 1983 is difficult for several reasons. First, there is the question "Compared to what?" One can compare the Reagan budget with the last Carter budget, the one submitted in January 1981. But the last Carter budget is not a good indication of the amount of expenditure that would have occurred if Jimmy Carter had been reelected. The common practice of outgoing Presidents is to leave behind a budget which shows low expenditures, setting a standard for frugality which the successor will find difficult to match. Second, the first complete Reagan year is fiscal year 1982, and even that largely reflects decisions that were made before he came into office.

Budget projections for 1983 and later may have represented Ronald Reagan's intentions more adequately, but these numbers were still only promises waiting to be realized. Third, expenditures for fiscal years 1982 and 1983 were increased by the fact that the country's unemployment was higher than Carter had assumed in his last budget. Finally, there was a change in statistical techniques for eliminating inflation from the dollar figures, and that reduced the comparability of the numbers.

A valid picture would probably show something like this. Between 1974 and 1980, real nondefense expenditures, excluding interest, rose at an annual rate of 5 to 6 percent, depending on the method of deflating dollar figures. When President Carter submitted his final budget he recommended measures which would hold real nondefense expenditures, excluding interest, about flat from 1980 to 1984. President Reagan's program, as it appeared when he submitted his budget in January 1983, would have reduced real nondefense spending by 1 percent a year from 1980 to 1984. The estimate of 1984 expenditures contained in the Reagan budget was increased, compared to the Carter budget, by the expectation of higher unemployment than had been assumed by Carter. Without that, nondefense, noninterest expenditures under Reagan would have fallen about 7 percent from 1980 to 1984. On the other hand, interest payments have risen under Reagan, partly as a result of the tax cuts he initiated. If we attribute the higher interest burden to Reagan, but do not charge him with the higher unemployment costs, it appears that his program, like Carter's, roughly stabilized nondefense expenditures from 1980 to 1984. Real nondefense expenditure in 1984 would be higher than in any year before 1980 no matter how unemployment costs and interest are treated. But in any case there had been a significant slowdown in the rate of increase.

During the campaign the reduction of expenditures had been put forward as a goal of obvious merit, identified as the elimination of waste, fraud and extravagance. But if the cut was to be large it could not be confined to that and required further justification.

Some elements of this justification were articulated more or less clearly. One was that government transfer payments to the poor did not really help poor people because they created incentives to avoid work and to break up families. Programs alleged to help disadvantaged people become self-supporting workers, such as training and employment programs, were also said to fall into that category, because federal programs did not really prepare their participants to work in the private sector but were only disguised welfare.

A second element in the justification was that much federal expenditure was only a shuffling of money between middle-income people in their capacity as benefit recipients and middle-income people in their capacity as taxpayers and income earners. The result was not to make the middle class better off but to make the whole society worse off by reducing incentives to work and produce income.

Third was the traditional argument that federal expenditures should be reduced by shifting functions back to the states, which would perform them more efficiently and finance them by taxes less burdensome on the economy without depriving people of essential benefits.

Thus, the expenditure policy was essentially a supply-side policy. It was supposed to strengthen incentives for work and for efficient use of resources, increase the national output and leave everyone, or almost everyone, better off. The authors of the program resisted characterization of it as an income redistribution program—shifting income from lower-income to upper-income people. But it was undoubtedly true that some of the motivation behind it was the natural and legitimate desire of taxpayers to be relieved of some of the burden of supporting other people, mostly poorer than themselves.

The justification for the expenditure-cutting policy indicated where the cuts would be made. There were sharp reductions in employment and training programs, reductions in the income levels at which food stamps and education assistance could be obtained, tightening of eligibility requirements for welfare and cuts in grants to state and local governments.

Achievement of these reductions was a political success in the sense that it ran counter to a trend of many years and to the conventional wisdom that the political forces behind expenditure growth were irresistible. Although the expenditure reductions were smaller than the tax cut, which was regarded as the great achievement, it was the expenditure side of the budget that showed the change of popular attitudes and President Reagan's political mastery.

The validity of the assumptions underlying the expenditure changes is still unclear. To what degree did tighter standards for aid to families with dependent children cause people to work or encourage families to stay together—and to what degree did these changes increase destitution? Did states really take up the slack left by federal government cutbacks? Did reduction in federal assistance reduce the number of college students, and, if so, will this reduction in the long run reduce economic growth or other qualities of American life?

To say that the outcome of the experiment is not clear is not to say that the experiment has failed or will. The change of policy resulted from years of accumulating dissatisfaction with many federal expenditure programs. That dissatisfaction was not conclusive evidence that the specific change of policy made in 1981 and 1982 would be an improvement, but it was sufficient basis for making the change and seeing what its effects would be.

The initial experience of implementing the change did, however, suggest some lessons:

1. To cut income assistance programs in a way which on the one hand protects the poor and on the other hand does not impair incentives to work is difficult. The most obvious procedure is to deny or reduce benefits for people who have more than a certain income. But that weakens the incentive to work and earn an income above the cut-off level. The alternative is to try to impose a work requirement. But that requires making fine distinctions between those able to work and those not able and risks injury to many "worthy" claimants for aid. In application the administration's policy involved greater use of means tests— lowering the income limits above which benefits were disallowed. This was true of Aid to Families with Dependent Children, food stamps and education assistance. This had the paradoxical effect of increasing the marginal tax rate on the working poor by increasing the benefit loss that resulted from earning more income at the same time that the marginal tax rate was being cut on the nonpoor.

2. The political obstacles to reducing benefits for the middle class are enormous, as might have been expected from the fact that they are most of the voters. The chief benefits involved are social security payments, which amounted to 38.5 percent of all nondefense expenditures in fiscal year 1982 and 67 percent of all transfer payments to individuals. (This includes Medicare.) President Reagan made a limited foray into this area in 1981 but quickly withdrew after his proposal for reducing outlays was unanimously rejected by the Senate. The problem of dealing with this vast block of expenditures is compounded by the identification of social security benefits as "entitlements." These benefits go only to people who have paid something for them, and this supports the notion that they are "entitled" to the benefits. But the fact is that most workers covered under social security have not paid enough to earn the benefits they have already received and will receive in the future under current provisions. This is evidenced by the fact that the funds accumulated from

social security contributions plus interest on these accumulations were near exhaustion in 1982. Although restraining the growth of this enormous part of the federal budget would have been consistent with the administration's philosophy, the administration did not feel able to tackle it. The subject was put off by referral to a bipartisan study commission to report after the 1982 election.

This commission, chaired by Alan Greenspan, produced a set of recommendations that were adopted with little change by Congress. These recommendations met the short-run fiscal problem of the social security trust funds almost entirely by methods that would raise the revenue. Scheduled future tax rate increases were advanced, part of social security benefits was made taxable under the federal income tax, and future federal workers were to be covered under the social security system. There were hardly any steps to restrict benefits in the near future. Some provisions were adopted, however, that would limit the growth of benefits in the longer run—after the year 2000. The chief of these was gradually to raise the age at which benefits would be payable.

3. State and local governments fiercely resist transfer of functions and responsibilities back to them, as many Presidents, beginning with Eisenhower, have discovered. This is true even if the proposal, on the whole, involves an offsetting transfer of revenue sources to the states and localities or transfer of expenditure functions to the federal government. One basic source of resistance is that even if states and localities on the average come out whole from the shift of functions and revenues, many states and localities will not come out whole. The losers complain bitterly, mobilizing the support of their Congressmen and Senators. The administration cannot adjust the program so that no one loses without greatly increasing the cost to the federal government. Even those units of government which probably will not lose are suspicious of the federal government's intentions for the future. The administration had made a major transfer of functions to the states and localities a central feature of its 1982 program, but it quickly disappeared without a trace.

4. There was danger that a supply-oriented approach to ex-

penditure cutting would sweep out some kinds of expenditures that might make a worthwhile contribution to economic growth, or prevent undertaking such expenditures. *Some* expenditures for research, education and such public works as port facilities may fit this description. Objective evaluation of such expenditures is difficult. Probably by the time Reagan came into office there had been twenty years of excessive willingness to make such expenditures and leaning in the other direction was a desirable correction. But that leaning can also go too far, and it becomes necessary to seek a more open-minded approach. There was no sign in its first two years that the Reagan administration recognized this need.

5. The administration's changes in expenditures were made in economic circumstances in which they would be least likely to yield their desired beneficial results. One of the administration's basic themes was that the improvement of the economy—the increase of employment, productivity and average incomes—would more than compensate poor and disadvantaged beneficiaries for the cut in their government programs. The theory was that the tax rate cuts would produce the improvement of the economy. But they did not, at least not in the early years, and should not have been expected to do so. Thus, people lost welfare payments, training slots and public service jobs in an economy where employment was especially difficult to find. It was also an economy where shrinking revenues limited the ability of states and localities to take up the slack. This raises the question whether the cuts in government programs might not better have been deferred until after the period of economic slack that would accompany the process of disinflation. This may not, however, have been politically feasible. The political support needed to make the expenditure cuts might not still have been there by the time the disinflation had been achieved.

In any case, the desired effects of the tax rate cuts and expenditure cuts did not appear in the first two years of the administration, which did not mean that they would not appear in time.

But one effect did appear quickly and became the object of enormous attention. That was the prospect of large budget deficits—between $175 and $200 billion a year from fiscal 1983 through fiscal 1985 and probably beyond. The administration tended at first to blame this prospect, so different from its early 1981 forecasts, on a recession due to the Carter administration but nevertheless unforeseen, and on its own success in getting inflation down. But it was much nearer the truth to say that the success of its own disinflation policy entailed the period of slow growth which contributed much of the unforeseen deficit and that the remainder which would persist even after economic recovery was achieved was due to failure to produce the expenditure cuts that had been promised.

Almost everyone agreed that the deficits were a bad thing. There were exceptions—mainly people who thought that the deficits were good because they would force reduction of expenditures—but this was confined to a very few. The assertions about the evils of the deficit, however, were not entirely convincing.

Two aspects of the deficit need to be distinguished. One is what the immediate consequences of the deficits of 1982–1985 were or would be. The other is what were the longer-run implications for fiscal policy of the fact that the country ran at least four more years of large deficits, larger than ever and more unwanted than ever, after twenty years of large deficits and in the administration of the most conservative President in fifty years.

Discussion of the immediate consequences of the deficit soon settled on one point. At first the automatic response was that the deficits were inflationary, because that had been the standard complaint about deficits for the preceding decades. But that was not a compelling proposition, since the inflation rate was rapidly falling. One could still assert that the future deficits would cause more inflation later, but that was too uncertain and remote to be interesting.

The common syllogism of the time went like this:

A. Budget deficits cause bad things.

B. The bad things that are happening to us are high interest rates, low output and high unemployment.

C. These bad things are caused by big budget deficits.

This went beyond rejecting Keynesianism. It stood Keynesianism on its head. Keynes had argued that an increase in the government deficit would stimulate the economy, by increasing the total demand for output. An increase in the deficit meant an increase in government payments to the private sector relative to government extraction from the private sector in taxes. Individuals and businesses in the private sector would have more income after tax to spend and would spend more—raising output and employment if the economy was not in a condition of full employment.

The monetarist counterrevolution, as we have already noted, denied that an increase in the deficit would stimulate the economy by increasing total demand: The argument was summarized in Milton Friedman's question: "Where do they think the money is coming from? The tooth fairy?" The implication was that if the government increased its deficit it might give money to people with one hand through higher expenditures or tax reductions but would have to take an equal amount of money from people by borrowing to finance the deficit. The Keynesians had an answer to that and the monetarists had an answer to the answer and so on. But the point is that the monetarists did not say that deficits would depress the economy. They only said that deficits would not stimulate the economy.

In 1981–1983, however, the common argument was that deficits did depress the economy. The causation was supposed to run through interest rates. Government borrowing to finance the deficit would raise interest rates and thus depress business investment, housing and the purchase of automobiles and other durable goods. The high interest rates would also raise the value of the dollar, and so depress net exports. But this was as one-sided an analysis as the original Keynesian one. It was open to the similar question: "Where do they think the money is going? To the tooth fairy?" If the government borrowed more, thus taking money out of the private sector, it was also giving more back to the private sector, through spending more or taxing less. There was nothing in this shift by itself that would necessarily depress output as a whole. There would be a depressing effect on some sectors—as already noted, housing, business investment, durable consumer goods and exports—as a consequence of the interest rate rise, but there would also be a stimulating effect on demand in other sectors as a result of larger government expenditures or lower taxes. This shift—away from private investment to consumption and defense—might be a legitimate subject for concern, but it would not explain low output and employment in total.

There were, as always, ingenious theories to explain the paradox—in this case that an increasing deficit was causing a recession. One was that resources, especially labor, did not move rapidly. The carpenters and bricklayers who lost jobs in the construction industry would not be immediately employed producing the video games that consumers wanted to buy with their tax cuts. This theory would have led to the expectation of labor shortages in many parts of the economy, which did not actually appear.

Another theory was that the prospect of large future deficits kept present interest rates higher than was consistent with high employment at present. The prospect of high future deficits led investors to expect that interest rates would be high in the future. In that case they would not lend at low interest rates today because they would suffer losses later when interest rates rose. This source of high interest rates, unlike today's borrowing by the government, did not have as its counterpart a flow of funds into the hands of taxpayers or beneficiaries of government programs. Thus, it might more plausibly be expected to have a new depressing effect on the economy. But this explanation left open the question of what the people who did not lend did with their money. The reasonable expectation would be that people who thought future deficits made long-term lending too risky would buy short-term securities. Then short-term interest rates should have been driven down to low levels. But in fact, short-term interest rates remained high during the period of maximum concern about future deficits.

An all-purpose explanation, good for whatever is wrong with the economy, is that the government's policy—in this case the deficit—has destroyed confidence, especially business confidence. Concern with business confidence had been a primary motivation behind Herbert Hoover's decision to raise taxes in 1932. The problem with this kind of explanation is that it doesn't explain why the particular policy in question impairs confidence or why the impairment of confidence has the particular consequence it is supposed to have. Thus, if deficits are not bad for the economy for reasons other than their effect on confidence, why do they affect confidence in a way that hurts the economy?

The fact is that the connection between the budget deficits and the low output and high unemployment of 1981–1983 was never clearly established, although some such connection may have existed. This connection was, however, the main reason advanced for acute concern about the deficit in those years. It was in response to this that the President reluctantly agreed to support a revenue increase in 1982, and in 1983 proposed at least a contingent future tax increase.

There was a more probable consequence of the large deficits which justified the concern about them. That was the effect of the deficits on the volume of private investment via the demands the deficits place on credit markets. Even though these effects may not depress employment or total output currently they mean that the total stock of productive capital rises less rapidly and therefore productivity and per capita incomes rise less rapidly. This effect would be small in any single year, but if continued year after year it can injure living standards seriously.

This kind of effect was recognized by supply-siders when the deficit resulted from increased expenditures. But they often had difficulty recognizing the point when the deficit was caused by tax reduction or when the deficit was to be reduced by a tax increase. They argued that increasing taxes reduced private saving so that the availability of funds for private investment was not increased. That is, the government would borrow less, but out of a smaller pool of private saving, so that the savings available for private investment would not be increased. The blind spot in this analysis is the assumption that taxes come dollar for dollar out of private saving. In fact, most taxes come out of private consumption. The net effect of raising taxes instead of borrowing is to reduce consumption and increase funds available for private investment and therefore to promote long-run economic growth.

An economy with a budget deficit equal to, say, 4 percent of GNP will probably have less private investment than one with a budget deficit equal to 2 percent of GNP, and, if other things are equal, it will probably have less growth of productivity. There is considerable disagreement among students of economic growth about how big this effect on productivity would be, but over a long period it would almost certainly be significant. There is, however, a more serious problem, which is that if the deficit is large relative to the GNP it will be difficult to keep it from getting still larger relative to GNP. The reason is that if the deficit is large relative to GNP the size of the debt will rise relative to GNP, and that will raise interest expenditures relative to GNP. Then unless noninterest expenditures can be reduced relative to GNP or taxes raised, the deficit will rise relative to GNP—which will raise the debt and the interest burden further. One can easily visualize this cumulative process reaching a point at which the temptation to repudiate the debt by inflation would be irresistible. Peacetime deficits of the size looming in 1983 raised this prospect. Since it was, however, a prospect for the distant future, it did not receive much weight in policy considerations.

The prospect of federal deficits approaching $200 billion a year for years to come did generate a scramble in the political arena to show aversion to deficits and to avoid responsibility for them, but no action on a sufficient scale to reduce the deficits significantly. Probably the outstanding lesson of the episode was that the United States did not have any fiscal policy. What I mean by fiscal policy is a policy which determines an appropriate size of the deficit or surplus to which decisions about expenditures and revenues are then adapted. Of course, any budgetary process will finally lead to a total of expenditures, revenues and, by subtraction, deficit or surplus. The distinctive feature of fiscal policy is that there is a rule or principle which determines the size of the deficit or surplus first and which requires the expenditures and revenues to conform to that.

Balancing the budget was such a fiscal policy. It involved a prior decision that expenditures should equal, or not exceed, revenues. The expenditure and revenue decisions were then supposed to fit that. Balancing the budget at high employment was also a fiscal policy. There was a Keynesian, or functional-finance, fiscal policy which said that the deficit or surplus should be high enough to yield high employment; once that had been determined the expenditure and revenue decisions would be made to conform.

Of course, the government never worked exactly like that. There was always a two-way adaptation, in which the size of the deficit or surplus adjusted to the requirements of the expenditure and revenue decisions, as well as vice versa. But we thought that the goal for the proper size of the deficit or surplus should be dominant and that it was too bad when that goal had to give way to limitations of revenues or demands for expenditures. The budget process, first in the executive branch and then in the Congress, was intended to give weight to the overall decision about the relation of total revenues to total expenditures and to force the parts of the budget to conform.

Conservatives complained about Keynesian fiscal policy on the ground that it was too "loose," did not define precisely and objectively what the proper size of surplus or deficit was and therefore left too much room for irresponsible behavior. They attributed the big increase of deficits in the 1970s to this, on the ground that even the "liberals" did not want those deficits but had no principles to resist the tendency of case-by-case expenditure decisions to add up to excessive total spending and excessive deficits.

The "conservative" fiscal policy was going to be "balancing

the budget." By the time the Reagan administration came, that was the only fiscal policy in sight. Functional finance had been discredited by experience, and synthetic standards, like full-employment balance, had been rejected by conservatives and liberals alike. History did not provide much reason to believe that "balancing the budget" would be an effective discipline either. As I said in *The Fiscal Revolution in America*, after reviewing the period 1929–1964, "the balanced budget is a flag more often saluted than followed." But there was a possibility that after disillusionment with the Kennedy-Johnson New Economics, and the growth of deficits that no one could defend, the balanced budget might regain its traditional position as the standard of fiscal policy. And Ronald Reagan was the man to do it.

Instead, the first two years of Reagan policy demonstrated that the balanced budget was indeed dead. Budget deficits were larger than ever and there was no plan for eliminating them at any foreseeable time. And that was not because anyone would say that deficits of the size in prospect for the indefinite future were a good thing. On the contrary, everybody said they were a very bad thing. And that was the conclusive evidence that we had no fiscal policy. Although everyone said that the big deficits were bad, hardly anyone was willing to give up anything he valued very much in order to reduce them. That was as true of President Reagan as of anyone else. His attitude was decisive. If the most "conservative" President in fifty years would not make any sacrifice in order to avoid the biggest deficits in history, who would?

This did not mean, to repeat, indifference to deficits. The Reagan administration disliked deficits and detested big deficits. But this attitude was not decisive. It was a factor taken into account in making other decisions but not a controlling, prior factor. The desirability of reducing the deficit by $1 billion had to be weighed against the desirability of spending $1 billion on food stamps or MX missiles or any of a hundred other things and against the costs of raising $1 billion from cigarette smokers or gasoline users or income tax payers in any of several dozen brackets and so on. This is a perfectly logical way to make a decision. It balances the costs and benefits of all items in the budget at the margin—running a deficit being just another source of funds like raising any tax or cutting any expenditures. But although logical, most people thought it was impractical. If the decision about the surplus or deficit was put on all fours with the other decisions in the budget the surplus-deficit decision would suffer because the consequences of the surplus-deficit decision, although important, were general and deferred whereas the consequences of other budget decisions would be immediately felt by beneficiaries of expenditures or by taxpayers. The essence of fiscal policy was to make a decision to balance the budget, or confine the deficit to a specified size, before constituencies knew who was going to pay for holding the deficit down.

By the fall of 1981 the Reagan administration knew that its plans for defense spending and tax cuts were inconsistent with balancing the budget, or coming close, anytime during the first term or probably for years thereafter. The budget submitted in February 1982 also revealed that the administration was not prepared to recommend cuts in nondefense expenditures that would be nearly sufficient to put the budget on a path to balance. The administration decided that it wanted a lot of other things more than it wanted to balance the budget. By 1983, facing still bigger deficits, the administration proposed a contingency tax increase for 1985–1988 that would reduce the long-run deficit to 2 percent of GNP—making the Carter achievement a target to aim at, no longer a failure to repudiate. But the contingent tax increase depended on the unlikely eventuality that Congress would approve all the President's desired cuts in nondefense spending.

This tolerance of deficits was not simply a bow to political convenience. When the administration faced the need for a serious sacrifice if the budget was to be balanced it had to ask itself why it wanted to balance the budget. And when this was asked as a practical matter, and not as a matter of ritual incantation, the answer was not compelling. During the campaign Mr. Reagan's chief argument against deficits was that they were inflationary because they caused monetary expansion. Once in office he learned that this was not a necessary conclusion. One argument for budget balancing was that it kept expenditures down. Now he heard the proposition that big deficits held expenditures down by frightening the Congress. Even the traditional argument that deficits impair growth by absorbing private savings was not open-and-shut, at least among his advisers. If the deficit had to be eliminated by raising taxes, that might have even a worse effect on growth. Also the deficit might, by one route or another, evoke a flow of additional savings to finance itself.

So, the case for balancing the budget, or even for drastically reducing the deficit, seemed too weak and uncertain to upset the commitment to the big tax reduction and defense spending increase. The administration thus put another nail in the coffin of the balanced-budget doctrine. Moreover, the administration made no effort to develop an alternative principle of fiscal policy which would acknowledge that it had found the balanced-budget principle impossible to live with. Instead, it took the position that the balanced budget was not dead but sleeping. In 1982, it supported a constitutional amendment designed to bring about balanced budgets in the future. But by 1983 that idea had fallen out of its lexicon. For the time being it must be said that the Reagan experience did not give us any rule of fiscal policy and the problem of creating one lies ahead.

Monetarism

Although the most conspicuous part of Reagan economics in 1981 and 1982 was his budget policy—the tax cut and the expenditure cut—the part that made the most difference in economic performance during those years and probably for some years thereafter was the monetary policy. It was this more than anything else which accounted for the greatest achievement of those years, which was the reduction of inflation, and the greatest disappointment, which was the rise of unemployment.

In fact, the monetary policy of this period was only in part

Reagan policy. It was under the independent control of the Federal Reserve, and the decisive step toward the kind of policy practiced during the first two years of the Reagan term had been taken earlier, in the fall of 1979. But this step surely deserved to be considered a major part of the turn to conservative economics. The Reagan team placed more reliance on monetary policy for the achievement of economic stability than previous administrations had done. And by and large the Reagan administration endorsed the policy, although with occasional misgivings, sometimes publicly expressed.

The policy that was adopted in 1979 is commonly called "monetarism." This is a term which stretches over a large number of ideas, not all of which are held by all the people who consider themselves monetarists or are considered such by others. As the policy was adopted by the Federal Reserve in 1979 and followed thereafter at least until late 1982, it included the following propositions:

1. The main contribution of monetary policy to good economic performance is price-level stability, but this does not mean that the approach to that goal cannot be tempered by other considerations temporarily. For example, starting from the high inflation rate of 1979 the Federal Reserve had to approach price-level stability with a certain gradualism.

2. In order to achieve price stability it would be necessary first to reduce the growth of the quantity of money and then prevent any future excessive rate of growth continuing over an extended period.

3. As guidance for itself the Federal Reserve should annually set and announce targets in the form of a range within which the year's growth of the quantity of money should be confined, for each of several definitions of the money supply. The Federal Reserve would set these targets each year as it considered appropriate for achievement of its disinflationary objectives. The target for the year did not imply that the money supply would be within the target range at all times during the year. Moreover, the Federal Reserve would retain discretion to decide where

within the range the money supply should actually be and also, in unusual circumstances, to change the target within the year.

4. In order to achieve the desired behavior of the money supply the Federal Reserve would try to provide the quantity of bank reserves which would permit the banks to supply the quantity of money the Federal Reserve was aiming at. This would be a change from the previous procedure in which the Federal Reserve tried to bring about a level of interest rates that it thought would be consistent with its desired money supply.

This policy of the Federal Reserve is best understood as an attempt to correct two previous biases of the previous system. One was a bias toward inflation resulting from the great emphasis previously given to other objectives, such as full employment, which in the short run often turned out to be inconsistent with price stability. The new policy did not imply indifference to unemployment. It did reflect the growing belief that the repeated efforts to pump the economy up to high levels of employment by monetary expansion were futile if not actually negative in their effects. The other bias was the tendency toward economic instability resulting from the emphasis on interest rates. When the economy was rising rapidly and inflation speeding up, interest rates would tend to rise and the Federal Reserve would find that its interest rate management policy led it to increase the money supply in an effort to keep interest rates down. In the reverse economic conditions it would be led to restrict the money supply.

The policy change of 1979 enabled the Federal Reserve to follow a more stable and persistently anti-inflationary policy. For this reason it was welcomed by many conservatives as an improvement over past practice. There were, however, several respects in which important conservative thinking departed from the new Federal Reserve doctrine and policy.

Stricter monetarists, of whom Milton Friedman was the leader, did not accept the policy as "monetarist" and regarded it as still too loose and discretionary. They distrusted the wide range of the annual targets, the freedom to change the targets from year to year and the lack of commitment to any path of monetary growth from month to month or quarter to quarter. In their view there was too much room for political pressure to push the Federal Reserve into inflation. There was too little reason for the private sector to believe that the Federal Reserve would stick to an anti-inflationary course. And there was just too much opportunity for the Fed to make mistakes in trying to estimate the appropriate behavior of the money supply.

Some monetarists carried thinking about the relation between inflation and unemployment one step beyond what had become standard doctrine. By 1980 the profession had largely abandoned the idea that inflationary policy could permanently keep unemployment low. As we have already noted, some people jumped from this to the extreme proposition that an ongoing rate of inflation could be substantially reduced without any, or with hardly any, temporary increase of unemployment. This view depended heavily on a large, prompt change of inflationary expectations as a result of a change of monetary policy, and such a change of expectations was most likely to come about if the new monetary policy was embodied in a precise and firm commitment.

Moving in another direction was another group of people who also considered money to be enormously important and who welcomed the change from pre-1979 policy. They did not, however, think that the Federal Reserve could ever estimate reliably what behavior of the quantity of money would yield price stability. Neither did they think that confidence could ever be created in the Federal Reserve's devotion to the goal of price stability. They wanted, therefore, to give up entirely the practice of attempting to achieve a predetermined target for the quantity of money. Instead they wanted a monetary policy that would directly stabilize the price of some thing, by standing ready to buy or sell it at a fixed price.

The thing, of course, was to be gold. The underlying theory was that the relation between the price of gold and the price of goods and services in general was rather stable, so that if the price of gold was constant the price level would also be constant.

Also, if the government adopted the gold standard it would not readily abandon it, and this would give the public the necessary confidence in the stability of the price level. The idea of the gold standard had few supporters among professional economists or in the financial community. It was, however, a favorite in a certain amateur cult. The Republican platform contained a veiled reference to it, and Ronald Reagan himself was known to be sympathetic to it.

The new monetary policy of the Federal Reserve was not successful in its first year, 1980. Faced by an upsurge of inflation at the beginning of the year, and reluctant to see interest rates in general skyrocket, the President induced the Federal Reserve to impose direct, selective credit controls in March. This led to a sharp curtailment of the money supply and contributed to a brief recession. When the recession caused a drop in interest rates the Fed was afraid to let the drop go "too far" and therefore did not increase the money supply up into its target range. Then in the summer the Federal Reserve began a vigorous expansion of the money supply so that at the end of the year it was near the upper end of the target range.

This highly variable behavior in 1980 left a good deal of uncertainty about the intentions of the Federal Reserve. Nevertheless there was reason to believe that the whole performance of 1980 had been badly distorted by the imposition of the credit controls, which was unlikely to be repeated in the Reagan Administration. After a rocky start, therefore, the disinflationary policy heralded in October 1979 might yet be carried through.

The new administration, placing, as I have said, unusual reliance on monetary policy, contained elements of all three of the deviant views I have described above. Probably most important were the stricter monetarists, represented in both the Treasury and the Council of Economic Advisers. They believed that they knew how rapidly money should grow not only in the current year but also each year into the future. They wanted the rate of growth of the money supply to decline steadily for several years until it reached a level consistent with price stability, after which the growth rate of money should be constant. They wanted the money supply to move steadily along that path and not oscillate violently around it from month to month. And they had in mind changes in Federal Reserve operating procedures which they believed would permit a smoother course to be maintained. The new members of the administration's team who held these views had been critics of the Federal Reserve for years and remained critics despite the partial turn of the Fed in their direction in 1979. They thought that with the new influence they had as administration officials they would be able to convert the Fed.

Not inconsistent with this attitude, but going beyond it, was the belief of some in the government that if monetary policy changed decisively the inflation rate would come down without any significant increase of unemployment. This was not a necessary corollary of strict, Friedman-type monetarism. Nevertheless, this idea, plus temporary political convenience, led the administration to forecast that its disinflationary policy would succeed with little transitional unemployment.

The third branch of administration monetarism—affection for gold—remained inconspicuous in the early months of the new term. It would only surface after economic trouble came.

The economic trouble came in the summer of 1981, as noted, with the rise of unemployment and interest rates, and the decline of output and the stock market. There were several possible explanations for this trouble. One was that the trouble was inevitable and did not result from any error of policy. Getting the inflation down by monetary restraint would cause a period of rising unemployment and high real interest rates until all expectations and contracts had adjusted. Whether the degree and timing of monetary restraint was the best it could be, no one could tell—certainly not in advance and probably not in retrospect. There was no reason to feel guilty about what was happening, since the government, including the Federal Reserve, was doing what had to be done. In my opinion that was the correct explanation.

A second explanation, which became increasingly common after the tax cut had been safely signed, was that the large budget deficits, actual and prospective, were causing the high interest rates which depressed the economy. I have already given reasons for thinking that the deficits were not depressing the level of total economic activity in the country, whatever other consequences they might have.

A third explanation focused on inadequacy of monetary policy. This explanation found adherents among Republicans and Democrats, conservatives and liberals, although the criticism of monetary policy and proposals for change took a variety of forms.

In the latter part of 1981 and early 1982 there was a wave of interest in gold as the key to correcting the inadequacies of monetary policy which were alleged to be preventing recovery. This was mainly stimulated by people who were also extreme supply-siders. There is no logical reason why a person who has the supply-sider view of the relation between tax rates and the supply of labor and capital should also believe that stabilizing the price of gold will stabilize the price level. The two propositions relate to different universes—the real world and the nominal world. There may, however, be a psychological link in that both the extreme supply-side view and the gold-standard view are rebellious against what had become the conventional moderate conservatism of the postwar period. In any case, many of the people most identified with the supply-side movement were also leaders in the effort to establish a gold standard.

The rise of interest rates in the fall of 1981 and the apparent sinking of the economy into recession was commonly regarded as a challenge to the supply-side argument. A large part of the supply-side budget program had been put into effect, and the economy was not responding in the positive way that the country had been led to expect. This was widely considered to reflect a failure of the supply-side theory.

With some justification the supply-siders could deny that their theory had been tested, as has been explained on p. 276. This response of the supply-siders did not, however, dispel the impression that the theory had failed. Certainly, the supply-siders had given no warning that the fiscal program adopted would still leave the country with several years of high unemployment and high interest rates to live through before the benefits of the program would be seen. In fact, the supply-siders had positively rejected such warnings.

Being thus on the defensive, the supply-siders found revival of the argument for gold a great convenience. The trouble in the economy, they maintained, was due to deficiencies of monetary policy which could be cured by return to the gold standard. The basic problem was lack of confidence in the steady conduct of a noninflationary monetary policy. After fifteen years of bad experience, no one would believe that the Federal Reserve could be relied upon to stick to a noninflationary course. Even if the Federal Reserve were determined to do so, there was no possible rule for the control of the quantity of "money" that would keep the economy on a noninflationary path. The financial system was exceedingly resourceful in creating uncontrolled substitutes for whatever kind of money the Federal Reserve chose to control, so the Fed could never know that its control of the designated "money" would actually serve to control inflation. In 1981 the depth of this problem was demonstrated by enormous growth of money market mutual funds, in which shareholders could hold assets with a degree of safety, liquidity and transferability that was hardly different from bank deposits.

Its supporters argued that gold would solve both of these problems, the problems of credibility and controllability. Once back on the gold standard the government could be counted on to stay there, because abandoning it would be a conspicuous and shocking action that a government would not want to undertake except in highly unusual situations. Moreover, the requirement that the government stabilize the price of gold would be a guide to monetary policy which escaped the difficulties of determining the proper quantity and definition of "money." If prices were tending to rise, people would want to convert their money, of whatever kind, into gold, and that would reduce the quantity of money to whatever degree was necessary to eliminate the expectation of inflation. The fact that people no longer wanted to exchange money for gold would by itself show that enough money had been withdrawn to eliminate the expectation of inflation. So there would be a device which would automatically signal the increases or decreases of the supply of money needed to keep the price level stable.

A stage for playing out the debate over gold was provided by the Gold Commission, established in 1981 pursuant to legislation enacted in 1980, of which Senator Jesse Helms had been the chief sponsor. The commission included representatives of the Congress, the administration, the Federal Reserve and the public at large. Although only a few members of the commission had a prior commitment to gold, they were, as is often the case, more zealous in the advocacy of their positions than people on the more conventional side. Moreover, there was in the background the President, known to have a certain leaning toward gold. So, the outcome of the commission's investigation was in doubt, and there seemed to be a real possibility that it might have recommended a "little bit" of gold standard. But in the end the concession to the gold enthusiasts was trivial—a recommendation that the Treasury issue a gold piece of defined weight but selling at the market price, so that there was no implication of a commitment to stabilize the price of gold. The commission's report laid to rest for all practical purposes and for the time being the question of a return to the gold standard.[6]

This left the supply-siders in need of an alternative monetary policy that would make supply-side theory work, or to the lack of which they could attribute its apparent failure to work. There was a certain flirtation with the idea of "commodity money," meaning that the government would undertake to stabilize the composite price of a basket of homogeneous products—like oil, wheat, tin, etc., possibly also including gold. This is an idea that has been floating around economics for at least sixty years, but it found no takers, essentially having the excess simplicity of gold without the aura. Attention of this school then shifted to the idea that monetary policy should be addressed to stabilizing interest rates, rather than meeting any target for the quantity of money. This was the last expression of the effort to substitute a price rule for a quantity rule of monetary policy. However, by the time this point was reached the original anti-inflation intent had been totally perverted. It was plausible to think that stabilizing the price of gold would tend to stabilize the price level because there would be a tendency for the price of gold to rise when the price level was rising and the rules of the gold standard would then require the monetary authority to sell gold and draw money out of circulation. But the relations would be reversed in a policy of interest-rate stabilization. Interest rates would tend to rise in a period of inflation, and an effort to resist the rise of interest rates by expanding the money supply would only make the inflation worse.

The transformation of the gold price stabilization doctrine into an interest rate stabilization doctrine brought this branch of "conservative" thinking into harmony, at least for the moment, with conventional "liberal" views of monetary policy. In the liberal view the emphasis on the quantity of money was always a mistake, and monetary policy should have concentrated on the management of interest rates, since it is through interest rates that monetary policy affects the economy. The application of this principle in 1981–1982 was that the money supply should be increased more rapidly in order to lower interest rates, which were the main obstacle to the recovery. (Interest rate policy almost always means policy to reduce interest rates. It is hard to think of occasions when people who want to manage interest rates wanted to manage them up.) Some of the more sophisticated or self-conscious proponents of this view in 1981–1982, aware that a proposal to increase monetary growth looked like a proposal to accelerate inflation, proposed that the monetary expansion be accompanied by a tighter budget. The usual prescription was to raise the revenue, offsetting or undoing some of the tax cut made in 1981. The proportions in which the easier money was to be accompanied by the tighter budget were never specified, and the impression was unavoidable that the mixture was intended to, or would, result in a faster rate of increase of total spending and at least the risk of more inflation.

Another kind of criticism of the prevailing monetary policy came from the conventional, rigorous monetarists, the disciples of Milton Friedman, who were to be found in the Treasury and the Council of Economic Advisers as well as in the academic branch of the economics profession. From time to time they seemed to be saying that the general trend of monetary policy was too restrictive, and that the Federal Reserve should be allowing money to rise more rapidly, or at least should be slowing down its growth more gradually. But this was an uncongenial position for them, since they had been preaching for so long about the inflationary bias of the Federal Reserve. Their more natural argument was to emphasize the damage done by the short-run oscillations of monetary growth around its trend, while accepting the trend as appropriate. Their evidence for the view was only then beginning to be developed and had not yet been subject to critical analysis.[7]

These deviant views, expressed by their supporters with so much confidence, provided little guidance for the Federal Reserve in the conduct of a disinflationary monetary policy. The notion that the path of monetary policy would not matter for the real economy—for output and employment—if the path were well understood by the private sector gave little comfort. It did seem to matter in 1981 and 1983, and if that might be disregarded as too short a period to deserve much attention, responsible officials could not take that position. Perhaps the problem was that the intentions of the Federal Reserve and the determination and ability of the Federal Reserve to carry out its intentions were not sufficiently believed in. But this only translated the difficulty into the realm of the creation of credibility; it did not eliminate the difficulty. The various price rules for monetary policy—gold or sensitive commodity prices—had little political support or analytical validity, and the interest rate rule had more political support but even less validity.

Monetarism was the Mother Church from which the monetary policy of 1979–1982 derived its inspiration, but that inspiration was not a rule of conduct. Monetarism said that the way to keep the rate of inflation low and stable was to keep the rate of increase of the money supply low and stable. It did not say that the rate of increase of the money supply should "never" change, in response to a change in financial institutions, or in the demand for money, or in the behavior of the real economy. It only said that the rate of increase of the money supply should "hardly ever" change, and should only change in the light of strong evidence of the need to change it. And monetarism did not say how strong that evidence would have to be. Also of great importance for 1979–1983 policy, monetarism did not prescribe a path for getting from a position of high inflation to one of reasonable price stability. It might say that the rate of growth of the money supply, which was about 8 percent per annum in 1979, should be reduced to, say, 2 percent. But it didn't say whether that reduction should occur in one year or in three or in five. It didn't say whether that reduction should be at a steady pace or should be faster at first or slower at first.

But these questions which monetarism didn't answer were precisely those which bedeviled policy in 1981 and even more in 1982 and 1983. The Federal Reserve until mid-1982 was following the prescription of reducing the rate of growth of the money supply. This was at least contributing to the decline of the inflation rate. It was also contributing, as an inevitable by-product, to a rise of unemployment. But was all of this going at the right pace? This question was usually raised with concern for the possibility that the growth of the money supply was too slow and was causing unnecessary increases of unemployment, high interest rates and risk of financial catastrophe. Each year the Federal Reserve had established target ranges for the growth of the money supply, and indicated its intention to keep the money supply, or various definitions of it, within the specified ranges. This was a "monetarist" kind of action, indicating a wish to let the private sector know in advance what the monetary policy would be and to resist the temptation to respond to every shift in the economic statistics. But this did not imply that the Federal Reserve would not run outside of the target range if the financial markets or the real economy developed in ways that provided strong evidence of the need to do so. And the Federal Reserve would be continually faced with the question whether the evidence was strong enough.

This question became acute in the summer of 1982, when the unemployment rate in the United States reached 10 percent and numerous financial institutions at home and countries abroad encountered serious financial difficulties which seemed to threaten much more serious difficulties for the U.S. economy. In fact, the Federal Reserve after June allowed the money supply to rise far above its target range. There were various explanations of this from the Fed, and many interpretations from outside observers, but the most common and probably correct interpretation was that, however monetarist Fed policy might have been after 1979, it was now, at least for a time, less so. But where monetary policy would go next, and how long its deviation might last, remained uncertain.

The turn of monetary policy in mid-1982, joined with the budget developments, signaled the end of Reagan campaign economics. Tax cuts were no longer relied upon to raise revenue. Balancing the budget was not confidently promised for any visible date. The administration seemed to be near the bottom of the barrel of practically, politically viable expenditure cuts. The instantaneous adjustment to disinflation which would avoid unemployment had not occurred. The gold standard had been rejected. And now we seemed to be leaving behind what there had been of steady monetary growth.

But if this was the end of Reagan campaign economics, it was not necessarily the end of conservative economics. The difficulties of Reagan economics did not mean that there was a "liberal" economics waiting in the wings that would solve our national problems. The country needed a new economic policy, and that would have to include a contribution from the conservative side.

9

Toward a New Consensus

BY 1983 THE CONSERVATIVE TURN in economic policy, begun in the Carter-Volcker administration and sharpened in the Reagan-Volcker administration, had a good deal to show. The inflation rate had fallen sharply. Defense spending was on an accelerating path. There had been important changes in the tax structure, including the reduction of the top marginal rate of individual income tax and the increase of allowances for depreciation of business capital. The rise of the total tax burden had been slowed down, and one step had been taken, indexing of the personal income tax, to prevent its future increase. The increase of nondefense spending had been restrained. There had been a few significant moves to reduce government regulation, notably with respect to energy.

But there had been no radical Reagan revolution. Total taxes and total expenditures were still as large as ever, relative to the GNP, and there was no prospect of any significant reduction for years ahead. Budget deficits, present and projected, were extraordinarily large. In fact, at the time the most distinctive feature of Reagan economic policy—aside from its language—was

307

the size of its budget deficits. The country was as far as ever, possibly farther, from having any agreed rules of fiscal policy that would limit particular spending and taxing decisions. There had been little movement toward establishing a predictable monetary policy. The pace of deregulation had been disappointing to its enthusiasts, and there had been some setbacks, notably protectionist moves with respect to steel, automobiles, and some other products.

Moreover, there was no sign in 1983 that a Reagan revolution lay ahead, or even that the trend was in the conservative direction. Indeed, there was a considerable possibility of turning in the opposite direction. The decline of inflation had been achieved in part at the expense of a serious recession. There was question about the willingness of the country to tolerate the slow pace of recovery that would prevent revival of inflation. Whether the country would be willing to pay the costs of the defense program as they increased was also in doubt; the President had already had to accept a cutback in his program. Even the administration was agreeable to a tax increase at some time in the future. After the 1982 elections it was very doubtful that the political tide was running toward the conservatives. The Democratic gains in the House of Representatives may have been no more than usual for the opposition in an off-year election. But if there was to be a Reagan revolution it should have been confirmed by Republican gains, as the Roosevelt revolution had been confirmed by the Democratic gains in 1934. Although the Republicans held to their majority in the Senate in the 1982 elections, the Senate Republicans were obviously becoming more independent of the President and more responsive to their own moderate leaders.

The basic reason why there was no Reagan radical conservative revolution in economic policy was that the 1980 election did not constitute a mandate for such a revolution. A small fraction of Reagan supporters claimed that there was indeed such a mandate. They complained bitterly that the administration was betraying its mandate, when it accepted tax increases in 1982, for example, and blamed that on moderate fellow travelers who had infiltrated the White House and kept Reagan from being Reagan. But in fact there was no such mandate.

Reagan did not have much of a mandate of any kind. Although he got 489 out of 538 electoral votes in 1980 he received only 51 percent of the total vote. He did not carry in a Republican Congress to help implement his program. The vote he did get was certainly in substantial part a tribute to his personal charm and even more to the general perception of Carter's personal inadequacy. Insofar as the vote reflected issues at all, there were issues other than economics that influenced many voters. Feelings about national security and status, intensified by the Iran hostage crisis, and the various "social" issues—abortion, school prayer, etc.—were important. But even where economics was concerned, Reagan's mandate was not to follow any specifically conservative policies or any specific policies at all. His mandate was to make things better. Reagan ran, like all challengers, on the negative proposition—that conditions were not satisfactory. No demonstration was needed that he would actually improve conditions.

Reagan's 1980 campaign promise was to reduce inflation, reduce taxes, reduce government spending and reduce government regulation. But it was not a promise to reduce inflation by increasing unemployment, to reduce taxes by increasing the government deficit, to reduce government spending by cutting benefits or to reduce regulation by increasing pollution. That would, at least arguably, have been a defensible conservative agenda. If Reagan had been elected on such promises he would clearly have had a mandate. But he was not. He had a mandate to provide a free lunch, or as used to be said in more agrarian days, a late fall and an early spring. And that is no mandate at all, because it is not a mandate to make any of the choices which must be made. He might as well have promised to fly from the top of the Washington Monument to the dome of the Capitol, unaided.

Mr. Reagan was known, of course, to be an ideological conservative, just as Mr. Carter was known to be a born-again Christian. But what that implied or promised in a President was unclear in any case. It didn't tell what a President would feel compelled to do when confronted with a specific problem.

What Mr. Reagan received in 1980 was not a mandate but an opportunity. He had an opportunity to try to create the radical conservative revolution from the commanding heights of the White House, and he might have succeeded.

There were several ways in which President Reagan might have brought about the conservative revolution once he was in the White House, even if his election was not a mandate for the revolution. One would have been to achieve the appearance of success. In his early days, during his presidential honeymoon, he had the opportunity to put into place distinctive policies, and to some extent he did. He got the big tax cut, for example, he made a number of expenditure cuts, and he deregulated oil prices. If such policies had been associated with the general feeling of improvement of the economy they might have become regarded as the way to go and still further steps in the same direction would have been accepted. It would not have been necessary that the policies actually succeed. We do not yet know whether Roosevelt's policies actually succeeded, but they acquired the appearance of success, and that was sufficient.

By and large the Reagan policies did not at first obtain the appearance of success. They were accompanied or followed by high unemployment, high interest rates and higher budget deficits. The positive accomplishments—mainly with respect to inflation—were insufficient when compared with the claims and promises the Reagan team had made. After the first few months, Reagan economics never had the momentum of success behind it. By 1983 there were signs that the economy was performing better. But by then it was at least as convincing to attribute that to the retreat from Reagan economics as to Reagan economics in its initial, pure form.

Even if Reagan economics was not working in the short run, the President might have used the early influence of his office, the desire of the public for a change and its willingness to give the new President a chance, all fortified by his personal popularity, to take steps that would fasten conservative economic policy irreversibly upon the country. Some of the Reagan supporters clearly had this idea. That explains the desire for constitutional amendments like the proposed amendment requiring the budget to be balanced or setting a limit to government expenditures. The rationale was that one could not count on the ordinary political process to keep the budget in balance or confine spending within limits but that it might be possible in the Reagan honeymoon to supersede the ordinary political process forever by amendment of the Constitution. Milton and Rose Friedman had a catalogue of seven constitutional amendments they proposed that would establish conservative (or free market) economics as the law of the land despite future political backsliding.[1]

There were other possibilities that might have had similar effects. For example, the idea of establishing the gold standard was to make a once-and-for-all step which would remove monetary policy from the control of human, and possibly "liberal," monetary authorities. Less extreme institutional changes were also designed to make difficult future reversal of Reagan's initiatives. For example, abolishing the Departments of Energy and Education would remove bureaucracies that would always be a force demanding more regulation and more money.

But the Reagan administration did only a little in this direction. Introducing indexing in the personal income tax reduced a built-in tendency for revenues to rise, a rise which generates a built-in tendency for expenditures to rise. The complete termination of oil price controls probably will be difficult to reverse. But there was little radical institutional change. One reason was that the effort to achieve such change conflicted with the administration's short-run objectives. The balanced-budget amendment was the leading example. Even before Ronald Reagan came into office, over thirty states had adopted resolutions calling for a convention to adopt such an amendment. This seemed to be the durable change in economic policy most likely to be adopted. The President placed great emphasis on it in argument during 1982 and the Senate did support it, but the House of Representatives did not. But by 1983 the idea was, if not dead, indefinitely postponed. The President no longer mentioned it. The idea was postponed because the President was unable to propose any combination of expenditures and revenues that would bring the budget close to balance even after five years, so that it would have looked extremely insincere to propose putting a straitjacket on his successors while he was disporting himself so freely with large deficits.

But the administration had put itself in that position, mainly by the big tax cut. Without the tax cut the Reagan budget would have been much closer to balance and the proposal for a constitutional requirement to balance the budget would have been much more believable. There would have been evidence that Reagan was willing to accept severe limitations on his own freedom of action for the sake of a permanent change that would limit the freedom of governments in the future. But this option was not perceived, or, if perceived, not accepted.

There were people, who thought that the big tax cut itself was the revolution, or at least a shot in the revolution. They believed that reducing the revenue sharply would force a sharp change of attitude toward government spending and a reversal of its upward trend—which they regarded as the key element of the revolution. But that was not a reliable expectation and in fact turned out to be true to only a limited degree. Congress proved willing to run a large deficit and also, though more reluctantly, to raise taxes.

There was, thus, this difference between the Roosevelt revolution and the Reagan would-be revolution. The Roosevelt revolution was incorporated in statutes, programs and agencies that were not subject to annual reconsideration and that developed constituencies—bureaucracies and beneficiaries—that resisted counterrevolution. The Reagan changes were changes in numbers, mainly budget numbers, that are the subject of redetermination every year. They would not have the lasting effect that the Roosevelt changes had.

A basic difficulty may impede the achievement of a radical conservative revolution. Such a revolution would be a sharp change toward limiting the role of government. But a revolution can hardly be engineered from outside the government, and even conservative governments when in office do not want to limit their own powers. So the radical conservative revolution is the dream of conservatives out of office, but not the practice of conservatives in office.

If unable or unwilling to take the steps that would establish a durable conservative revolution during his time in office, a President might be able to use the "bully pulpit" of his office to change national thinking in a way that would permit a future conservative revolution or evolution. In fact, President Reagan did not do that. The notion of the "bully pulpit" is much over-rated. Presidents have an excellent vantage point from which to preach to the people. They rarely, however, use this opportunity to try to change popular conceptions or values. Rather they take those conceptions or values for granted and try to show that they, or their programs, are most in conformity with what the public already thinks and wants.

Reagan was no exception to this. He did not try to preach the real conservative doctrine that there is no free lunch, and that while conservative economics would yield beneficial results in the long run there would be some costs to be paid by some in the short run. As difficulties appeared—mainly in the form of unemployment—President Reagan had to abandon his earlier position that all good things were simultaneously possible and to begin telling the people that there was no "quick fix." But by that time the proposition that there was no quick fix looked like a politically motivated effort to escape blame. It did not have the educational value, or the credibility, that it might have had if it had been said when there was a risk in saying it.

Perhaps that is the key to the failure of Mr. Reagan and of Presidents generally to use the bully pulpit to change people's minds. To change people's minds it is necessary to say things that people do not already believe and to explain why what they formerly believed was wrong. This is a risk few politicians want to take. Mr. Reagan as the Great Communicator was skillful at pressing the conservative buttons that were already there in the American mentality. He was not much concerned with changing the liberal buttons or installing new conservative ones.

So, there was not to be a radical conservative revolution in economic policy during the Reagan administration. The country did not need that or want it, and the Reagan team itself, once in office, did not strive to accomplish it. But this did not mean that the conservative movement in economic policy was over. The problems which had turned the country in that direction even in the Carter administration remained, and so did the opportunity to seek the support of the American people. What was required was a conservative policy that realistically promised to solve the problems and that could be explained to the electorate with a reasonable possibility of being approved. In other words, the operational and understandable features of the conservative policy still had to be developed.

Despite the failures of Reagan economics the liberal alternatives were not promising and did not seem to generate any enthusiasm in public opinion. These liberal alternatives had two main ingredients. One of these was basically Kennedy-Johnson-Humphrey economics. That meant first of all expansionist demand-management policies accompanied by incomes policies to prevent inflation. Again, as in the past, expansion of demand would be relied upon both to achieve high employment and to promote strong long-term growth of productivity. Some of the cuts in social programs would be undone—food stamps, educational assistance, etc.—and some social programs would be introduced or expanded—catastrophic medical insurance, for example. Taxes would be raised again, mainly by closing "loopholes" of greatest value to middle-income and upper-income people. The regulations installed in the 1970s, especially environmental and safety regulations, would be more rigorously applied. Defense spending would be slowed down.

This standard brand of liberalism had changed in several "conservative" ways since the mid-1970s, under the impact of events and argument. In general it was less ambitious. Notions of the goal for the reduction of unemployment were more moderate—something like 6 percent being accepted as satisfactory—and more concern was expressed about inflationary dangers. The pace at which new spending programs were being invented had slowed down, most liberal requirements for an issue on that front now being satisfied by resistance to the Reagan cuts. New emphasis was placed on the evils of budget deficits, which was easy since the deficits could be blamed on Reagan's defense program and tax cuts.

This movement of the mainstream liberals held out the hope of achieving a consensus with the mainstream conservatives—the pre- and post-Reagan conservatives. That was important in itself. The country needed a more stable and predictable economic policy and that would be more achievable if the gap between the dominant wings of the political array was not great.

But still, despite these changes of attitude, the standard brand of liberalism retained the seeds of its old inadequacies and evils. It still called upon the country to entrust the powers of government to the wisdom and goodwill of a group of people who promised to deliver all good things, but especially high employment and "fairness," meaning income redistribution. That is, it was still undisciplined, still devoid of guidelines and limits. The main implication of this was too much danger of inflation. All the old mistakes which had contributed to the inflation remained. There had to be a numerical goal for unemployment, and while the number now accepted was higher than previously no one could be sure that it was an uninflationary number. Moreover, unless the idea of a numerical goal was rejected, political competition would almost certainly lead to promises to achieve a goal which would be inflationary. Also, the standard liberal doctrine accepted an inflation rate of 5 or 6 percent and had no interest in getting the rate down further. This was not a sign of strong determination to end inflation. And what would be needed, if inflation was to be reduced and held down, would be a general belief in the strength of the government's determination to accomplish that.

The liberal approach to inflation relied heavily upon the notion that there is in reserve an incomes policy that will directly restrain price and wage increases even if conditions in the markets would tend spontaneously to cause such increases. It is this reliance which leads to the belief that no great cost in unemployment ever has to be borne, even temporarily, to control inflation. But there is much experience to show that this belief seduces governments into overly expansive monetary policies, creating inflationary pressures that temporary or voluntary incomes policies cannot withstand. This strategy then leads to another wave of inflation or, worse, to long-continued, mandatory, comprehensive controls, which would be extremely debilitating to the economy.

By the early 1980s the standard brand of liberalism had come to assign much more importance to monetary policy than it had done earlier. But it had not accepted any rules for the conduct of monetary policy except that the monetary authorities should do their best, in view of their perception of all the conditions in the economy, to achieve the best combination of economic goals. This freewheeling attitude to monetary policy was the necessary counterpart of the commitment to a preset goal for unemployment, which has already been mentioned. It was also the engine that would create the inflation that the approach made probable.

By the early 1980s the standard brand of liberalism had left behind its primitive Keynesian ideas of functional finance—of a budget policy exclusively determined by the requirement of meeting a known goal of "full employment." But that left the guiding principle of liberal fiscal policy quite unclear. Many liberals, both economists and politicians, discovered during the Reagan administration that they were greatly alarmed by the size of the actual and prospective budget deficits. Economists maintained that the large present and prospective deficits were contributing to the recession—or at least, they maintained that view while the economy was in recession, especially in 1982. This was not only a departure from previous liberal doctrine, it was a reversal of that doctrine. The liberal argument against deficits began to look like the former conservative argument against deficits—mainly a cover for opposition to particular expenditures and taxes. The liberals tried to mobilize what they believed was a popular fear of budget deficits in support of their desire to cut the Reagan defense program and to restore some of the taxes on business and upper-income people that had been cut in the Reagan program. Whether they had a commitment to balanced budgets or small deficits which would make them willing to limit expenditure increases of a kind they liked was in doubt. They did not seem to have a theory or policy for determining the acceptable size of budget deficits that they could live with or that the private economy could count on.

Thus the standard brand of liberalism by the 1980s was neither intellectually satisfying nor politically appealing. It still retained most of the features of the Humphrey-Carter economics that were associated with the dismal economic performance of the 1970s and that, moreover, by then had become banal. Insofar as it incorporated departures from this earlier orthodoxy they were pale imitations of old-fashioned conservatism, for which the liberals were not credible champions.

Aware of the insufficiency of their standard doctrine, liberals began after the 1980 election to look for an alternative or supplementary economic policy. What emerged was a new strategy, or slogan, called "high technology" or "industrial policy." Insofar as this idea emerged from anything more than the political need for a new slogan it was stimulated by two observations. Within the United States, employment and output were sluggish or declining in older American industries—such as steel and automobiles—but rising within certain newer industries, mainly connected with electronics. At the same time output of these newer industries was rising elsewhere, notably in Japan, and so were U.S. imports of these high-tech products.

These observations led to several conclusions.

1. The United States economy would benefit from the shift of more resources to high-tech industries. There would be less unemployment, more income per hour and less inflation.

2. This shift would not occur under present policies.

3. This shift should be promoted by policies which encouraged investment and enterprise in general, such as reduction of the budget deficit and of business taxes, in the expectation that market processes would direct the investment and enterprise to

those industries in which the private gains were greatest and those would also be the industries in which the social gains were greatest.

4. The shift to high-tech industries should be promoted by policies which promoted high tech in general—such as government financing of research or technical education. This would not require the government to select particular industries or particular firms for promotion.

5. Private markets would not effectively select the industries that would contribute most to national economic growth. Therefore the government should select these—presumably, high-tech—industries and promote their development by subsidies, loans, protection against import competition or in other ways.

It was the last of these points that constituted the new "liberal" look in economic policy. The others, whether or not valid, were not particularly alien to conservative thinking. In fact, President Reagan absorbed the first four of these ideas. The last point, the central selection and promotion of "winners"—the industries that would be the carriers of growth—was the 1980s version of a theme that recurs in American thinking about economic policy. That is the need for a "plan." This notion had been prominent in the New Deal, in the early Kennedy days of fascination with French indicative planning, and in the 1975–1978 period when Humphrey-Javits and Humphrey-Hawkins bills were under discussion. The planning idea never got very far with the American public, who were prepared to welcome government regulation in any specific case but who reacted against the idea of a comprehensive plan, which seemed theoretical and Rube Goldberg-like. The high-tech version might be more popular, however, because it seemed more specific and involved the image of hard science (engineering, physics) rather than soft science (economics, sociology).

But the fact is that "industrial policy" had little to offer. With respect to most of the problems besetting the American economy, it was almost totally irrelevant. It would do nothing about inflation and almost nothing about unemployment. On this latter point there was much confusion. People saw, via television or otherwise, that there was little unemployment in cities and towns that produced personal computers or video games and they thought that there would be less unemployment nationally if more cities and towns produced such high-tech products. But all the unemployed could not be employed to produce high-tech products, and it was not necessary for any of them to produce such products in order to get unemployment reduced. At the existing prices there was a certain market for high-tech products, and if more was produced in Lowell, Massachusetts, less would be produced in San Antonio, Texas. If the price of these products could be reduced, more of them would be sold, which might or might not increase employment in their production. That would depend on how the price was reduced; if that was done by increasing productivity, employment would not rise if the productivity increase exceeded the output increase. But even if employment increased in the high-tech industries, total employment might not increase. The effect on total employment would depend on whether the purchase of additional high-tech products was a substitute for other purchases. And if total employment could be increased by, for example, subsidizing the output of high-tech products, it might be equally possible to increase employment by subsidizing the output of anything else.

Countries with low productivity or slowly growing productivity can have full employment without inflation—just as well as countries with high productivity or rapidly rising productivity. What happens to employment in these cases will depend on what happens to wages. A country with low productivity and high real wages will have high unemployment, because it will not pay to hire all the workers. A country with high productivity and still higher real wages will also have high unemployment, and for the same reason. If there is a mechanism, either in the private markets or by government controls, that keeps real wage demands from exceeding productivity there will be high employment, whether productivity is high or low. If there is no such mechanism an effort to make productivity keep up with wages is hopeless, because even the most effective policy can change productivity only little and slowly, compared with possible changes of wages.

A similar point must be made about inflation. If the growth of demand is kept moderate by monetary and fiscal policy, there will be no inflation even if productivity rises slowly. And if demand is not kept from rising rapidly, no productivity-stimulating policy can prevent inflation.

Where high-tech policy could make a difference is in real wages and real incomes. If high-tech policy could direct more of the nation's resources of labor and capital into industries with high and rising productivity than would result without such policy, it could make real wages and incomes higher and more rapidly rising than they would otherwise be. The question is whether high-tech policy would do that. There already is a powerful force tending to direct resources into uses where their productivity is high. That is the incentive of the owners of the resources—workers and investors—to maximize their incomes by using them in a productive way. This force has been highly effective. It has been a major element in a process that gave the United States the highest average per capita income in the world. Although the rate of productivity growth had slowed down in the 1970s, there was no evidence that this was due to a weakening of this private productivity-seeking force.

This is not to deny that government has played an important role in the American growth process, by such general means as the provision of education, research, roads, etc. It has also made a contribution to the development of particular industries, such as agriculture, which turned out to be a contribution to national economic development. To be skeptical about high-tech policy does not imply rejection of the function of government to create general conditions conducive to economic growth, or in *exceptional* cases to promote a particular industry.

But this is not what high-tech policy or "industrial policy" means as a serious entry in the discussion of national economic policies. What these words mean is more comprehensive surveillance of the industrial distribution of the national resources and a more positive federal policy to guide the distribution of resources in order to accelerate growth. If high-tech policy does not mean that, it may be acceptable but no strong claims can be made for it as a novel approach that will significantly change and improve the performance of the American economy. Viewed in its more radical aspect, high-tech policy is unpromising for two reasons. There is no reason to think that the government officials making the decisions will be intellectually more capable than the private people who would otherwise make the decisions. There is every reason to think the contrary. The private people will be closer to the conditions and opportunities and will know more about them; risking their own resources, they will be more highly motivated to learn as much as possible, and the market will tend to select out those private people who are most capable of making decisions and to attract the most capable people because the rewards are greater. Even more important, in fact, the government's decisions will be less single-mindedly devoted to the increase of productivity because the government decision-makers have less to gain personally from the increase of productivity and more to gain from devoting the programs to their personal political advantages. Experience with government economic development programs for depressed regions, with small-business-assistance programs and with tariff protection demonstrates, what should be obvious *a priori,* the dominant influence of personal or regional political considerations. Thus, even if it were likely that sophisticated government bureaucrats could out-think the market in discovering where resources should go, it would be extremely unlikely that the political decisions would conform to these scientific findings.

"Industrial policy" was to the liberals of 1983 what supply-side economics was to the conservatives of 1980—attractive because it promises more of everything but without any grounds for fulfilling the promise.

A New Consensus

The failure of the Reagan administration to inaugurate a radical right revolution in economic policy and the obvious inadequacy

of the liberal approaches in either their Johnson-Humphrey standard version or in the newer high-tech version reveal the vacuum
which exists in economic policy. The old postwar consensus had
been carried too far—into too much expansion of demand, too
much spending and taxing and too much regulation—by the time
of President Carter. But Reaganism was more a shriek of horror
than a program for solving real problems. It did not make use of
the opportunity to find better solutions, but the opportunity and
the need remain.

There is no logical necessity for these solutions to be "conservative." The important thing is to find policies that have a reasonable chance of improving the performance of the economy
and also of being acceptable to a sufficient range of interests and
opinions. From the latter standpoint, pure or extreme conservatism is not a promising route, even if, as does not seem likely
anyway, it contains all the truth. But still the lessons of experience and economic analysis will cause the new consensus, if one
is achieved, to differ from that of the 1960s and 1970s in many
respects that may be called conservative. The new consensus
would place more weight on restraining inflation and less on generating full employment by expansionary means, more on promoting economic growth and less on redistributing the available
output among industries, more on monetary policy and less on
fiscal policy for stabilization of the economy, more on markets
and less on government regulation.

Probably a great many people who once considered themselves liberals, and some who still do, would agree with this general prescription. But as was seen in the last two years of the
Carter administration and in the early years of the Reagan administration, translating these general leanings into a specific
policy is difficult. It is intellectually difficult and politically difficult. That is not surprising, of course. If it were easy it would already have been done. The intellectual difficulty is that economists
do not know enough even to say with much confidence and pre-
cision what the effects of different economic policies would be.
Even if one is able to describe what effects are desired he cannot
be sure of the prescription of policy that would yield those ef-

fects. The political difficulty is that even if it were possible to identify the policy that would be best, or probably best, from the standpoint of most of the persons concerned, it might not be possible to get that policy adopted. The best policy for most is unlikely to be the best policy for all, and those who would lose from the best policy may be able to prevent its adoption. This becomes obvious if many of the people who would gain from the best policy are still unborn and therefore unable to influence the decision.

These difficulties must be recognized in an effort to improve or develop national economic policy. It is not sufficient or even very helpful to lay out "ideal" programs as if their ideal character could be objectively demonstrated and as if their implementation could be confidently expected once they had been promulgated. There is a need first of all to try to learn more. That is a slow process, however, and the world cannot wait for its completion. Policies must be developed that take account of our ignorance and uncertainties, and which provide assurance against catastrophe even if they do not guarantee optimum results. That is what prudence means. Even about that we will be uncertain and there will be different views about what is prudent. There must be an effort to reconcile these views, and to reach a compromise if that fails. "Compromise" is a bad word in some contexts, but agreement on policy is important for the sake of stability and predictability. Compromise may be the only way to achieve that. Otherwise policy can oscillate uncertainly and violently between different views in response to election results that may not indicate a need or popular desire for change. Stability of an agreed-upon policy may be more important than the selection of the particular policy.

The search for a policy is a search for rules or principles or guidelines and procedures which will restrain the political bias toward short-run and special interests. The basic assumption is that it is possible to get general assent to rules and procedures believed to be in the long-run national interest even by individuals or groups who recognize that these rules and procedures will sometimes prevent them from pursuing their own perceived interest. There have been such rules in the past, such as the rule that required the government to balance its budget or the rule that required the government to stand ready to convert its money into gold. These rules turned out, in the end, not to be in the long-run national interest and they did not survive. But for a considerable period they did limit and discipline the behavior of governments and therefore of the groups that had political power.

The balanced-budget and gold-standard rules originated spontaneously sometime in the distant past and were preserved by the respect paid to tradition. They were not the product of deliberate decisions. Perhaps it is not possible to create rules of policy by discussion and conscious agreement. If so, we are destined to be governed by accident and by the shifting balance of political power among competing interests. But I do not believe that is inevitable. There have been times when, driven by a feeling of national crisis, decision-makers in and out of government did carry on a responsible discussion which led to useful consensus. Conditions call for an effort to do that today.

We are not having such a discussion. Although there is much talk about economic policy, there is no debate. People say what they have always believed, or what they find it convenient to say, but there is no confrontation of the arguments. There is no effort to find the sources of disagreement or to reach agreement, perhaps because the participants think that the effort to change minds and reach agreement is hopeless. Talk about economic policy has become only a way of rallying one's own troops.

Discussion by economists is either incomprehensible or incredible—incomprehensible because conducted in a language that few but experts can understand or incredible because so obviously partisan that no one can take it seriously. The Employment Act of 1946, which established the President's Council of Economic Advisers and the Congressional Joint Economic Committee, was supposed to bring economic science into the political process. Whether or not it has succeeded in that, it has certainly brought politics into economics. It has helped to raise up a cadre of economists whose association with government—experienced in the past or hoped for in the future—gives their views a strong partisan cast. And these are the economists who get attention in the media, because they are believed to be important. This conveys the impression to the public that economic argument consists entirely of briefs for one or another political party.

Private institutions show little desire to break out of this superficial, ritual, parochial mold of economic discussion. There was a time when private institutions behaved more open-mindedly and constructively. I have already described some of these conditions in Chapter II. Around the end of World War II the businessmen of the Committee for Economic Development exposed themselves to both Keynesianism and Chicago classical free market economics. The National Planning Association worked to find the areas of constructive agreement among representatives of business, labor, agriculture and the general public. The American Economic Association organized group efforts to produce statements on major issues of policy that could be communicated to Congress. Nothing like that goes on today. The action-oriented institutions concentrate on promoting the immediate and parochial interests of their members. It is symptomatic that the most prominent business organization today, the Business Roundtable, is short on research and public discussion but long on lobbying. Thinking is relegated to "think tanks" where like-minded people gather together to comfort each other. The calendar is full of conferences of people with diverse views, but the last thing that happens at such conferences is any "conferring"—any more than the bears and the elephants at a zoo may be said to confer with each other because they are on the same ground.

One would hope that the needed discussion would arise spontaneously in the country in response to the evident uncertainties and inadequacies of economic policy. As this does not seem to be happening, the process might be stimulated by an initiative in Congress. The Congressional debate over what became the Employment Act of 1946 forced an exploration of the limits of possible agreement on goals, instruments and procedures of economic policy. Attention was focused on large issues, and the national mood of concern about the economy forced the participants to try to make a constructive contribution.

Congressional consideration of a significant revision of the Employment Act of 1946 could precipitate a new serious and possibly constructive debate over economic policy. The Employment Act of 1946 was enacted in an atmosphere of obsession with the unemployment problem and naive confidence in the ability of macroeconomic policy, mainly fiscal policy, to solve the problem. The act served to improve economic policy, on the whole, for a considerable period. But it is now irrelevant or misleading in the light of our current problems and understanding. The attempt to revise it would require an attempt to formulate in a realistic and precise way what should now be the objectives and procedures of economic policy, especially of fiscal and monetary policy. Although revision of the act is not strictly necessary for reform of policy, a new synthesis arrived at by national discussion is necessary, and revising the act can be a way to force that discussion.

The following suggestions for reforming economic policy are offered as a contribution to the needed discussion. They are not offered as the only or final solutions for our problems. They are put forward to help advance the discussion, not to end it. I am not under the illusion that I know what the best answers are or that if I did know them that would be the end of the matter. Second-best answers on which we agree may be more valuable than first-best answers on which we don't agree.

Inflation

The great economic trauma of the 1970s was inflation. That more than anything else created the feeling of anxiety about the economy, the dissatisfaction with the existing management of policy and the demand for a change. It was primarily the fact that the old course, inaugurated under Roosevelt, had led into an acceleration of inflation that signaled the end of that course.

Economists for a long time belittled the common hysteria about inflation. They insisted on looking behind the veil of prices to see what was happening in the "real" world of output and employment. Much of the time in the 1970s that real world looked good. But people were unhappy. At a press conference in 1973 I explained that although prices were rising, incomes were rising even faster, so people were better off. A reporter asked me why, in that case, the administration was so concerned about inflation. I answered that inflation made the people unhappy and the administration, contrary to a common view, did not want the people to be unhappy. That was meant as a joke but it contained a basic truth. People were unhappy. They felt cheated because their rising income did not make them as rich as they thought. They were worried because they weren't sure that their incomes would continue to keep up with prices. This unhappiness was a real thing, even if it did not show up in the economists' measurements of the real economy. It was probably the dominant real consequence of the inflation. There were other real consequences, later, which would show up in the measurements, including the unemployment that would be involved when the public's resentment of the inflation required that it be brought to an end.

Inflation was not the problem of the 1980s as it was of the 1970s. By 1983 the inflation rate had been reduced below 5 percent. Some people looked at that and said that the inflation was over. Fighting the anti-inflation fight was fighting the last war, in their opinion. They may have been right. But such talk had been heard before, several times since 1965, and it always turned out to be wrong. Inflation accelerated again. To think that there had been some radical change in the economy or in politics which was about to hand us a generation of price stability was risky. If there has been such a change it will appear, and will make economic life easier. But to assume it would only expose us to the danger of another wave of inflation. And that wave, if it occurs, could be worse than the previous ones. A revival of inflation after the pain that had been induced from 1979 to 1983 to bring it down, and after the efforts of our most "conservative" combination of President and Federal Reserve chairman, would confirm the view that accelerating inflation is inevitable in the United States. There would be a rush for protection against inflation, by demanding bigger wage increases, raising prices, accumulating commodities and buying real estate, selling bonds, perhaps even getting out of dollars. That would produce a much more rapid inflation than we have yet suffered.

U.S. economic policy for the 1980s needed to take control of inflation as its first priority: in fact, controlling inflation was the necessary condition for achieving other objectives. As a practical matter that meant, first, that the control of inflation had to be the dominant objective of monetary policy, to which other objectives must be subordinated if they conflict and, second, that monetary policy had to be the chief instrument for controlling inflation. Earlier there would have been considerable disagreement about both of these propositions, but they acquired much wider acceptance in the 1970s.

There have in the past been two main approaches to the causes and cures of inflation. Everyone agreed with the tautological statement that inflation results from an excess of the demand for output over the supply at existing prices. The conventional view, almost two hundred years old, has emphasized the demand side of this equation. But there have always been some people who insisted that the demand explanation and prescription was too simple and that the supply side must also be considered. During the Napoleonic wars there were economists who maintained that the cause of the British inflation was not the government's printing of money but Napoleon's sinking of ships bringing grain to England. In the 1970s and early 1980s the supply-side explanations became more numerous. They included the power and greed of unions or corporations—depending on who was telling the story—the increased number of women and youths in the labor force, the rise of acquisitiveness, the increased absorption of the national output by government, bad crops and the operations of the oil cartel. For a time a number of politicians and publicists, and a few economists, gained attention with the idea that the way to check inflation was to increase the supply of output, mainly by cutting taxes. They scoffed at the idea that restraint of demand could cure inflation, maintaining that demand-restraint would be counterproductive because it would cut output.

The supply-side approach is, however, seriously deficient both as explanation and as prescription. The difference between the

noninflationary years 1955–1965 and the inflationary years 1965–
1980 was on the demand side, not on the supply side. In the former period, real output rose by 3.5 percent per annum, total
spending rose by 5.6 percent per annum, and prices rose by
2.0 percent per annum. In the latter period, real output rose by 3.1
percent per annum, total spending rose by 9.3 percent per annum, and prices rose by 6.0 percent per annum. The big difference was that total spending—which is the demand side of the
equation—rose much more rapidly in the second period. A possible explanation is that monetary policy generated a much more
rapid expansion of demand in an effort to keep output rising at
its previous level, and that the effort turned out to be unsuccess-
ful and inflationary. But that only means that the inflation was
due to a mistaken demand-management policy. And in fact, the
inflation was well underway before output growth began to slow
down. Some people, especially business people, maintained for a
long time that the inflation was caused by excessive wage demands of unions. But actually wage demands followed the inflation, rather than leading it. The strongest case for an exogenous
supply-side effect on inflation relates to the oil price increases.
But again, the inflation was well under way, and was sufficiently
worrisome to give rise to mandatory price and wage controls, before the oil price increases began. The big oil price increases
of 1973–1974 and 1978–1979 undoubtedly contributed to the
surges of general inflation at those times, but it was the rise of
demand which explained the extent to which the oil price increases were subsequently translated into inflation in the rest of
the price structure. With more restraint of demand, the increase
in the *relative* price of oil could have been accommodated within
a much slower overall inflation rate. Some countries, like Japan
and Switzerland, absorbed the same energy prices that the United
States did with much less total inflation.

Whatever the division of responsibility for past inflation may
be, there is no question that policy for preventing inflation in the
future must rely predominantly on demand management. The
reason is simple. Demand management is the only anti-inflation
policy that the government can push to whatever degree is neces-

sary. Whatever is happening on the supply side of the economy, there is some demand-management policy that will keep it from being inflationary—if not in a particular quarter or year then surely over a reasonable period of time. For example, if total demand does not rise over a period of, say, ten years, it is almost inconceivable that there should be any substantial rise of prices over that period. On the other hand, if demand rises rapidly it is almost inconceivable that any supply-side policy could prevent inflation. The power of the government to influence the supply side of the economy is small, much smaller than the possible spontaneous or managed variation of demand. It is unlikely that any government policy could change the rate of growth of supply, within a time period measured in decades, by as much as one percentage point—for example, from 3 percent a year to 4 percent a year—whereas government policy can, over a reasonable period of time, make the growth of demand anything it wants. Demand management is not only essential for the prevention of inflation, it can also be sufficient.

This does not by itself mean that some supply-side policies may not be helpful in preventing inflation. It does mean that they cannot very much change the responsibility of demand-management policies. There was a time when this judgment would have been challenged with respect to incomes policy. That is, some economists would have said that a feasible policy for direct government restraint would permit a more expansive demand policy than would otherwise have been consistent with the avoidance of inflation. After disappointing experience with incomes policy, probably many of those who retain some hope for it would put the proposition differently. That is, they would advocate a demand-management policy that would avoid inflation without any contribution from incomes policy, supplemented by an incomes policy which, if it had any effect, would reduce the unemployment associated with general price stability. They recognize that the effectiveness of incomes policy is too uncertain to rely upon it as an anti-inflationary instrument but hope that it may still contribute something to reducing unemployment. The possible usefulness of incomes policy will be discussed below. The point being made here is that the potentialities of incomes policy, even if they are real—which I don't believe—do not qualify the proposition that demand-management must be the basic and ultimate reliance for achieving price stability.

This is only the beginning of a strategy for dealing with inflation. Difficult questions remain. By what standards and objectives should demand-management policy be guided? By what means are these objectives to be achieved? Is a demand-management policy directed to the avoidance of inflation politically viable?

The standard statement of the objectives of demand management—of fiscal and monetary policy—is that it should seek high employment and price stability. The problem arises if these two goals do not lead to the same policy. The standard statement assumed that a number of combinations of unemployment and inflation rates were possible. We could have—for example—6 percent unemployment and 2 percent inflation, 5 percent unemployment and 3 percent inflation and so on. Then the managers of fiscal and monetary policy would select one of these combinations which it thought best met the nation's objectives.

There are two difficulties with this strategy. First, no such menu of choices exists. We cannot choose, except temporarily, to have a lower unemployment rate by accepting a higher inflation rate. The unemployment rate will be the same at any continued and predictable inflation rate (although that unemployment rate will vary with changes in other factors, such as the age-sex composition of the labor force, and may be altered by government policies, such as the provision of training for unemployed workers). The second difficulty is that we don't know what that unemployment rate is, because it changes from time to time, with demographic and other factors. Therefore, a government that aims at this sustainable unemployment rate—sometimes called the "natural" rate—can easily make an error in estimating what that rate is. And the political temptation, to which governments have commonly yielded, is to promise too low a rate of unem-

ployment and to seek to achieve it by expansion of demand that
will be inflationary—and that will yield the promised unemployment rate only temporarily, if at all.

To aim demand-management policy at a target unemployment
rate, or employment rate, or level or rate of growth of total output, will not affect those "real" variables for any long period, but
runs a great risk of being inflationary. But aiming at a low and
stable inflation rate, or rate of growth of nominal GNP, will, if
successful, also yield whatever results in unemployment, employment or total output are possible to obtain over a sustained period. A policy that takes as its target a real variable cannot yield
better results in terms of the real variable than would be obtained
from a policy that succeeds in achieving a stable, predictable,
low rate of inflation, but aiming directly at a real target can yield
more inflation, unless the real target is chosen with a moderation
that cannot be expected. Thus, to aim at a goal for inflation
rather than at a goal for unemployment is not to subordinate the
unemployment goal but to seek to achieve the achievable unemployment rate in the best possible way.

One of the main lessons of the experience of the 1960s and
1970s is that demand management policy should aim at a nominal
goal—basically the price level or, as we shall discuss later, GNP
in nominal terms or the money supply in nominal terms. The adoption of nominal rather than "real" goals for demand management
policies is more important than what nominal goal is chosen. Nevertheless, the choice of the nominal goal is of some significance,
especially after a period of rapid inflation.

Between 1978 and 1981, inflation as measured by the GNP
deflator ran around 9 percent per annum. By 1983 that rate had
been reduced to less than 5 percent. This decline had been aided
by a decline of oil prices and by an increase in the exchange value
of the dollar, which reduced the prices of imports. It had also been
associated with the restraint of demand, which had also caused the
recession of 1981–1982.

The question then was whether to take as a goal the stabilization of the inflation rate at a level around 5 percent or to push
on to reduce the rate "essentially" to zero—say to 1 or 2 percent.

The case for "settling" for a 5 percent inflation rate was that it represented a substantial improvement over the experience of the recent past and that to try to push the figure down further would involve prolonging or even deepening the recession. This is not inconsistent with the statement made above that the unemployment rate does not depend on the inflation rate. That only said that as low an unemployment rate could be achieved with 2 percent inflation as with 5 percent inflation. It does not deny that getting from a 5 percent inflation rate to 2 percent would involve a transitional period of higher unemployment. Many economists would have said that this additional cost of reducing the inflation rate below 5 percent was not worth paying.

There is, however, a contrary argument. What the foregoing argument says is that once the inflation rate has risen as a result of accident or an error of policy the government should not pay the temporary cost of getting the inflation down again. But since there will be inflationary accidents or errors this means that government policy accepts, accommodates and perpetuates each increase of the inflation rate. Expectation of such a policy will have an inflationary effect on the behavior of private businesses, labor unions and investors. It will also make a transition to a lower rate of inflation more painful if the government should ever seriously undertake such a transition.

Clearly, the government's policy cannot be to accept and perpetuate whatever rate of inflation happens to occur. Whether, having reduced the rate from 10 percent to 5 percent, and accepted considerable cost in doing that, it could credibly "settle" for 5 percent is a more difficult question. Perhaps that would be accepted as evidence of the government's determination to avoid an inflation rate higher than 5 percent or undo it if one does occur. On the other hand, skepticism about the government's intentions may have been so solidified by fifteen or more years of inflationary experience that credibility would only be restored by a more radical demonstration, such as would be involved in reducing the inflation rate to a negligible level. In 1976 I thought that settling for a 5 percent inflation rate, and avoiding the unemployment and other costs that would be associated with reducing it further, was a prudent and feasible policy. After another big wave of inflation my opinion has changed and I think it desirable to aim for a much reduced rate. But the choice, it seems to me, is a close one.

In either case, the government should declare its goal for the inflation rate—whether 5 percent per annum or 2 percent or some other number. That will serve to guide the private sector in its expectations about inflation. It will also serve as a commitment by the government, in the sense that the government can be seen to have failed if inflation does not meet the goal, unless there is sufficient explanation for not doing so. If the goal is a lower inflation rate than the one currently being experienced the commitment might be to approach it gradually but with sufficient speed so that progress or the lack of it will be visible.

The demand-management policy that will be used to achieve the inflation goal is fiscal and monetary policy. The senior member of that partnership is monetary policy. That is not to deny that fiscal policy—taxation, expenditures and the deficit or surplus—can affect aggregate demand. There is disagreement about whether or not it can. We have also seen that there is disagreement about the direction in which the fiscal policy affects aggregate demand. In 1981 and 1982 there were some economists who thought that cutting the deficit would stimulate the economy and others who thought it would depress the economy. These uncertainties are not, however, the reason for giving fiscal policy a subordinate role in demand management. Relying on fiscal policy to play an active part in demand management is not efficient. Fiscal policy has other important objectives to serve. It implements important decisions about the way the national output is allocated—between public and private uses, among public uses between, say, defense, and education, between consumption and investment and among different private persons. To put upon fiscal policy the further responsibility of actively contributing to the maintenance of price stability will divert it from carrying out well the functions that only it can carry out. To decide whether building the MX missile will contribute to the national security is difficult enough. To encumber that decision with responsibility for helping to control the behavior of aggregate demand will only make the decision worse from the national security standpoint. And it is not necessary to do that. Monetary policy has no function other than to manage aggregate demand. Therefore monetary policy can be devoted unreservedly to that purpose.

This implies that monetary policy alone is sufficient to achieve the desired noninflationary path of aggregate demand or, at least, can achieve it as well as if it were "assisted" by fiscal policy. If the noninflationary path refers to the behavior of the economy over a number of years, and not quarter by quarter, that is certainly correct. This point must be recognized. For sixty years the American monetary authorities have used the deficiencies of fiscal policy as an explanation or excuse for the inadequacy of their policies to stabilize the economy. This has diverted attention from the need to improve the performance of the monetary authorities. Their responsibility needs to be clearly identified.

A common argument is that monetary policy cannot control inflation if there are large budget deficits. This proposition is, however, groundless. The claim is sometimes made that if the government runs large deficits the monetary authority must expand the money supply in order to help the government finance the deficits. But there is no such need, and little evidence that the monetary authorities in recent years have acted as if there were such a need.[2] An alternative argument is that a large budget deficit makes interest rates higher than they would otherwise be, which reduces the quantity of money people want to hold and thus reduces the quantity of money that is appropriate for the noninflationary path. This only means—at most—that monetary policy needs to be different if there is a large budget deficit from what it is if there is not, but monetary policy can be adapted to that. Monetary policy may have difficulty adapting to sharp and unpredicted swings in the budget deficit. It may not be possible to keep such swings from causing unwanted fluctuations of the economy. That is a reason, as will be discussed later, for trying to avoid such swings in the budget position unless there is a strong need for them, like the need to respond to a national security threat. In any case, such short-term fluctuations in the budget position need not prevent achievement of the long-run anti-inflation goal.

The belief that the inflation rate can be controlled by monetary policy rests upon three propositions:

1. Monetary policy can control the quantity of money.

2. There is a relation between the quantity of money and aggregate demand (or total spending or nominal GNP) which permits aggregate demand to be controlled by controlling the quantity of money.

3. There is a relation between aggregate demand and the inflation rate which permits the inflation rate to be controlled by controlling the quantity of money.

If all of these propositions were correct and if the relations assumed were invariable and predictable, the conduct of monetary policy would be perfectly simple. If the objective was a zero inflation rate and we knew that inflation would be 2½ percent less than the rise of nominal GNP—because output would rise steadily by 2½ percent per annum—we would know that nominal GNP should grow by 2½ percent a year. And if we knew that nominal GNP always grew at the same rate as the money supply, we would know that the money supply should grow by 2½ percent a year. And we would know how to produce just that rate of growth of the money supply.

Unfortunately, the relations are not constant and predictable. A constant rate of growth of the money supply will not yield a constant rate of growth of nominal GNP, and a constant rate of growth of nominal GNP will not yield a constant rate of inflation.[3] The question is what to do about this. There are two extreme answers to this question. One is that the rate of growth of the money supply should be set now at the best estimate of what will yield the desired rate of inflation on the average and kept constant at that rate forever. The argument is not that this policy will assure stability of the inflation rate but that this policy will come closer to achieving stability than would the attempt to adapt the money supply to necessarily imperfect forecasts of the future relations between money and the price level. At the other extreme is the position that the decision about the money supply should be constantly open for revision in the light of new information about the relation between the money supply and the price level. In this view there is no reason to think that the initial estimate of the required money supply will be good for any period of time; it is only reasonable to give weight to information as it subsequently becomes available.

Neither of these extreme positions is satisfactory. The possibility cannot be denied that changes in the economy might significantly and durably change the relation between the money supply and the inflation rate. Three percent annual growth of the money supply might have produced, on the average, price stability from 1950 to 1980. No one can be so sure that this relation will hold from 2000 to 2030 that he would reject the possibility of looking at the evidence again. On the other hand, to be continuously reestimating the money growth that would yield the desired inflation rate will yield erroneous and probably inflationary results. The reasons for that are psychological and political. In theory a monetary authority trying to estimate the relation between the money supply and inflation each month could conclude that the past relation was the best estimate. But this is very unlikely to happen. The temptation to try to do better than extrapolate the past, and to try to bring to bear current information and insights, will be irresistible. This can lead to variations of monetary policy that are at best random. But they probably will not be random. There will be great uncertainty about what current information and insights mean for monetary policy. In the presence of this uncertainty—when economic analysis does not tell just what to do—decisions will be politically determined, and will have an inflationary bias.

Policy about the rate of growth of the money supply should be open to change when there is strong evidence that the relation between the money supply and the price level has changed, but policy should not be altered in response to weak and transitory evidence. It does not seem to be possible to describe objectively what evidence is sufficiently strong. Therefore, it is not possible to dispense with judgment of live officials. The problem is to try to arrange the organization of these officials, their legislative mandate and the public's understanding of their role in such a way that they will exercise their discretion in a cautious and self-restraining way.

What is proposed here is a major change from the past practice of the Federal Reserve in two respects. First, the Fed would aim only at *nominal* targets—price level and nominal GNP. It would not aim at real targets—like employment, unemployment or output—except insofar as a stable noninflationary growth of the nominal variables would indirectly contribute to good performance of the real variables. Second, it would derive its money-supply targets from its nominal GNP targets and a prediction of velocity—that is the ratio of nominal GNP to the money supply. It would alter the prediction of velocity in response to strong evidence that a durable change had occurred, and only in response to strong evidence. As contrasted with traditional practice, this means rejecting "real" targets and rejecting "fine-tuning."

I visualize the monetary authority as operating in the following way. Suppose that we have arrived at 1995 after the disinflationary transition: The price-level goal is that the price level should rise by 2 percent per annum, on the average. On the assumption of a normal trend of real output rising 2.5 percent per annum, the goal is that nominal GNP should rise by 4.5 percent per annum. If the expected velocity is constant (for M_2), then the money supply should rise by 4.5 percent per annum. Thus, there are the following goals:[4]

	A. Price Level (GNP Deflator) 1987 = 100	B. Nominal GNP $ billion	C. Money Supply, M_2 $ billion
1995	132	6,730	3,740
1996	134.6	7,033	3,908
1997	137.3	7,349	4,084
1998	140.1	7,680	4,268
1999	142.9	8,026	4,460

Even if the money supply is kept on its target path, nominal GNP will not remain exactly on its target path. That would mean that velocity had deviated from its estimated path. That would not ordinarily call for a revision of the money-supply target. It is not to be expected that the money supply can be adapted to all variations of velocity and the business cycle thereby eliminated. But there may be occasions on which there is strong evidence that the path of velocity has probably changed. On such occasions the money-supply targets should be altered, in an effort to keep nominal GNP on its target path.

Similarly, even if nominal GNP is kept to its target path, the price level may depart from its desired path. The relation between nominal GNP and the price level is not absolutely fixed in the short run. Such a deviation would not necessarily call for altering the nominal GNP target. But if the deviation is exceptionally strong, revision of the nominal GNP target would have to be considered in order to achieve the price-level target.

The kind of policy I am describing here is not likely to be adopted by the Federal Reserve on its own initiative, and if it were so adopted it would probably not last for long. The policy I am describing is totally at variance with the tradition and organization of the Federal Reserve, with its legislative mandate and with the public image of it. The Federal Reserve as now constituted is viewed as a body dealing with mysteries, continuously scanning an enormous body of information to make complex decisions addressed to a number of objectives, but not sufficiently powerful to achieve any of its objectives and not to be held responsible for their achievement.

The Federal Reserve Board consists of seven members appointed by the President for staggered terms of fourteen years, one of whom serves as chairman for a term of four years. The board is assisted by an exceedingly large economic research staff—350 people—the leading members of which serve for a long time. The staff is so large because the board operates on the premise that it must be continuously informed about everything that goes on in the economy and must be continuously able to reappraise its policy in the light of this incoming information.

The staff naturally clings to this view of the board's function because that is what justifies the size and status of the staff. Moreover, the staff, which serves even longer than most members of the board, carries the tradition of the system, which is of continuous surveillance and fine-tuning.

Major decisions are made by the Federal Open Market Committee, consisting of the seven members of the board and five of the twelve presidents of the regional Federal Reserve Banks. The participation of the presidents reflects a certain view of the way in which monetary policy decisions should be made. These regional representatives are supposed to bring to the process a knowledge of what is happening in the economy at the grass roots—to expand the range of information beyond that available to the economic staff. It is part of the notion of taking "everything" into account, which is the antithesis of the strategy of living by a few objective rules in the absence of strong contrary evidence. The practice of holding a meeting of the Federal Open Market Committee each month also reflects the belief that the monetary instruments are in constant need of fine-tuning. Although some of the regional presidents have brought their own views of monetary policy into the discussions it is common for them to get their first serious introduction to the subject from briefings by the staff.

The members of the board are well-informed, not only about monetary matters but also about fiscal policy and other aspects of economic policy and developments. The chairman, because he is so well-informed, is respectfully listened to on a range of subjects beyond monetary policy. He regularly testifies, for example, before the budget committees of the House and the Senate. This encourages the propensity of the Federal Reserve to give great weight to nonmonetary solutions for the economic problems of the country. It is standard practice of the Federal Reserve chairman to emphasize the crucial role of fiscal policy as an explanation of the limited achievements or promises of monetary policy. Federal Reserve chairmen have also been prominent advocates of incomes policy to restrain inflation.

The Federal Reserve operates with only a loose legislative

statement of the objectives it is to pursue with the powers granted to it. The Federal Reserve is not mentioned in the Employment Act of 1946, but the board has said that it feels itself included in the mandate of the act that the government should use all of its powers to achieve "maximum employment, production and purchasing power." Although nothing is said in the act about inflation, the term "purchasing power" has been, rather generously, interpreted to mean something about avoiding inflation. So the net of the Employment Act is that the Federal Reserve, like other parts of the government, is to pursue both real objectives and price-level stability.

In 1974, Congress made an effort to tie the Federal Reserve down with a resolution requiring the board to notify Congressional committees four times a year (later changed to twice) of its goals for the money supply. The Fed unsuccessfully resisted adoption of the resolution. While the resolution probably helped to turn the Fed in the direction of using monetary aggregates as an instrument of policy it was not binding about that and was entirely silent about the objectives toward which the Fed was to aim its control of the money supply. The Fed conformed to the resolution by specifying target ranges for a number of definitions of money, which left it a great deal of latitude for changing its mind from time to time while still remaining within the target range for at least one of the definitions. Moreover, the Fed frequently ran outside its announced targets. Congress never criticized the Fed for the targets it announced or for missing the targets when it did so. Thus, the resolution was not a serious guide or limitation for monetary policy.

The Full Employment Act of 1978 (Humphrey-Hawkins) required the President to specify his five-year objectives for employment, output and the price level and also stated goals for each of these variables that he should plan to achieve. The Federal Reserve resisted a similar injunction and it was only required to state whether its monetary targets were consistent with the President's objectives. The Fed meets this requirement by submitting a range of the forecasts of the seven members of the board, a range which always encompasses the President's objectives but also leaves room for considerable deviation from them. The board as a body presents no forecast and it does not accept any of the forecast quantities as a goal which it will try to achieve. In any case, the Humphrey-Hawkins goals are so unrealistic and inconsistent that they are not taken seriously by anyone.

The basic fact is that there is no general understanding in the Congress or in the country of what the proper goals of Federal Reserve policy are or of what are reasonable expectations for performance. This leaves the Federal Reserve exposed to criticism for failing to deliver what it cannot and should not be expected to deliver and on the other hand under no strong compulsion to deliver anything. The Federal Reserve thus has a great deal of freedom and a strong incentive to deny responsibility.

Reform of monetary policy will require two things. There must be a fundamental change in the country, in the Congress and in the monetary authority in the understanding of what monetary policy is to do. This understanding will have to emphasize the focus on nominal targets—ultimately the price level—and on continuity of policy. There must be a fundamental change in the structure of the monetary authority to break out of the Fed's traditional pattern of thought and action.

To bring about a new understanding of the function of monetary policy, legislation should be adopted which would amend the Employment Act of 1946 and the Full Employment Act of 1978 insofar as they give instructions to the Federal Reserve. This is not because the legislation is essential or even important. But a proposal to amend the legislation would precipitate a serious discussion of the objectives of the Federal Reserve that would raise public understanding of the issues, and if the legislation was amended after such a discussion the Federal Reserve would have a new understanding of its responsibilities.

The Employment Act of 1946, as I have already noted, calls upon the government to use all of its powers to achieve maximum employment, production and purchasing power. This is interpreted as applying to the Federal Reserve. The 1946 Act should be amended to specify that the Federal Reserve is to contribute to the achievement of these objectives by managing the money supply so as to stabilize the price level. The intent of such an amendment would be to relieve the Fed of responsibility for influencing employment, unemployment and total output except as they are influenced by the behavior of the price level.

The Full Employment Act of 1978 (Humphrey-Hawkins) requires the Federal Reserve to report to the Congress on its targets for the growth of the money supply in the current year and to give its opinion on the consistency of these money-supply targets with the economic assumptions on which the administration's budget is based. These assumptions cover both nominal variables—nominal GNP and the price level—and real variables—output and employment. The result is to give the impression of Fed responsibility for all kinds of goals. The act should be amended to require the Federal Reserve and the administration to submit targets for the nominal variables on which they have agreed—or separate targets if they have not agreed. The purpose again is to commit the Federal Reserve to specifying nominal targets for a moderate period by which they will be guided in managing the money supply. The agreement of the Federal Reserve and the administration on the targets will also provide the basis for improving fiscal policy, as we shall see.

Legislative changes alone, however, will not sufficiently alter the conduct of monetary policy, because legislative rules cannot be specified so precisely as to leave the Federal Reserve with no discretion. Satisfactory results will still depend on how the Fed exercises this discretion. It will be important to try to wean the Fed from its traditional approach of fine-tuning policy based on continuous surveillance of a universe of information while constantly disclaiming responsibility for the outcome.

The most common suggestion for reorganizing the Federal Reserve is to make it an administrative agency like any other, directly responsible to the President, perhaps as a bureau of the Treasury. This is believed to be a way to assure "coordination" of monetary policy with other economic policies and to centralize responsibility for economic performance on the President. This idea has a certain attraction in that it would remove the present mystique of the Fed. But it is not, in my opinion, a desirable direction in which to move. Monetary policy should not be "coordinated" in the sense that it becomes one of several instruments to be used interchangeably to achieve a common package of objectives. Monetary policy is a unique instrument to be directed to unique objectives. Moreover, it is doubtful that we want the President to be unequivocally responsible for the performance of the economy and so forced to window-dress that performance in time for November every fourth year. The President *should* be able to say that there are long-run considerations which limit his ability to deliver all good things within a four-year term.

The advantage of the present system is that the members of the board have fourteen-year terms. This permits and encourages, although it does not require, a long view of their actions and objectives. It also inevitably implies a certain degree of independence of Presidents, who are elected for four-year terms. This should be preserved. The problem is how to preserve the long term of board members while changing the organization of the Federal Reserve in a way that will encourage a more stable policy more narrowly focused on price-level stability. The following changes would be helpful, partly because they would indicate the seriousness of the desire to break up the old pattern and begin a new approach:

Remove from the Federal Reserve all functions not directly related to controlling the quantity of money. This primarily means that the responsibility for examining and supervising banks would be transferred elsewhere, to the Federal Deposit Insurance Corporation or possibly to a newly created bank supervisory agency. This would not only help to concentrate the attention of the Federal Reserve on the primary objective. It would also be a rejection of the notion that the Federal Reserve needs detailed hands-on experience with the internal affairs of banks in order to discharge its monetary functions.

Abolish the Federal Open Market Committee and place all of the functions of the Federal Reserve in the seven-member board. This means removing the presidents of the regional Federal Reserve Banks from the policymaking process. Some of these bank presidents have made valuable contributions to the thinking of the system. But fundamentally the role of the Federal Open Market Committee is a symptom of the belief that the conduct of monetary policy requires close and continuous personal contact with what is going on in Cleveland and St. Louis and Dallas.

Greatly reduce the size of the Federal Reserve staff, again to concentrate the attention of the Fed on its primary macroeconomic functions. The Federal Reserve Board does not need to be advised by specialists on the automobile industry or on agricultural policy. The idea that the board needs to think about such things is part of the pattern of fine-tuning adaptation to the real short run of the economy—and also to the pattern of the Federal Reserve advising the President, the Congress and the public on all aspects of economic policy.

The hope of all of this, both the legislative mandate and the reorganization, is to emphasize that the Federal Reserve has a vitally important but limited function for which it must assume responsibility. Failure to discharge this function, to manage the money supply so as to achieve a low and reasonably predictable rate of inflation, has been the chief failure of policy since the late 1960s. Correction of that failure would be the greatest contribution policy can make to economic performance in the next twenty years. There may be disagreement about what needs to be done in other areas. It should be possible to reach agreement on the need for basic reform in the monetary field.

The Significance of Budget Deficits

Nothing better reveals the vacuum in economic policy than the gap between the nearly universal statements of aversion to budget deficits and the prospect of exceptionally large deficits for as far ahead as the eye can see. No one any longer talks about balancing the budget. There is a tacit agreement that the things that would have to be done to eliminate the deficit cannot be done—which means only that the necessary action is considered worse than the deficit.

But if zero has been abandoned as a goal for the size of the deficit no other goal has received any general support. Everyone in the political process wants to be known as supporting a lower deficit than his rivals, but hardly anyone tries to justify any particular size of the deficit as a proper target. All the participants are willing to do something to reduce the prospective deficits, but each is willing to do only things that he was willing to do anyway, without regard to the size of the deficit. In the 1980s, President Reagan was willing to cut social programs he wanted to cut even when the deficits did not loom so large. Many "liberals" were prepared to cut the defense program, or to raise taxes on the "rich," in order to reduce the deficit—never having felt much need for a large defense program or much concern about the after-tax incomes of the upper-income minority.

The fact is that talk about reducing the budget deficit has become largely a ritual. Everyone believes that there are other people out there who are greatly worried about budget deficits and it is therefore necessary to show that one shares that worry. But the reasons for the worry are not cogent or agreed-upon and do not lead to any clear idea about the proper size of deficit, if it is not zero, or to much action.

There are people who believe that deficits don't really matter. They believe that the size of government expenditures matters. Government spending subtracts from the output available for private use. They are concerned about that subtraction—mainly to keep it as low as possible. But whether that subtraction is financed by taxation or by borrowing seems to them of no great importance. This attitude leads to a certain anomaly. People who hold this view are usually reluctant to avow it when expenditure decisions are being considered. Wanting to hold expenditures down, they would like all decision-makers to believe that they should not spend money unless they raise taxes to pay for it. But the decision-makers are not likely to accept that discipline unless they see some reason why they should raise taxes, and they will not see that unless they think that the difference between taxing and borrowing matters.

Our present situation is that we talk as if deficits were terribly important, we act as if they didn't matter very much, and we really don't know what the nature and size of their effects are. It is not easy to be positive in laying down principles for deciding on policy toward deficits. All one can do is to try prudently to adapt policy to a rather cautious and moderate view of what the effects are.

In my opinion the present state of economic analysis tends to support this view of the effects of the size of the deficit: Short-run variations in the size of the deficit have short-run effects on nominal GNP, the price level, output and employment. That is, an exogenous increase in the deficit—one not resulting from a decline of the economy—will tend temporarily to raise the rate of increase of nominal GNP and the price level and also to raise output and employment. In the long run the size of the deficit— whether large or small—if it is stable will not affect nominal GNP or the price level or employment. It will, however, affect the long-term growth rate of output and of productivity, because the larger the deficit is in the long run the slower will be the growth of private productive investment.

The proposition about the short-run effect of the budget deficit does not contradict what has been said earlier about the dominant role of the money supply in determining the long-run behavior of nominal GNP and the price level. Even the most extreme monetarist would recognize that velocity can fluctuate in the short run, which means that the economy can fluctuate even if the money supply does not. Variations in the deficit or surplus are among the possible causes of variations in velocity.

The key question is whether this short-run influence of fiscal policy should be used actively or only passively in an effort to achieve desired behavior of the economy. Almost everyone will now agree on at least the passive use. That is, the variations in the size of the deficit or surplus that come automatically with variations of the economy will be accepted. To try to offset those automatic variations by changing tax programs or expenditure programs is disturbing to the planning of taxpayers and government agencies, and certainly not helpful to the stability of the economy. There are some economists who retain a longing for more than that—for varying the deficit in a countercyclical direction. They cling to the early Keynesian idea of cutting tax rates to stimulate the economy when it is depressed or, more realistically, is expected to be depressed, and vice versa. But the number who believe this with confidence has greatly diminished. The effort to stabilize the economy by variation of fiscal policy has a high risk of being destabilizing because of the difficulty of forecasting the economy accurately. This destabilizing effect is likely to have an inflationary bias, because of the short-run preoccupation with reducing unemployment. For the same reason the short-run decisions about the budget are likely in the long run to add up to larger deficits than would be desirable.

This comes down to a short-run policy of keeping the size of the deficit stable from year to year, or even for longer periods, except insofar as the size of the deficit responds automatically to variations of the economy. This leaves two problems. First, how are we to distinguish between the automatic, passive variations of the deficit, which are to be accepted, and the active, purposely generated variations of the deficit, which are to be ruled out by the policy? This distinction requires us to identify a condition of the economy at which the deficit will be kept constant and from which deviations can be observed and measured. The CED in 1947 identified this condition as "high employment" and said that taxes and expenditures should be such that they would yield a constant surplus when the economy was at high employment. (In 1947 one still talked of a surplus.) This prescription was deficient in several respects. No one really knew what "high employment" was, the definition used turned out, as might have been expected, to be more ambitious than could be actually achieved on the average, and the prescription did not recognize the importance of the price level as an aspect of the condition of the economy. But the "high employment" notion, although crude, did reflect the correct basic idea. This was that tax and expenditure programs should be set so that they would yield a stable and desirable surplus (or deficit) when the economy was in a desirable and, on the average, probable condition. If this is done, variations in the surplus resulting automatically from variations of the economy will help to keep the economy near its desirable condition. The long-run size of the surplus will probably be the desired size because the budget has been set to yield that surplus when the economy is in its long-run probable condition. In the past, "practical" conservative people tended to scoff at the idea of balancing the budget at high employment because it promised to balance the budget under hypothetical conditions which might not exist whereas they were interested in "actual" balance. But the valid interest in the actual size of the surplus or deficit is an interest in the actual size of the surplus or deficit over a period of years. If we aim to get the desired surplus or deficit when the economy is on its most probable path we will probably realize that actual surplus or deficit on the average over a period of years, although not in every year.

The desirable, feasible, and probable condition of the economy at which we should plan to get the target surplus or deficit is the level of nominal GNP at which monetary policy is aiming. I have suggested above that the Federal Reserve should try to control the money supply so that it will on the average achieve growth of nominal GNP that is low and predictable. That is the desirable path of the economy, because if it is achieved there will be little inflation and the economy will fluctuate moderately about a high employment level. It is a feasible path because monetary policy can on the average keep the economy on it. And it will be the probable path, about which the actual economy will fluctuate, if the monetary policy is directed to achieving it. Therefore, if tax rates and expenditure programs are set so that they would achieve the desired surplus or deficit when the economy is on the target path, the actual surplus or deficit over a moderate number of years will be the desired one.

This implies that it should be the responsibility of the administration to submit an annual budget that would achieve the desired surplus or deficit when the economy is on the nominal GNP path set by the Federal Reserve. The present system in which the administration submits a five-year budget based on economic assumptions that the Federal Reserve may not share and to which it has no commitment is unsatisfactory. It encourages irresponsible window-dressing by the administration in making up its assumptions and permits anyone to challenge the policy by making up his own assumptions. Moreover, if it is not known whether the budget assumptions conform to the Federal Reserve's intentions no one can tell whether or not the budget describes the probable outcome for the deficit or surplus.

The interaction between monetary and fiscal policy would work something like this: The Federal Reserve would be directed to submit to the Congress each year its targets for nominal GNP for the next five years and its plan for the money supply in the next year to keep the economy on that path. Presumably the Fed will discuss these plans with the administration before it submits them to Congress. Congress can, if it wishes, comment on the Fed's plans. In extreme circumstances Congress could enact legislation which would instruct the Fed to do something different. This is quite unlikely to happen, however. Although many members of Congress like to be able to criticize the Fed, few Congressmen have shown any disposition to accept the responsibility for managing monetary policy. The administration would submit a budget for the next five years that would yield the desired surplus or deficit when the economy is on the Fed's target path. The desired surplus or deficit should be stable from year to year, so that variations of the size of the surplus or deficit will not disturb the economy from the path the Fed is seeking to maintain.

This brings us to the second question. What is the desirable size of the surplus or deficit, on the average, aside from cyclical fluctuations? That depends, of course, on what the effects of surpluses or deficits are. This has been the subject of much controversy over the years. Argument over this issue has, I believe, now properly led to the conclusion that the important effect of the absolute size of the deficit or surplus is the effect on private investment. That is, I think, the view now held by most, although not all, economists.

The argument is simple. Private savings equal the sum of private investment plus the government deficit. Private saving is totally absorbed in these two uses. The larger the government deficit is, the smaller private investment will be—unless the larger government deficit is matched by an equally larger total of private savings. There is some debate over this qualification. That is, there are people who contend that an increase in the deficit will be matched by an increase in private saving and so will not reduce private investment. There have been three kinds of argument for this position. The Keynesian argument is that the increase in the deficit will increase the national income and so increase saving enough not only to finance the deficit but possibly also to finance an increase in private investment. Hardly anyone would hold to that as a long-run proposition anymore. An older view recently revived is that if the deficit is increased people will realize that they will have to pay more taxes in the future and they will save to be able to pay those future taxes. But no one has been able to verify that people do respond in that way. The third argument is part of supply-side economics. This holds that if the deficit is higher because taxes are lower the after-tax return to saving will be higher and people will save more. There is probably something in that. But estimates of how much an increase in the after-tax return will increase saving do not come close to showing that the increase of saving would be as large as the increase of the deficit.

So while some uncertainty must be recognized, the most probable basis for thinking about the absolute size of the deficit or surplus over a period of time is that the primary effect is on the cumulative amount of private investment over that period. This effect on private investment is a matter of serious concern because the amount of private investment over time affects the level of total output and productivity.

One may ask why it is any business of the government to try to influence the rate of economic growth by a decision about the size of the government surplus or deficit. The national rate of economic growth is the statistical summation of the results of the decisions and efforts of millions of individuals and households, each seeking to manage its affairs so as to achieve the rate of personal income growth that seems feasible and desirable. There is no reason for the government to have a goal about that except to create conditions in which individuals can freely make their own choices. Therefore the government should only choose some arbitrary goal for the size of the deficit or surplus—like zero—and leave the private parties free to make whatever adjustment they like to that decision. If the private parties on the whole feel that the rate of their personal income growth is too low under these conditions, they can work more, save more, study more or do whatever else they think worthwhile. No one could say that the resulting rate of economic growth would be "wrong."

This is a conceivable position, and indeed I took this position in the 1960s.[5] It does not seem to me a reasonable position today, however. At that time one might think that there was a position about the budget—namely, that it should be balanced—which although arbitrary had a great deal of public support. That satisfied the need for a standard to which politics would conform, and probably satisfied it better than any alternative that might seem less arbitrary. Also, in the 1960s one could be more complacent about the prospects for the growth of the American economy than one can be today—simply because our rate of productivity growth has fallen significantly.

The government does have to decide the size of the surplus or deficit. There is no free market solution for that. Neither is there any longer a traditional standard—like the balanced budget—for making the decision. A new standard has to be created and defended against alternatives, and it will have to be defended by showing that it has good effects. The most important of these effects is on the future rate of economic growth via the influence on the rate of private investment.

So it seems clear that in thinking about the desirable size of the deficit or surplus one should be thinking primarily about the desired rate of growth of national output and productivity. But once that has been said it is hard to say more. There is no objective way to determine how much the nation should forgo current government services and private consumption in order to make the future national income greater.

The problem is the same at the national level as at the household level. There is no objective way to determine how much a household should save in order to have more income in the future. One can list some things that the household should think about—the probable trend of its future income and the income prospects of its children, whether it has extraordinary expenses now or foreseeable in the future, what the costs of various levels of living after retirement would be and so on. But when all such information is assembled, different people will make different judgments about how much is to be saved. The best one can get is an informed feeling.

So at the national level all one can hope to achieve is a procedure in which a deliberate decision is made on the size of the surplus or deficit in the light of the relevant information by responsible people who represent the national feeling about the matter. The decision should be made for several years at a time—at least five. The effect of the budget decision on the stock of productive capital is very small in any one year, because the volume of investment in any one year is small relative to the capital stock. It is only the accumulated size of the deficit or surplus over a number of years that significantly affects the stock of capital and therefore the levels of output and productivity. Moreover, the considerations which affect what the size of the surplus or deficit should be will not ordinarily change much from one year to another, although they may change gradually over a longer period of time.[6]

Thus, one can visualize the administration in its annual budget setting a target for the size of the deficit or surplus in the ensuing five years. In deciding on this target it would take into account the recent and predicted trends of productivity growth. Even though one cannot objectively say what is the "proper" rate of productivity growth, forcing the population to adapt to a slow-down of real income growth relative to expectations is disruptive and should be avoided if possible. Therefore the case for a high surplus or low deficit will be strong if needed to prevent a slow-down of productivity growth. If current expenditure requirements are exceptionally high, as in a period of defense buildup, the case for deficits is strong, to avoid the necessity for tax rates which

raise difficult questions of incentives and equity. This is traditionally recognized in wartime, of course. The composition of the budget may also make a difference in the decision. That is, the more
the expenditure side of the budget provides for growth-promoting
programs, like research, the more justification there is for borrowing rather than taxing.

The important point is that the decision about the deficit or
surplus should be regarded as a decision about the allocation of
the national output, like other decisions in the federal budget.
Federal expenditures influence how much of the national output
is devoted to defense and research and education and highways
and so on. There are no precise objective formulas by which to
determine the right amount in any of these cases. But we seek
informed and responsible judgments. So the decision about the
size of the surplus or deficit is a decision, positive or negative,
about the share of the national output that goes to private investment, and it should be made and explained in that way.

In 1983 one could see the beginnings of thinking about the
deficit in this way. The deficits in prospect were large by historical standards, but no one any longer took seriously the notion of
balancing the budget. How big should the deficit be? Three considerations seemed to provide an answer. The growth of productivity in the 1970s had been disappointingly low. It was important to stop that trend of deterioration and if possible to reverse
it. This pointed to the desirability of seeing that the deficits were
at least no larger relative to GNP than they had been in the previous decade—about 2½ percent of GNP—rather than the 6 percent experienced in 1983. On the other hand, we were planning
an increase of defense spending relative to GNP, which meant
that to get the deficit down below 2½ percent of GNP would require high marginal tax rates that might endanger economic efficiency. Moreover, to avoid disturbing the economy's recovery
from the recession it would be desirable that the reduction of the
deficit should come gradually. This combination of factors led to
the recommendation that the deficit be reduced gradually to 2½
percent of GNP by 1988. The Reagan budget issued in January

contained such a recommendation, and some of the foregoing argument was implicit in the report of the President's Council of Economic Advisers at that time.[7]

In circumstances different from those of the early 1980s a different conclusion about the desirable size of the deficit might be reached. If, for example, defense requirements should diminish, because the rebuilding of the armed forces had been completed or for some other reason, it might be appropriate to aim for a smaller deficit or even for a balanced budget. A radical change in the rate of productivity growth would also affect the surplus-deficit target. The desirable size of the surplus or deficit is not fixed forever. That is why it should not be incorporated in a constitutional amendment. The choice of a surplus or deficit target is a political decision to be made from time to time in the light of long-run growth considerations. The problem, of course, is to get them made in this way, rather than for short-run political expedience. There is no alternative to trying to develop understanding of the need for this, in the government and in the public. This should be one of the main objectives of the national reconsideration of economic policy that is now required.

The Undertaxed Society

One of the basic premises of Reagan economics was that politicians liked to raise taxes, or at least had no great aversion to raising taxes. The standard political philosophy was thought to be "tax and tax, spend and spend." Because the politicians had no proper appreciation of the evils of taxes they were willing to raise taxes to pay for increases of government expenditures that were clearly excessive. If this propensity to tax was resisted and indeed if, with strong presidential leadership, taxes could be reduced, excessive expenditures would also be reduced and other good things would happen. (Of course, the idea that politicians like to raise taxes and had to be restrained by the Reaganites was simply wrong. Politicians hate to raise taxes.)

When the President proposed a big tax reduction in 1981, although Congress resisted some parts of the reduction it readily accepted the idea. But within a year the President was joining those, a majority in the Congress, who believed that taxes were too low. As already noted, in 1982 and 1983 he supported a number of tax increases. He only resented efforts to limit the income tax cut scheduled to take effect in 1983 on the essentially Keynesian grounds that the *timing* was bad from the standpoint of the cyclical recovery.

Between 1981 and 1983 the country moved from a flush of enthusiasm for tax reduction to a sad recognition that taxes were too low—that we were, as George F. Will put it, an undertaxed society. The basic reason for this change was experience with the effort to cut government expenditures. Until Reagan became President it was always possible to believe that a determined budget-cutter in the White House could find vast amounts of money in expenditure programs that could be eliminated—and that Congress would be forced to eliminate them if some of the revenue was removed. But we have seen that "even" President Reagan could not propose a budget that cut expenditures enough to hold deficits down without more taxes than were left after the 1981 tax cut. This may have been in part for political reasons. That is, there may have been bigger cuts that he would have liked to make if the Congress and the country would have accepted them. But undoubtedly he and his colleagues, once in office, discovered that the needed or justifiable expenditures were larger than they thought. And the political reason is not to be disregarded either, because it is an indication of the public's wishes, which should not be disregarded.

No one likes tax increases. What was recognized by 1983 was that the consequences of failure to raise taxes—which were to forgo certain expenditures or to accept a larger deficit—were worse than the consequences of a tax increase. But this recognition did not assure the result. As indicated earlier, although almost everyone thought the prospective deficits were too large there was not any compelling agreement on the proper size of deficit. This raised the strong possibility that when it came right down to the hard decision the President and Congress would settle for a token tax increase and token deficit reduction. There would always be a question whether now was the right time for a tax increase, however much the long-run need was recognized.

Moreover, the nature of the tax increase is critical—whether individual income taxes, corporate taxes, selective excises or general consumption taxes. There will be much disagreement about that, which may prevent achievement of a tax increase of adequate size. The nature of the tax increase will also influence its effects. Any tax increase will have adverse economic effects—if considered in isolation from the beneficial effects of reducing the budget deficit. But some tax increases will have more adverse effect per dollar of revenue than others.

The conditions that give rise to the need for more revenue suggest what is the nature of the appropriate tax increase. A tax increase was needed because it was necessary to devote a larger share of the national output to private investment and undesirable to reduce the share devoted to the consumption of the very poor. That means basically that it was necessary to reduce the share of the national output devoted to the consumption of middle-income people, the consumption of the rich absorbing only a tiny part of the national output.

It would also have been desirable to raise additional revenue without raising marginal rates of taxation very much, if possible. This element in the supply-side argument, that the marginal rate—the rate of tax on a dollar of additional income—is most important in determining the incentive effects of taxation, is true. The trouble with the 1981 tax cut was that it combined some highly useful cuts in marginal rates with a number of other changes which were of no great incentive benefit but lost a great deal of revenue. Reducing the 70 percent marginal tax rate to 50 percent—approximately a 30 percent cut—is a significant cut. It raises the after-tax return on $1 of additional income from 30 cents to 50 cents, or by 66⅔ percent. Reducing the 14 percent rate to 10 percent, however, is not a significant change from that standpoint, even though it is also approximately a 30 percent tax cut. It raises the after-tax return on $1 of additional income from 86 cents to 90 cents, or by less than 5 percent. But still this tax cut and others in the low and medium brackets accounted for much of the revenue loss in the 1981 act.

So we needed a tax increase to restrain the consumption of the middle-income people without serious impact on the very poor and without raising marginal rates at the levels where marginal rates have a significant effect on incentives to work, save or invest. This was made more difficult than it had to be by the nature of our tax system. The federal government relies heavily on the personal income tax, which includes within taxable income less than half of the gross national product and only about 60 percent of personal income.

The remainder of GNP is excluded by personal exemptions and by a long list of deductions, or because it is retained by corporations or by government. As a result, to raise 10 percent of the GNP in personal income taxes requires an average tax equal to about 20 percent of taxable income. Since the system is progressive, taxpayers pay a higher rate of tax on their highest dollar of income than on their average dollar. Thus, in 1982 a married couple with two dependents and an income of $50,000 paid about 22 percent of its income in personal income tax and faced a marginal tax rate of 39 percent.

To raise, for example, another 2 percent of the gross national product in taxes by raising the rates of the personal income tax would require raising the average rate on taxable income from 20 percent to 24 percent. That is a 20 percent increase, and if applied across the board would raise the marginal rate on the $50,000 family from 39 percent to almost 47 percent, which is a significant increase.

To raise the revenue collected from middle-income people without significantly raising marginal tax rates in a harmful way, it is necessary either to increase the proportion of the middle incomes that is subject to tax or to raise the rates while reducing the degree of progression. The extreme of the second approach may be illustrated by imagining that instead of maintaining a structure of personal income tax rates running from 10 percent to 50 percent and yielding revenue equal to about 20 percent of taxable income we were to institute a flat tax of 24 percent on the present income tax base. This would raise the revenue while reducing marginal rates where they are most burdensome and raising them where they are lowest and the raised rates would probably still not be very harmful. Less extreme solutions are possible. For example, all existing tax rates could be raised by an equal percentage of the amount by which they fall short of 50 percent. Then the 10 percent rate would be raised a great deal and the 50 percent rate would not be raised at all. This would avoid having to raise the marginal rates where the incentive effects of doing that would be most adverse.

The alternative to concentrating rate increases in the income levels where the existing rates are low is to broaden the tax base so that the necessary average rate increase would be small. If the tax base was not 50 percent of GNP but, say, 75 percent of GNP, the average tax rate needed to yield a given amount of revenue would be reduced by one-third. This fact has revived interest in a comprehensive income tax and in the value-added tax.

The comprehensive income tax now goes under the name "flat tax," but in most variants the adjective "flat" is an exaggeration. The proposals generally have two ingredients. One is to broaden the income tax base by reducing or eliminating deductions other than personal exemptions, such as deductions for interest and taxes paid, and by including some income now excluded, such as unemployment benefits or interest on state and local securities. The other part of the flat tax idea is to lower the average tax rate and reduce the number of different tax rates, but only in the extreme versions is that number reduced to one, making the system genuinely flat.

The amount of additional revenue that could be obtained from the personal income tax by limiting deductions, without any rate increases, is large. The table below shows the estimated revenue losses in fiscal year 1993 caused by some of the larger exclusions, other than those that might have a close connection with private business investment.

Example of Revenue Loss Caused by Exclusions
from Income Tax Base[8]

Fiscal Year 1993

Deductibility of mortgage interest on owner-occupied houses	$42.9 billion
Exclusion of social security benefits	24.5 ''
Deductibility of nonbusiness state and local taxes, other than on owner-occupied homes	23.8 ''
Exclusion of employer contributions for health insurance	43.1 ''
Exclusion of interest on life insurance savings	8.6 ''
Deductibility of property tax on owner-occupied homes	12.6 ''

The political difficulty of changing the provisions of the income tax law that generate these revenue losses is obvious. This
political difficulty is not to be considered mere timidity on the
part of government decision-makers. To close these "loopholes"
would impose a large burden on some taxpayers and leave others
unaffected. And although it may be true that those who would be
most injured have been for some years the beneficiaries of unjustified privileges, a sudden undoing of these privileges, legally
granted, is not fair either. Moreover, many of the people who
would now be hurt by closing these loopholes did not fully benefit
from them in the first place. The present owners who bought
houses when interest rates and taxes were deductible paid over
part of the benefit in higher prices to sellers and higher interest
rates to lenders, for example.

Partly because of these difficulties, people look for a more
even-handed way of broadening the tax base which would raise
revenue with a low rate applied fairly equally across the board.
That is one of the main attractions of the value-added tax
(VAT). In its usual form, VAT is a tax on the production and
distribution of consumer goods and services, levied at each stage
of production and distribution but in a way that avoids double-
counting. If no exceptions were provided, the base of such a tax
could be very large—say 65 percent of GNP compared with less

than 50 percent for the taxable income which is the base of the personal income tax. In practice, provision would almost certainly be made to provide a rebate for very low-income families. Very probably there would be exclusions for the imputed rent of owner-occupied homes, for medical costs and for the purchases of charitable and religious institutions. Thus the base of the VAT is likely to wind up not very different from the base of the personal income tax.

If this is true, the revenue yield of, say, a 4 percent value-added tax would be about like the revenue yield of adding 4 percentage points to each rate of the income tax—making the 10 percent rate 14 percent and the 50 percent rate 54 percent. The economic effect of the two approaches would be somewhat different—the VAT probably reducing consumption more and saving less—but that difference is probably not very great. There would also be a difference in the administrative burdens. VAT would impose a whole new, large burden of paperwork on the taxpayers and on tax collectors, which would not be necessary if additional revenue was obtained within the structure of the personal income tax. The main differences are in the realm of politics. The VAT would look like a consumption tax, and that would be considered unfair to "the poor." On the other hand, an equal percentage point increase in income tax rates would also look unfair to the poor. It would raise the 10 percent rate by 40 percent, in my previous illustration, while the 50 percent rate was raised by only 8 percent. Which impression will be most compelling in the political process is hard to say. One possibility is that the VAT would be harder to get established in the first place than an increase in income tax rates or even a revision of the income tax base, but once established it may be a politically easier source of additional revenue. This may be the worst combination possible, making it difficult to raise the revenue when we need it but providing a continuing enticement to more spending in the future by opening up a new source of revenue.

The relative merits of these approaches are less important than the need to get acceptance of the idea that somehow the taxes on the middle-income American must be increased and that this must be done without increasing the tax burden on the very rich or the very poor. This becomes clear once one abandons the notion that growth of the economy, perhaps under the stimulus of supply-side tax cuts, will provide for all our wants. Once that is accepted, priorities must be established. Our priorities, I am suggesting, should be the defense of the country, the promotion of economic growth and support of the living standards of the very poor. If that is the case we must look to the consumption of the middle-income American as the source from which we tend to these priorities. That does not mean a decline in middle-income living standards. It does mean that the share of middle-income consumption in the rising national income will have to decline, so that the absolute standard of living rises more slowly than it otherwise might for a while.

For a while in 1982 there seemed to be a possibility that the restraint on middle-class consumption might be achieved by cutting back government expenditures that mainly transferred income to middle-class people—social security being the largest case. This was the period of great attention to the "entitlement" programs. But the bipartisan commission on reform of the social security system showed little appetite for this and, as already noted, relied heavily on tax increases, for the coming years.

One can easily be skeptical of the possibility of achieving an increase in the taxation of middle-class people, especially if the increase is not extended to the upper-income people, since the middle-income people are the large majority of the voters. But such skepticism would not be entirely justified. The public, including the middle class, has shown a capacity to learn some things about the tax policy that serve the national interest and to accept the implications of them. The 1981 tax cut was an indication of that. True, almost everyone got something out of that act. But still the public accepted with equanimity some tax changes that in other times would have been strongly resisted as handouts to the rich. These included the reduction of the top individual income tax rate from 70 percent to 50 percent and a rather generous treatment of capital depreciation. Perhaps that was an isolated occasion, but politicians and leaders of opinion should not act on the assumption that the citizens are incapable of farsighted and public-spirited action.

I do not want to suggest that it is only the middle class that must sacrifice. The tens of billions probably needed to reduce the deficit can only come from the middle class, because that is where the money is. To try to get any significant amount out of upper-income people would be futile and counterproductive. There has been some lessening in the resentment and envy toward the rich and powerful that animated tax legislation in the past, as well as greater recognition of the economic folly of the taxation those feelings inspired. But the upper-income people, corporate heads and their representatives have an obligation not to exploit the situation by using their influence to defend tax preferences that are unjustified in equity or economics. Percentage depletion and provision of excess loss reserves by financial institutions are examples. If we enter a period of more stable prices it may even be necessary to think again about that perennial blister, the taxation of capital gains. For a long time the closing of such loopholes was resisted on the ground that the high rates of taxation made them necessary if the economy was to function. Now that the highest rates of individual income taxation, and the effective rate of corporate profits taxation, have been substantially reduced it is time to reconsider the loopholes.

The Nature of the System

The preceding discussion deals with the traditional functions of government in the economy—with monetary policy, the decision about the size of the budget surplus or deficit and the level and composition of taxes. These are things that all but the most extreme free marketer would accept as necessary functions of government. But even in as free market a country as the United States today the government makes many more economic decisions than are involved in these functions. The government operates upon the economy selectively through controls, subsidies, tariffs, loans and many other ways. Calls for more of this are always present, and these calls become especially insistent when the economy is believed to be in trouble, as is now believed to be the case.

There is a common belief that the expansion of government controls and consequent limitation of the free market is inevitable, even though proceeding at an irregular pace. Some welcome this alleged development and others regret it. But the facts are not at all clear. The size of government has expanded by almost any measure. But the size of the economy has also expanded, and it is not possible to determine whether the area of freedom has expanded or contracted. Government revenues have increased, but private incomes after tax have also increased. Government regulations have proliferated, but there have also been powerful developments increasing freedom of choice in the economic sphere, including the spread of knowledge and the reduction of transportation costs. The future of the free market is still to be determined. One can regard what has been going on as a race between the political tendency to expand the role of government and the dynamic forces of the private sector that expand the free domain. The race has proceeded irregularly, with occasional spurts of government controls, and the net outcome is hard to measure. The Reagan administration came into office determined to accelerate the expansion of the free sector and to undo some of the earlier increase of government controls. The results of its efforts in these directions in the early years of the administration were mixed, although the net was almost certainly to slow down the expansion of controls. But the national contest about the role of government did not come to an end with the advent of Ronald Reagan.

Issues about particular controls or subsidies will continue to arise and the outcomes will be determined by the locus of political power and by the costs and benefits of the specific measures in question as well as by general attitudes to government. There are, however, problems that could lead to a more radical change in the nature of the economic system. One of these is the alleged structural problem of the American economy, as evidenced principally by the concentration of high unemployment in the automobile, steel and other "smokestack" industries. This is commonly taken to show the inability of the free market system to adapt the use of labor and capital to changing markets and technologies and leads to the conclusion that the government needs to take more responsibility for directing American industry into greener pastures. Various proposals to this end have arisen under the name of "industrial policy," mainly promising to move us into a high-technology future. I have discussed this line of thinking earlier and indicated why it promises no contribution to improving the performance of the American economy. Talk of such a policy will undoubtedly have a period of prominence in politics, because it meets the politicians' need to sound modern and intellectual but is sufficiently vague to avoid sharp analysis and criticism. There is unlikely to be an attempt to implement this idea on a comprehensive scale, partly because its extreme implausibility will appear as soon as its specific features are spelled out. Nevertheless the idea is dangerous and needs to be be rejected. It provides the rationale for *ad hoc* interventions to "assist" American industry in the adjustment that a changing world economy requires. Experience shows that this assistance overwhelmingly takes the form of protecting existing industries rather than promoting adaptation to new ones. It is no accident that this has happened. That is the nature of politics and of the bureaucracy.

The "general" economic measures described above are, in fact, the best and most promising "industrial policy" the United States can have. The main requirement is an environment in which private enterprise will invest in change, providing attractive opportunities to draw workers out of the fading industries. To reduce the economic uncertainties that accompany inflation, to avoid absorbing an enormous share of the national saving in financing a deficit and to relieve the tax burdens that have borne most heavily on investment—these things will most surely contribute to the adaptation of the American economy. With a stable and nonhostile environment, American private enterprise has been quite energetic in moving into new technologies and new markets. In retrospect one can point to cases in which these adjustments seem to have been too slow. But that is not the same as saying that government intervention in the process would have made these adjustments better or quicker.

Americans have recently been fascinated by what they think to be Japanese economic practice, including the image of the energetic, farsighted and public-spirited bureaucrat who sees the proper direction of economic development and unerringly guides labor and capital to what will be their most productive uses. This picture is undoubtedly exaggerated. But even if it were not, the lesson for the United States would be unclear. Perhaps in Japan, talent is greater in the government than in the private sector and the bureaucracy is more dynamic than the private market. That is not true in the United States.

The idea of "industrial policy" has possible ramifications that could seriously impair the efficiency and adaptability of the American economy. I do not, however, believe that this idea will get beyond the stage of *ad hoc* interventions that will be sand in the cogs of the economic system but will not much change the system.

Another danger lies in the appeal that "incomes policy"—meaning some kind of wage and price controls—recurrently has to many American intellectuals and to the public at large. The decline of the inflation rate after 1980 was accompanied by a substantial rise of unemployment. Critics of the time did not deny that the decline of inflation was important but maintained that they knew a way to do it better—with less unemployment. That way was incomes policy, to induce business and labor to slow down prices and wage increases without having to go through the wringer of a recession.

The brisk recovery from the 1981–1982 recession, without the revival of rapid inflation, suppressed interest in such policies of direct wage and price restraint. But one should not assume that the idea will not return. It has the perpetual attractiveness of all ideas that promise painless solutions of real problems. As time passes, the officials who had direct experience with the failure of incomes policies and direct controls to curb inflation in the 1960s and 1970s will leave the scene. Public memory of such things is notoriously short. The kinds of circumstances that give rise to the demand for incomes policies can easily recur. As a result of mistakes of monetary policy or for other reasons, we may find ourselves with an inflation rate that is intolerably high. But the process of reducing it may entail a temporary increase of unemployment. Then the suggestion will be heard that incomes policy could resolve our dilemma. Or we could go through a period in which the unemployment rate seems to be stuck at a level that politicians can tell the public is intolerably and unnecessarily high. Then we would get promises from politicians to rescue us by recourse to the magic formula, "incomes policy."

It is worthwhile, therefore, to recall some of the arguments and experiences of the 1960s and 1970s that should be in the public memory as we face economic developments of the future.

Controls over prices and wages have more appeal to the American people than controls that affect the production process more directly. A proposal that the government should direct the movement of labor and capital from Pittsburgh to San Antonio would be rejected as impractical and improper. A suggestion that the government should set ceilings on prices and wages is much more acceptable. Opinion polls regularly show a majority of the public in favor of price and wage controls. The public seems to regard price and wage controls as having an exclusively distributive function, protecting the weak against exploitation by the strong, and in this context a majority think of themselves as weak. They regard the setting of prices and wages as separate from decisions about production and employment, which go on grinding out the same goods and services and employment regardless of the prices and wages. Moreover, incomes policy is commonly thought of as the imposition of a uniform standard for prices and a uniform standard for wages—such as 2½ percent annual increase for prices and 5 percent annual increase for wages. That does not involve the government in making specific decisions about specific businesses and unions and seems a less powerful government intrusion. Finally, incomes policy is commonly portrayed as relying upon voluntary cooperation by business and labor, so that little or no exercise of government power is required. This distinction between mandatory and voluntary seems important to many economists who retain a professional disposition toward free markets. The distinction seems not to bother the public at large.

All of these perceptions which make "incomes policy" attractive or at least acceptable are wrong. The decisions about prices and wages do importantly affect not only how incomes are divided but also what gets produced, where and by whom. What people do not understand is that the incomes policy inevitably affects *relative* prices—the price of steel relative to the price of aluminum, for example. Even if all prices were frozen, or permitted to rise only by the same percent, the policy would be affecting the relative prices because the relations would not have remained constant in an uncontrolled world. And these relative prices are going to affect how much steel and how much aluminum is used in cans and in automobiles, and therefore how much employment is in Pittsburgh, Pennsylvania, or Massena, New York. The dominant and efficient influence of relative prices in directing real economic activity is one of the great lessons of economics, a lesson of which the population in general is ignorant and which some economists choose to disregard.

The neglect of relative prices is the fundamental flaw in the case for incomes policy. If prices are rising on the average by 10 percent per annum and wages on the average by 13 percent it seems perfectly obvious that we would be better off if prices rose on the average by 2 percent and wages by 5 percent. The next step is to order or suggest that no price should rise by more than 2 percent and no wage by more than 5 percent. But there is a big difference between an increase of 2 percent in the *average* level of prices and an increase of 2 percent in *each* price. We may want the average to rise by 2 percent. We do not want each price to rise by 2 percent, because that would suppress the changes in relative prices that the free market would generate and that are essential for the efficiency of the economy. The problem that incomes policy does not solve is how to get noninflationary behavior of the average level of prices while retaining the necessary flexible adaptation of relative prices.

In fact, any incomes policy that lasts for more than a few months must begin to grapple with the determination of particular prices and wages. It loses its character of a general rule that falls equally upon all wages and all prices like the gentle rain from heaven. The managers of the system must begin to make specific decisions about the extremely large number of cases in which the general rule does not fit, possibly because of unusual cost changes. At this point the managers of the system change from neutral administrators to the wielders of large discretionary power.

During the Nixon price and wage control days, when I had a role in drawing up the rules of the system, even though I did not deal with particular cases, I was besieged by visits from businesses and trade associations that wanted special consideration. I remarked to President Nixon that one could come to like the system because it gave him such a feeling of power over all these supplicants. The President thought that was funny, because he knew that I had a strong distaste for the controls. But the feeling and the power itself are both real, and the power is dangerous because it could easily be used to reward friends and punish enemies. This is aside from the fact that no one knows how to make efficient decisions from Washington about particular prices and wages.

For some proponents of incomes policy the distinction between mandatory and voluntary is critical. They reject, or say they would reject, the notion that the government should compel businesses and workers to keep prices and wages within limits set by the government. But they find the economic and political defects of such a system absent if the government only makes "suggestions" that private parties may choose to follow or to leave alone. This always turns out to be a weak distinction. However initially determined to keep the system voluntary, the government cannot remain uninvolved if its suggestions are conspicuously disregarded by businesses and unions. At the least the transgressors are subject to public opprobrium, which is likely to be increased if the government calls attention to the transgression. But the government invariably is drawn into using other influence to "persuade" businesses or unions to comply, such as the allocation of government contracts or institution of antitrust suits. In fact, the difference between mandatory and voluntary systems is not great. In both cases there will be a high degree of compliance motivated simply by the desire to do what the authorities say should be done, strengthened by fear of sanctions. There will be a certain amount of noncompliance, but this cannot be relied upon to correct the economic inefficiencies caused by the arbitrary setting of relative prices. One difference is that when the system is mandatory the private parties have an opportunity to go to court to seek relief from what they consider arbitrary treatment. In this respect the mandatory system is more respectful of private rights.

For a while in the 1960s, the fashionable version of incomes policy was the tax-based incomes policy, or TIP. In TIP the government would establish limits to wage increases, or, in some versions, both wage and price increases, and exceeding the limit would subject the transgressors to a tax proportional to the amount of the transgression. Thus, exceeding the limit would not be prohibited but it would be costly, and the cost would presumably be great enough to make transgression rare. But if the cost is that great, provision would have to be made for administrative exceptions.

The main reason for the persistent interest in TIP, though, is that it has never been tried and so has no failures to its account. But fundamentally, TIP changes nothing from previous incomes policies or wage and price controls. The fundamental point is that arbitrary limits are set to the ability of prices and wages to respond to market conditions and that the government assumes tremendous power to determine the economic fortunes of the citizens.

Most of the policy questions discussed in this chapter are fit subjects for negotiation and compromise. That includes such matters as the objectives and techniques of monetary policy, the size and stability of budget deficits and the distribution of the tax burden. These are matters on which liberals and conservatives, Keynesians and monetarists, Democrats and Republicans disagree. But if they are candid they will recognize that they are not sure of the one right answer, that the differences among them are matters of degree and that reaching agreement and consequent stability of policy may be more important than continually striving for one's preferred solution.

But that is not true of wage and price controls, euphemistically called incomes policy. Of course, there can be a little bit of it, in the sense that a few specific prices, like utility rates, can be, and are, controlled. I am talking here, however, of controls on a scale that might be relevant to the macroeconomic problems of inflation and unemployment. With respect to such controls there can be, from the standpoint of conservative economics—in its classic, free-market sense—no middle ground and no compromise. Such controls are fatal to the conservative vision of a good society and a good economy, which is regularly described as the "free price system." Their adverse effects on economic efficiency, which would surely compound as the controls were prolonged, are not the main reason for rejecting them. They provide the government with a weapon by which it can single out for control, for reward or punishment, any industry, firm or union, violently disturbing the balance between the sphere of government and the sphere of private life. The adoption of general and lasting controls of prices and wages would be a statement that the idea of the self-regulating economy is through.

This judgment of the controls is not invalidated by the fact that our most thoroughgoing experience with controls came during a conservative administration. That experience only confirmed these judgments. It was only kept from being disastrous by being terminated, even though the termination was itself painful.

The national-consensus economic policy that we need cannot include price and wage controls, in whatever guise. Those who share this aversion to controls should recognize that it imposes certain obligations on them not to create but to help to avoid the conditions that strengthen the demand for controls.

Promises that create expectations unlikely to be satisfied must be avoided. Such a promise—to end inflation without an increase of unemployment—was one of the main errors of the Nixon administration. It led to disappointment with the Nixon policy and clamor for controls as a way to make the promise good. Similar promises made during 1980 and 1981 were a danger, but the

Reagan administration moved to more realistic ground by 1982, warning the public that a noninflationary policy would entail a considerable period of universally high unemployment.

There should be no illusions about the possibility of moderating the controls to keep them harmless while at the same time achieving the results that proponents of controls seek for them. Once initiated, the controls have a strong tendency to assume all of their harmful features. What was intended as the statement of guidelines to be voluntarily observed becomes the rationale for more and more compulsion. Plans for limiting only wage increases inevitably lead to controls over prices. Ninety-day freezes turn into elaborate systems lasting for years.

Businessmen must restrain their understandable claims for protection, subsidies and other preferential treatment in their own particular cases. They cannot credibly wrap themselves in the flag of the free price system while pushing such claims. Proposals for economic "planning" in the United States invariably are described as simply efforts to rationalize the chaos of government intervention that already exists. Much of this intervention is a response to demands of people who consider themselves champions of free markets.

Price and wage controls are most popular when unemployment seems to be the consequence of the effort to reduce or restrain inflation by traditional monetary policy. The controls are not a good solution for this problem. But the problem is a real one. Those who are most determined to avoid the controls should recognize it and be prepared to support constructive measures to deal with it. I have already indicated that it is dangerous to promise that anti-inflationary policy can be painless. But still, things can be done to shelter those who would be most severely injured in the anti-inflationary process. A safety net of income assistance programs for low-income people—such as unemployment compensation, food stamps, aid to families with dependent children—can assure that necessary macroeconomic policies do not force people into poverty. Public employment programs can support the income, work experience and morale of persons who would be most hurt by unemployment without interfering with the anti-inflationary policy—if the wages paid in those programs are not too high. Such measures are not only a matter of political pragmatism—of making the free market acceptable to people who do not appreciate its value. They are important for their own sake just because avoiding human misery is important.

There is a more general point here. The free market system is the most assured route to strong economic growth and thus to raising the standard of living of all the people. Conservatives love to say that the best way to care for the very poor is to assure that the overall productivity of the economy improves. In some backward countries it may be true that to attempt to use part of the meager resources to care for today's poor would prevent later generations from rising out of poverty. But that is not true of the United States. The national income of the United States is so great and the number of the very poor is so low that a minimum income can be provided for all by the application of a small fraction of our resources. That would not prevent our children and grandchildren from being still richer than we are, on the average. Conservatives should be concerned that assistance for the poor and disadvantaged takes forms that are consistent with a free market system. That means basically that there should be as little interference as possible with decisions on production and pricing. But conservatives should not be in the position of forcing the society to choose between freedom and growth on the one hand and compassion on the other. That is worse than politically unwise. It is unnecessary and unworthy of conservative values.

We need a responsible, open-minded national discussion of economic policy, addressed to our real problems and seeking to reach agreement. Such a discussion should start with the undeniable fact that the American economy has worked well. The difficulties we have experienced recently are serious only in relation to earlier periods of our own greatest achievements. The economy has continued to provide extremely high living standards, growing at a moderate pace, including on the average a reduction of poverty from already low levels. Discussion of economic policy should also start with a clear picture of the economy that delivered these results. It has not been a laissez-faire economy and it has not been a planned economy. The common term is that we have a "mixed" system, but that does not indicate the nature of the mixture. The mixture consists of three elements: a free market to govern production and the initial distribution of income, macroeconomic policy of government to provide a stable overall environment within which the free market can work, and government measures of assistance to the poor.

Our economic difficulties since the early 1960s do not indicate that this three-way division of functions has failed. The experience does not suggest the need for a radical change of policy—to substitute government planning for the free market or to deprive government of its macroeconomic or redistributive responsibilities. Our difficulties mean that the system has not been run very well, not that that system needs to be replaced. The main deficiency has been in macroeconomic policy, which in my view is mainly monetary policy. This was responsible for the inflation of the years after 1965, and that in turn was the main source of the anxiety that overcame the American people in those years. The inflation contributed in various ways—including the escalation of marginal tax rates—to the slowdown in productivity growth in the same period. Our other troubles, less serious but still real, were also the results of mistakes in the management of the system. The proper function of the government in providing assistance to the poor was allowed to mushroom into a vast transfer of income to middle-income people—mainly old people—that required financing by high tax rates on the working population. An increasingly large fraction of the national saving was absorbed by budget deficits. Excessive government interference with the free market obstructed the adaptation of the economy to changing conditions—energy policy being the leading example.

These mistakes of economic policy have been partly due to the deficiencies of economics. Economists have not known how to describe the path of the economy that would most surely and efficiently prevent inflation. They have not known just what monetary policy would keep the economy on that path. They have not been able to say with confidence how much difference a certain structure of taxes or a certain size of budget deficit would make for long-run economic growth.

But these inadequacies of economics, although serious, have not been the fundamental problem. Enough was known to permit avoidance of long-continued cumulative inflation, even if not enough was known to keep the price level stable from year to year. Probably enough was also known to point to better policies about deficits, taxes and controls than we followed to yield a higher rate of economic growth.

The fundamental difficulty was political. Parochial and short-run interests dominated over national and long-term interests. It was, in my opinion, the domination of the short-run view that was most harmful. Inflationary policies were followed because they seemed to have, and often did have, a quite general short-run benefit whereas the adverse consequences would come only later. We run excessive deficits because the bad effects come only later, in the form of lower productivity and lower economic growth, whereas the bigger government programs and lower taxes that yield the deficits are enjoyed now. We use the wrong kinds of taxes because their bad effects appear slowly.

Economists have some responsibility for this preoccupation with the short run. Too many have forsaken the economists' traditional role of emphasizing the long view. Some may have been taken in by Keynes' remark that in the long run we are all dead. Others, probably more numerous, have been seduced by the attraction of participating in politics. But it is not only or mainly the economists who are to blame. Others who influence public opinion, and mainly the politicians, are more important. No one wants to incur the unpopularity of telling the American people that there is a choice between the present and the future. All politicians like to say that they are calling upon the people to make sacrifices, because they believe that among the present things that people enjoy is the virtuous feeling of sacrifice. But no one really calls for sacrifice—even the trivial sacrifice of the present that would be involved in a country as rich as ours if a more stable and productive future were to be assured.

The politicians say that it is impractical for them to take the long view, because the voters will not stand for it. The common argument of incumbent politicians is that if they do the right thing—the forward-looking thing—the voters will bring in the opposition, who will do even worse. Nothing is more natural than for the incumbent to identify the long-run national interest with his reelection. But the implied view of the public is too cynical and unjustified. There is at least a chance that the public will respond to candid talk and farsighted policy and will appreciate the politicians who offer that.

But we cannot rely mainly on politicians to change the tone of the discussion and practice of economic policy. Others who are concerned, and who do not have political office at stake, will have to take the lead. They will have to make the world safe for politicians to do the right thing. They can accomplish that, or at least try to do so, by initiating and carrying on a discussion out of which will emerge new understanding and new principles of policy that give proper weight to the long-run national interest.

10

Ten Years of the U.S. Economy and Economic Policy, 1977–1987

The "Real" Performance of the Economy

DISTINGUISHING BETWEEN THE "REAL" AND THE "NOMINAL" performance of the economy is important, especially in the ten years under review. By "real" is meant those aspects of the economy that are actually or conceptually measurable in physical quantities—like the volume of output or the number of workers, or relations among these measures like the volume of output per worker. By "nominal" is meant those aspects of the economy that are measurable in dollar amounts or ratios of dollar amounts—like the average of prices or the sum total of dollar expenditures.

This distinction is especially important for the years 1977–1987 because the most striking fact about this period is that the real performance has been in most respects quite ordinary, whereas the nominal performance has been extraordinary.

To look at the real performance first:

1. Total output, as measured by real GNP, increased between 1977 and 1987 at an average annual rate of 2.6 percent. This rate has

---

This chapter originally appeared in slightly different form in the *AEI Economist*, in 1988.

prevailed since 1973. It is significantly smaller than the rate of 3.6 percent from 1950 to 1973 and smaller even than the longer-term rate of 3.1 percent from 1929 to 1973.

2. The ten-year period is too short to permit any confident statement about whether there has been a change in the trend of output, as distinguished from cyclical fluctuations. But at least one can say that there has been no clear evidence of a change in trend. From 1977 to 1981 output rose by 2.3 percent per year, whereas from 1981 to 1987 the increase was 2.7 percent per year. This difference almost disappears, however, if the dividing point is moved from 1981 to 1980. From 1977 to 1980 the annual rate of growth was 2.48 percent and from 1980 to 1987 was 2.54 percent.

3. The period 1977–1987 includes one serious recession, which began in the third quarter of 1981. The pattern of this recession was similar to the pattern of the recession that began in the second quarter of 1974. The decline of output from peak to trough was 4 percent in the 1974 recession and 3 percent in the 1981 recession. Six years after the beginning of the 1974 recession, output was 16 percent above the previous peak. Six years after the beginning of the 1981 recession, output is 17 percent above its previous peak. By 1980 the recovery from the 1974 recession was near its end. If common forecasts are correct, the recovery now continuing will significantly outstrip the earlier one. But those are forecasts.

4. The rate of growth of productivity, measured by output per hour of work, which had slowed down markedly after 1973, remained low during the years 1977–1987. The rate fluctuated cyclically, but at the end of the period there was no evidence that the trend had increased.

5. Total employment increased rapidly between 1977 and 1987— by about 2 percent per year. This rate of growth was the continuation of a 2 percent growth rate that began around 1960. It reflected rapid increases in the working-age population and in the labor-force participation of women in the more recent period. Cyclical fluctuations aside, the growth of employment was fairly steady, at a rate of 2.2 percent between 1977 and 1981 and 1.9 percent between 1981 and 1987. The unemployment rate was 7.3 at the beginning of 1977. It fell to a low of 5.5 percent during the recovery of that cycle, rose to 10.6 percent at the depth of the 1981–1982 recession, and fell

again to 5.9 percent in July 1987.

6. One respect in which the period 1977–1987 was extraordinary was that in the latter years of it the United States used significantly more goods and services than it produced. In other words, the United States was a net importer of goods and services. To be a net importer was not in itself unusual for the United States. It was in that condition in seventeen of the twenty-six years from 1950 to 1976. But the amounts were usually small. In 1984, 1985, and 1986, however, the amounts were quite large—2.4 percent, 3.0 percent, and 3.9 percent of GNP.

7. At the end of the period 1977–1987, the amount of goods and services the United States used was larger than the amount of gross national product. The distribution of the available goods and services among major uses was quite stable. Consumption regularly took about 63 percent of the total, private investment about 17 percent, and government (federal, state, local) about 20 percent. The most important change was in the composition of the government uses. The share of available goods and services going to defense rose from 5.3 percent to 6.7 percent, whereas other federal uses fell from 2.4 to 1.8 percent, and state and local uses fell from 11.9 percent to 11.0 percent.

8. Gross private saving as a percentage of GNP for the ten years as a whole was a little lower than earlier in the postwar period and was lower at the end of the ten years than at the beginning. In the fiscal years 1984–1987, an exceptionally large part of these savings was absorbed in financing the federal budget deficit. The availability of savings to finance domestic private investment, despite the drain into the budget deficit, was supplemented by the inflow of capital from abroad, permitting private investment to maintain a fairly stable relation to GNP. But, of course, some of this investment belonged, directly or indirectly, to the foreigners who provided the capital inflow. The increase in the capital owned by Americans, net of their foreign liabilities, fell significantly as a fraction of GNP. (See table.)

9. The division of output among types of products and industries remained almost unchanged during the period. Despite much alarm about the "deindustrialization" of America, manufacturing output grew along with the rest of the economy. In 1977 manufacturing

TABLE : SAVING AND INVESTMENT AS A PERCENTAGE OF GNP, 1977–1986

Calendar Year	(a) Gross Private Saving	(b) Federal Budget Surplus	(c) State and Local Budget Surplus	(d) Gross Private Domestic Investment	(e) Net Foreign Investment	(f) Gross Private Domestic Investment by U.S. Residents
1977	17.8	−2.3	1.4	17.3	−0.4	16.9
1978	18.2	−1.3	1.3	18.5	−0.4	18.1
1979	17.8	−0.6	1.1	18.1	0.1	18.2
1980	17.5	−2.2	1.0	16.0	0.5	16.5
1981	18.0	−2.1	1.1	16.9	0.3	17.2
1982	17.6	−4.6	1.1	14.1	0	14.1
1983	17.4	−5.2	1.4	14.7	−1.0	13.8
1984	18.0	−4.5	1.7	17.6	−2.4	15.2
1985	16.6	−4.9	1.6	16.0	−2.9	13.1
1986	16.1	−4.8	1.3	15.8	−3.4	12.4

NOTE: Column (f) = (d) − (e); column (f) also equals (a) + (b) + (c), except for statistical discrepancy.
SOURCE: *Survey of Current Business*, July issue, various years.

CHART: LEVELS OF MANUFACTURING OUTPUT
AND EMPLOYMENT, 1960–1986

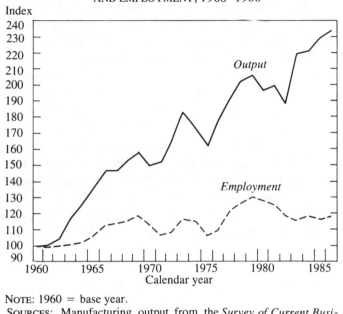

NOTE: 1960 = base year.
SOURCES: Manufacturing output from the *Survey of Current Business;* manufacturing employment from the Bureau of Labor Statistics.

output was 21.8 percent of the GNP; in 1986 it was also 21.8 percent (see chart).

10. The proportion of the population in poverty—that is, with incomes below the official poverty line—varied cyclically but showed no trend during the years 1977–1987. The poverty rate continued a leveling out that began in about 1973 after a long period in which it had declined substantially. The leveling out of the poverty rate occurred despite a 21 percent increase in real per capita disposable income between 1973 and 1986.

Performance in the "Nominal" Economy

On the nominal side of the economy, the distinguishing feature was the high rate of inflation in the early part of the period and the much lower rate near the end of the period. One should note, however, that even the "much lower" inflation rate of the mid-1980s was high in comparison with the inflation rate during most of our history.

From 1977 to 1981 the consumer price index rose at an annual average rate of 10.7 percent; from 1981 to 1986 the average rate was 3.8 percent. In the earlier period labor compensation per hour rose by 9.5 percent per year, on the average; in the latter period the average rate was 4.9 percent. The average yield on a ten-year Treasury security rose from 7.42 percent in 1977 to 13.91 percent in 1981; it then fell, along with inflation, to 7.68 percent in 1986.

The inflation rate had fallen substantially during the recession from 1974 to 1976, but rose sharply thereafter in the recovery. The distinctive feature of the 1982–1986 recovery was the continuing drop in the inflation rate. In the first half of 1987 the consumer price index rose at an annual rate of 5.4 percent, and by June the yield of the ten-year bond had risen to 8.62 percent. Concern was being expressed about a new wave of inflation. But still, there was little doubt that a marked, if not necessarily eternal, change in the inflation rate had occurred since the late 1970s.

The Role of Policy

The key question about economic policy in the decade under review is what caused the most spectacular development of the period— namely, the sharp reduction of inflation. The behavior of the real economy might seem to require less explanation, since it was so ordinary. But still one might ask why it was so ordinary. Why did the real economy behave in such an ordinary—not to say dull—way despite "supply-side" policies intended to reinvigorate it?

One must first say, or confess, that many questions about the connection between economic policies and economic performance remain mysteries even for years after the events. Economists are still arguing about what the Kennedy-Johnson tax cut had to do with the economic expansion of 1961–1966, as well as about the connections between Hoover and Roosevelt policies and the 1929–1939 depression and recovery. They will surely be arguing for a long time about what caused what in the experience of 1977–1987. Still it is worthwhile to reveal some of the uncertainties in the story.

Just as the decline of the inflation rate is the central story, the recession of 1981–1982 and the subsequent recovery are the main events in the story. Although other factors were involved, the character of that recession and that recovery were critical for the decline of inflation.

The American economy, like others, fluctuates for numerous reasons, not all of them positively related to government policy. There were probably ample grounds for thinking that the United States would go into a recession sometime in the early 1980s. The expansion had been going on for an exceptionally long period, since early 1975, with only a brief and peculiar interruption in the second quarter of 1980. More important, the rapid rate of inflation was a source of great uncertainty and made it inevitable that at some point the expectations on which businessmen made their investment and inventory plans would turn out to be wrong and there would be a correction, probably of a recessionary character.

But beyond that, policy makers at the beginning of 1981 wanted to slow down the economy in order to reduce the inflation rate. The means for slowing down the economy was to be monetary restraint. Everyone was agreed on this strategy—the outgoing Carter administration, the incoming Reagan administration, and the Federal Reserve under the continuing leadership of Paul Volcker.

They were, moreover, agreed on a policy of gradualism employing a minimum dose of restraint. At the time, in a mood of despair about subduing the inflation, there was a good deal of talk in academic economic circles about the possible need for a "sudden death" strategy. The idea was that monetary growth would be sharply cut with the announced intention of getting the inflation rate down to zero, or close to it, in one step no matter what the cost in output and employment might be. Underlying this idea was the belief that such a move would quickly eliminate inflationary expectations and then allow the real economy to recover while prices remained stable.

No responsible officials supported this strategy, however. The final economic report of the Carter administration envisaged two quarters of slow growth in the first half of 1981, after which growth would accelerate, but the brief moderate slowdown would be enough to set the inflation rate on a gradual downward path. The

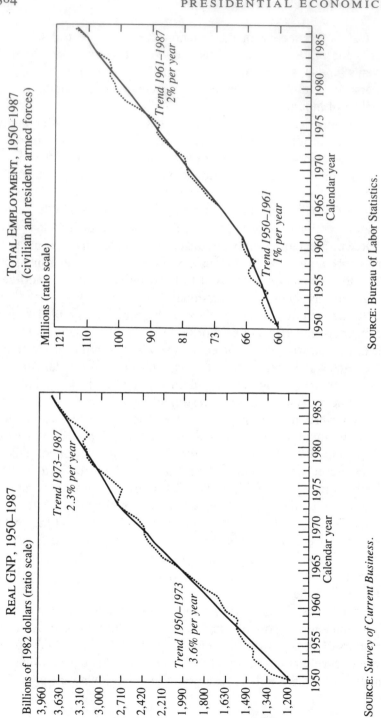

REAL GNP, 1950–1987

Billions of 1982 dollars (ratio scale)

*Trend 1973–1987
2.3% per year*

*Trend 1950–1973
3.6% per year*

SOURCE: *Survey of Current Business.*

TOTAL EMPLOYMENT, 1950–1987
(civilian and resident armed forces)

Millions (ratio scale)

*Trend 1961–1987
2% per year*

*Trend 1950–1961
1% per year*

SOURCE: Bureau of Labor Statistics.

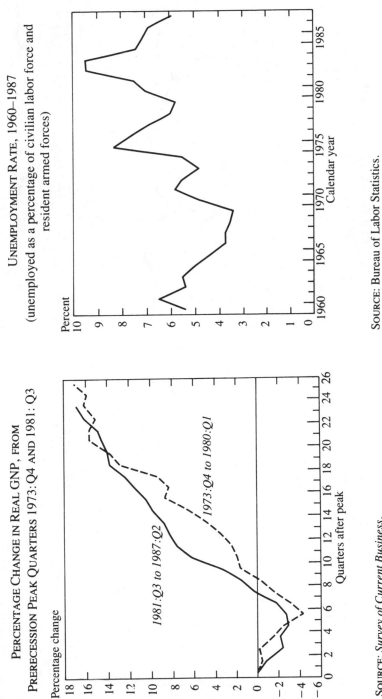

PERCENTAGE CHANGE IN REAL GNP, FROM
PRERECESSION PEAK QUARTERS 1973:Q4 AND 1981:Q3

1981:Q3 to 1987:Q2

1973:Q4 to 1980:Q1

Percentage change

Quarters after peak

SOURCE: *Survey of Current Business.*

UNEMPLOYMENT RATE, 1960–1987
(unemployed as a percentage of civilian labor force and
resident armed forces)

Percent

Calendar year

SOURCE: Bureau of Labor Statistics.

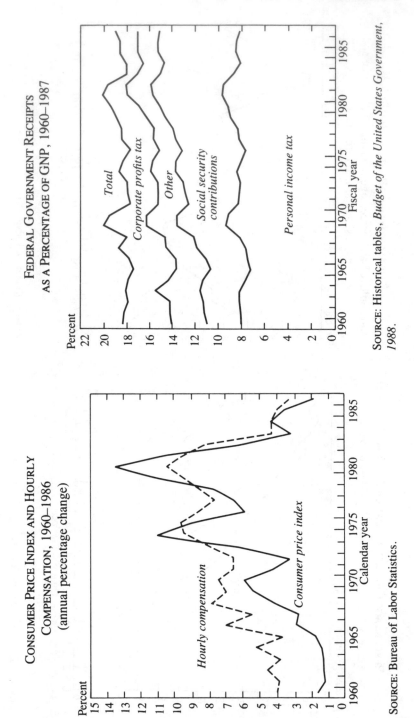

CONSUMER PRICE INDEX AND HOURLY
COMPENSATION, 1960–1986
(annual percentage change)

Hourly compensation

Consumer price index

SOURCE: Bureau of Labor Statistics.

FEDERAL GOVERNMENT RECEIPTS
AS A PERCENTAGE OF GNP, 1960–1987

Total

Corporate profits tax

Other

Social security
contributions

Personal income tax

SOURCE: Historical tables, *Budget of the United States Government,
1988.*

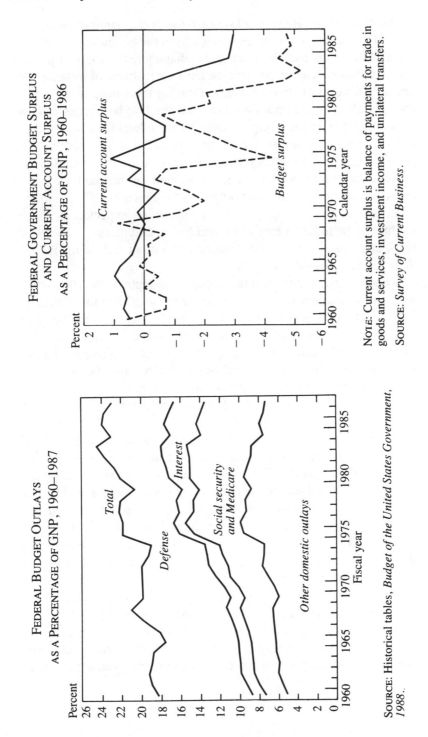

FEDERAL GOVERNMENT BUDGET SURPLUS
AND CURRENT ACCOUNT SURPLUS
AS A PERCENTAGE OF GNP, 1960–1986

NOTE: Current account surplus is balance of payments for trade in goods and services, investment income, and unilateral transfers.

SOURCE: *Survey of Current Business.*

FEDERAL BUDGET OUTLAYS
AS A PERCENTAGE OF GNP, 1960–1987

SOURCE: Historical tables, *Budget of the United States Government, 1988.*

economists of the Reagan administration had a similar view, but pushed the period of "sogginess" back from the beginning of 1981 to the middle. (This pattern seems to be characteristic of governments facing inflation. They recognize the need for restraint of inflation but are unwilling to predict a recession during their time in office; so they hopefully count on a slowdown too small to be a recession but big enough to turn the inflation down.) The Federal Reserve was less precise and less optimistic in its promises, but it also described a policy of gradual monetary restraint to achieve gradual disinflation.

None of the responsible parties wanted or planned as much reduction of total demand and output and as much rise of unemployment as we got in 1981 and 1982, and none expected as much decline in the inflation rate as we had by the end of 1982. There are two questions: (1) Why did demand and output fall so much? (2) Why did inflation fall so much?

Some observers attributed the unexpected depth of the 1981–1982 recession to an unexpectedly sharp contraction of the money supply. This explanation does not hold, however. In fact, the slowdown of monetary growth was quite moderate. As the 1983 Annual Report of the Council of Economic Advisers pointed out, if historic relations between the money supply and nominal GNP had persisted, the actual growth of the money supply would have led to a 10 percent increase of nominal GNP in 1982 instead of the actual 4 percent that occurred.

Neither can the depth of the recession be attributed to fiscal policy, at least according to any standard theory of the way fiscal policy works. By the fall of 1981, after the big tax cut had been enacted, the deficit was rising rapidly and it was becoming clear that unusually large deficits were here to stay for some time. In the standard theory of the past fifty years large deficits should have been expansionary, at least for a time, and in earlier, classical theory they should have had no effect on total demand and total output, although they would affect the composition of output.

There was, and may still be, a theory that the tax cuts contributed to the recession because the cuts were phased in over three years and people were waiting for the lowest tax rates to take effect before they engaged in income-earning activity. This does not, however, seem credible as a description of the 12 million unemployed at the end of

1982 or of many other people either.

The depth of the recession can be "explained" by pointing to the decline in the velocity of money—the relation between nominal GNP and the money supply—that occurred after 1981. But this is not really an explanation; it only restates the question of why nominal GNP grew so much less than was expected. Part of the explanation may be the decline of interest rates during 1981 and 1982, which reduced the cost of holding money. Some recent studies suggest that the common forecasts of economists underestimated the degree to which velocity would be affected by the decline of interest rates. The size of the drop in interest rates was caused in part by the depth of the recession, which it cannot therefore explain. The decline of interest rates may also have been caused by a marked change in expectations about the future rate of inflation—a subject to which I shall return.

In part the decline in velocity was caused by a change in banking regulations and practices, which increased interest payments on checkable bank deposits and so increased the desire to hold them. Even so, the size of the decline in velocity probably cannot be explained without invoking the magic word—expectations.

We are in a similar condition in trying to answer the second question. Why, given the decline in velocity and in nominal GNP, did the inflation rate decline so far so fast? Before the disinflation began economists had estimated how much recession, as measured by unemployment, would be required to get the inflation down by any given amount—say, by one percentage point. The estimates varied a good deal, but it is probably fair to say that the inflation rate fell more in 1982 than most of the estimates would have predicted even in a recession of the kind we experienced. Part of the explanation is the rise in the exchange rate of the dollar, which reduced the prices of imports and intensified competition for American producers. The rise of the dollar in turn requires explanation, which is not definitely available, but the answer surely includes the rise of the budget deficit and the tax cut of 1981, both of which attracted capital to the United States. So in a peculiar and rather unexpected way the administration's fiscal policy contributed to the decline of the inflation rate.

Whether the rise of the dollar is sufficient to explain why the inflation rate fell more than was conventionally predicted is a subject of dispute among economists. One possibility, of course, is that the estimates of economists were simply wrong and that they had exaggerated the amount of recession that would be required to get the inflation down, so that there is really no mystery, even without the added factor of the rising dollar. But it can be convincingly argued that something more was involved. (See Phillip Cagan, "Containing Inflation," in *Contemporary Economic Problems,* American Enterprise Institute, 1986.) This something more was a change of expectations about inflation.

A plausible story is that sometime in 1981 the private sector came to expect with confidence that the inflation rate would come down soon and significantly. This expectation made people willing to hold more money and therefore caused the decline of velocity. It also made businesses and workers willing to set and accept smaller price and wage increases and so contributed to the decline of the actual inflation rate.

But the source of this change of expectations as a cause of the disinflation and not as a consequence of it is difficult to see. The Reagan administration did not come into office with strong credentials as inflation fighters. The only specific economic program of the Reagan campaign in 1980 had assumed a high rate of inflation continuing for five years. The budget revisions submitted by the Reagan administration soon after entering office implied a very slow reduction of the inflation rate. By the fall of 1981 general recognition that the administration's fiscal policy implied large budget deficits for a long time would ordinarily have been a signal of more inflation. The main contribution of the administration to the idea of a marked change in the economic outlook in 1981 was probably the president's refusal to give in to the wage demands of the air traffic controllers when they went on strike.

The Federal Reserve may have had more to do with a change of inflationary policy expectations. Paul Volcker's appointment in 1979 as chairman of the Federal Reserve was quite explicitly tied to the need to curb inflation. His shift in operating procedures, with more emphasis on the supply of money and less on interest rates as a target, was interpreted in some circles as a sign of more disciplined focus on fighting inflation. But still, in both 1981 and 1982 the forecasts, and presumably also the objectives, of the Federal Reserve for reducing the inflation rate were moderate—significantly less than was actually achieved.

A change in inflationary expectations may have contributed more to developments during the expansion after the fall of 1982 than during the recession up to that point. If we consider the period 1981 to 1987 as a whole, the failure of inflation to rise during the expansion is more remarkable than the decline of inflation during the recession. By the time of the expansion, expectations were being influenced by the experience of the recession. This experience was not only the actual decline of the inflation rate in 1982. It was also the rather calm response of the administration, the Federal Reserve, and the public to the recession as the unemployment rate rose to almost 11 percent in 1982. The view developed that in the Reagan-Volcker regime the danger of being stampeded into inflationary monetary policy by fear of unemployment was less than it had been in earlier regimes. This perception helped to keep inflation low during the expansion.

The low actual and expected inflation during the 1982–1986 expansion is somewhat ironical because the growth of the money supply was extraordinarily rapid during this period. But there was growing recognition, in and out of the Federal Reserve, that changes in financial regulations and structures had broken previous relations between the money supply and inflation, at least temporarily and within some limits. The Federal Reserve seemed to be operating pragmatically, trying to adapt its course to observed events, with heavy emphasis on the rate of inflation.

To recapitulate, despite general avowal of a policy of gradualism, there was a disinflationary shock to the economy in the form of a recession whose depth was unplanned and unexpected by both the fiscal and the monetary authorities. If the depth of the recession had been foreseen, the authorities almost certainly would have tried to avert it by expansionary measures. In that sense the disinflation was triggered by accident. The main contribution of the policy makers was to tolerate the disinflationary recession they had not caused or wanted and not to try to get out of it quickly.

A more general explanation may be offered of our disinflationary experience. Back in 1974 I incautiously said that the American people got the inflation they deserved. I was widely criticized for that, but I only meant that if the American people had demanded or even had seemed willing to tolerate noninflationary policy they would have had it. By 1980 the people had experienced more than a decade of inflation trauma and had learned that nostrums like price controls did not work. They then "deserved" anti-inflationary policy; President Reagan and Chairman Volcker were the instruments by which they got it. This turn in public attitude was self-reinforcing. The public's willingness to tolerate anti-inflationary policy supported the expectation that inflation would come down, and that expectation made the decline of inflation easier and less costly in output and employment.

Policy and the Real Economy

In many dimensions the performance of the real economy in the past ten years was a continuation of earlier trends. Total employment (and employment as a percentage of the working-age population) rose more or less as they had since 1961. Total output and total output per hour of work rose at the slow rate that had begun after 1973—slow at least by comparison with the previous twenty-five or fifty years.

The shift to a slower trend of output and productivity growth, now seen to have come after 1973, was not clearly recognized until around the beginning of the period under review here. It became a matter of increasing concern in the first half of our decade. Students of productivity trends were unable to reach any agreed and confident explanation of the slowdown of productivity growth. Among the factors commonly listed as causes were a slower rate of growth of capital per worker, the debilitating effects of rising marginal tax rates, the costs of regulation, the costs of adapting to higher energy prices, and the uncertainties resulting from inflation.

Some of the alleged causes seemed open to correction by policy. The concern with the slowdown of growth and the belief that it had major roots in policy helped to rationalize the "supply-side" turn of policy, or policy rhetoric, associated with the advent of the Reagan team. This turn focused on two things: (1) reducing marginal tax rates, which would increase saving, investment, and labor-force participation as well as a less-measurable ingredient like innovativeness; and (2) reducing government regulation of the economy, which would allow the private sector to function more efficiently and relieve it of heavy compliance costs. Perhaps a third route to strengthening the supply side of the economy should be added—reducing the uncertainties caused by rapid inflation.

It appears that the results sought were not achieved. One has to say "appears" because the statistics about total output, productivity, and saving, are all in dispute; but still the judgment is supported by the best information we now have. National saving did not rise but declined as a fraction of GNP. Investment in the United States in real terms did not rise as a fraction of GNP. (Investment declined relatively in current dollars but remained a constant fraction in real terms because the prices of investment goods rose less than the general price level.) Labor participation rates continued their rising trend but did not accelerate. The growth of output and productivity fluctuated cyclically but did not rise above its low growth trend.

This lack of response should not be surprising. For one thing, the steps in tax reduction and deregulation came slowly. Although reduction of marginal income tax rates began in 1981, the lowest rates will not be reached until 1988. For many taxpayers, the effect of a reduction in the income tax rate was offset by higher rates of social security payroll taxes. The total ratio of federal taxes to GNP leveled out after 1981 but did not fall. Deregulation consisted mainly of slowing down the pace of new regulation, rather than severely curtailing existing regulation. Indeed, when account is taken of increased regulation of international trade, total regulation may not have decreased at all.

Moreover, some of the gains from supply-side increases may appear only after a long period has passed, especially if patterns of participation in the labor force are to change. And there may be benefits or consequences of some of these measures that do not show up in total output and productivity. For example, airline deregulation benefits travelers by making lower fares available, partly at the expense of the earnings of airline employees, which may be a gain or a loss depending on one's point of view.

Still, the enthusiastic expectations of the beneficial effect of supply-side measures were almost certainly unjustified. These expectations relied on a strength of response of savings and labor that was not supported by information available at the time and that has not been demonstrated since.

The key test is the behavior of saving and investment. Experts disagree on the size of the effect of the national investment rate on the growth of productivity. But almost everyone would agree that the investment rate, and the saving rate upon which it depends, is important and that it is probably the most important element on which policy can have a substantial and prompt effect. The Reagan administration program relied heavily on an increase in private saving. Private saving had to increase sufficiently to exceed the rise in the federal budget deficit, so that the total of national saving (private and public) would rise, permitting an increase in private investment by Americans. In fact, this did not happen, as can be seen in table 1. Private saving as a percentage of GNP fell while the federal deficit rose, so that the *United States* saving available to finance private investment fell sharply, from 17.4 percent of GNP in 1977–1981 to 13.7 percent in 1982–1986. A large inflow of foreign capital partly offset this decline as far as the amount of investment *in* the United States was concerned, but could not offset the decline in the amount of investment *owned* by Americans.

The saving picture has two parts—the decline in private saving and the rise in the federal deficit. The decline in the ratio of private saving to GNP is a mystery. The rise in the federal deficit is the subject of a rather silly debate between people who say that expenditures rose relative to revenues and those who say that revenues did not keep up with expenditures. These are two ways of saying the same thing. But the big change between the early part of the decade and the latter part was in the rate of increase of revenues. Between 1977 and 1981 total federal revenues in real terms rose at an annual rate of 4.1 percent. Between 1981 and 1986 they rose by 1.1 percent. Revenues other than social security taxes rose by 3.9 percent per year from 1977 to 1981, whereas they declined by 0.6 percent per year from 1981 to 1986. In real terms federal expenditures rose by 3.6 percent per year from 1977 to 1981 and by 3.9 percent per year from 1981 to 1986.

I have already noted that the deficiency of U.S. saving was in some degree made up by an influx of capital. This had as its counterpart a large net inflow of goods and services, commonly called the trade "deficit." This deficit was widely regarded as a great problem of the Reagan administration. In my opinion it was not a problem at all but a condition that helped to ease the real deficiency of capital caused by our budget deficit and low saving rate. I mention this condition, the trade deficit, only to show that I have not forgotten it.

Nations do not live by GNP alone. What they do with GNP is also important. The most significant change in the use of output during the decade was the rise in the share of GNP going to defense—from 5.4 percent in 1977 to 7.0 percent in mid-1987. (The share of total goods and services used is slightly smaller because the United States used more goods and services than it produced in both periods, importing the difference.) The increase in the defense share was, of course, the result of policy initiated in the latter days of the Carter administration and accelerated in the Reagan administration.

Relative to the total GNP or total private consumption this is a trivial change. But relative to saving and investment, or to government expenditures or to the budget deficit, these numbers are significant. To put the matter a little differently, given the unwillingness to reduce the share of additional resources going to consumption, by far the largest claimant of total resources, the increase in defense had a measurable effect on other resource uses and on the economy.

The real significance of the increase in defense spending is, of course, not in these obviously "economic" dimensions but in its contribution to the national security. This is often considered a noneconomic consequence. But nothing is more vital to our future economic growth and prosperity than provision for the national security.

●　●　●

Economic developments of the past ten years had three main elements—two things that changed and one that did not. The changes were the reduction of the inflation rate and the increased devotion of resources to defense. What failed to change was the rate of growth of output and productivity. The relations of these developments to economic policy were different. Real growth failed to accelerate in spite of policy measures intended to achieve growth. Defense expenditures increased clearly as a result of policy. The reduction of inflation was in part accidental from the standpoint of policy. The recession of 1981–1982, which set the stage for the disinflation that continued thereafter, was not intended or expected by policy makers. But by the early 1980s the public aversion to inflation may have been so strong that ways to get the inflation rate down would have been found even if the accidental reduction of 1981–1982 had not occurred.

At the end of 1965, after five years of noninflationary growth, there was a belief in the country that economists and the politicians they advised had discovered the key to managing the economy. The key was an American 1960s version of Keynesianism. The country spent the next fifteen years learning that the belief of 1965 was wrong.

We are, one must hope, unlikely to make the same error again. The recent performance of the economy, although good in some respects, is mixed, the record of policy is unclear, and economists are much less confident than they once were of the state of their own knowledge. There is much to do and the instruments to do it with are uncertain.

11

Economic Fashions
of the Times,
1977–1987

FASHIONS IN ECONOMIC IDEAS COME AND GO, like fashions in women's clothes. Economics can offer an explanation for this. Having a new idea is profitable; its originators, the publicists who first write about it, and the politicians who first exploit it get advantages in fame, votes, or money. But once the idea is commonplace there is no great gain in having it—like a K-Mart copy of a Lauren original. Also, there is no completely reliable way of demonstrating that one economic idea is better than another—or, at least, of demonstrating it to everyone who feels entitled to have an idea. So there is nothing to keep any idea from being displaced by another one. The market is always open for new ideas.

The foregoing is something of an exaggeration. But certainly the history of economic thought is closer to the history of women's fashions than to the history of astronomy or physics. Many of the economic ideas that are "new" today are rediscoveries. The monetarists rediscover Irving Fisher, Simon Newcomb, David Hume. Protectionists rediscover Friedrich List, Alexander Hamilton, the 17th century mercantilists. And so on. Aside from the mathematics, "it's all there" in the writings of an earlier generation.

This chapter originally appeared in slightly different form in the *AEI Economist*, in 1988.

397

I do not intend here to take such a long view of the matter. Continuing the review of the ten years 1977–1987, I want to recount some of the ups and downs of talk about economic policy in that decade.

Fashions of 1977

Looked at from 1987, the 1977 discussions of economic policy seem quaint. We can hardly remember that we used to talk about such subjects and say such things.

Five examples stand out:

1. We were still in the era of *fine tuning fiscal policy* to stabilize the economy. As distinguished from earlier days, the main instrument of this fine tuning was on the tax side, rather than the expenditure side, of the budget. But still, what now seem to us rather small changes in the size of the budget deficit were proposed and evaluated in terms of the effort to affect the level of total demand, output, and employment in the very short run.

Skepticism about this approach, on both political and economic grounds, had been growing for some time. When the Nixon administration took office in 1969 it specifically disavowed this policy of ad hoc fiscal management. In early 1971 President Nixon tried to introduce a more stable policy of balancing the budget at high employment. But this idea was not widely understood or accepted, and it fell by the wayside when the government confronted the necessity to do something about a recession. So the Nixon administration proposed a tax cut in the fall of 1971. The Ford administration did the same in 1975, and the Carter administration did the same in 1977. These proposals were defended and debated by reference to models of the economy in which the fiscal changes would quickly and durably affect total economic performance. They were also discussed in the context of the belief that monetary policy would be insufficient to achieve the desired result or would not be available for the purpose.

We no longer even hear discussion of such proposals. This is not because economists have learned more about their effectiveness than they knew ten years ago, or because the problem of instability has gone away, or because we have learned better ways to deal with it.

The reason, I believe, is that the problem of the counter-cyclical use of fiscal policy has been drowned out by what is conceived to be the greater problem of the persistent deficit. Thus, it now seems to be conventional wisdom that if the deficit is $200 billion in good times, any deliberate move to increase the deficit in a recession is out of the question. But I have seen no argument at all in support of this proposition, which I suppose is why it is conventional wisdom and not some other kind.

2. In 1977 *incomes policy* was widely considered to be an available option for achieving price stability. Probably the standard doctrine of the time was that full employment and price stability could not be simultaneously achieved or maintained without some direct government intervention in the process of determining prices and wages.

We had implemented an extreme version of this doctrine with the comprehensive, mandatory price and wage controls of 1971–1974. That effort was agreed to have been a failure, although there was disagreement about whether the failure revealed an intrinsic defect of the policy or a deficiency of a Nixon administration that did not really "believe" in the controls. But the idea remained common among economists, politicians, and assorted intellectuals that something short of comprehensive mandatory controls was feasible and essential. That something was incomes policy. The idea was that the government, possibly in consultation with representatives of business and labor, would set out some general guidelines for wages and prices. These guidelines would not be mandatory, but certain sanctions were contemplated. Offenders would at least be exposed to public shame. They might lose defense contracts. In one version popular among economists there would be tax penalties for noncompliance.

President Carter tried to implement these ideas in various forms, with repeated calls for a partnership of government, business, and labor. Some may still vaguely remember that Robert Strauss was once Mr. Carter's inflation czar and that Alfred Kahn later held that position. It was big headline stuff. But that has all disappeared—at least for the time being. Just when and why it disappeared is hard to say. Surely it was still around in 1980 and surely it was not around in 1982. The arrival of Reagan probably had much to do with it, but that did not by itself seem sufficient. I thought at the time, in 1981, that Mr. Reagan's promise to get the inflation down painlessly might yet trap him into some version of incomes policy. Moreover, Mr. Reagan's arrival does not explain why the Democratic opposition gave up an idea to which they had been devoted for over twenty years. The decline of inflation in 1982 surely had much to do with it also, but the inflation was coming down with a painful recession, just the condition that incomes policy was supposed to avoid.

To say that incomes policy has been tried and failed is too simple. There are always versions of an idea that have not yet been tried and therefore have not yet failed. Probably boredom with the idea had some effect, as did the association of incomes policy with Carterism —itself a synonym for ineffectuality, at least in the early 1980s. This history does not mean that incomes policy is dead forever, any more than the long dismal history of price controls has killed that idea permanently. But incomes policy is in a deep sleep.

3. Ten years ago almost any list of the three or four most important economic policies of government would have included *energy policy*. Any list of the three most important economic concerns would have included inflation, unemployment, and the energy supply. That is, energy was not just another micro problem, even a big one, like housing or agriculture. It had been elevated to the macro level, as one of the things intimately tied in with the inflation rate, the unemployment rate, the growth rate, and the balance of payments.

The oil shock of 1973 and its continuing repercussions was the main explanation of the emphasis placed on energy. Probably if the price of a bushel of wheat had risen to $50, wheat would have been given a central place in economic thinking. But the brute fact of the big increase in oil prices had to be combined with a certain perception of what the government's proper response should be before energy policy could assume its central role. That perception, which called for direct action by the government to control prices, subsidize production, and allocate supplies, was perhaps natural but not self-evidently correct.

Energy policy has now receded from the front ranks of governmental concerns and responsibilities because of the decline in the relative price of energy. At some prices of oil, energy would again be regarded as a serious problem by some people. Probably a price of oil below \$15 a barrel or above \$25 a barrel would generate calls for government action from some people, the people being different in the two cases. Whether there has been any change in the general perception of the government's responsibility—so that the reaction to a supply-price shock of great magnitude now would be different than it was ten to fifteen years ago—is unclear.

4. Ten years ago *economic planning* was still fashionable in some circles. These were not the innermost circles of decision making but were nevertheless "respectable." The fashion was fading, having probably reached its peak in 1975 or so, but it had still not passed entirely. This was the period of the Humphrey-Javits bill and the Humphrey-Hawkins bill, both of which seemed important at the time but have now been forgotten even though Humphrey-Hawkins was enacted.

In an article published in 1975 I pointed out that interest in economic planning had fluctuated over the years, reaching peaks when things seemed not to be going well, as in the 1930s, the immediate postwar period, and the period beginning in 1974. But what was meant by planning was never very clear, except that the government was to manage or "influence" the economy in more detail and to do so in line with some comprehensive top-down view of the way the economy should behave. Although the word "plan" had favorable resonance to many people (and set others' teeth on edge), the idea was too abstract and vague to get much support outside intellectual circles or to be implemented even if it were supported. The interest in economic planning in the mid-1970s passed away, but aspects of it would return with other names before the ten years were out.

5. Economic planning was the pet idea of intellectuals, with some support from fashionable business people. The pet idea of the business and financial community was *capital shortage*, and that had some support from intellectuals. That the economic policy of government was depressing private investment and so restraining economic growth had been the chronic complaint of business people for a long time and their main argument for less taxation of the return to capital. This complaint was given added weight by several developments in the mid-1970s. The slowdown in the rate of growth of

labor productivity was becoming increasingly clear. The rate of increase of the capital stock, and especially of capital per worker, was diminishing. Inflation was increasing the tax burden on capital by reducing the real value of depreciation allowances. (This was to some extent offset by the reduction in the real value of business debt as a result of inflation, but this point was not widely recognized until later.)

This combination of developments made the complaint about capital shortage look like something more than the self-serving argument of business people who wanted to pay less taxes. It became a more or less national concern and was reflected in several proposals made during the Carter administration for reducing taxes on investment income.

The issue of capital shortage has disappeared, at least in the terms of the mid-1970s discussion, and has been swallowed up in the budget deficit issue. As an argument for cutting the tax burden on investment, the capital shortage complaint, while possibly still valid, is no longer promising. The burden on investment has been reduced, and the budget deficit seems to rule out more tax reduction. When the Reagan team concentrated its influence on the across-the-board reduction of individual income tax rates the possibility of relieving investment income of tax burdens ran into a limit. The only hope was in a substitution of a general consumption tax for part of the income tax, a platform that few found attractive. Moreover, analysis of the consequences of the budget deficit was revealing that the main limitation on investment was not tax deterrents but the available supply of saving. Furthermore, the Reagan administration, whose supply-side orientation would logically have made them supporters of the capital shortage idea, found themselves on the other side of the argument. They had to show that "their" deficit had not crowded out private investment and that private investment was indeed as high as ever—although more than ever of it was owned by foreigners. So the hot "conservative" idea of the mid-1970s was left without its natural supporters.

Fashions of Mid-Decade

1. Of course, the most spectacular example in recent history of an economic idea that rose like a rocket and then fizzled out was what I

call *punk supply-sidism.* The adjective is important. That the supply
of resources and output is important, that it is affected by government policy, including tax policy, and that the growth of supply is
one of many legitimate objects of government policy—these are old
ideas. Even the idea that a general reduction of tax rates in the
United States would raise the revenue was not new. It was regularly
put forth by the older Republican members of the House Ways and
Means Committee, people usually not considered sources of ideas,
let alone new ones. What was new in 1980 was that the idea was
embraced by people who had national attention—academics, editorial writers, and most important of all, the presidential wing of the
Republican party.

Punk supply-sidism is also an example of the paradoxical implications of the proposition that ideas have consequences. The proposition is true, but it means that people choose the ideas whose
consequences they want. The idea that cutting taxes would raise the
revenue was attractive to many people not because there was evidence of its validity but because it had consequences they wanted. It
enabled them to appeal to those voters who wanted their taxes
reduced—which is surely 100 percent of them—without alienating
that fraction who had an attachment to balancing the budget.

Punk supply-sidism is not entirely dead. There are still people
who rely on it in a negative sense by insisting that a tax increase will
not raise the revenue. But despite the large budget deficit, which
"everyone" wants to reduce, no one, not even the president, suggests that cutting taxes would raise the revenue.

If one is strict about evidence, the decline of punk supply-sidism
is puzzling. It was a *ceteris paribus* proposition, saying that if
everything else remained constant a tax cut would raise the revenue.
But, of course, everything has not been the same since the
1981–1983 tax cuts, as it never is. And, of course, revenue has risen
since the tax cut, as it does in almost every year in a growing and
somewhat inflationary economy. So to isolate the effects of the tax
cuts on the revenue is not easy. The dazzling rise of the public or
political use of the idea was due to its convenience, and its subsequent fall was due to its lack of intuitive credibility. As far as the
mainstream of economics is concerned, the situation is different.
The original claims of punk supply-sidism were not believed to be
supported by the evidence available at the time. An extraordinary

surge of revenue after the 1981 tax cut might have cast doubt on the earlier evidence and supported the supply-side view, but no such surge occurred.

2. *Monetarism* in some sense is a very old idea. At least the idea that the quantity of money is a major determinant of the price level is very old. A more specific version of this proposition that became popular among economists held that the relation between the quantity of money and the price level was sufficiently stable that a constant rate of growth of the money supply would come closer to stabilizing the price level than any other policy. It also held that stabilizing the price level should be the prime objective of monetary policy.

These ideas seemed to become national policy between 1979 and 1982, which is why I include them in the fashions of that period despite their longer history. When Paul Volcker became chairman of the Federal Reserve, the Federal Reserve's description of its operations began to concentrate on its management of the money supply, rather than on other variables. Also, disinflation clearly became the top priority. The Fed was less outspoken about its plans for the rate of growth of the money supply. But the economists of the new Reagan administration filled that gap by describing their preferred strategy as one of gradually reducing and then stabilizing the rate of growth of money.

Through 1981 and much of 1982 monetary policy seemed to be following the monetarist prescription. But by mid-1982 the economy was clearly falling much faster than monetarist analysis would have predicted. That is, the velocity of money was falling with unexpected speed. By the fall of 1982 the Federal Reserve had given up any pretense of stabilizing the growth of the money supply. A rapid but variable growth of money began, which was accompanied, at least through 1986, by a gradual decline of the inflation rate and a strong steady recovery of the real economy.

Attempts have been made to show that the experience of 1982–1986 did not contradict monetarist analysis. Some have shown that the 1982–1986 relation between the money supply and the inflation rate does not look so unusual if one takes a different definition of the money supply than what used to be the most common one. Others have said that the relation is reasonably stable if other variables, like interest rates and inflation rates, actual and expected, are introduced. Monetarism came to look more and more like the definition I flippantly gave of it in 1979: "The theory that there is a stable and predictable relation between the price levels as effect and the supply of money as cause. This theory has firm empirical support if the definition of the money supply is allowed to vary in an unstable and unpredictable way."

Monetarists could convincingly say that they had never promised that the relation between money and inflation was exact and invariant or even that the variations would always be within a certain range. They had only maintained that relying on this stability and therefore stabilizing the growth of the money supply would yield better results than the fine-tuning, discretionary strategy that had been followed earlier. What was most embarrassing for monetarism was the generally admirable performance of the economy during the four years from 1983 through 1986 when monetarist rules were ignored.

The attempt to discover or create a reliable relationship between the money supply and the rate of inflation goes on, as it must, because without it we will have no free-market anchor for the price level. But for the time being monetarism has been recalled to the factory for repairs.

3. For a long time almost all American economists—conservatives and liberals, Keynesians and monetarists—have agreed that *deregulation* of the economy, or at least of some aspects of it, would be a good thing. In a survey of economists taken in 1978, 47 percent agreed with the proposition that "reducing the regulatory power of the ICC, CAB [Interstate Commerce Commission, Civil Aeronatics Board], et al. would improve the efficiency of the U.S. economy," 31 percent agreed with provisions and 22 percent said that they generally disagreed. After all, the virtue of "the market" is one of the first things every American economist learns. Even Walter Heller, the epitome of the "liberal" economist, once said that he appreciated the free market, even though he didn't make a "fetish" of it. The interest of economists in deregulation grew during the 1970s for two reasons. They were looking for ways to deal with what they thought was "cost-push" inflation, and deregulation seemed a way to get costs down. They were also looking for

explanations of the slowdown in productivity growth, and government regulation seemed to belong on the list.

Deregulation became a popular theme, as distinguished from an economist's theme, late in the 1970s. Probably the best sign of this was Senator Kennedy's becoming a champion of airline deregulation. The popularity of deregulation at that time was greatly enhanced by the recognition that much regulation was protecting established businesses, such as airlines, banks, and trucking companies. Thus, one could be for deregulation without being probusiness.

By the time the Reagan administration came into office some major steps had been taken in deregulation and "everyone" was for it. The new administration made it a main plank in its platform. But after a few years—say by 1984—public interest in the subject faded and the policy effort languished. Probably the subject was not one that could have maintained popular interest for very long, because the economic logic supporting deregulation was difficult and counterintuitive. Moreover, the policy soon brought the deregulators into a number of unpopular positions, even though they were correct by economists' standards. Thus they had to be "for" brown lung disease and environmental pollution. Even where consumers benefited from deregulation, in some respects the public got an unclear picture. Airline fares dropped, for example, but concerns about safety, delays, and discomfort rose. Some telephone rates fell, but complaints about service increased. These negative effects may not have been necessary consequences of the deregulation, but to reach that conclusion required finer distinctions than many people would make. Moreover, notorious scandals in financial markets led to disillusionment about the virtues of unregulated markets. None of this means that the analysis underlying the case for deregulation was wrong, although it probably means that this analysis had to be more discriminating, more aware of conditions creating exceptions, than it had been. But popular and political enthusiasms faded.

4. Supply-side, monetarism, and deregulation were ideas supported by the Reagan administration, but not held exclusively by it. Since "new ideas" had become as essential a part of political campaigning as make-up men, the opposition also had a need for new ideas. The new opposition idea of the early 1980s was *industrial policy*. This reached its height of fashionableness in Robert

Reich's 1983 book, *The Next American Frontier*, which was endorsed by Senators Mondale and Hart.

But industrial policy was not a new idea at all. It was a new version of the recurring idea that the American economy needed planning. Industrial policy was economic planning without a plan. It called for government action to promote industries believed to be carriers of future progress and adjustment assistance for industries in difficulty. The whole idea was stimulated by Japan, in two ways. Japanese competition was causing trouble for some American industries, and Japanese economic success seemed to be due to a Japanese industrial policy that we were urged to emulate.

Industrial policy had its period in the media limelight, but it disappeared without a trace. The idea was not accepted by "mainstream" economists, even on the Democratic side. Charles Schultze, who had been chairman of the Council of Economic Advisers in the Carter administration, wrote one of the most powerful critiques of industrial policy. Moreover, the industries that were to be the presumed beneficiaries of the policy were not much interested. The "leading" industries that were to be stimulated did not need or want the government intervening in their affairs. The "lagging" industries did not want adjustment—they wanted protection.

Fashions of 1987

Fashions in economic ideas differ from fashions in women's clothes in at least one respect. Women presumably know that this year's fashions will pass just as the fashions of earlier years have. But while we are aware that earlier fashions in economics have passed, we tend to think of this year's ideas as the last and lasting word. Of course, that is a mistake. I will not speculate on the future of this year's ideas except to suggest that they too will yield to the vicissitudes of history.

1. The hot idea in budget policy these days is what I call *robotic budgeting*. Some people have discovered that governments are not very good at governing—or at least that governments do not govern the way they would like. Therefore, they seek ways of getting the government out of governing. The standard suggestion for doing this has been a constitutional amendment requiring that the federal

budget be balanced. While this suggestion was still hovering over the country an interim version was adopted—the Gramm-Rudman-Hollings Act of 1985. This not only prescribed a path for the size of the deficit over the next five years. It also prescribed an exact arbitrary pattern for distributing expenditure cuts among each of several thousand items of the budget in the highly probable event that the deficit targets were not met otherwise. With the assistance of the Constitution and the Supreme Court, however, the government broke back into the process of governing and neither the deficit targets nor the expenditure cuts were achieved. But as this is written our governors are again engaged in trying to devise new ways to avoid the necessity of governing.

2. *Competitiveness* has become the banner under which a variety of people justify a variety of measures for influencing the behavior of the economy. For some it has merely superseded "growth" as the reason for supporting rather traditional kinds of government activity —education, research, or the tailoring of tax policy to encourage investment. For others it has replaced economic planning and industrial policy as the explanation for a variety of new government activities in support of selected industries by procurement policy, protection, loans, adjustment assistance, and other means. No one has yet given any compelling explanation of what competitiveness is, why the country should be concerned about it, or how the recommended measures will correct it. The constant recourse to competitiveness is an outstanding example of the use of an appealing association to sell irrelevant policies, like the association of beer with good fellowship and sports cars with sexiness.

3. Economists have had a keen interest in the *international coordination of economic policy* ever since they discovered the joys of French cuisine while attending meetings of the Organization for Economic Cooperation and Development in Paris. Interest at higher levels of government has grown recently, as shown by the attention paid to the Plaza Agreement, the Louvre Agreement, and others. This interest has been stimulated by the unusually large changes in balances of payments and exchange rates of the past five years. Governments found that if they devoted their monetary and fiscal policies to achieving their objectives for inflation and the allocation of the national output they did not have instruments available for

managing their exchange rate or their balance of payments. So each country thought it would be assisted in achieving its goals if it could have the assistance of the policies of other countries. Thus, the United States would have a better chance of achieving its goals if it could employ German monetary policy in its service. Germany would have a better chance of achieving its goals if it could manage America's budget for Germany's purposes.

So it seemed natural to believe that if the governments could get together and pool their instruments they could achieve results they could not achieve separately. But the effort to do this ran into the difficulty that getting together did not increase the number of instruments. If America's budget were to be used to help solve Germany's economic problems, it could not also be used to solve America's problems—or at least that would often be the case. For this and other reasons efforts at international coordination have so far been disappointing. That does not deny the usefulness of the effort, but it does suggest that what can be achieved under what conditions has not yet been realistically defined. And there is a good possibility that the subject of international coordination will recede as concern over "imbalances" in the international economy subsides, either (a) because the imbalances subside or (b) because we realize that they are not imbalances after all. (The subject of international coordination was discussed at greater length in the August 1987 issue of the *AEI Economist*.)

4. From time to time people find it necessary to demonstrate that despite the "superficially" good performance of the American economy, Marx's predicted "immiseration" of the population is proceeding. The current version of this demonstration is the allegation of a *decline of the middle class*. This notion has become popularly accepted, as disseminated on national TV and elsewhere. The basic claim is that although employment has been increasing rapidly, more and more of the employment has been in low-paying, dead-end jobs—symbolized by the hamburger server. As a consequence, while average real incomes are increasing in America the number of poor is increasing and the few rich are getting richer.

The proposition is on its face incredible. One has to ask, If the middle class is disappearing who is buying the new houses, automobiles, restaurant meals, airline tickets, and all the other paraphernalia of middle-class life? Not just Bill Cosby and Ivan Boesky. A more scientific evaluation of the case is provided in the conclusion of a recent article by Marvin Kosters (*Public Opinion*, July/August 1987, p. 46), director of Economic Policy Studies at AEI:

> The enviable record of the U.S. economy for creating new jobs in recent years is increasingly haunted by fears that the quality of jobs is deteriorating. These fears have been generated and nurtured by works with provocative titles like these: "The Shrinking Middle Class," "The Deindustrialization of America," "The Grim Truth about the Job Miracle," and "American Job Machine Has Begun to Sputter." These titles might suggest that the evidence is firm and conclusive.
>
> That this view can be seriously challenged has gone largely unrecognized, even though much of the evidence supporting it is subject to serious criticism. Support for fears that a widespread deterioration in the quality of jobs is occurring rests on analytical foundations that are extremely weak. Evidence that points in the opposite direction suggests that concerns about declining job quality are not just exaggerated, they are instead essentially unfounded.

The fact is, nevertheless, that definitions are so flexible, data so limited, the possibilities of statistical manipulation so great, and standards of scholarship so elastic that almost any argument in this field can be said to have empirical support and a Ph.D. to certify it. So the idea of the declining middle class will probably persist, at least through the 1988 election.

5. *The decline and fall of America* is the highbrow version of the competitiveness and declining middle-class propositions, espoused by people who have read, or at least heard of, Edward Gibbon. Reflections of the idea that the United States faces imminent decline and fall are found in articles in *Foreign Affairs*, the *Atlantic Monthly* and the *New Yorker*. The basic proposition is an extension from economic developments to political-security developments. The economic developments involved are the slowdown of economic growth as compared with earlier periods, lower economic growth in America than in some other places, budget deficits and budget "stringency," balance of trade deficits, and inflow of capital. As a

consequence the United States is said to be losing its "hegemonic" (their favorite word) power—as leader of the free world coalition and bulwark against the Soviet barbarians.

This is all rather puzzling—the twilight of America setting in so soon after President Reagan carried forty-nine states on the thesis that it was morning in America. Some of the economic developments cited are indeed facts, but their significance is misinterpreted. Our budget deficits and "stringency" are the result of political priorities and decisions, not of economic necessities. Our trade deficits and capital inflows were for many years the result of the high confidence of foreign private investors in the United States as a place to put their money. More recently the trade deficit and influx of capital result from the desire of other governments to prop up the dollar rather than expose their economies to competition from the United States, as they would with market-determined exchange rates. The economic growth rate in the United States has declined since 1973, as it has in most of the advanced world. But the United States is still by far the world's strongest economy and has much greater resources than any other country to devote to its international political and security needs without satisfying other essential claims on the national output.

If one wants to find economic deficiencies and difficulties that are weakening political-security leadership, one can surely look to the Soviet bloc. The economic strength of the United States is rising vis-à-vis the Soviet bloc, and the economic strength of the free world is rising even more relative to the Soviet bloc. The U.S. leadership of the free world is not derived from economic dominance of other free-world countries. It is derived from greater ability and willingness to bear the responsibilities of leadership in defending free-world values. Insofar as that ability derives from the economy, it is not declining.

There is more to America than economic strength. The possibility of an American decline may lie in political, cultural, or moral spheres. This possibility deserves attention and is being discussed by serious commentators. But economics is the area of our greatest, not least, strength and the source from which decline, if it is coming, is least likely to come.

12

A Look Back at Bush

IN HIS ECONOMIC REPORT OF JANUARY 1989, as he was leaving office, Ronald Reagan said:

> Today, it is as if the world were born anew. Those who doubted the resolve, and resilience, of the American people and economy doubt no more. The tide of history, which some skeptics saw as ebbing inevitably away from Western ideals of freedom of thought, expression, and enterprise, flows in our direction. By strengthening our military posture and reaffirming our commitments to the cause of freedom throughout the world, we have restored respect for America and have achieved the first arms control agreement in history to eliminate an entire class of nuclear missiles. And by reducing taxes and regulatory bureaucracy, we have unleashed the creative genius of ordinary Americans and ushered in an unparalleled period of peacetime prosperity. The world today is safer, and more prosperous, than it was 8 years ago. And the America of today is, once again, brimming with self-confidence and a model for other countries to emulate. To be sure, there are challenges for the future, but I leave office confident that, with continued cooperation between the President and the Congress, America will meet these challenges and, in

partnership with its allies, will continue to lead the world toward peace, prosperity, and freedom.

Four years later, as Mr. Reagan's successor, George Bush, was leaving office, these words would sound sadly romantic. The country was not brimming over with self-confidence. It was more in the mood to sing "Brother, Can You Spare a Dime?" than "Over There!" The part about the dismantling of nuclear missiles seemed real enough, but the rest of the story seemed a fantasy.

What happened? How to explain the big difference between Mr. Reagan's picture of America in 1989 and the very common view of the picture in 1993?

There are three parts to the explanation. First, the Reagan picture of 1989, the picture of sunrise in America, was an illusion; there were many more problems in the legacy he handed on to George Bush than he recognized. Second, the Bush administration struggled with these problems but did not alter them very much. Third, the perception common in 1993 was bleaker than the facts warranted.

Clouds in Mr. Reagan's Sunny Picture

Mr. Reagan's picture of the American scene in 1989 suffered from a basic defect: it assumed that there were two ways to organize a society—Stalin's way and Reagan's way—and that the obvious failure of Stalin's way proved the virtue of Reagan's way. But there are many non-Stalinist ways of running a society, and the choice among them is and always has been the choice we have to make.

The idea that "reducing taxes and the regulatory bureaucracy" is the formula for running a successful economy and society is simpleminded. Reducing taxes and the regulatory bureaucracy is a good thing, and it is what the American people want, especially the reduced taxes. But the American people also want some other things—their social security benefits, their Medicare benefits, some provision for the poor, better health care and education, a cleaner environment, safer streets, and so on. These wants may or may not be "legitimate"; that is, everyone may not agree that they are wants that should be recognized. But they are real wants, which is important in a democracy, and these wants must be reconciled with the desire for lower taxes and less regulation. Reaganism had only one way to effect this reconciliation: a large budget deficit. Reducing the budget deficit, however, was also a real want. President Reagan thus left behind him the need to reconcile (1) the aversion to taxation and regulation, (2) the benefits the public expected from government, and (3) a widespread feeling that reduction of the deficit was important.

Something less tangible was also at work—boredom with passive government. The American people seem to go through swings of attitude about how government should behave. For a time, they want government to be busy doing things. Watching government is one of America's chief activities, and part of the time, probably most of the time, they want government busily at work. They do not want a scoreless football game. But then they get tired of it and want to be left alone. Mr. Reagan came into office when people were ready for a rest from government—after the hyperactivity of Lyndon Johnson, the bitter fights of the Nixon period, and the fussiness of the Carter days. They were ready for Reagan to come to town and read them bedtime stories. But after eight years they were ready for action again, even though Reagan was good at making inaction seem like action. That was to be a demand on George Bush.

To say that Reagan's policy had "ushered in an unparalleled period of peacetime prosperity" was surely an exaggeration. Although we had enjoyed a vigorous recovery from the deepest postwar recession, there was no sign that the rapid rate of long-term growth the country had enjoyed before 1973 had been restored. Neither was there anything in the situation as Reagan left to promise that the economy would not fall into another recession or that we would know how to deal with it if that happened.

In fact, already forces were at work that could easily initiate another recession. One was the greatly overbuilt condition of commercial real estate, resulting in part from the combination of large-scale deposit insurance and lax regulation. Connected with that was the weakened state of many financial institutions. In addition, the reduction of defense expenditures, a welcome consequence of the end of the cold war, would cause some disruption. During the Reagan administration, and indeed for some years before that, the question of antirecession measures had completely fallen out of the discussion of national policy. The country was left with no strategy for dealing with a possible recession.

Moreover, the end of the cold war contributed, ironically, to unease rather than to satisfaction about the state of the economy. Attention turned to the idea that we were in hostile competition with other industrial countries that we had previously considered allies in the cold war. And as we looked abroad, especially at Japan, many people believed that we were losing—falling behind—especially in economic growth but also in some other arenas such as education and control of internal violence. The feeling of decline was fortified by the observation that we were running trade "deficits" with the rest of the world, and again especially with Japan. The significance of this fact was commonly misunderstood and magnified by people with a special interest in protectionism, but the fear was real nevertheless.

Opinion polls about the state of the nation around the time of Mr. Reagan's departure from office are mixed but surely do not convey the feeling of overwhelming optimism suggested in his farewell statement. According to the Gallup Poll of February 1989, 50 percent of the population was dissatisfied with "the way things are going in the United States at this time," while 45 percent was satisfied. A poll by ABC News/*Money Magazine* in the same month showed 8 percent more thinking the U.S. economy was "not so good, poor" than thinking it "excellent, good." A poll by TIME/CNN, however, reported that in February 1989, 71 percent of the respondents said that things were going "very/fairly well" in the country these days.

How President Bush Coped

When he came into the presidency, George Bush inherited a difficult economic and political situation, part of the difficulties having been caused by his predecessor and part having simply been sidestepped

by his predecessor. How much Mr. Bush felt committed to contin- /
uing the policies of Ronald Reagan is unclear. As far as can be
judged from his history before he became vice president, he was not
then a strict antigovernment Reaganite. (Possibly Ronald Reagan
was not before 1980, either.) George Bush would probably have
been described as a "country-club" Republican, perhaps a Rockefeller Republican, and certainly no more conservative than a Nixon
Republican. His most notable utterance about economic policy had
been to call the supply-side rhetoric of Ronald Reagan "voodoo
economics" during his 1980 campaign for the Republican nomination.

During the 1988 campaign for the presidency and after, Mr. Bush
showed some awareness of the need for change. He spoke of wanting to help make this a "kinder, gentler" society. He said that he
wanted to be "the education President" and "the environmental
President." At the same time, he showed considerable attachment
to some of the ideas of the radical Right, most noticeably with respect to taxes. His challenge to Congress at the 1988 convention,
"Read my lips—no new taxes!" defined and inhibited much of his
policy during his administration.[1] Greeted with cheers at the convention, these words may have become the ironic epitaph of his
presidency.

Before returning to the tax question, I want to take note of another
significant early statement of his position. In his inaugural address,
after recognizing the existence of some problems in America—
homelessness, abandoned children, drugs, crime, welfare dependency, and others—President Bush said:

> The old solution, the old way, was to think that public money alone
> could end these problems. But we have learned that that is not so. And
> in any case, our funds are low. We have a deficit to bring down. We
> have more will than wallet, but will is what we need.
>
> We will make the hard choices, looking at what we have and perhaps
> allocating it differently, making our decisions based on honest need and
> prudent safety.
>
> And then we will do the wisest thing of all—we will turn to the only

resource we have that in times of need always grows: the goodness and
the courage of the American people.

The idea that our funds were low and that we had more will than
wallet reflected a common attitude at the time. The notion that
America was a poor country, unable to meet its needs, was then
more associated with "liberals" and "declinists" than with people
celebrating the glorious days of Ronald Reagan, but it affected conservatives as well. Its meaning for them was not that the country
was poor, which it was not, but that the government was poor, as
evidenced by its deficit.

We would have to allocate what we have to meet the needs the
President recognized, that is, reallocate something *away* from
somebody or something. We could not reduce the allocation to private consumption, however, because that would entail new taxes.
We could not reallocate by cutting social security; that was taboo.
We could not reallocate to the new problems by borrowing, thereby
restraining private investment, because reducing the budget deficit
was the highest priority. So as far as economic resources were concerned, the "new priorities" would be subordinate to many old priorities.

This left us with the "noneconomic" resources—the goodness
and courage of the American people. To mobilize these resources,
Mr. Bush called on the American people to become "a thousand
points of light" shining into the dark corners of American life.
(Bartlett's *Familiar Quotations* includes only three utterances of
George Bush. One is "Read my lips," another is "kinder, gentler,"
and the third is "a thousand points of light." These three epitomized his presidency.) He wanted to make America a kinder, gentler
place, but he did not want the government to pay for it: he wanted
private individuals to rally around and deal with the problems of
making America kinder and gentler voluntarily. That was what the
thousand-points-of-light was about. But he had no means to get the
private individuals to rally around, either. In fact, as he also said in
his inaugural address: "A president is neither prince nor pope, and
I don't seek a window on men's souls." He thus withdrew from the
business of making America a kinder, gentler place.

We turn now, however, from the thousand-points-of-light to the struggle over the budget, which was act one of the economics of the Bush administration; act two would be the recession that began in 1990. There would be no act three. Although there would be several other issues and accomplishments—the Clean Air Act, the Americans with Disabilities Act, the effort to advance the Uruguay Round of negotiations on trade, the initiation of negotiations for a North American Free Trade Area, for example—they were not the special events that established the character of the Bush presidency.

George Bush's no-new-taxes pledge was obviously unrealistic when he made it. It was unrealistic because he also had balancing the budget as one of his main priorities and promises. Balancing the budget without raising taxes was not arithmetically impossible, but the preconditions were extremely difficult and improbable. The Bush team reacted to this criticism in several ways:

• They said that raising taxes would not reduce the deficit because "they," the Congress, would spend any additional revenue. Having said this, they, in effect, gave up on the promise to balance the budget and focused instead on holding expenditures down.

• They wanted to impose a "flexible freeze" that would hold expenditures down despite the strong built-in tendencies for expenditures to rise, especially for Medicare, Medicaid, social security, and the savings and loan rescue operation. As campaign rhetoric, this idea had the merit that it avoided the need to specify any program that would be frozen or cut. After the inauguration, the Bush administration gave several examples of how the flexible freeze might work—that is, how some expenditures would be cut to make room for increasing others. But the examples were trivial in size. In fact, the administration never came anywhere near proposing specific cuts that would keep the total from rising, let alone make room for new programs.

• The American people do not want any more taxes, Mr. Bush and his associates said. That was true, of course, but it threw no light on the problem. The American people did not want any number of other things; the problem was that these things could not all be simultaneously avoided.

• The Bush team had in mind one final escape hatch. The Gramm-Rudman Act then in force mandated achievement of a balanced budget by fiscal 1993, and that was the date Bush had in mind when he promised to balance the budget. But the Bush economic team believed that if necessary that date could be slipped back somewhat. If they could just restrain the growth of expenditures to a rate below the growth of revenue generated by the growth of the economy, in time the budget would come into balance. This strategy required that the Gramm-Rudman Act be amended to stretch out the date for achieving a balanced budget. It probably also required a credible showing that the deficit was on a path toward zero, even if slowly.

Unlike *some* in the Reagan team in 1980, the Bush team in 1988 did not hold out the possibility that tax reduction would increase the revenue and contribute substantially to balancing the budget.[2] It remained a firm tenet of the Bush administration that cutting the tax rate on capital gains would increase the revenue, but the amounts expected were small in comparison with the size of the deficit.

By the time of Mr. Bush's election, the political difficulties in dealing with the budget problem were obvious. Substantial deficit reduction could not be achieved without seriously cutting the rate of increase of expenditures for Medicare, Medicaid, and social security, or raising taxes, or both. For all their talk about cutting expenditures, the Republicans would not fight the Democrats to cut these extremely popular programs. The Democrats were certainly not going to initiate such cuts without at least some support from the Republicans. Moreover, the Democrats would not even participate in such cuts unless they were accompanied by tax increases—not because the Democrats loved tax increases but because they could distinguish between expenditure cuts that hurt their primary constituents and tax increases that did not. They would not impose pain on the low- and middle-income beneficiaries of government programs and let the upper-income taxpayers, predominantly Republican, off scot-free. Democrats may have felt a special pleasure in requiring the Republicans to cooperate in raising taxes, because the Republi-

cans had made so much political hay out of picturing the Democrats
as the party of high taxes.

Without the Gramm-Rudman law, the two parties might have tac-
itly agreed to finesse the whole problem, postponing the date for
deficit reduction until sometime in the future. But Gramm-Rudman
specified a five-year deficit path and imposed a sanction in the form
of across-the-board expenditure cuts if the path was not followed by
the routine budget decisions. The authors of the law had expected
the sanction never to take effect, but to frighten Congress into making its own expenditure cuts to avoid it. The sanction, however, was
also painful to the administration. To avoid the across-the-board cut,
the administration was forced to deal with Congress on a plan to
revise the Gramm-Rudman targets, to cut the deficit, or both. In this
deal, Congress would require Republicans to share in responsibility
for higher taxes.

Recognizing the ultimate need for such a deal, in December 1987
Congress established a mechanism for allaying the political pain on
all sides. Following a suggestion by Governor Mario Cuomo of New
York, Congress created a bipartisan National Economic Commission to develop recommendations for reducing the deficit without
impairment of economic growth or inequitable distribution of burdens. The commission was led by Robert S. Strauss (Democrat) and
Drew Lewis (Republican). The theory behind it was that if a group
of respected, responsible, independent people from the two parties
could agree on a plan, the more timorous and vulnerable politicians
might embrace it, telling their constituents that this was the word of
God and they could not do otherwise. The two parties could also
hold hands and jump together, so that neither could blame the other
for the pain. Enough of the members of the commission probably
recognized that an agreed plan would have to include both increases
in taxes and cuts in the big spending programs.

Since the members of the commission were selected by the Republican and the Democratic leadership of Congress and by the
president, the outcome would depend on whether that leadership
wanted an agreement that would provide political cover for them in
carrying out the unpopular measures needed to reduce the deficit.
The initial membership of six Republicans and six Democrats con-

sisted of persons who were not extremely partisan or ideological and included some known "deal makers." There was at least a chance then that an agreement could have been reached among them. But the plan for the commission also provided that the new President, who would be inaugurated on January 20, 1989, could select two additional members. Thus the new President would have a great deal of influence, because the commission members from his party would regard the two new members as representative of his wishes.

Senator Daniel Patrick Moynihan, a Democratic member of the commission, later said that the outcome was determined as soon as it was known that George Bush had been elected. Bush was resolute that the Republican members reject any agreement that included a tax increase, but the Democrats could accept an agreement only if it did include one. The outcome was a divided report, with a majority Republican part and a minority Democratic part. Both sides agreed on the importance of reducing the deficit. The Republicans, however, averred that could be accomplished without a tax increase, while the Democrats said that it could not. Neither side proposed any specifics, either tax increases or expenditure cuts.

Whether the outcome would have been different if Michael Dukakis had been elected, we will never know. His appointees might have been adamantly opposed to the cuts of expenditure that the Republicans considered the sine qua non of an agreement.

Bush's no-new-taxes pledge would not be tested in 1989 but would in 1990. In February 1989, the new administration presented a budget that showed the deficit declining in line with the Gramm-Rudman targets and vanishing in 1993. Almost everyone knew at the time that the budget results had been achieved by "smoke and mirrors." The future costs of Medicaid and income security programs were greatly underestimated, while the future revenues from the existing tax system were overestimated. The administration also both minimized the costs of bailing out the savings and loan institutions and proposed to place those costs outside the budget, by a device that was deceitful and costly.[3] There was, however, little desire to confront the new President over these matters so early in his term, resulting in a common agreement to look the other way.

How unrealistic the 1989 budget estimates were can be seen by

comparing the results then forecast for 1992 with the actual outcome. In 1989, the Bush budget looked forward to a deficit of $30.6
billion in 1992: the actual deficit was $290.2 billion. About half the
difference was on the expenditure side of the budget and about half
on the receipts side. To some extent, the actual 1992 deficit was the
result of the recession that began in 1990, which the administration
could not have been expected to foresee in 1989. But the Congressional Budget Office has estimated that the actual deficit in 1992
would have been $201.5 billion if the economy had been at high
employment. Even that was $170 billion above the estimate made in
1989. Two-thirds of this difference was on the expenditure side of
the budget. Unforeseen increases in Medicaid, in other transfer programs, and in interest and a shortfall of revenue—effects of the
recession aside—accounted for most of the difference.

In January 1990, the Bush administration again presented a
budget with a deficit, based on existing programs, within shooting
distance of the Gramm-Rudman targets. But by spring the picture
looked enormously different. For fiscal year 1991, the deficit looked
like $200 billion rather than the $85 billion the administration had
estimated. This difference was largely the result of the unexpectedly
high costs of the savings and loan bailout. But for later years, after
this factor had diminished, there was a big gap because of lower
revenue estimates, higher interest rates, and the increase of interest
costs due to the growing debt.

This excessive deficit compared with the Gramm-Rudman targets
was too big to sweep under the rug. A revision of the budget goals
and a substantial change of budget policy were required, but these
could not be achieved without a positive statement from the Bush
administration of the need for new taxes. In May, a statement to this
effect was issued from the White House, and a long, difficult process of negotiation between the administration and various factions
in the Congress began. The whole process seemed on the verge of
breakdown several times before a package with tax increases, expenditure restraints, and some new budget rules was agreed upon in
November.

The President vacillated considerably in his own explanation of
the package. Immediately after its adoption, he said that although it

did not comport with all his wishes, he believed that on the whole it would be very good for the country. In the statement issued when he signed the new budget, he omitted reference to the fact that the package included a tax increase. In his economic report of February 1991, he said: "The budget law enacted last fall gives fiscal policy a strong and credible medium-term framework." He emphasized his commitment to a tax system that would promote growth and repeated his proposal for a cut in the tax rate on capital gains. He did not mention the tax increase included in the 1990 agreement.

By 1992, however, he was agreeing with all his Republican critics that the 1990 package had been a serious mistake. He seemed to apologize for having accepted a tax increase in 1990, even arguing that this mistake was a reason for reelecting him, because he could be counted on not to repeat it.

In 1990, after the package was adopted, I hoped that the agreement would wean the Republicans from their fixation on avoidance of tax increases and open the door for a more pragmatic evaluation of the relative merits of specific tax increases and specific expenditure reductions. This hope has so far been disappointed. In fact, the Bush experience may have solidified the Republican opposition to tax increases. President Reagan had shown how it was possible to agree to a tax increase in almost every year between 1982 and 1988 and still retain the politically popular posture of opposing taxes. President Bush showed that President Reagan was probably the only one who could do that.

The 1990 agreement has been criticized on the ground that the deficit has continued large despite it, with the implication that the agreement has been ineffective. That, however, reflects a misunderstanding of the agreement. Unlike Gramm-Rudman, the 1990 agreement did not set any deficit targets. Although there were estimates of how the deficit would behave under the agreement, the plan only prescribed certain policies that the government had to follow. That is, it set a ceiling on discretionary expenditures and required that if there were policy actions that raised the expenditures on entitlements, they would have to be matched by revenue increases. But if revenues from the existing tax laws fell short of expectations because of incorrect estimates or because of less favorable economic conditions, the deficit would rise above the estimate. Similarly, on the expenditure side of the budget, if interest rates turned out to be higher than estimated, if the costs of the savings and loan bailout were larger, or if the utilization and costs of medical care under the various health entitlement programs surpassed expectations, the deficit would exceed the estimates. The Congress and the President did in fact observe the requirements of the 1990 agreement, which made the deficit less than it would otherwise have been, but external factors raised the deficit above the estimate. Perhaps, if the future deficits had been more accurately foreseen in 1990, the agreement would have been stricter. At the time, though, no one was arguing for a tougher agreement; the whole argument was over the division of the package between expenditure cuts and tax increases.

In retrospect, the 1990 agreement was not sufficiently ambitious. Even on its own assumptions, the significant reduction of the deficit would not begin for two years, and balance would not be achieved for six years. But, as many were pointing out at the time, "balance" would come only with the assistance of a large surplus in the Social Security Trust Fund, which was a loose and possibly inadequate notion of balance. The package left no room for expansion of the programs that might have contributed to Bush's goal of a "kinder, gentler" society. And it left no room for error in the original estimates and provided no mechanism for correction if those estimates were wrong. That is, if the receipts turned out to have been overestimated or the entitlement expenditures underestimated—both of which were high probabilities given the natural bias in the estimates—the 1990 agreement did not require any correction. The excess would simply be added into the deficit to be accepted—or left for a subsequent administration to deal with, which is what happened.

A larger and more secure package, however, could not have been obtained without much more aggressive, even heroic, leadership. Perhaps it could not have been obtained even then. But the leadership was not forthcoming. The size of the package was not even seriously discussed. As I said at the time, "It looks like the result of a search for the smallest deficit reduction that will be accepted by the public and the financial community as a great achievement, despite the fact that it leaves large deficits for a long time."

Because the 1990 agreement was enacted after the economy entered recession, the date of this entry now being placed at the second quarter of 1990, the agreement could hardly have precipitated the economic downturn. But critics of the agreement later ascribed the recession, or at least its depth (which was not great) or its persistence (which was long) to the agreement, particularly to the tax increases contained in it.

We do not know enough about the magnitude, or perhaps even the direction, of the short-run effects of budget changes to be sure of the connection between the 1990 package and the 1990 recession. By the time the agreement was reached, the administration was sufficiently concerned about the possible negative effects to talk plaintively about the need for the Federal Reserve to support the economy by reducing interest rates. And in its 1991 report, the Council of Economic Advisers pointed to the fact that the deficit reduction in the package came mainly near the end of the fifth year, to show that it would have small negative effects on the weak economy.

There were certainly plenty of causes for the 1990 recession other than the budget package, including the weakness of financial institutions, the overbuilding of commercial real estate, the efforts of the Federal Reserve to get inflation down further, and the uncertainties caused by the Gulf War and the increase in oil prices. While the budget package may have contributed to the recession, it does not follow that it was therefore a mistake. It was designed to deal with a problem that had been going on for a long time and that threatened to continue or grow worse if not addressed. The political obstacles to dealing with it—the political temptations to put off dealing with it—were great. If one were to look for the optimum moment in a dimly foreseen business cycle to initiate steps to correct the long-run problem, one might wait a very long time. When the President initiated the negotiations that led to the agreement in May 1990, we did not know that we were in a recession. Even when the agreement was signed in November, the recession did not seem so serious as to require jettisoning a long-run program that had been so hard to work out.

One should regard the 1990 agreement as an exogenous event, like the Gulf War, that may have had a short-run destabilizing effect on the economy but whose timing cannot be well adapted to the needs of economic stability. The real issue is how economic policy deals with such events to minimize their bad consequences.

I have written about the policy response to the 1990 recession in the next chapter. The conclusion of that review of the story is that neither fiscal nor monetary policy responded to the recession, or to the dragging out of the recovery, as vigorously as they might have done. But that was not necessarily a mistake on either side. Prolonged fiscal irresponsibility had created the danger that any move toward countercyclical fiscal expansionism would undermine confidence in the future control of the deficit. Monetary policy was inhibited by the twenty-year record of inflation and the fear that monetary expansionism would revive inflation and the expectation of inflation. These evaluations of the situation may have been wrong, but no one can yet say with confidence that they were.

Mr. Bush could not reject the 1990 Budget Agreement in the fall of 1990 despite the weakness of the economy because getting the budget on a more satisfactory long-run path was more important than responding to a mild recession. For much the same reason, the importance of staying on the long-run path, he could not try to deal more vigorously with the sluggishness of the recovery.

George Bush was the prisoner of his inheritance. He inherited a large budget deficit. More important, he inherited popular cynicism about promises to reduce the deficit, as the result of years of experience with insincere promises and ineffective performance. He also inherited a Republican tax phobia. To some extent, he had contributed to that phobia, probably mainly to show his loyalty to his inheritance. Once in office, he struggled responsibly to loosen the bonds of the legacy, compromising on his no-new-taxes pledge at great pain and at some political risk for himself. But he did not, and probably could not, do enough to change the trend of the deficit significantly, to make room for the expansions of programs that might have supported his ambition to make America a kinder and gentler place, and to permit an attempt to use the budget countercyclically.

In the end, Bush fell victim to that inheritance. Those who had idolized Reagan despised Bush because they considered him an apostate. Those who had most disliked Reagan disliked Bush because they considered him to be only a continuation of Reagan. He deserved better, but he could not escape the shadow of his predecessor.

The Economy after Bush

During the 1992 campaign, the common picture was that the American economy was in a dismal state. That the opposition, the Democrats and the followers of Perot, should try to paint that picture was no surprise. But to a surprising degree the picture seemed to have been accepted by the media and by the public.

In fact, the economy in 1992 was not fundamentally in worse condition than it had been in 1988, when the economy had not been an obstacle to continuing the Republicans in office. True, the economy had entered into a recession in 1990, but almost every president encounters a recession at some time during his term. Bush's recession was milder than Reagan's or Ford's. At its high point in July 1991, in fact, the unemployment rate was only 7.5 percent, compared with 10.8 percent in November 1982 and 9.0 percent in May 1975. The recovery was slow, but by election time the economy was clearly recovering and total output had exceeded its prerecession peak. Moreover, no one had a politically acceptable recipe for accelerating the recovery, as would be clear during the first year of Mr. Clinton's term.

During the twenty years before Bush left office, total output and output per capita had grown much less rapidly than in the earlier years after World War II. But still it had grown, and in 1992 real output per capita was 30 percent higher than in 1972. That was a rate of increase of 1.3 percent per year, which would double real per capita output in fifty-two years. Even though that was slower growth than in some earlier periods, it was still exceptionally high when viewed against the long record of human history. It did not seem to be a rate of growth that should cause anguish.

A major contributor to growth in the preceding two decades had been a significant increase in the proportion of the population at work. In fact, in 1992, despite the recession, civilian employment as a proportion of the population was higher than in any year before 1987. That meant that we were working more than previously to get the real output. But at a time when jobs per se seemed to be a primary goal of policy, that record might have been considered a success.

Total worker's compensation per hour, in real terms, had increased by about 15 percent between 1972 and 1992. The common perception that real wages had declined resulted mainly from failure to take account of the large increase in noncash benefits received by workers—such as health insurance and pensions—and by reference to an inferior method of converting compensation into real terms.

In 1992, much attention was given to the idea that the rich were getting richer and the poor were getting poorer. Although some shift in the distribution of income had occurred in the past two decades toward more inequality, the size of this shift was small. The proportion of the population in poverty remained about what it had been during most years since 1973.

Despite all the worries about America's decline, per capita income in the United States was the highest in the world. America's balance-of-payments deficit with the rest of the world—which I do not regard as a sign of weakness but others do—was smaller in 1992 than in any of the years between 1984 and 1992.

None of this is to deny that there were problems. To grow more rapidly, to reduce the poverty rate, and to recover more quickly from the recession would be highly desirable. While these were a sufficient challenge to public policy and private behavior, it was a mistake to consider that these were the problems of a poor, incompetent economy, that they were in a peculiar way the fault of Mr. Bush or even of Mr. Bush and Mr. Reagan combined, or that someone had in his briefcase a feasible program to solve them all.

13

This Peculiar Recovery

ECONOMISTS STILL DO NOT KNOW what caused the deep depression and slow, halting recovery of the 1930s. To claim now to explain the shallow recession and slow recovery of 1990–1993 would be presumptuous. Even as I am writing this, the economy may be starting a strong surge that will change the perception of this cycle. But still it may be helpful to place some of the facts about this economic cycle as it has proceeded so far in historical perspective and to offer some speculative hypotheses about what has been happening.[1]

A Historical Perspective

The figures in this chapter compare various aspects of the U.S. economy in the eleven quarters from the second quarter of 1990 through the first quarter of 1993, with the similar period of decline

An earlier version of this chapter was first published in *The American Enterprise*, July/August 1993; it has been slightly revised for inclusion in this book.

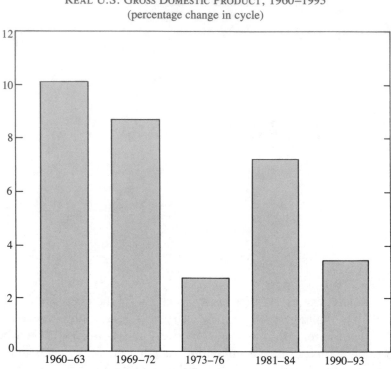

FIGURE 13–1
REAL U.S. GROSS DOMESTIC PRODUCT, 1960–1993
(percentage change in cycle)

NOTE: Cycle, eleven quarters.
SOURCE: U.S. Department of Commerce.

and rise that followed the recessions of 1960, 1969, 1973, and 1981.
I exclude the cycle that began with the recession in 1980 because
its recovery ran into another recession before eleven quarters had
passed.

Several key facts stand out:

• After eleven quarters, total output in the first quarter of 1993
was only 3.3 percent above its prerecession peak, a much smaller
gain than in any of the previous cycles except that which began at
the end of 1973 (see figure 13–1).

• Despite a sharp rise in employment in May 1993, total employment had still risen less compared with the prerecession peak than
in any of the previous cycles (see figure 13–2).

FIGURE 13–2
TOTAL U.S. EMPLOYMENT, 1960–1993
(percentage change in cycle)

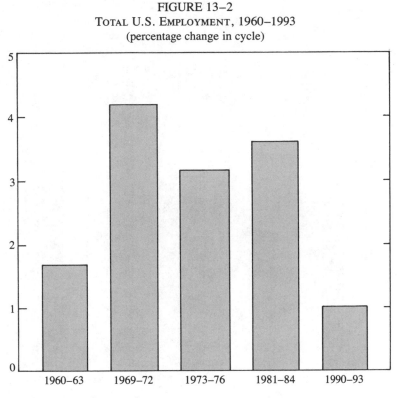

NOTE: Cycle, thirty-four months.
SOURCE: U.S. Department of Labor.

• Nevertheless, the unemployment rate in May 1993, 6.9 percent, was lower than at a similar stage in the two previous cycles, partly because this cycle started with a lower rate and partly because the labor force has been rising slowly (see figure 13–3).

• Prices, as measured by the consumer price index, rose somewhat less during this thirty-three-month period than in the 1969–1972 and the 1981–1984 cycles and much less than in the 1973–1976 cycle. Comparison with the earlier periods is distorted by the fact that the 1969–1972 period included wage and price controls and the 1973–1976 period included the first oil shock. Still, by comparison with the experience of two decades, inflation in the current cycle seems mild.

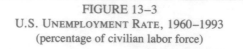

FIGURE 13-3
U.S. UNEMPLOYMENT RATE, 1960–1993
(percentage of civilian labor force)

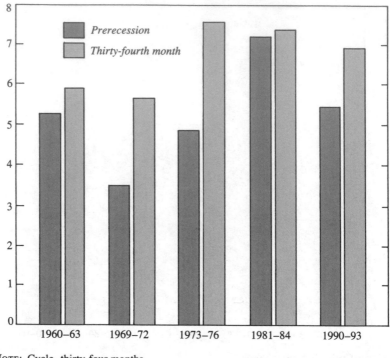

NOTE: Cycle, thirty-four months.
SOURCE: U.S. Department of Labor.

The rate of inflation declined during the current cycle, compared with the rate before the recession began. That fall had also occurred in the previous cycles, and the decline in inflation this time was smaller than in the three previous cycles, at least in part because it started from a lower level (see figure 13-4).

• The low and reduced increases of output and prices in the current period were accompanied by a low and reduced increase of total expenditures for the purchase of goods and services (see figure 13-5). This, of course, is an arithmetical necessity, since total expenditure is the arithmetical product of total output and the average price level. It seems reasonable to say, however, that the combination of the slow rise in output and the slow rise in prices was *caused*

FIGURE 13–4
CHANGES IN THE U.S. CPI, 1960–1993
(percent)

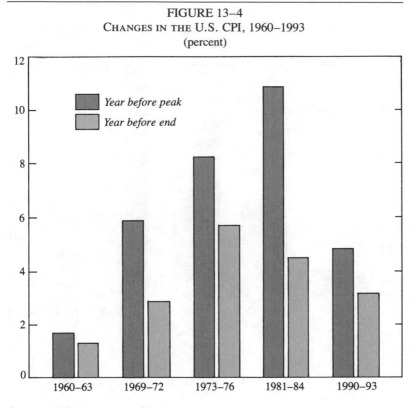

SOURCE: U.S. Department of Labor.

by the slow rise in expenditures. Conceivably, total output might have reached a ceiling in 1990 set by capacity to produce, beyond which it could rise only slowly. But the decline in the inflation rate and the rise in the unemployment rate make this interpretation implausible.

If the behavior of the economy has been due to the slow growth of spending—which we may call the growth of demand—how do we explain it? The relative rates of growth of various categories of expenditure provide an explanation of a sort. In the current cycle, federal real expenditures for defense have fallen, and expenditures for private investment have risen slowly, compared with other recoveries except for the one following the 1973 recession.

FIGURE 13-5

ANNUAL RATE OF CHANGE OF NOMINAL GDP IN THE UNITED STATES, 1960-1993

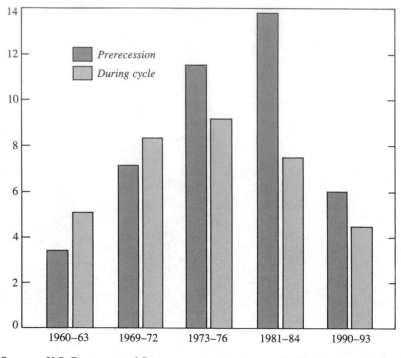

Prerecession
During cycle

1960-63   1969-72   1973-76   1981-84   1990-93

SOURCE: U.S. Department of Commerce.

The reason for the decline in defense expenditures is perfectly obvious; the reason for the slow growth of investment seems fairly clear as well. In the years before the recession began, investment had surged, mainly in residential and commercial structures, propelled by continued expectations of inflation, favorable tax treatment up to 1986, and extremely lax lending practices by financial institutions. But by 1990, the determination of the Federal Reserve to bring inflation down further and the collapse of many financial institutions and severe troubles of others had changed these conditions. Much of the earlier investment proved redundant and unprofitable, and the demand for new investment dried up. Moreover, the investment had been financed by borrowing to a high degree. Debtors were then forced to sell properties, which reduced market prices, further weakening financial institutions, discouraging new investment, and shrinking the net worth of many investors.

Such explanations in terms of the behavior of particular sectors are not fully satisfactory, however. There are always parts of the economy that are declining or lagging. In the 1969–1972 cycle, defense spending fell more than in the current one. In the 1973–1976 cycle, private investment fell sharply, whereas in the current cycle it only stopped rising. In the 1981–1984 cycle, net imports rose sharply, much higher than in the current cycle.

Equilibrating Forces

These large declines or especially slow rises, however, are partly offset and in time completely offset by rises elsewhere, so that the economy recovers. These offsets are not entirely accidental. The equilibrating forces of the economic system tend to bring it back to high employment. These forces do not work instantaneously; if they did, there would be no recessions. But they do seem to work in time. What appears peculiar about this cycle is that in eleven quarters these forces have not brought total output as high above the previous peak as they did in the earlier cycles.

The equilibrating forces are of two kinds—market forces and policy forces. The main market forces are the behavior of the price level and the behavior of interest rates; the main policy forces are fiscal and monetary measures.

Whether a decline in prices, or slowdown in their rise, induced by slack in the economy, would help to cushion a decline in output and produce a recovery depends on several factors: the contemporary behavior of monetary policy, the expectations of future inflation, and the general understanding of the intentions of government policy. In the circumstances of 1990–1993, a more rapid slowdown in inflation might have contributed to a more rapid revival of production. But the slowdown in inflation was probably as much as could have been expected, and a deficiency in that regard was probably not a cause of the slow recovery.

The decline in interest rates when aggregate demand for output declines or slows can also cushion or reverse the fall in output. In the current cycle, interest rates, on both long- and short-term assets, have declined. But short-term interest rates when measured in real terms—that is, when adjusted for inflation—did not fall as low as in previous recessions. During the 1973–1976 recession, for example, the real short-term rate became negative; that is, the nominal interest rate was lower than the inflation rate. Moreover, long-term interest rates did not fall as much as in previous cycles, absolutely or in relation to short-term rates. The spread between long- and short-term rates remained unusually large. And for most investment decisions, it is the long-term rates that count.

The Federal Reserve can, by sufficient expansion of the money supply, probably make short-term rates as low as it chooses. Therefore, explanation of the failure of short-term rates to decline further must involve consideration of monetary policy. The failure of long-term rates to fall more, and the consequent opening up of the spread between long-term and short-term rates, is a greater puzzle. Various explanations can be offered:

• Foreign interest rates remain high, mainly because the German Bundesbank is holding the rates up. Whether this is a sufficient explanation for what is happening in the United States is unclear, but in any case it only expands the puzzle from the United States to the world.

• Investors may be expecting inflation to rise, in contrast with the 1975–1976 or the 1982–1983 situations when inflation was high but a declining trend was expected. But if today's long-term rates are high because of expected future inflation, today's *real* long-term interest rates are not as high as they seem and should not be depressing investment.

• Investors may be expecting a boom in the private economy after, say, five years, that would raise interest rates then; they may therefore be unwilling to make commitments now to long-term assets that would decline in price when interest rates rose. Other signs of an expected boom are not in evidence, although the level of the stock market may point in that direction.

• Investors may be looking at the federal budget deficit as it will be beyond the next five years. The deficit may not rise much, or may actually decline relative to gross domestic product (GDP), in the next five years. But a common and growing opinion is that after about five years, when the phase down of defense spending has been completed, rising built-in expenditures, mainly for health, will greatly boost the deficit, forcing interest rates up.

Despite uncertainties about the explanation, the natural forces of the market certainly failed to bring about a prompt and strong recovery from the recession of 1990–1991. Why, then, did fiscal and monetary policy measures not bring about such a recovery? One part of the answer must be that the shape of the cycle always left it unclear whether stimulative measures were required, or could be safely employed. Total output never declined sharply, nor did the unemployment rate rise to a new peak, such as precipitated stimulative action in 1974 and 1982. Instead, output declined moderately and always looked as if it was about to be followed by an upturn.

The initial decline in output was influenced to an unknown degree by a factor expected to be temporary—the Gulf War. The summary of the forecasts of leading economists published by *Blue Chips Economic Indicators* in February 1991 bore a headline saying, "Short War—Prompt Economic Recovery, Long War—Delayed Recovery." The consensus at that time was that by the end of 1991 total output would be a little above its previous peak, whereas in fact it turned out to be 1.3 percent below.

Almost to the end of 1991, many believed that stimulative policy was unneeded because the economy had already begun a revival that, although slow, would speed up to the rate of earlier cycles. By December, when that evaluation looked somewhat doubtful, the Federal Reserve took the major step of reducing interest rates. At the beginning of 1992, too, the administration proposed a fiscal package to promote recovery. But by the middle of the year, with more signs of recovery, the administration and the Federal Reserve perceived less need to follow up with stimulative measures.

Proposals of the Clinton Administration

In early 1993, the new administration proposed its package of fiscal measures to stimulate the economy—against the background of a strong rise in the fourth quarter of 1992. This encouraging performance probably helped keep the proposed package small and at least contributed to its rejection by the Senate.

Several other factors contributed to the failure to take more vigorous fiscal or monetary measures. For one thing, many economists have by now become skeptical that we can design a fiscal stimulus so precise in its timing and size that it is more likely to promote stability than instability. Probably more important than the opinions of economists, however, were the conflicting wishes of politicians. When Mr. Bush presented his stimulus package in 1992, it had as a key element a reduction of the tax rate on capital gains, which was anathema to Democrats in the Congress and which they could portray as benefiting only the rich. When Mr. Clinton presented his stimulus package in 1993, it relied heavily on increased government expenditures, which were anathema to the Republicans in Congress and which they could portray as only more "tax and spend" politics. Both packages were thus defeated.

Hanging over all consideration of fiscal stimulus in this period has been the problem of the size of the deficit and the debt. Although it is sometimes said that fiscal measures that would increase the deficit are not feasible now because the debt is so large, that is probably not the real problem. Thirty years ago, when the Kennedy-Johnson administration achieved the big tax cut that is still regarded as a model of fiscal management, the debt was as large relative to GDP as it is today. Neither is the fact that the debt-to-GDP ratio has been rising, rather than falling as it was thirty years ago, the real problem. If we had shown any ability to stick to a chosen path for the deficit and the debt over the long run, we would be able to make a temporary departure for the purpose of cyclical stabilization without generating an adverse reaction. But with our record, no deficit-controlling plan could be counted on (although the experience with the 1990 Budget Act may have been misinterpreted), so that every step toward enlarging the deficit seemed permanent and irreversible,

FIGURE 13–6
CHANGE IN DEFICIT, NATIONAL INCOME ACCOUNTS
(as percentage of peak GDP)

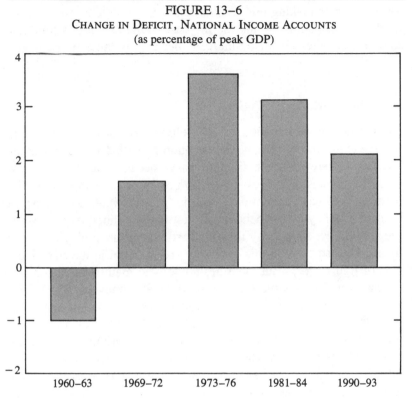

NOTE: Cycle, eleven quarters.
SOURCE: U.S. Department of Commerce.

whatever the authorities might promise. That made the government reluctant to embark on "temporary" deficit increases and strengthened the chance that the reaction of capital markets would be unfavorable if such increases were attempted.

As is shown in figure 13–6, the increase in the budget deficit, as a percentage of prerecession GDP, has been much smaller in the 1990–1993 cycle than it was in the two previous cycles. It would be instructive to see what is variously called the "high-employment deficit" or the "cyclically adjusted deficit," which would reveal how much of the increase in the deficit was due to policy changes as distinct from the automatic effect of the recession itself on revenues and expenditures. Unfortunately, the Department of Commerce stopped making this calculation in the middle of 1991. But a crude estimate suggests that the increase in the deficit this time due to policy changes was also much smaller than in the earlier cycles.

Behavior of Monetary Policy

Evaluation and explanation of the behavior of monetary policy in this cycle are made difficult by the plain facts that we do not know whether money has been tight or easy, because we do not know what that means, and because we do not know what money is. For many years, many economists have judged the tightness or ease of monetary policy by the behavior of a broadly defined monetary aggregate known as M2. By this standard, monetary policy has been unusually restrictive in this cycle, as may be seen in the right-hand side of figure 13–7. But there are some who maintain that the significant variable is a more narrowly defined money known as M1, and that has increased rapidly, as can be seen in the left-hand side of that figure. Others would say that the important test is the behavior of interest rates, which have fallen substantially, at least for short-term credits. But when adjusted for the contemporary rate of inflation, interest rates have not fallen as much as in earlier recessions. Moreover, interest rates tend naturally to fall in a recession, and that fall does not indicate the extent to which monetary policy is resisting the decline in the economy or promoting its recovery.

It is clear, though, that monetary policy has not been sufficiently expansive to promote a rapid recovery. It is not that the Federal Reserve is devoted to a particular target for the money supply, however defined, or for interest rates, but that the Fed seems to adapt its policy from month to month, or even from week to week, to its understanding of the present and probable course of the economy relative to its idea of the desirable course. When it believes the economy is falling below the desirable path, it eases by expanding the reserves of the banking system, an action with consequences for interest rates and for the supplies of different kinds of money. Conversely, when the economy appears to be expanding too quickly, it reduces the reserves of the banking system.

FIGURE 13–7
CHANGES IN REAL M1 AND M2, 1960–1993
(percent)

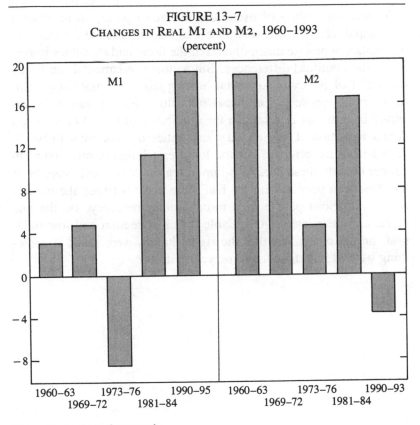

NOTE: Cycle, thirty-four months.
SOURCE: U.S. Federal Reserve and author's calculations.

The critical question is how the Federal Reserve viewed the course of the economy in comparison with the desirable path. The Fed's behavior strongly indicates that it was not greatly displeased with the course the economy was following, or seemed to be following, in the past two years. The Fed or many of its members have said for a long time that they were not satisfied with a permanent rate of inflation as high as 3 or 4 percent a year and was surely determined to prevent it from escalating above that rate. Apparently, as long as the fall in output and the rise in unemployment were not too great, the Fed would not be diverted from the effort to reduce the inflation rate further, even if that meant that the recovery would be slow.

In part, the failure of fiscal and monetary policy to promote a more rapid recovery was attributable to inadequacies of forecasting, difficulties of precise manipulation of the fiscal and monetary instruments, and political differences. But a more fundamental cause was the belief of policy makers that other goals were more important than a rapid recovery. The fiscal authorities did not want to be diverted from trying to establish the credibility of a path of long-run deficit reduction. The monetary authorities did not want to be diverted from the effort to get the long-term inflation rate down. In neither case do these decisions imply neglect of the real interests of the American people. Choices had to be made between the interest of the American people in a more prompt recovery, on the one hand, and their interest in reliable deficit reduction and low inflation, on the other. Whether the right choices were made is something we will not know for some years, if ever.

14

Another New Economics

So ANOTHER NEW ECONOMICS has come into Washington with the Clinton administration. In my fifty-five years in Washington, this is the third New Economics, or possibly the third-and-a-half. There are certain similarities among them. In each case, there was a strong feeling of confidence among the bearers of the New Economics that they knew what they were doing, unlike their predecessors. And in the cases that are now history, there was a subsequent discovery that this confidence was not justified, or at least not fully justified. Whether this will also be true of the New Economics of 1993 remains to be seen.

New Economics, 1961

The first New Economics within my experience came into Washington in 1961, with President Kennedy and his Council of Economic Advisers (CEA) under the chairmanship of Walter Heller. This was the New Economics of J. M. Keynes. Its main feature was belief in the possibility of keeping the economy close to full employment with rapid growth of total output by flexible adjustment of the size of the budget deficit.

Keynesianism became the New Economics in 1961 after twenty-five years of gestation and evolution, since the publication of Keynes's *The General Theory of Employment, Interest and Money* in 1935. The economists who came with Kennedy—not only Heller but also James Tobin, Kermit Gordon, and others—were of the generation that had been fascinated by Keynes as graduate students in the 1930s. Although he did not come to Washington with them, their mentor was Paul Samuelson, whose textbook had revealed the Keynesian magic to millions of college sophomores. By 1961, they were of an age to "take over"; they, like Kennedy, were part of a generational shift, as we call it today.

Keynesianism had had to survive a number of difficulties, and undergo some transformations, before it became the New Economics. The early pretensions of Keynesian economists in Washington had been dealt a blow by their wildly wrong forecast of a severe recession after World War II. Neither President Truman nor President Eisenhower had much interest in the Keynesian idea. Surprisingly, the four economists who served as chairman of the CEA under those two Presidents either did not understand or did not like the Keynesian theory and its policy prescriptions. The theory was dominating the economics profession, and in some quarters outside the profession a kind of watered-down or domesticated version of it was gaining acceptance. But the time was not ripe for the pure medicine until Kennedy came to the White House.

The 1961 New Economics came into Washington with a considerable history of thinking behind it, unlike the 1993 New Economics. That does not mean that the 1961 version was correct. Indeed, it had many flaws that were revealed in the coming years. The economy prospered through the end of 1965, and many people were led to declare that the key to stability and growth had been found. But after 1965 this confidence began to evaporate. There were many reasons, but two were of most importance. One was the failure of the Keynesian ambition for full employment to deal with the likely emergence of inflation; the other was the political problem. Presidents Kennedy and Johnson had enjoyed the Keynesian prescription when it called for cutting taxes and increasing expenditures. As might have been expected, President Johnson was very reluctant to follow the prescription when it called for raising taxes and cutting expenditures.

New Economics, 1969

In 1969 came what might be called a half–New Economics, with Richard Nixon as President and Paul McCracken as chairman of the CEA, on which Hendrik Houthakker and I were members. We were, I believe, more modest than our predecessors, but still we thought that we knew where they had gone wrong. We were the moderate and sensible version of what had gone before. We would be restrained Keynesians, eschewing fine-tuning, monetarist but not dogmatic about it—determined to stabilize the price level, balance the budget, and above all avoid the price controls with which the Johnson team had been flirting. As is now well known, things did not work out that way. The fault was that economists did not know enough. Moreover, the goals of stabilized prices and high employment were probably not consistent in the short run, while political considerations did not permit waiting for the long run.

New Economics, 1981

A more definitely "new" economics came in 1981. Its distinctive feature was supply-sidism, the main credo of which was that reduction of marginal tax rates would solve much of what was ailing the economy. Of course, the idea that high marginal tax rates had some adverse effects was old, but in the extreme version espoused in 1981, it had no roots in the history of economics. Just what was meant by supply-side economics is still the subject of dispute. According to one interpretation, reduction of tax rates would increase the revenue and balance the budget. According to others, it meant only that the reduction of tax rates would increase the national output and the tax base and also increase the propensity to save. As a result, although the deficit would increase, private saving would increase by more than the deficit increased, and the total supply of saving available to finance private investment would rise.

There are still people who believe that this prescription worked, or that it would have worked if followed more rigorously or if Congress had not interfered. There are also people who believe that if Napoleon had not been fifteen minutes late at the battle of Waterloo, there would be a Bonaparte emperor of France today. But the number of true believers in the extreme version of supply-sidism has surely diminished. Because of or in spite of it, after 1981 the deficit grew, private saving declined, and there was no significant revival of the long-run growth of output and productivity.

New Economics, 1993

Now we come to the New Economics of 1993. Of course, it is not entirely new. It contains vestiges of Keynesianism in its short-run "stimulus package." Its goals for health care sound much like Lyndon Johnson's Medicare and Medicaid generalized to the country at large. But what is new about Clinton's New Economics is the degree to which it is willing to intervene in the market. This is seen in the talk about managed international trade, in proposals for price control in the health industry, and in numerous plans for "targeting" investment. All of these ideas have precedents in past practice as well as in the writings of economists. But they seem to have a centrality in the 1993 New Economics that they have not had before, either in practice or in American economic thought.

In a way, the New Economics of 1993 appropriates—or, as some would say, misappropriates—the arguments of its predecessor. The previous argument was that accelerating growth is the prime economic objective, accelerating growth requires more investment, and, therefore, policy should be kind to private savers and investors—above all by not taxing them too much. The New Economics of 1993 goes along with the primacy of growth and the need for investment. But it does not accept the desirability of leaving the investment to the private savers and leaving them to reap the main returns from the investment. Instead, it would tax private income recipients more and have the government do more of the investing. And it rejects the claim that private investment guided by the market will be better, more productive investment. Instead, it maintains that the government can do a larger share of the investment better.

Skepticism toward the New Economics

The New Economics of 1961 and the somewhat–New Economics of 1969 brought into Washington what was already the conventional wisdom of economists. That was not true in 1981 and is not true today. It is not necessarily a defect of today's New Economics not to be a part of the conventional wisdom. After all, the term *conventional wisdom* was originally used ironically, to suggest that it was more conventional than wise. But still, today's unconventional wisdom deserves a skeptical examination.

What was New Economics in 1961, 1969, and 1981 turned out to be a disappointment for two main reasons. The first was that economists did not know enough. In a classroom or a textbook, it was sufficient to know that if a certain action is taken the result will be in a certain direction—the curve in the diagram will go up or down. To put that into practice, it was necessary to know "how much," and they did not know that. They did not know in the Kennedy-Johnson period how much fiscal stimulus could be exerted without an inflationary result. In the Nixon period, we did not know how far or how long the economy would have to be restrained to eradicate inflationary expectations. The Reagan era economists did not know how much additional private saving and effort would result from any specific cut of tax rates.

These deficiencies might not have proved so serious if the political process had been more evenhanded and patient in applying the economic prescriptions. But the politicians always wanted too much of the happy part of the prescriptions and wanted the good results too soon. Keynesianism legitimized for President Johnson his natural preferences for low taxes and high expenditures. President Nixon was not inclined to wait for the long run in which the "old time religion" of his economic advisers might have worked. President Reagan and Congress pushed the reduction of tax rates beyond the point where the economic argument was valid.

There are, I believe, some lessons here for the 1993 New Economics. One is not to embark on policies whose successful execution would require knowledge that economists and policy makers do not have. The second is to recognize that economists' ideas take on a life of their own when introduced into the political process and may be used in ways the economists did not contemplate. These are lessons of modesty and caution. But there is another lesson as well: coming into Washington for the first time as "the government," having won an election, is not conducive to modesty and caution. On the contrary, it leads to a feeling of knowing everything and being able to do everything. Sometimes I think that we would be better off being governed by the party that just lost the election: they might be more humble.

Appendix

TABLE A–1
U.S. Gross Domestic Product, Gross Domestic Product per Capita, and Output per Hour, 1929–1992

	GDP (in billions of 1987 dollars)	GDP per Capita (in 1987 dollars)	Output per Hour (1948 = 100)
1929	821.8	6,743	n.a.
1930	748.9	6,079	n.a.
1931	691.3	5,569	n.a.
1932	599.7	4,800	n.a.
1933	587.1	4,671	n.a.
1934	632.6	5,001	n.a.
1935	681.3	5,349	n.a.
1936	777.9	6,069	n.a.
1937	811.4	6,292	n.a.
1938	778.9	5,993	n.a.
1939	840.7	6,416	n.a.
1940	906.0	6,857	n.a.
1941	1,070.6	8,026	n.a.
1942	1,284.9	9,528	n.a.
1943	1,540.5	11,266	n.a.
1944	1,670.0	12,067	n.a.
1945	1,602.6	11,453	n.a.
1946	1,272.1	8,997	n.a.
1947	1,252.8	8,692	n.a.
1948	1,300.0	8,866	100.0
1949	1,305.5	8,750	100.9
1950	1,418.5	9,352	109.8
1951	1,558.4	10,101	114.5
1952	1,624.9	10,352	118.3
1953	1,685.5	10,563	122.9
1954	1,673.8	10,307	124.7
1955	1,768.3	10,699	128.7
1956	1,803.6	10,722	130.7
1957	1,838.2	10,733	134.3
1958	1,829.1	10,503	138.3
1959	1,928.8	10,892	143.2
1960	1,970.8	10,903	145.7
1961	2,023.8	11,014	151.2
1962	2,128.1	11,405	156.1

	GDP (in billions of 1987 dollars)	GDP per Capita (in 1987 dollars)	Output per Hour (1948 = 100)
1963	2,215.6	11,704	162.6
1964	2,340.6	12,195	169.9
1965	2,470.5	12,712	175.3
1966	2,616.2	13,307	180.0
1967	2,685.2	13,510	185.5
1968	2,796.9	13,392	191.3
1969	2,873.0	14,171	192.0
1970	2,873.9	14,013	193.8
1971	2,955.9	14,232	200.0
1972	3,107.1	14,801	202.0
1973	3,268.6	15,422	211.4
1974	3,248.1	15,185	207.3
1975	3,221.7	14,917	211.8
1976	3,380.8	15,502	218.0
1977	3,533.3	16,039	222.0
1978	3,703.5	16,635	224.1
1979	3,796.8	16,867	221.6
1980	3,776.3	16,584	220.9
1981	3,843.1	16,710	224.3
1982	3,760.3	16,194	222.7
1983	3,906.6	16,672	228.3
1984	4,148.5	17,549	234.3
1985	4,279.8	17,944	239.2
1986	4,404.5	18,299	244.5
1987	4,539.9	18,694	247.7
1988	4,718.6	19,252	253.2
1989	4,838.0	19,556	252.1
1990	4,877.5	19,513	251.1
1991	4,821.0	19,077	251.4
1992	4,922.6	19,217	258.4

n.a. = not available.
NOTE: Output per hour refers to the business sector.
SOURCE: Department of Commerce for GDP and GDP per capita; Department of Labor for output per hour.

TABLE A–2
U.S. Employment, Unemployment, and Price Level, 1929–1992

	Total Employment (millions)	Unemployment (percent)	Consumer Price Index (1982–84 = 100)
1929	47.9	3.2	17.1
1930	45.7	8.7	16.7
1931	42.7	15.9	15.2
1932	39.2	23.6	13.6
1933	39.0	24.9	12.9
1934	41.2	21.7	13.4
1935	42.5	20.1	13.7
1936	44.7	16.9	13.8
1937	46.6	14.3	14.3
1938	44.6	19.0	14.1
1939	46.1	17.2	13.9
1940	48.1	14.6	14.0
1941	52.0	9.9	14.7
1942	57.7	4.7	16.3
1943	63.5	1.9	17.3
1944	65.4	1.2	17.6
1945	64.3	1.9	18.0
1946	58.7	3.9	19.5
1947	59.4	3.9	22.3
1948	60.6	3.8	24.0
1949	60.0	5.9	23.8
1950	60.1	5.3	24.1
1951	62.1	3.3	26.0
1952	62.6	3.0	26.5
1953	63.4	2.9	26.7
1954	62.3	5.5	26.9
1955	64.2	4.4	26.8
1956	65.8	4.1	27.2
1957	66.0	4.3	28.1
1958	64.9	6.8	28.9
1959	66.4	5.5	29.1
1960	67.6	5.5	29.6
1961	67.6	6.7	29.9
1962	68.8	5.5	30.2
1963	69.8	5.7	30.6

454

	Total Employment (millions)	Unemployment (percent)	Consumer Price Index (1982–84 = 100)
1964	71.3	5.2	31.0
1965	73.0	4.5	31.5
1966	75.0	3.8	32.4
1967	76.6	3.8	33.4
1968	78.2	3.6	34.8
1969	80.1	3.5	36.7
1970	80.8	4.9	38.8
1971	81.3	5.9	40.5
1972	84.0	5.6	41.8
1973	86.8	4.9	44.4
1974	88.5	5.6	49.3
1975	87.5	8.5	53.8
1976	90.4	7.7	56.9
1977	93.7	7.1	60.6
1978	97.7	6.1	65.2
1979	100.4	5.8	72.6
1980	101.9	7.1	82.4
1981	102.0	7.6	90.9
1982	101.2	9.7	96.9
1983	102.5	9.6	99.6
1984	106.7	7.5	103.9
1985	108.9	7.2	107.6
1986	111.3	7.0	109.6
1987	114.2	6.2	113.6
1988	116.7	5.5	118.3
1989	119.0	5.3	124.0
1990	119.6	5.5	130.7
1991	118.4	6.7	136.2
1992	119.2	7.4	140.3

TABLE A–2 (continued)

SOURCE: Department of Labor.

TABLE A–3
U.S. Government Expenditures and Receipts as a Percentage of Gross Domestic Product, 1929–1992

	Total Expenditures	Federal Expenditures	Net State and Local Expenditures	Total Receipts	Federal Receipts	Net State and Local Receipts
1929	9.7	2.6	7.1	10.7	3.7	7
1930	11.9	3.1	8.8	11.6	3.4	8.2
1931	16.0	5.5	10.4	12.1	2.8	9.4
1932	17.9	5.5	12.4	14.8	3.1	11.7
1933	18.7	7.0	11.7	16.4	4.9	11.5
1934	19.2	9.7	9.5	15.8	5.5	10.3
1935	18.3	9.1	9.1	15.5	5.5	10.0
1936	19.3	10.6	8.7	15.5	6.2	9.3
1937	16.3	8.1	8.1	16.7	7.8	8.9
1938	19.2	9.9	9.3	17.6	7.8	9.8
1939	19.4	10.2	9.1	16.7	7.5	9.3
1940	18.1	9.9	8.2	17.6	8.8	8.8
1941	23.0	16.5	6.5	19.9	12.4	7.5
1942	40.2	35.3	4.9	20.5	14.6	5.9
1943	48.5	44.8	3.8	25.5	20.5	5.0
1944	48.7	45.3	3.4	24.2	19.5	4.7
1945	43.7	40.0	3.7	25.0	20.1	4.9
1946	22.3	17.7	4.6	24.7	19.3	5.5
1947	18.5	13.2	5.3	24.6	18.9	5.7
1948	19.2	13.4	5.8	22.8	16.9	5.9
1949	22.9	16.2	6.7	21.7	15.2	6.5
1950	21.6	14.7	6.8	24.0	17.6	6.4
1951	24.0	17.7	6.3	25.7	19.5	6.2
1952	26.7	20.4	6.4	25.7	19.4	6.3
1953	27.1	20.6	6.4	25.5	19.1	6.5
1954	26.2	19.0	7.2	24.2	17.3	6.9
1955	24.2	17.1	7.2	25.0	18.1	6.9
1956	24.4	17.0	7.4	25.7	18.4	7.2
1957	25.6	17.9	7.7	25.8	18.4	7.4
1958	27.6	19.4	8.2	25.2	17.5	7.7
1959	26.7	18.9	7.8	26.1	18.3	7.7
1960	26.3	18.2	8.1	27.0	18.9	8.1
1961	27.7	19.1	8.5	27.1	18.6	8.5

456

TABLE A–3 (continued)

	Total Expenditures	Federal Expenditures	Net State and Local Expenditures	Total Receipts	Federal Receipts	Net State and Local Receipts
1962	27.8	19.3	8.4	27.3	18.8	8.5
1963	27.5	19.0	8.5	27.8	19.2	8.6
1964	26.9	18.3	8.6	26.7	17.9	8.8
1965	26.4	17.7	8.7	26.6	17.9	8.7
1966	27.5	18.8	8.7	27.4	18.6	8.7
1967	29.5	20.3	9.2	27.8	18.7	9.1
1968	29.9	20.4	9.4	29.3	19.9	9.5
1969	29.6	19.9	9.7	30.6	20.8	9.8
1970	30.8	20.6	10.2	29.7	19.3	
1971	30.8	20.4	10.4	29.1	18.5	10.6
1972	30.5	20.7	9.8	30.2	19.2	11.0
1973	29.8	20.0	9.7	30.3	19.5	10.7
1974	31.2	21.0	10.3	30.9	20.2	10.7
1975	33.5	23.0	10.5	29.4	18.6	10.8
1976	32.3	22.2	10.1	30.1	19.2	10.9
1977	31.2	21.6	9.6	30.3	19.5	10.9
1978	30.0	21.0	9.0	30.2	19.8	10.4
1979	29.9	20.9	9.0	30.3	20.3	10.0
1980	31.8	22.6	9.2	30.5	20.4	10.1
1981	32.1	23.0	9.1	31.1	21.1	10.0
1982	33.9	24.5	9.5	30.5	20.2	10.3
1983	34.0	24.7	9.3	29.9	19.4	10.5
1984	32.6	23.6	9.0	29.7	19.2	10.5
1985	33.2	24.0	9.2	30.1	19.5	10.6
1986	33.7	24.1	9.6	30.2	19.4	10.9
1987	33.4	23.5	9.9	31.0	20.1	10.8
1988	32.5	22.6	9.8	30.5	19.8	10.6
1989	32.4	22.5	9.9	30.9	20.2	10.7
1990	33.3	23.1	10.3	30.9	20.1	10.8
1991	34.2	23.5	10.7	30.8	19.8	11.0
1992	35.4	24.5	10.9	30.7	19.5	11.2

NOTE: Receipts, expenditures, and deficit are as measured in national income accounts. Federal grants to states and localities are excluded from state and local receipts and expenditures.
SOURCE: Department of Commerce.

TABLE A-4

Federal Government Deficit and
Debt as a Percentage of Gross Domestic Product, 1929–1992

	Federal Deficit as Percentage of GDP	*Federal Debt as Percentage of GDP*
1929	−1.1	16.9
1930	−0.3	16.7
1931	2.8	20.2
1932	2.4	29.1
1933	2.2	39.6
1934	4.1	44.9
1935	3.6	41.8
1936	4.5	43.6
1937	0.3	42.0
1938	2.1	42.3
1939	2.8	46.0
1940	1.1	44.8
1941	4.1	42.9
1942	20.8	47.8
1943	24.3	72.8
1944	25.8	91.7
1945	19.9	111.0
1946	−1.6	113.9
1947	−5.7	100.8
1948	−3.5	87.7
1949	1.0	81.7
1950	−2.9	82.5
1951	−1.8	88.4
1952	1.0	63.1
1953	1.6	60.1
1954	1.6	61.1
1955	−1.0	59.0
1956	−1.5	53.5
1957	−0.5	50.2
1958	1.9	50.6
1959	0.5	49.0
1960	−0.7	46.8
1961	0.5	46.1
1962	0.6	44.7

	Federal Deficit as Percentage of GDP	Federal Debt as Percentage of GDP
	TABLE A–4 (continued)	
1963	−0.2	43.4
1964	0.4	41.0
1965	−0.2	38.8
1966	0.2	35.7
1967	1.5	33.7
1968	0.5	34.1
1969	−0.9	30.0
1970	1.3	28.7
1971	2.0	28.8
1972	1.4	28.1
1973	10.5	26.7
1974	0.8	24.5
1975	4.4	26.1
1976	3.0	28.3
1977	2.1	28.6
1978	1.3	28.2
1979	0.6	26.3
1980	2.2	26.8
1981	1.9	26.5
1982	4.3	29.4
1983	5.3	34.1
1984	4.4	35.2
1985	4.5	37.8
1986	4.7	41.2
1987	3.3	42.4
1988	2.8	42.6
1989	2.3	42.3
1990	3.0	44.1
1991	3.7	47.7
1992	5.0	51.1

NOTE: Debt to GDP ratios before 1940 not strictly comparable with later data and partly estimated by author.
SOURCE: Department of Commerce, Office of Management and Budget, and the Department of the Treasury.

TABLE A-5
FEDERAL EXPENDITURES AS A PERCENTAGE OF GROSS DOMESTIC PRODUCT, FISCAL YEARS 1940–1992

	Total	Payments to Individuals	Interest	Defense	Other
1940	9.9	1.4	0.7	2.3	5.5
1941	16.5	1.1	0.6	11.0	3.7
1942	35.3	0.9	0.6	31.2	2.6
1943	44.8	0.6	0.8	41.5	1.8
1944	45.3	0.9	1.0	41.5	2.0
1945	40.0	2.0	1.4	34.6	2.1
1946	17.7	4.3	1.8	7.7	3.8
1947	13.2	3.8	1.7	4.3	3.4
1948	13.4	2.9	1.6	4.3	4.5
1949	16.2	3.4	1.7	5.4	5.8
1950	14.7	3.8	1.5	5.0	4.5
1951	17.7	2.6	1.4	10.2	3.6
1952	20.4	2.5	1.3	13.2	3.3
1953	20.6	2.6	1.2	13.2	3.6
1954	19.0	3.1	1.2	11.2	3.4
1955	17.1	3.1	1.1	9.6	3.2
1956	17.0	3.1	1.2	9.5	3.1
1957	17.9	3.5	1.2	9.9	3.3
1958	19.4	4.3	1.1	10.2	3.7
1959	18.9	4.1	1.3	9.4	4.1
1960	18.2	4.2	1.3	8.8	3.8
1961	19.1	4.7	1.2	9.0	4.2
1962	19.3	4.5	1.2	9.1	4.6
1963	19.0	4.5	1.2	8.5	4.7
1964	18.3	4.3	1.2	7.8	5.0
1965	17.7	4.3	1.2	7.3	5.0
1966	18.8	4.4	1.2	8.1	5.2
1967	20.3	4.9	1.2	9.0	5.1
1968	20.4	5.2	1.3	8.9	5.0
1969	19.9	5.3	1.3	8.2	5.1
1970	20.6	6.1	1.4	7.6	5.5
1971	20.4	6.7	1.3	6.8	5.8
1972	20.7	6.7	1.2	6.4	6.3
1973	20.0	6.9	1.3	5.7	6.0
1974	21.0	7.9	1.4	5.7	6.0
1975	23.0	9.3	1.5	5.6	6.6

TABLE A–5 (continued)

	Total	Payments to Individuals	Interest	Defense	Other
1976	22.2	9.0	1.5	5.3	6.4
1977	21.6	8.6	1.5	5.1	6.4
1978	21.0	8.2	1.5	4.9	6.4
1979	20.9	8.3	1.7	4.9	6.1
1980	22.6	9.1	1.9	5.3	6.3
1981	23.0	9.3	2.4	5.5	5.8
1982	24.5	10.0	2.7	6.2	5.6
1983	24.7	10.0	2.7	6.3	5.7
1984	23.6	9.1	3.0	6.2	5.4
1985	24.0	9.1	3.1	6.4	5.4
1986	24.1	9.0	3.1	6.5	5.5
1987	23.5	8.9	3.0	6.4	5.2
1988	22.6	8.7	3.0	6.0	4.9
1989	22.5	8.8	3.1	5.7	4.9
1990	23.1	9.1	3.2	5.7	5.1
1991	23.5	9.7	3.3	5.7	4.8
1992	24.5	10.2	3.1	5.3	5.8

SOURCE: Office of Management and Budget.

TABLE A–6
FEDERAL RECEIPTS AS A PERCENTAGE OF GROSS DOMESTIC PRODUCT, 1940–1992

	Total Receipts	Individual Income Taxes	Corporate Income Taxes	Social Insurance Contributions	Other
1940	6.6	0.9	1.2	1.8	2.7
1941	7.0	1.1	1.7	1.6	2.6
1942	9.2	2.1	3.0	1.6	2.5
1943	12.5	3.4	5.0	1.6	2.5
1944	20.7	9.3	7.0	1.7	2.7
1945	21.2	8.6	8.0	1.6	3.0
1946	18.5	7.6	5.6	1.5	3.8
1947	16.4	7.7	3.7	1.5	3.5
1948	16.0	7.4	3.7	1.4	3.4
1949	15.2	6.0	4.3	1.5	3.4
1950	13.7	5.5	3.6	1.5	3.1
1951	15.6	6.5	4.3	1.7	3.1
1952	18.9	8.0	6.1	1.8	3.0
1953	18.8	8.1	5.7	1.8	3.1
1954	18.8	8.0	5.7	1.9	3.2
1955	16.2	7.1	4.4	1.9	2.7
1956	17.5	7.6	4.9	2.2	2.8
1957	17.8	7.9	4.7	2.2	2.9
1958	17.5	7.6	4.4	1.5	4.0
1959	16.0	7.4	3.5	1.4	3.7
1960	18.0	7.9	4.2	1.9	4.0
1961	17.8	7.8	3.9	3.1	3.0
1962	17.4	7.8	3.6	3.0	3.0
1963	17.7	7.9	3.6	3.3	2.9
1964	17.4	7.5	3.6	3.4	2.9
1965	16.6	6.9	3.6	3.2	2.9
1966	17.0	7.2	3.9	3.3	2.6
1967	18.3	7.6	4.2	4.0	2.6
1968	17.2	7.7	3.2	3.8	2.4
1969	19.5	9.1	3.8	4.1	2.5
1970	19.1	9.0	3.3	4.4	2.4
1971	17.1	7.9	2.4	4.3	2.4
1972	17.2	8.9	2.7	4.4	1.2
1973	17.1	7.7	2.7	4.7	2.0
1974	18.1	8.2	2.7	5.2	2.0

	Total Receipts	Individual Income Taxes	Corporate Income Taxes	Social Insurance Contributions	Other
	TABLE A–6 (continued)				
1975	17.6	7.7	2.6	5.3	2.0
1976	18.6	7.4	2.3	5.1	3.7
1977	18.0	8.0	2.8	5.4	1.8
1978	17.9	8.1	2.7	5.4	1.7
1979	18.6	8.8	2.6	5.6	1.6
1980	19.1	9.0	2.4	5.8	1.9
1981	19.8	9.4	2.0	6.0	2.3
1982	19.6	9.5	1.6	6.4	2.1
1983	17.6	8.5	1.1	6.1	1.9
1984	17.6	7.9	1.5	6.3	1.9
1985	18.2	8.3	1.5	6.6	1.8
1986	18.0	8.2	1.5	6.7	1.6
1987	18.8	8.7	1.9	6.7	1.5
1988	18.6	8.2	1.9	6.8	1.6
1989	18.9	8.5	2.0	6.8	1.6
1990	18.7	8.5	1.7	6.7	1.8
1991	18.6	8.2	1.7	7.0	1.6
1992	18.3	8.0	1.7	7.0	1.6

SOURCE: Office of Management and Budget.

TABLE A–7
FEDERAL OUTLAYS IN BILLIONS OF CONSTANT 1987 DOLLARS, 1940–1992

	Total	Defense	Payments for Individuals	Net Interest	Other
1940	96.8	18.6	13.4	7.8	57.0
1941	135.3	64.9	13.4	7.9	49.1
1942	315.1	222.7	12.5	8.3	71.6
1943	655.2	537.9	10.7	11.7	94.9
1944	787.1	670.1	10.5	16.8	89.7
1945	812.6	731.6	12.9	22.9	45.2
1946	463.0	380.4	30.9	26.5	25.2
1947	230.6	101.6	44.7	22.7	61.6
1948	192.9	72.0	42.3	22.2	56.4
1949	245.5	97.1	46.0	22.3	80.1
1950	260.5	101.1	62.7	24.0	72.7
1951	285.9	171.5	44.8	22.1	47.5
1952	416.0	310.4	45.8	21.9	37.9
1953	444.5	322.1	45.0	23.4	54.0
1954	401.4	305.6	51.2	21.7	22.9
1955	380.0	261.8	57.7	21.4	39.1
1956	370.4	243.7	60.3	21.7	44.7
1957	379.7	245.0	65.7	22.1	46.9
1958	388.0	241.6	78.9	22.8	44.7
1959	409.5	233.2	84.4	22.6	69.3
1960	392.1	220.1	87.8	26.6	57.6
1961	406.0	221.2	98.5	25.5	60.8
1962	436.0	228.0	102.3	25.7	80.0
1963	437.6	222.9	107.8	28.4	78.5
1964	456.6	224.0	110.3	29.6	92.7
1965	446.1	203.9	111.4	30.4	100.4
1966	482.4	225.9	121.7	32.2	102.6
1967	560.0	269.1	137.8	34.1	119.0
1968	608.6	295.5	153.9	35.5	123.7
1969	593.9	282.5	169.4	38.7	103.3
1970	596.1	262.9	183.8	41.5	107.9
1971	599.1	236.9	218.2	40.8	103.2
1972	617.5	219.7	241.4	40.4	116.0
1973	620.3	197.2	260.5	43.1	119.5
1974	625.4	185.3	277.4	49.6	113.1
1975	698.5	183.9	322.4	48.9	143.3

TABLE A–7 (continued)

	Total	Defense	Payments for Individuals	Net Interest	Other
1976	729.3	177.8	354.7	52.2	144.6
1977	740.9	176.8	357.6	54.0	152.5
1978	773.9	177.2	358.9	59.5	178.3
1979	781.7	180.4	365.7	65.9	169.7
1980	832.1	187.1	394.9	74.4	175.7
1981	867.7	198.2	420.5	88.4	160.6
1982	891.1	214.3	435.6	101.8	139.4
1983	921.1	230.4	459.8	103.2	127.7
1984	933.5	241.7	446.5	122.3	123.0
1985	1,001.3	261.2	458.6	137.3	144.2
1986	1,017.3	276.4	467.5	140.1	133.3
1987	1,003.9	282.0	471.3	138.7	111.9
1988	1,027.1	283.3	480.0	146.5	117.3
1989	1,057.2	285.9	490.4	156.3	124.6
1990	1,110.1	272.3	509.5	163.2	165.1
1991	1,122.0	240.1	540.4	165.2	176.3
1992	1,138.4	253.6	589.3	164.6	130.9

NOTE: "Other" includes some off-budget payments for individuals.
SOURCE: Office of Management and Budget.

TABLE A–8
Federal Taxes and Income, 1929–1992

	Federal Individual Income Tax as Percentage of Estimated Personal Income[a]	Federal Corporate Profits Tax as Percentage of Book Profits	Federal Corporate Profits Tax as Percentage of "Real" Profits[b]
1929	1.45	11.32	11.76
1930	1.35	16.28	10.14
1931	0.81	100.00	16.67
1932	0.63	−20.00	−42.86
1933	0.90	29.41	−71.43
1934	0.78	19.35	31.58
1935	1.04	19.05	23.53
1936	1.08	18.84	23.21
1937	1.82	17.33	20.31
1938	1.83	20.45	20.93
1939	1.29	17.11	22.03
1940	1.33	25.00	28.26
1941	1.73	39.89	49.32
1942	3.32	50.45	55.22
1943	10.63	53.13	55.97
1944	10.30	51.02	51.23
1945	11.13	51.00	51.52
1946	9.67	34.54	50.00
1947	10.41	33.23	45.89
1948	9.05	32.31	38.03
1949	7.85	31.76	33.10
1950	8.06	39.35	48.30
1951	10.26	47.87	53.23
1952	11.38	45.52	48.16
1953	11.16	45.91	50.13
1954	9.94	42.35	44.62
1955	10.05	41.85	43.61
1956	10.41	40.76	44.18
1957	10.50	40.70	43.26
1958	10.16	40.75	42.23
1959	10.32	40.45	41.30
1960	10.70	40.31	40.63
1961	10.56	40.78	40.31

	Federal Individual Income Tax as Percentage of Estimated Personal Income[a]	Federal Corporate Profits Tax as Percentage of Book Profits	Federal Corporate Profits Tax as Percentage of "Real" Profits[b]
1962	10.80	38.48	36.41
1963	10.84	38.73	36.41
1964	9.44	36.18	34.12
1965	9.69	35.03	33.29
1966	10.18	35.02	33.63
1967	10.47	34.35	32.67
1968	11.38	37.09	36.29
1969	12.49	37.08	36.83
1970	11.43	34.57	34.97
1971	10.35	33.41	33.33
1972	11.33	31.96	32.36
1973	10.77	29.72	33.42
1974	11.43	27.73	37.89
1975	10.31	27.21	31.34
1976	10.89	28.04	33.11
1977	11.24	27.40	31.70
1978	11.52	27.07	32.25
1979	12.15	24.90	32.15
1980	12.28	24.33	32.98
1981	12.76	22.59	28.41
1982	12.32	19.17	22.31
1983	11.26	22.35	22.14
1984	10.64	24.62	22.41
1985	11.04	26.00	20.83
1986	10.82	30.30	24.30
1987	11.43	29.66	26.70
1988	10.86	26.94	25.64
1989	11.39	27.82	26.30
1990	11.18	25.41	24.97
1991	10.74	24.41	23.59
1992	10.39	26.02	24.56

a. Personal income less transfer payments plus employees' contributions for social security.
b. Book profits plus inventory valuation and capital consumption adjustment.
SOURCE: Department of Commerce.

NOTES

CHAPTER 1 (15–26)

1. Carter-Reagan Debate, October 28, 1980, Cleveland, Ohio.
2. For example, in 1980 real per capita disposable income was 7.5 percent higher than in 1976 and the unemployment rate was lower than in 1976.
3. *The Constitution of Liberty* (Chicago: Henry Regnery, 1960), pp. 397–411.
4. See Henry C. Simons, "Introduction: a Political Credo," in *Economic Policy for a Free Society* (Chicago, University of Chicago Press, 1948), p. 1.
5. See Herbert Stein, "New York, Chicago, Main St. . . ." *Washington Post,* November 29, 1964, p. E1.
6. There were such moments, for example, in 1972 and 1975. In the spring of 1972 I held a press conference on the economic statistics for the first quarter, which showed little inflation and a large increase of output. I said that this was the best combination of economic statistics in recorded history and then, not wanting to seem boastful, added the qualification "at least in the Christian Era." But those good statistics did not last, of course.

CHAPTER 2 (27–63)

1. As estimated many years after the fact from fragmentary data.
2. See Jude Wanniski, *The Way the World Works* (New York: Basic Books, 1978), p. 125.
3. They were looking through a set of glasses that *never* saw a reason for a tax increase.
4. For an explanation of this decision see Herbert Stein, *The Fiscal Revolution in America* (Chicago, University of Chicago Press, 1969), pp. 26–38.
5. I have done so in *Fiscal Revolution,* pp. 39–130.
6. New York: Harcourt, Brace, 1936.
7. Extreme supply-siders believed that there was unemployment because high tax rates curtailed incentives to work and high welfare benefits increased incentives to idleness.
8. One example of the revival of Say's Law is George Gilder, *Wealth and Poverty* (New York: Basic Books, 1981), once regarded as the Bible of the Reagan administration.
9. See p. 47.
10. "Mr. Keynes on the Causes of Unemployment," *Quarterly Journal of Economics,* 1937, p. 149.
11. Milton Friedman, *A Theory of the Consumption Function* (Princeton: Princeton University Press, 1957), p. 235.
12. Martin Feldstein, various articles, *Journal of Political Economy,* 1974, pp. 905–926, 1982, pp. 630–642, *Journal of Public Economics,* 1980, pp. 225–244, *Review of Economics and Statistics,* 1979, pp. 361–368.
13. Speaking of inequality in the distribution of income or power, Simons said: "Surely there is something unlovely, to modern as against medieval minds, about marked inequality of either kind." "A Positive Program for Laissez-Faire," 1934, reprinted in *Economic Policy for a Free Society* (Chicago: University of Chicago Press, 1948), p. 51.
14. State and local economic regulation has been pervasive throughout our history, but its influence is limited by interstate competition. See Jonathan R. Hughes, *The Governmental Habit: Economic Controls from Colonial Times to the Present* (New York: Basic Books, 1977).
15. Some of the "conservative" farm organizations criticized the farm programs, but many supported them.

CHAPTER 3 (65–87)

1. Friedrich A. von Hayek, *The Road to Serfdom* (Chicago: University of Chicago Press, 1944).

2. John Maynard Keynes, *How to Pay for the War* (New York: Harcourt, Brace, 1940).

3. Personal income is here defined as in the national income and product accounts except that government transfer payments are excluded, because they are not taxable, and employee contributions to social insurance are included.

4. One evidence of the national concern was the Pabst contest. The Pabst Brewing Company had celebrated its fiftieth anniversary in 1894 by giving away tin trays for serving beer. In 1944 it thought that the national situation called for something more serious. Therefore it sponsored a contest for essays on how to achieve high employment after the war. Forty-six thousand essays were submitted, the more eligible ones were selected by staff of Columbia University, and the winners were chosen by a jury of four distinguished persons. Much national publicity attended the announcement of the winning plans. In terms of the classification of positions given above in this chapter, the winning essay, by the present author, fell in the category of conservative macroeconomics, and the second-place essay, by Leon H. Keyserling, was in the category of reformers and planners, whereas many of the honorable mentions were strictly Keynesian. (Both Keyserling and I later became chairmen of the President's Council of Economic Advisers.) *The Winning Plans in the Pabst Postwar Employment Awards, 1944.*

5. Paul T. Homan and Fritz Machlup, eds., *Financing American Prosperity: a Symposium of Economists* (New York: Twentieth Century Fund, 1945).

6. *American Economic Review,* 38: 248 (June 1948).

7. Theodore O. Yntema, Howard B. Myers, Herbert Stein.

8. See Stephen K. Bailey, *Congress Makes a Law* (New York: Columbia University Press, 1950).

9. New York: McGraw-Hill, 1948. There are many later editions, which adapted to the subsequent evolution of economic thought.

10. Committee for Economic Development, New York, 1947.

11. U.S. Congress, Joint Committee on the Economic Report, Subcommittee on Monetary, Credit and Fiscal Policies, *Report,* 81st Congress, 2nd Session, 1950.

12. Milton Friedman and Anna Jacobson Schwartz, *A Monetary History of the United States* (Princeton: Princeton University Press, 1968).

13. *Journal of Political Economy,* Vol. 52, No. 1 (March 1944), pp. 1–25.

14. See Chapter 4, note 3.

CHAPTER 4 (89–131)

1. For an evaluation of the economic growth problem as it looked in 1960, see Edward F. Denison and Herbert Stein, "High Employment and Economic Growth," in *Goals for Americans* (Englewood, N.J.: Prentice-Hall, 1960), pp. 163–190.

2. J. K. Galbraith, *The Affluent Society* (Boston: Houghton Mifflin, 1958), p. 257. Another influential book of this period that dramatized the alleged deterioration of the quality of American life through the abuse of the environment was Rachel Carson, *Silent Spring* (Boston: Houghton Mifflin, 1962).

3. Professor James Tobin, who was a member of President Kennedy's Council of Economic Advisers, estimated the percentage of families with real incomes below what was considered the poverty level in 1965 as follows:

Percentage of families with annual incomes below $3,000
1965 dollars

Year	Percent
1899	67
1918	63
1935–36	51
1950	30
1960	20
1965	17

Cited in James J. Patterson, *America's Struggle Against Poverty 1900–1980* (Cambridge, Mass.: Harvard University Press, 1981), p. 79.

4. Joseph A. Schumpeter, *Capitalism, Socialism and Democracy* (New York: Harper, 1942).

5. A. W. Phillips, "The Relation between Unemployment and the Rate of Change of Money Wage Rates in the United Kingdom, 1861–1957," *Economica*, November 1958, pp. 283–299.

6. See *Goals for Americans* (Englewood, N.J.: Prentice-Hall, 1960).

7. *Annual Report of the Council of Economic Advisers*, January 1962, pp. 185–190.

8. Stein, *Fiscal Revolution*, p. 372.

9. As Walter Heller later wrote: "As early as May, 1963, Kenneth O'Donnell told me: 'Stop worrying about the tax cut. It will pass—and pass big. Worry about something else.' We did. We turned to the question of those whom the tax cut would leave behind. By mid-1963, I had sent President Kennedy our economic and statistical

analysis of the groups beyond the reach of the tax cut and had offered some groping thoughts on 'an attack on poverty.' " Walter W. Heller, *New Dimensions of Political Economy* (Cambridge, Mass.: Harvard University Press, 1966), p. 20.

10. Herbert Stein, "Curriculum for Economics, 1981: Poverty and the Budget," *AEI Economist*, October 1980. Calculation based on data in G. William Hoagland, "The Effectiveness of Current Transfer Programs in Reducing Poverty," April 19, 1980, paper presented at Middlebury College Conference on Economic Issues.

CHAPTER 5 (133–207)

1. Mr. Nixon loved these football metaphors. "Three yards in a cloud of dust" referred to a style of cautious, slow-moving play in which the offense plows methodically along the ground. The "long bomb" refers to a more daring attempt to gain rapidly by a long pass.

2. In 1966 and 1967, before the surcharge, federal receipts were 18.8 percent of GNP. In 1980 they were 20.5 percent of GNP and in 1981 21.4 percent.

3. During the 1972 campaign President Nixon preferred to discuss economic questions on the radio at noon, thinking that his audience would be mainly farmers on tractors and not people who would be diverted from anything more absorbing.

4. "The Role of Monetary Policy," *American Economic Review*, March 1968, Vol. 58, pp. 1–17.

5. There were people at that time who considered an unemployment rate of 4 percent as too high and aiming at it as evidence of lack of compassion. For example, Mr. Whitney Young, head of the National Urban League, called a 4 percent unemployment goal "unacceptable." *New York Times*, October 27, 1969.

6. Members were the President, Vice-President, Secretaries of Treasury, Agriculture, Commerce, Labor, Housing and Urban Development, counselors to the President (Burns and Moynihan), director of the Bureau of the Budget, Deputy Under Secretary of State for Economic Affairs and chairman of the CEA.

7. "Inflation, The Fundamental Challenge to Stabilization Policies," remarks to the American Bankers Association, May 18, 1970, reprinted in *Reflections of an Economic Policy Maker* (Washington: American Enterprise Institute for Public Policy Research), pp. 91–102.

8. The annual rates of change of the consumer price index were: December 1969 to December 1970, 5.5 percent; December 1970 to March 1971, 2.8 percent; March 1971 to June 1971, 5.3 percent; June 1971 to August 1971, 2.5 percent.

9. *Public Papers of the Presidents: Richard Nixon, 1970*, pp. 502–509.

10. Address to the National Association of Manufacturers, December 4, 1970 (*Presidential Papers, 1970,* pp. 1085–1095).

11. In a statement on July 18, 1970, the President said: "In raising the issue of budget deficits, I am not suggesting that the Federal Government should necessarily adhere to a strict pattern of a balanced budget every year. At times the economic situation permits—even calls for—a budget deficit. There is one basic guideline for the budget, however, which we should never violate: Except in emergency conditions, expenditures must never be allowed to outrun the revenues that the tax system would produce at reasonably full employment. When the Federal Government's spending actions over an extended period push outlays sharply higher, increased tax rates or inflation inevitably follow. We had such a period in the 1960's. We have been paying the high price—and higher prices—for that recently." *Public Papers of the Presidents: Richard Nixon, 1970,* p. 60, *Presidential Papers, 1970,* p. 601.

12. *Public Papers of the Presidents: Richard Nixon, 1971,* p. 52.

13. He is usually erroneously reported as having said, "We are all Keynesians now." It was Milton Friedman who said that, in 1965. See p. 113.

14. Walter Heller, testifying before the Joint Economic Committee on July 27, 1972: "As I say, now that we are again on the move the voice of overcautious conservatism is raised again at the other end of Pennsylvania Avenue. Reach for the brakes, slash the budget, seek an end to wage-price restraints."

15. See President Nixon's message signing this bill on July 1, 1972. *Presidential Papers, 1972,* pp. 723–724.

16. In connection with the President's defense I prepared a statement of the economic argument to show that the Employment Act of 1946 which directed that the government use all its powers to achieve maximum production, employment and purchasing power implicitly authorized the President to impound funds. The statement was written with unusual concern for the qualifications and uncertainties of the argument, perhaps because I had to swear to it before a notary, an exceptional procedure for a statement of an economist.

17. See Chapter 3, note 3.

18. *Survey of Current Business,* April 1982, p. 26.

CHAPTER 6 (209–233)

1. *Public Papers of the Presidents: Gerald Ford, 1974,* p. 228.

2. Joseph J. Minarik, "The Size Distribution of Income During Inflation" (Washington: Brookings Institution, 1980).

3. In 1979 married couples with two dependents and incomes below

$25,000 in 1980 dollars paid less federal income tax than similar families with the same real income had paid in 1960, but families with $35,000 or above paid more. Marginal rates had been reduced for families with incomes below about $20,000 1980 dollars and raised for higher-income families (with an exceptional marginal-rate increase for low-income families who were near the point at which the refundable earned income credit phased out). For many low- and middle-income families the increase in social security taxes was larger in dollars than the increase in income taxes, but that seemed to generate less resentment.

4. See Herbert Stein, "What Margaret Thatcher Knows," *AEI Economist,* August 1979.

CHAPTER 7 (235–262)

1. See Herbert Stein, "Some Supply-Side Propositions," *Wall Street Journal,* March 19, 1980.
2. Paper entitled "The Decline of the Budget-Balancing Doctrine or How the Good Guys Finally Lost" (March 25, 1976), published in James M. Buchanan and Richard E. Wagner, eds., *Fiscal Responsibility in a Constitutional Democracy* (London/Boston: Martins Nechoff, 1978).
3. See Don Fullerton, "On the Possibility of an Inverse Relationship between Tax Rates and Government Revenues," National Bureau of Economic Research, Working Paper No. 467, April 1980.
4. Herbert Stein and Murray F. Foss, "Taxes and Saving," *AEI Economist,* July 1981.
5. See Arthur B. Laffer in "Two Views of the Kemp-Roth Bill," *AEI Economist,* July 1978.
6. Wanniski, *The Way the World Works.*
7. Report of the Joint Economic Committee, Congress of the United States on the January 1980 Economic Report of the President together with Additional Views, February 28, 1980.
8. Barry Goldwater, *The Conscience of a Conservative* (Woodland Hills, Calif.: Victor Publishing Company, 1960), pp. 62–63.
9. I had an encounter with Reagan's optimism the first time I met him, which was at the first meeting of the President's Economic Policy Advisory Board in February 1981. Sitting across the table from him in the Cabinet Room of the White House I wondered what was the essential thing to say to this powerful person. I decided to say that although we all hoped that his program was going to work, economists could not forecast well enough to be sure that the inflation would come down without a recession. I thought he should warn the country of that, to prevent future public disappointment that might

force him to do things he would prefer not to do. He was unmoved by my advice and seemed not to want to consider the possibility.

10. Most of the preceding three paragraphs is based on Rowland Evans and Robert Novak, *The Reagan Revolution* (New York: Dutton, 1981).

CHAPTER 8 (263–306)

1. "Avoiding a GOP Economic Dunkirk," December 1980. This memo was unsigned but widely "known" to be by David Stockman and unpublished but widely distributed. One purpose of starting the new program quickly and decisively was to avoid Thatcherization. By 1983, after Mrs. Thatcher was reelected as British Prime Minister by a wide margin, Thatcherization did not look like such a bad fate.

2. By mid-1983 the administration's estimate of this increase was 2.5 percent, which would leave real GNP in 1985 6.5 percent below the figure forecast by the Reagan administration in March 1981.

3. See Herbert Stein, "Another New Economics," *AEI Economist*, April 1981; also Rudolph G. Penner in *New York Times*, February 22, 1981, and Rudolph G. Penner, "A Loyalist Reflects on the Reagan Plan," *New York Times*, August 16, 1981.

4. Signing the budget and tax bills on August 13, 1981, the President said that "they represent a turnaround of almost a half a century of a course the country's been on and mark an end to the excessive growth in government bureaucracy, government spending, government taxing." *Presidential Papers*, 1981, p. 706.

5. Reported in Herbert Stein, "Why Deficits Matter," *AEI Economist*, January 1982.

6. "Report to the Congress on the Role of Gold in the Domestic and International Monetary Systems," U.S. Treasury, March 1982.

7. See Milton Friedman, "What Could Reasonably Have Been Expected From Monetarism: The United States," paper for Mont Pelerin Society Meeting, Vancouver, August 29, 1983.

CHAPTER 9 (307–376)

1. Milton Friedman and Rose D. Friedman, *Free to Choose: A Personal Statement* (New York: Harcourt Brace Jovanovich, 1980), pp. 301–309. In addition to limiting government spending the amendments dealt with international trade, wage and price controls, occupational licensure, tax structures, the money supply and inflation protection.

2. It is conceivable that if the government runs very large deficits for a long period the total debt will rise substantially relative to the GNP, and government interest payments will rise substantially relative to

the GNP. In that case there is danger that deficits will rise continuously relative to the GNP. But there is a limit to this process. The deficit cannot exceed the gross saving of the country (aside from capital imports) and before that point is reached there would be a slowdown of economic growth, or even a decline of output, that the society will find intolerable. There would then be a strong temptation to escape from this situation by inflation that would reduce the real value of the debt. But it is one thing to say that inflation may be a politically tempting alternative to taxation in certain budgetary positions. It is another thing to say that inflation is a necessary alternative. In any case, the argument against allowing an endless escalation of deficits relative to the GNP is compelling, even if the result is not inflation.

3. The use of the expression "the money supply" requires explanation now that everyone is conscious of a number of different definitions of money. There are several kinds of assets that serve some of the functions of money—currency, checkable deposits with various interest rates and subject to various limitations on their activity, deposits that are not checkable but instantly convertible to checkable deposits, other liquid assets of different maturities. Whatever list of assets we combine and call "money" the relation between it and nominal GNP will depend on the proportions in which the different kinds of assets exist. Thus, if we define money as currency plus checkable deposits, now called M_1, the relation between M_1 and nominal GNP will depend in part upon the quantity of the liquid assets that are excluded from M_1. There is a considerable range of professional opinion about how much difference this makes. In any case, I include the existence in variable proportions of a variety of money-like assets as one of the reasons for saying that the relation between the supply of money, however defined, and nominal GNP is not constant and predictable.

4. B. divided by A. = real GNP and rises by 3 percent per annum, the assumed normal growth of real GNP. B. divided by C. = velocity, and rises by 3 percent per annum, the predicted trend of velocity.

5. Herbert Stein, comment on paper "Economic Growth as an Objective of Government Policy" by James Tobin, Proceedings of American Economic Association, December 27–29, 1963 (published May 1964), pp. 24–27.

6. In thinking about the proper size of deficits it is necessary to look out even beyond the five-year period suggested here for setting targets. The deficits run during one five-year period will determine the size of the debt with which the next five-year period begins, and that will affect the difficulty of holding deficits in that next five-year period to a level that may be consistent with national growth objectives. This

only means that it is desirable to avoid deficits of a size that, although tolerable or helpful today, excessively limit the freedom of action of future generations.

7. A more explicit use of this reasoning to arrive at this recommendation appeared in an article by Cagan, Fellner, Penner and Stein, "Economic Policy for Recovery and Growth," *AEI Economist,* January 1983.

8. Special Analyses, Budget of the United States Government, Fiscal Year 1993, pt. 2, pp. 25–28.

CHAPTER 12 (413–429)

1. The idea that Congress loves to raise taxes and would be trying to get a reluctant President to go along is one of the peculiar myths of our times. Congressmen hate to raise taxes, as much as anyone or more. But they are pragmatic also. They know the difference between taxes that bear heavily on their constituents and those that do not. They would rather raise a tax that does not burden their constituents than give up an expenditure program that benefits them.

2. I emphasize the word *some* because there is now dispute over whether this was the official position of the Reagan team.

3. Many people argued at the time that expenditures for paying depositors in closed financial institutions did not have real effects, because those expenditures only liquidated federal costs that had been incurred when the institutions made the bad investments that ultimately required the federal government to pay. By that logic, the accruing liability to the federal government should have been recognized in the budget earlier, during the Reagan and Carter eras. The Bush proposal was to postpone recognition of these costs to some later day, or possibly not to recognize them at all. The means by which this was to be done was to create an entity formally outside the federal budget that would pay off the depositors and raise the money to do so by issuing bonds issued by the federal government. Since those bonds would have to carry interest a little higher than bonds issued by the government itself, the process involved higher interest costs than if the costs of the bailouts had been included in the budget.

CHAPTER 13 (431–444)

1. Revisions of the national income data since this chapter was originally written, in June 1993, have shown the recovery to have been somewhat more rapid than was first thought, although still slower than most postwar recoveries. In the present chapter, I continue to refer to the period ending in the first quarter of 1993, or April for monthly data, but I have incorporated revisions reflecting data available as of August 31, 1993.

Index

ABOUT THE AUTHOR

Herbert Stein earned his B.A. from Williams College and his Ph.D. from the University of Chicago. He was a member of the President's Council of Economic Advisers from 1969 to 1974 and was chairman from 1972. He is the A. Willis Robertson Professor of Economics Emeritus of the University of Virginia and a senior fellow of the American Enterprise Institute (AEI). He writes regularly for *The American Enterprise,* the magazine of AEI. He is also a member of the board of contributors of the *Wall Street Journal,* for which he writes frequently.

Among his publications are *An Illustrated Guide to the American Economy* (1992, with Murray Foss), *The Fiscal Revolution in America* (1969, rev. ed. 1990), *Washington Bedtime Stories* (1986), and *Governing the $5 Trillion Economy* (1989).